MW01041617

SEXUALITY AND CITIZENSHIP:
METAMORPHOSIS IN
ELIZABETHAN EROTIC VERSE

Sexuality and Citizenship

Metamorphosis in Elizabethan Erotic Verse

JIM ELLIS

UNIVERSITY OF TORONTO PRESS
Toronto Buffalo London

© University of Toronto Press Incorporated 2003
Toronto Buffalo London
Printed in Canada

ISBN 0-8020-8735-3

Printed on acid-free paper

National Library of Canada Cataloguing in Publication

Ellis, James Richard, 1964–

Sexuality and citizenship : metamorphosis in Elizabethan
erotic verse / Jim Ellis.

Includes index.
ISBN 0-8020-8735-3

1. English poetry – Early modern, 1500–1700 – History and
criticism.   2. Erotic poetry, English – History and criticism.
3. Metamorphosis in literature.   I. Title.

PR539.E64E44 2003   821'.3093538   C2003-900211-X

University of Toronto Press acknowledges the financial assistance to
its publishing program of the Canada Council for the Arts and the
Ontario Arts Council.

This book has been published with the help of a grant from the
Humanities and Social Sciences Federation of Canada, using funds
provided by the Social Sciences and Humanities Research Council
of Canada.

University of Toronto Press acknowledges the financial support for
its publishing activities of the Government of Canada through the
Book Publishing Industry Development Program (BPIDP).

Contents

vi   Contents

Conclusion:
Nymphs and Tobacconalias   224

Acknowledgments

In Book X of the *Metamorphoses*, Venus transforms Hippomenes into a lion for failing to acknowledge her contributions to his efforts. Ingratitude is a serious sin, then as now, and so I wish to thank here the benevolent deities who have helped this study along, as well as those who have been a source of pleasure and inspiration for me while I was writing.

Two teachers of early modern poetry at York University in Toronto have been particularly influential: Ian Sowton, who supervised the dissertation out of which the idea for this study emerged, and Heather Ross, who introduced me to the epyllion in the first place. Elizabeth Harvey encouraged me to write a book on this topic, and has been an unflagging source of advice and support for the duration of the project.

Colleagues and friends have read some or all of the book and offered valuable advice, in particular, Mary Polito, Peter Sinnema, Stephen Guy-Bray, and Susan Rudy; these and others, including Jackie Jenkins, Eric Savoy, Susan Bennett, and Penny Farfan, have provided a stimulating intellectual and social environment in which to live and work. My friends in London, particularly Caroline Duncan and Graeme Marsden, have been unfailingly generous in their hospitality during my visits there.

Thanks are owed to the University Research Grants Committee at the University of Calgary, who provided a start-up grant at the beginning of the project and to the Vice-President (Research) for two research grants mid-way through. A Killam Resident Research Fellowship gave me time off to complete the manuscript, for which I am grateful. Among other things, these grants funded the work of two research assistants early on in the project, Linda Howell and Nusya Campbell; later, Karen Walker provided invaluable help while I was preparing the manuscript for the Press.

Portions of this book have previously appeared in print. Part of section 2 in the second chapter originally appeared in 'Embodying Dislocation: *A Mirror for Magistrates* and Property Relations,' *Renaissance Quarterly* 53 (2000): 1032–53; some of chapter 3 appeared in a different form in 'Imagining Heterosexuality in the Epyllion,' in *Ovid and the Renaissance Body*, edited by Goran Stanivukovic (Toronto: University of Toronto Press, 2001), 38–58; two sections of chapter 5 are a revised version of 'Orpheus at the Inns of Court,' from *The Affectionate Shepherd: Essays in Celebration of Richard Barnfield*, edited by Kenneth Borris and George Klawitter (Selinsgrove: Susquehanna University Press, 2001), 283–304. My thanks to the editors and readers of those essays, who offered invaluable advice and guidance. Similarly, a large debt of gratitude is owed to the two anonymous readers for the Press, whose close, thoughtful readings of the manuscript helped me to make this a better book.

My parents, Ross and Mary, and my three sisters, Joyce, Joanne, and Jennifer, have provided love and encouragement from afar. My largest debt of gratitude is to my partner, Glenn Mielke, who has wrought many metamorphoses in my life, all for the better.

SEXUALITY AND CITIZENSHIP:
METAMORPHOSIS IN
ELIZABETHAN EROTIC VERSE

Introduction: Heterosexuality and Citizenship in the Elizabethan Epyllion

In the 1590s, spurred on by the success of Thomas Lodge's *Scillaes Metamorphosis* (1589), a series of comic, erotic poems was written on mythological tales, most often from Ovid's *Metamorphoses*. These poems, now generally labelled 'epyllia,' were produced for the most part at the Inns of Court, a crucial training ground in Elizabethan England for those with political aspirations. Ambitious young men of the kingdom came to the Inns, sometimes after studying at the universities, sometimes direct from the counties, to experience life in London and learn the common law. Not coincidentally, given their primary audience, the poems frequently retell myths concerning the transformation of youths such as Adonis, Narcissus, and Hermaphroditus. We have then in the epyllion a group of poems concerning the metamorphoses of young men, written by and for a group of young men at the centre of a culture and a nation that were rapidly changing. Exploring change from within change, the genre offers a unique perspective on the metamorphosis of subjectivity within early modern England.

This book explores the connections between literature and social change, and between erotic narratives and political narratives. How might stories about the dalliances of goddesses and shepherds be at the same time stories about the nature of citizenship? In particular, how do these tales of the transformation of youths bear witness to the emergence of new forms of male subjectivity in the period?

These may seem to be inappropriately serious questions to direct at what is often characterized as a 'self-consciously trivial' genre,[1] but when we consider the original milieu of the poems, the political dimensions of the epyllion are less surprising. Because of the centrality of Ovidian texts in Elizabethan education, Ovid was subsequently deployed in a whole range of cultural sites, and as Valerie Traub observes, the 'gendered and erotic dynamics internal to these sites' yielded different versions of Ovidian eroticism.[2] Thus the Ovid of the Inns of Court will necessarily have a different tone and content than the Ovid of the playhouse or the court. I will argue that the poems produced at the Inns use Ovidian myth to produce a certain kind of subject, one suited to participating in newly emerging forms of economic and political relations. To be more precise, the epyllion invents, through its reinterpretation of Ovidian mythical narratives, a new version of heterosexuality.

An immediate qualification should be raised here. By 'heterosexuality,' I mean to denote as much a political relation as an erotic one. As Gregory Bredbeck observes of the genre, 'These poems are concerned not so much with erotic behavior as with the implications of power and social order underpinning it.'[3] Of course, social commentary was never far from Ovid's mind, and R.W. Maslen argues of earlier Elizabethan retellings of Ovid that they are both 'more sophisticated – and more politically engaged – than scholars have been willing to concede.'[4] Not surprisingly, then, these poems that initially seem to be about desire are often, on closer examination, about other, more political questions: the formation of national literary canons, the justification of English over-seas trade, and, most centrally, the re-imagining of citizenship according to a fraternal and contractual model. What is interesting about the epyllion is how it shows that these stories are not in fact separate. We can see in these poems the erotic underpinnings of political subjectivity, and the political implications of erotic scenarios.

The epyllion is an odd genre. Its flourishing is linked to a single decade, and to a fairly well-defined cultural milieu, the Inns of Court. After its brief period of popularity it never resurfaced again.[5] The time span is not in itself unusual; the Elizabethan vogue for the sonnet sequence, after all, didn't have an appreciably different longevity, but sonnets and sequences were written before and would continue to be written long after. Not only did the epyllion not survive, it is not even clear that it existed as a genre in the first place. The label was first applied to classical poetry in the nineteenth century, and only later to English examples.[6] Whether the Elizabethans viewed these poems as a group is unknown, as is whether they would have drawn any distinction between the epyllion and the Ovidian complaint, which (if in fact it is a separate genre) has had a longer life.

From another perspective, the question of genre is immaterial: a group of poems based on stories from Ovid was written by writers who clearly knew each other's work. Lodge's *Scillaes Metamorphoses*, Marlowe's *Hero and Leander*, and Shakespeare's *Venus and Adonis* were widely read and admired, and subsequently imitated by writers such as John Marston (*The Metamorphosis of Pigmalions Image*), John Weever (*Faunis and Melliflora*), and Thomas Heywood (*Oenone and Paris*). The poems share an interest in rhetorical display, lush erotic description, and self-conscious wit; they typically contain about nine hundred lines of pentameter verse, most often structured in rhyming couplets or sixains. Similar kinds of narratives from Ovid are favoured, with certain key figures, notably Orpheus, Adonis, and Narcissus, appearing in poem after poem. In other words, the poems share enough to be sensibly discussed together. Most importantly, as Clark Hulse points out, the poems share a distinctly Ovidian tone: the ironic, studied amorality with which they retell stories of love and transformation, a tone William Keach identifies as 'the Elizabethan epyllion's ironic self-consciousness.'[7] As Lynn Enterline argues, this is one of the key differences between Ovidian and Petrarchan poetry, the distance of the narrator from the desire in the poem.[8] Adopting an Olympian perspective on desire allows the narrator to absent himself from the trivial ethical concerns of mortals.

The question of genre no doubt surfaces because of the self-consciously literary nature of the poems. Like any genre, the epyllion exists in relation to literary systems that extend both synchronically and diachronically, although the epyllion is unusual in the extent to which its connections to other genres are central to its functioning. One reason for the epyllion's quick rise and fall might be found in its essentially reactive nature: while it partakes of the long tradition of Ovidian translation and adaptation, it is most immediately a response to and a rejection of a long-standing urge to Christianize and moralize Ovid. The epyllion is the ironic heir of the medieval tradition of the *Ovide moralisé*, the influences of which could be seen at least as late as the 1560 publication of T[homas] H[owell]'s *The Fable of Ovid tretyng of Narcissus, in Englysh Mytre* (which was accompanied by a 'Moralization of the Fable' approximately three times as long as the poem itself) and beyond that, to George Sandys's 1632 publication of *Ovid's Metamorphosis Englished, Mythologiz'd and Represented in Figures*.[9] In the latter, each book is followed by a prose commentary that offers some of the traditional moralizing, in addition to speculation on the historical origin of each tale. Arthur Golding's 1567 translation, *The .xv. Bookes of P. Ouidius Naso, entytuled Metamorphosis*, was a major influence on the genre; although moralizing to some degree, Golding moved away from the more explicitly Christian-izing medieval tradition.[10] Jove's abduction of Ganymede is no longer read, for example, as the story of Christ embracing Saint John the Evangelist.[11] Nonetheless, in 'The Epistle' and 'The Preface' that accom-pany the work, Golding still feels compelled to offer quick allegorical readings of the tales contained in each book. By contrast, the writers of the epyllion abandon instruction, delighting instead in rhetorical play and sexual adventure, much in the spirit of Ovid himself. As far as translations go, epyllia, like the gods they describe, are spectacularly unfaithful, typically rewriting thirty or so lines of the *Metamorphoses* into nine hundred lines of witty, digressive, and rhetorically ornate verse.

The genre does not simply react against its own tradition, however; more pointed is its satire of Petrarchan poetic conventions, which pro-vided the dominant literary love conventions of the period.[12] While Petrarchan poetry contains within itself anti-Petrarchan sentiments, the epyllion tends to ignore this complexity and characterizes the Petrarchan poet as idealistic, self-deluded, and immature. The Ovidian lover, by contrast, takes what the genre characterizes as a frank and mature attitude towards love and sex, acknowledging the hypocrisies and cruel-ties of desire as an unavoidable, indeed central, part of existence. Like their source, the epyllion delights in what might be called ironic aetiol-ogy, featuring in a semicomic way tales of how things came to be the way they are. The most frequent explanations concern men and women, and gender norms. The poems are stories of sexual difference, sexual desire, and gender protocol. Readers are taught, for example, 'That nimphs must yeeld, when faithfull louers straie not' (Thomas Lodge, *Scillaes Metamorphosis*, envoy).[13] George Chapman tells us that no does not mean no, and that when female minds 'Breake out in fury, they are certaine signes / Of their perswasions' (*The Divine Poem of Musaeus: Hero and Leander*, 190–1); John Weever concurs: 'In womens mouths, No is no negatiue' (*Faunus and Melliflora*, 310). We learn that women are ruled by the moon, and 'That as of Plannets shee most variable, / So of all creatures they most mutable' (Michael Drayton, *Endimion and Phoebe*, 421–2). Within the poems characters are instructed on behaviour appro-priate to their sex and to sex itself, and are schooled in the differences that mark out male and female: 'Wert thou a mayd, and I a man, Ile show thee, / With what a manly boldnesse I could woo thee' (Francis Beaumont, *Salmacis and Hermaphroditus*, 715–16), says the bold nymph Salmacis to the bashful Hermaphroditus. Venus says similarly to the reluctant Adonis,

Would thou wert as I am, and I a man,
My heart all whole as thine, thy heart my wound!
For one sweet look thy help I would assure thee.

(369–71)

The education of youths is a central concern of the genre (hence the multitude of truisms about women), which is bound up with a recurring warning that 'youth forespent a wretched age ensu'th' (Lodge 6.6). All of this schooling on sex and gender is bound up with the epyllion's rejection of Petrarchan poetry and its gender protocol, as the genre attempts to install a new version of (literary) sexual relations. One of the central projects of the current study is to show that the poems' concerns with both of these kinds of conventions – gender and poetic—have larger political implications.

While it is easy to dismiss these comic, erotic poems as light literary exercises on mythological themes, the political dimensions of the genre become more visible when viewed in relation to the epic. Epyllia are sometimes referred to as minor epics ('epyllion' means 'little epic'), most obviously because they are moderately lengthy narrative poems. But as we shall see in the later chapters of this book, the epyllion shares with the epic a predilection for many of the same rhetorical devices (catalogue, ecphrasis, digression), some common subject matter, and a concern with nationhood. The epyllion, like the epic, works to establish the basis of community or nation; unlike the epic, its primary concern is the psychology of national belonging as opposed to the ideal subject of nationhood (the epic hero). While we do occasionally get the matter of epic in these poems, such as the fall of Troy, the fall of Constantinople, and the voyages to Virginia, these tend to function as the backdrop to more intimate stories. The concern is not with the foundation of the nation as such but with the re-imagining of political subjectivity. The epyllion and the epic thus share a complementary project in the Elizabethan world, where the idea of the English nation was newly emerging.[14]

A qualification is in order about the poems to be discussed. The difficulty in naming, defining, and drawing the boundaries of the genre is perhaps the reason that neither of the two existing studies of the genre actually use the word 'epyllion' in their titles (although they do in their texts).[15] William Keach's *Elizabethan Erotic Narratives*, whose understanding of the genre is closest to that of the present study, defines it rather narrowly, and focuses on the interplay of eros and satire in the six best-known examples of the genre (excluding *The Rape of Lucrece*). By contrast, Clark Hulse's *The Elizabethan Minor Epic* takes a rather capacious view of the genre in studying metamorphosis as a literary and cultural system. The present study falls somewhere in between and takes a slightly idiosyncratic approach to the genre, excluding poems based on Ovid that do not invoke the usual Ovidian sensibility (such as Chapman's philosophically arcane *Ovid's Banquet of Sense*[16] and Drayton's Neoplatonic *Endimion and Phoebe*) and including some narrative poems that are not based on Ovid, but which are clearly indebted to their Ovidian precursors (such as Beaumont's *The Metamorphosis of Tobacco* and Barksted's *Hiren, or the Faire Greeke*). My own interest is in reading the poems within their historical milieu in order to understand the cultural work accomplished by these retellings of myths.

The Elizabethan epyllia share a theory of desire that is frequently defined against what is recognizably Petrarchan, or at least a particular English version of Petarch. This scheme of desire, which critics have reasonably named 'Ovidian,' involves what the genre sees as a more frank and more emphatically masculine approach to sex: 'Ladies, thinke that they nere loue you, / Who doe not vnto more then kissing moue you' (Marston 20.5–6). This sort of desire the genre characterizes as natural, as opposed to the manifest artificiality of Petrarchan compliment ('the foolery / Of some sweet Youths' [Marston 19.1–2]), and it bolsters this identification through a wealth of metaphors drawn from the natural world. Love is seen to be, like the gods of the *Metamorphoses*, capricious and cruel, not the ennobling and spiritualizing love of the Neoplatonists (although we see precisely this Neoplatonic version of love in Drayton's very un-Ovidian *Endimion and Phoebe*). Desire is as frequently humiliating as it is gratifying. Although these anti-Petrarchan sentiments occur in Petrarchan poetry as well, they do not dominate as they do in this genre. Whereas in Petrarchan poetry they figure as interruptions within the frame, in this genre they are the foundation.

Petrarchanisms most often surface in the poems in the mouths of youths, and thus typically come to be associated in the genre with immaturity. Characters such as Glaucus, Leander, and Narcissus spout Petrarchan clichés until they learn better. The Petrarchan lover, the poems suggest, is in love with the idea of love, whereas a mature Ovidian male believes that love should lead to sex. The Petrarchan lover falls for an idea, prostrating himself before the fantasy of an ideal woman, whereas the Ovidian prefers engagement with actual women. The Petrarchan mistress shows up with startling regularity in the epyllion, as either a woman, in the case of Hero, Scilla, Mirrha, and Pigmalion's statue or, almost as frequently, as a male youth, such as Adonis, Narcissus, and Hermaphroditus. If the Petrarchan mistress is female, she will generally be rejected, silenced, humiliated, or converted by the end of the poem. The male youth who finds himself in the position of the Petrarchan beloved must either advance beyond his childishly moral objections to desire, or risk being cut off forever from adult masculinity. In the more satiric examples of the genre, the rejection of Petrarchanisms takes a different form. In William Barksted's *Mirrha the Mother of Adonis*, for example, the Petrarchan lovers are Cupid and a satyr named Poplar, figures one does not readily associate with idealized love. In these burlesque treatments, Petrarchan compliment is revealed to be simply a hypocritical discourse of seduction that can be adopted and abandoned at will.

Situated serenely above all of these tragicomedies of desire is the Ovidian narrator. One of the hallmarks of the Ovidian voice is its certainty, expressed in the sententiae and aetiological myths that are always on offer ('*Æsopian* snakes will alwaies proue vnkind' [Edwards, *Cephalus*, 446]; 'since Heroes time hath halfe the world beene blacke' [Marlowe, *Hero and Leander*, 50]). Part of the genre's interest in sententiae might simply be fashion; John Hoskyns writes to his Inns of Court protégé, 'Sententia (if it be well used) is a figure (if ill & too much) it is a style, whereof none that writes humorously or factiously nowe adayes can bee cleare.'[17] The fashion may be related to the maxims of the common law, which I will discuss in the next chapter. But the use of sententiae is also linked to the origins, interests, and tone of the genre (and indeed, the fashion for this figure and the popularity of the genre no doubt went hand in hand). The confident pronouncements that so often appear might seem to contradict another characteristic gesture of the poems, that of offering two possible explanations for a phenomenon, and then refusing to decide between them (some say ... others assert). This, however, is a display of certainty of a different kind: the narrator is certain he could not care less which version is true. Uncertainty is, at least in some areas of knowledge, not particularly troubling. When we remember that the majority of these poems were written by young men, sometimes not yet twenty years old, we might begin to question the purpose of these rhetorical moves. The confident posture (however comically intended) may in fact be a defence against the very uncertain times in which the poets lived or more simply the inevitable uncertainties attendant upon entering society as an enfranchised political subject. At the very least, the comic position of certainty serves to control the anxiety encoded in the narratives of the poems themselves, in which youths are often subject to unpleasant metamorphoses.

The Ovidian narrator takes his cue from Orpheus, who was for the humanists one of the chief models of the supreme rhetorician. Like Orpheus, the Ovidian narrator looks back on desire and converts stories of loss into rhetorical mastery. Unlike Hercules, the other major contender for supreme rhetorician in humanist culture, Orpheus is less interested in leading men by the golden chain of rhetoric than in charming his auditors with pastoral songs. It is no doubt significant that Orpheus is the singer of Bacchus's mysteries and that the other figure for rhetoric that shows up in the poems is Mercury, patron of thieves and translation (among other things). Orpheus as rhetorician is a figure more often for the *power* of rhetoric rather than for the *civilizing* power of rhetoric, which for humanist culture is a crucial difference.[18] He therefore makes a more suitable hero than Hercules for a genre that positions itself in opposition to a whole tradition of moralizing pagan myth.

This does not mean, however, that the rhetoric of the Orphic narrator has no effect on the polis. Quite the contrary. As we can see in Ovid's version of the Orpheus myth, Orpheus introduces the practice of pederasty to Thracian culture and inflames the women to the point where they are compelled to destroy him. This leads Bacchus to punish the women and abandon the fields of Thrace. Clearly desire has effects beyond the individual. New historicist critics have insisted for some time upon the political dimensions of erotic verse, arguing, for example, that 'love is not love' in Elizabethan sonnets but rather a literary displacement of political concerns.[19] Arthur Marotti's deservedly famous argument drew a certain amount of criticism, and while these objections were to some degree justified, they were perhaps misplaced. It is certainly reductive to read Sidney's sonnets as only a displacement of his failed political ambitions, converting political failures into literary successes, and to read Stella as merely a representation of Elizabeth. This is not the same, however, as asserting that Sidney's experiences with power (within a heavily eroticized power structure at that) would necessarily influence his view of eroticism, in which power inevitably plays a large role. But to reduce the question to an individual poet's experience with political power is misleading. Petrarchan poetry, with its emphasis on an idealized, powerful mistress, may have had a unique appeal to Elizabeth's subjects (and this appeal was exploited by Elizabeth herself) but this was only a minor (and accidental) part of its cultural resonance. Similarly, the appeal of Ovidian verse in England does have to do with changing conceptions of power, but this has to be understood more broadly. The epyllion's warnings about the powerful female wooer have less to do with the final years of Elizabeth's reign (as some have argued) than with larger political, economic, and social changes that were redefining power structures within the culture at large.

Exploring the ways in which power structures coincide with erotic structures has been one of the chief contributions of queer theory to early modern studies. Michael Warner's essay 'New English Sodom,' for example, exposes the ways in which political discourse in Puritan New England depends upon imagining the community as loving brothers. Warner argues that in re-imagining social relations, Puritan leaders drew upon such discourses as male friendship and contract theory: 'Implicitly male contractual relations – for that is what covenant theology was modeled on – were becoming paradigmatic of God's own behavior. At least in part, mutuality and interest were becoming the principles of the social bond, not hierarchy and divine command.'[20] Warner's argument builds to some degree on the pioneering work of Alan Bray, which demonstrated how early modern conceptions of friendship, an eroti- cized relation, corresponded to a particular political system. When the economic situation that fostered one particular model of friendship underwent some change, relations that were formerly regarded as exalted suddenly were open to accusations of sodomy. The particular model of friendship that Bray outlines did not in fact survive much later than the sixteenth century, precisely because of a shift in power structures.

One of the recurring narratives of the epyllion is closely related to the social shift that Bray explores. Although the narratives frequently de- scribe or enact a homosocial circuit of conversation, the poems are deeply suspicious of desire directed at a youth. Adonis's objections to Venus are the most obvious example, with Adonis objecting that Venus's desire will, in effect, stunt his growth:

Who wears a garment shapeless and unfinish'd?
Who plucks the bud before one leaf put forth?
If springing things be any jot diminish'd,
They wither in their prime, prove nothing worth;
    The colt that's back'd and burthen'd being young,
    Loseth his pride, and never waxeth strong.

(415–20)

Because Venus is at times in the poem coded masculine, it is not too much of a stretch to see anxieties about sodomy surfacing here. Adonis's fundamentally economic objections are in accordance with studies of sodomy by scholars such as Jonathan Goldberg, Valerie Traub, and Alan Stewart, which show that accusations of sodomy were centrally concerned with disruptions in various reproductive economies. In her discussion of how female homosocial relations in Shakespeare are displaced by heterosexual ones, Traub argues that 'the gendered and erotic scenarios enacted in these plays do not exemplify psychosexual necessity – that is, a developmental movement through progressive erotic stages – but an economic, political imperative: as each woman is resecured in the patriarchal, reproductive order, her desires are made to conform to her "place."'[21] In other words, heterosexualizing individuals involves coercing them into certain socially reproductive organizations. It thus has less to do with their souls or their desires than it does with their political alignments.

The epyllion frequently warns youths about the danger of being the object of desire, and seeks to position adult males as autonomous subjects of desire. This narrative is often overlaid on the rejection of Petrarchanism, which results in a parallel distinction. The Petrarchan poet is ruled by desire, whereas the Ovidian poet is in control of his desire. The strictures on adult males are not entirely novel. Even in earlier cultures that either institutionalized or tacitly accepted the phenomenon of pederasty as a form of initiation rite, this acceptance is generally accompanied by an insistence on the impropriety of an adult male being the object of another man's desire; this can be seen, for example, in Michael Rocke's account of same-sex desire in fifteenth-century Florence.[22] The novelty in the epyllion is the notion that desire directed at a youth is similarly outrageous, and will likely prevent the youth from becoming an enfranchised adult male. What is changing here is not actual practice but rather the political meaning of sexual practice (if one can separate meaning from practice). And this change, I will argue, has to do with the definition of a political subject within a particular culture. The rejection of Petrarchan poetry has less to do with the power of women than it does with power relations between men, and by this point, we must understand 'men' to mean 'politically enfranchised men.'

Here is where we must look outward to the culture and to the shifts in thinking around political relations and political community. One of the most profound changes in the legal system at this time is the development of the contract, which will be discussed in more detail in the following chapter. The contract will in fact become, in the next century, a model both for political association, in Hobbes's theory of the social economy, and for religious association, in the rise of contract theology. When Hobbes, following scientific principles, resolves society into the smallest political unit, it is not the family or the manor that is the foundation of society, as one might have seen in earlier centuries, but rather the individual.[23] In the development of contract theory we can see the law functioning as an interpretation and codification of shifts in societal consensus. As Christopher Pye argues, 'The appearance of the abstractly defined, freely acting human subject – the contractual subject – is coterminus with the emergence during the early modern era of society understood as an autonomous, impersonal domain, the domain of state and law.'[24]

The individual is at least partly defined by its relative freedom from the relations of submission and domination that characterize the feudal system. In a feudal economy, virtually every subject owes some debt of service or obligation to a superior, and is similarly owed a debt by an inferior. The experience of power differences is completely familiar to the feudal subject, and indeed, to a large degree constitutive of it. The shifting power relations that Heather Dubrow identifies in Petrarchan poetry would in no way be alien to the experience of such a subject, however much it might prefer power to powerlessness.[25] A similar argument was made (in different terms) by C.S. Lewis regarding the connection of courtly love poetry to its own social milieu.[26] Petrarchanisms only offend the subject who believes that it is, or at the very least that it should be, free of relations of submission and domination: precisely the subject we see emerging in early modern England. Not a subject free of power relations, but rather a subject whose power relations are increasingly predicated on equality, in the political, economic, and social sphere, a subject who imagines political association according to a fraternal rather than hierarchical model. The fraternal model is an intermediate step between the feudal political subject and the citizen of a nation state, the latter a category that was only just beginning to be imagined.[27] This intermediate step is the autonomous subject – or rather, the subject that fantasizes its autonomy – that we see narrating the epyllion.

The following chapters look at the ways in which the writers of these poems persistently and directly explore the phenomenon of change. This change is most immediately an alteration of the self, visualized through bodily metamorphosis. However, the poems are interested in far more than simply physical transformations; the transformations are often connected to alterations in the subject's relations to others. These others are most often objects of desire or unwanted suitors, but they can also be groups of others. For example, the defeat or rejection or loss of the woman is sometimes connected with the formation of male communities. While the following chapters are a study of how a genre rewrites dominant male subjectivity, subjectivity and sexuality must be understood as being bound up with other societal discourses: with education, law, economics, and political relations.

The chapters of this book are arranged to take in an increasingly broad view of the relation between individuals and culture. The book will move, then, from fantasies of selfhood, through erotic relations with others, to literary affiliation, political relations, and finally to international issues, such as exploration, settlement, and trade. Underlying this structure is the belief that these issues exist on a continuum, that the subjectivity outlined in the earlier chapters is one that is amenable to the kinds of political relations being theorized in the early modern period.

The first chapter will lay out some of the cultural context and the theoretical underpinnings of the study. Because of the poems' relation to the law schools, this chapter considers how the style of thought of the epyllion, particularly its use of myth, is linked to early modern legal thinking. Both the law and myth are centrally concerned with definitions of subjectivity; using a combination of legal theory and psychoanalytic discourse, I look at how shifts in the definition of property – which is arguably the foundation of the law – will necessarily be bound up with changes in the outlines of normative subjectivity. Finally, I will consider how the development of the contract, a crucial element of the economic changes of the period, leads to a re-imagining of the subject's relations to others, in both the economic and political realms.

Chapter 2 continues the exploration of the cultural context of the epyllion by looking in greater detail at the Inns of Court educational system and the Inns' connections to literary culture. I then move on to discuss two early poems that were explicitly addressed to the young men of the Inns, Peend's *Hermaphroditus* and Lodge's *Scillaes Metamorphosis*, which set the pattern for many of the poems that follow. Whereas Peend's poem offers an admonitory tale about the dangers of the city, Lodge's poem, which has a similar narrative, talks about the dangers of Petrarchan poetry. This will be a common theme in the poems, which tend to associate Petrarchan schemes of desire with immaturity, and Ovidian verse with adult masculinity.

The third chapter looks at the most famous examples of the genre, Marston's *Metamorphosis of Pigmalions Image*, Shakespeare's *Venus and Adonis*, and Marlowe's *Hero and Leander*. This is the most explicitly psychoanalytic of the chapters, and it seeks to identify the fantasy at the heart of the genre. What we see in all of these poems is the danger for the young man of being the object of desire. If he is to move from being a youth to a man, the young man must avoid or repulse the attentions of older men or women, and establish a particular relation to desire, which the poems associate at the same time with a mastery of rhetoric. The poems attempt to naturalize this particular developmental narrative by associating it with a more basic one: the emergence of the speaking subject from the Imaginary into the Symbolic order. According to the logic of the poems, becoming a man, becoming heterosexual, and becoming a rhetorician are all part of the same project.

The lesser-known poems discussed in chapter 4 take up similar stories of youths and goddesses, while at the same time making arguments about the importance of a national literary culture. Edwards's *Narcissus*, his *Cephalus and Procris*, and Weever's *Faunus and Melliflora* all demonize Petrarchan poetry to some degree, associating it with corrupt Italian literary culture and sodomy. This allows these poems both to assert a proper male sexuality and to claim that the true heir of the classical literary tradition is contemporary English writing. In a group of epyllia that take as their most immediate inspiration Marlowe rather than Ovid, we can see a consciousness of this tradition emerging.

In the fifth chapter I look at poems that use Ovidian myth to think in new ways about community or political association and the subjectivities that are implied by these new political forms. Francis Beaumont's *Salmacis and Hermaphroditus*, which retells the story from the most significant precursor of the genre, does not seem initially to lend itself to political readings. However, in his satire of the Elizabethan justice system and his portrayal of a world essentially ruled by bargains, he figures in a comic way the social contract. A similar tendency can be seen in the use of the Orpheus myth in both R.B.'s *Orpheus His Journey to Hell*, and in the writings of Inns of Court lawyer and essayist, Sir Francis Bacon. In particular, we can see how the Orpheus myth is being used alongside contract law to theorize a political community based on fraternity rather than hierarchy.

Chapter 6 looks at sexual violence in Barksted's *Mirrha the Mother of Adonis*, Heywood's *Oenone and Paris*, Shakespeare's *The Rape of Lucrece*, and Barksted's *Hiren, the Faire Greeke*. In particular, the chapter explores how the representation of rape works to consolidate male communities, and serves to provide a dividing line between different political regimes and different versions of the self. Stephanie H. Jed has remarked on how rape frequently appears in foundational political tales; in looking at these poems, which can be seen as foundational narratives of a different kind, I want to identify the implications for the male selves that correspond to the political communities being thus founded. The chapter considers what is at stake in the changes in the rape laws during the sixteenth century, and finds some of the same anxieties at work in the representation of England's fraught relation with the Ottoman Empire in Barksted's poem. The solution posed by the poems is a subject who can successfully accommodate contradiction, a self divided from the self. The perfect model for this is the Ovidian narrator, with his detached perspective on (his own) desire.

The final chapter extends the usual geographical trajectory of the genre from Rome to England further westward. John Beaumont's *The Metamorphosis of Tobacco* is unusual in that it does not retell an Ovidian myth, but recounts instead a series of myths about the most fashionable and controversial commodity of the New World. This chapter argues that the attitudes at work in the earlier, less obviously topical poems are amenable to and even supportive of colonialist enterprise. That is, the particular attitude promoted by the poems towards rhetoric, desire, the self, and the other is fully congruent with political attitudes necessary to resolve the contradictions attendant upon foreign trade and settlement.

As might be expected with a genre in love with digression, this study itself digresses fairly frequently to consider issues that may at first seem unrelated to the poems in question. These digressions are most often used to explore the genre's rhetorical obsessions. The genre's interest in ecphrasis leads to a discussion of the implications of perspective painting for the bodily ego; its play with aetiological digression is related to the development of the concept of the fact in legal proceedings; and its use of chiasmus is linked to the contract. As in the poems, the digressions in this study do contribute to the overall project of the work. The study as a whole aims to consider the genre in its historical moment and to read its rewritings of myth as attempts by these young poets to understand pressing cultural dilemmas. For these young men at the centre of a changing culture the appeal of the *Metamorphoses* is perhaps clear; the following chapters will attempt to bring into clearer focus the use they were able to make of it.

CHAPTER ONE

The Metamorphosis of the Subject

In the opening stanzas of Thomas Heywood's *Oenone and Paris*, the grieving nymph comes upon the man who abandoned her and addresses him thus:

> And art thou come to prosequute the cause
> Of well or woe? my loosing or my winning?
> > Say, gentle Troian, wordes that may delight me,
> > And for thy former lust I will acquite thee.

(57–60)

Oenone's speech begins what is a typical scenario in the epyllion, a discussion of love that is conducted like a debate, hingeing upon an effective use of rhetoric ('words that ... delight,' rather than logic or justice), and frequently employing legal language. The use of legal terminology in a mythological tale is, to the modern ear, a little surprising, but nonetheless appropriate: both law and myth function to map out the intersection of communal expectation and individual members of a group. It is fitting, then, that a genre of poetry produced at the Inns of Court, where the common law was studied, should take up mythical narratives to explore the metamorphosis of subjectivity.

This chapter will discuss the cultural background to the poems and establish the theoretical underpinnings of this study. The first section, 'Law and Society,' looks at the links between the intellectual culture of the Inns of Court and the dominant concerns of the epyllion, and some of the parallels between law and myth. The next section on 'Property and Subjectivity' uses the work of legal theorist Margaret Jane Radin, particularly what she calls the personhood perspective on property, to explore the implications of property law on selfhood. Radin's theories can be used as a new avenue into two of the more hotly debated topics in early modern studies: the historical dimensions of subjectivity, and the outlines of the early modern body. Her insights into the connections between persons and things can be productively combined with the early work of psychoanalyst Jacques Lacan on the bodily ego in order to explore the subjective implications of the changes in the legal system in the early modern period. The final section, 'Contract and Sovereignty,' outlines in brief the rise of contract theory in English law, and the connections between the contract, the psychology of absolutism, and the emergence of the individual.

Law and Society

Thomas Lodge's *Scillaes Metamorphosis* (1589) is generally acknowledged to be the first example of the genre, but it was itself heavily influenced by Thomas Peend's *The Pleasant fable of Hermaphroditus and Salmacis* (1565). *Hermaphroditus* retells the tale from Ovid and then offers a long explication of it, recasting it in the terms of the popular London story of the green youth who is not sufficiently guarded against the seductions of the city's many vices. Both Peend's poem and Lodge's are dedicated to the young men of the Inns of Court, and the genre over the course of its production was associated with this milieu. (Ovid himself studied rhetoric and law and acted for a time as a minor justice official.)[1] Peend, Lodge, John Marston, John Beaumont, and Francis Beaumont are all known to have attended one of the Inns; among the lesser-known writers, Richard Barnfield, William Barksted, and Thomas Edwards are thought by scholars to have been associated with the Inns of Court and Chancery. Ironically, the two best-known poets to write epyllia were also the least typical; neither Shakespeare nor Marlowe attended the Inns, although both were certainly familiar with and familiar to this world. Perhaps because of the prominence of these two writers, the influence of the Inns on the epyllion has not been fully examined, although it is frequently mentioned.[2] Exploring the milieu out of which the genre emerged will help to illuminate the cultural interventions the poems are making.

For the duration of the sixteenth century, the Inns of Court were an important site of literary activity and translation, producing some of the earliest English drama, the first English tragedy (*Gorboduc*, by the Inner Templars Thomas Norton and Thomas Sackville), many of England's finest poets, and its most comprehensive statement of poetic theory, George Puttenham's *Arte of English Poesie* (Puttenham attended the Middle Temple).[3] Epyllia, however, are unusually well suited to this environment, featuring bravura displays of rhetoric and legalistic argument against a backdrop of mildly licentious behaviour. Not only were the Inns central to English literary and intellectual life, they were also, through their stewardship of the common law, an important guardian of Englishness.

For early modern legal thinkers Sir John Davies and Sir Edward Coke, the common law was central to an English national mythology.[4] For both writers, the common law was both ancient and quintessentially English, one of the key points of difference from the continent, where Roman civil law prevailed. The common law was associated by many with English custom and relied upon the 'common erudition' of the legal profession rather than a codified system of principles. Thus not only was the common law itself mythologized, it also functioned analogously to a mythological system of knowledge.

To the modern eye (and probably to the sixteenth-century eye as well), the English legal system is bewildering, with its various systems of law and types of courts with overlapping jurisdictions.[5] The three kinds of law in use at the time were the common law (taught at the Inns of Court), the civil law (taught at the universities), and the canon law (taught at the universities and used in the church courts). The ecclesiastical courts, according to *De Republica Anglorum* (1583), had jurisdiction in four areas: 'Testamentes and legations, Tythes and mortuaries, mariage and adulterie or fornication and also of such things as appertaine to orders amongest themselves and matters concerning religion.'[6] Most minor criminal and civil matters were dealt with by the local courts, which held petty and quarter sessions presided over by Justices of the Peace. At Westminster rested the three principal common law courts: the Court of Common Pleas, the Court of King's Bench (a higher court), and the Court of the Exchequer. The financial courts, including the Courts of Augmentations, First Fruits, and Wards, also employed the common law to some degree. Finally, there were the prerogative courts, principally Chancery, Star Chamber, and Requests, which were often seen as a rival or threat to the common law courts. The jurisdictional distinctions between these courts were by no means clear-cut, and even among the common law courts there was a certain amount of jostling for clients.

The most active common law court was the Court of Common Pleas, and its main business was civil litigation concerning real property, tres-pass, and debt.[7] All action in the court originated in a writ obtained from Chancery outlining the suit. The writ formed the basis of the pleading in court, which would serve to establish the legal issue at stake in the case. From there, the case would proceed to an examination of the relevant facts. J.H. Baker writes, 'Since the writs governed the whole course of the action, and varied according to the form of action, they were tradition-ally regarded not only as the foundation of every action but as the foundations upon which the whole law depended.'[8] If the writs were the foundation of the system, for the common lawyers, 'the most important part of the whole law was the science of pleading.'[9] Legal historian T.F.T. Plucknett writes, 'The whole business of pleading orally, in the face of the court and with opponents ready to pounce at any moment, was an immensely skilful and recondite game, conducted with great virtuosity by the leaders of the bar, and keenly relished by all others who were sufficiently learned to understand what it was all about.'[10] Not surpris-ingly, then, the first two parts of the law student's education were mas-tery of the system of writs followed almost immediately by elementary mooting practice.

During the latter half of the sixteenth century, judges exercised a fair amount of latitude in interpreting the statutes, either restricting or expanding the scope of the legislation, most often by speculating on the intent of the law-makers. In reaching decisions, common law justices relied on what was known as the 'common erudition' or 'common learning,' which would include, among other things, previous interpre-tations of the statutes, common law maxims, and to some degree prec-edents (which were not considered binding). In *The Common Law Mind*, J.W. Tubbs argues that the primary way in which the common law can be understood to be based on custom is in its dependence upon this common erudition, which can be understood as the customs of the legal profession, 'the thinking of the very small elite group of lawyers and judges who try cases in the king's courts ... carried forward mainly through oral tradition.'[11] Following Frederick William Maitland, Baker argues that 'the common law was the creature of the inns of court. It is not just that the judges were chosen from the serjeants, and the serjeants from the readers in court. The "common learning" of the profession was generated and nurtured in the halls of the inns rather than in the hall of Westminster Palace, where it was put into practice.'[12] Because of this emphasis on the common erudition, Baker argues that Readings, moots, and lectures held at the Inns of Court, as well as informal discussions over dinner among the barristers or serjeants, could conceivably exert just as much influence on the interpretation of the common law as a decision at court.[13]

In addition to common erudition, argues Tubbs, early modern common lawyers also understood the law as embodying 'common reason.'[14] As with the identification of the common law with custom, the identification of it with reason must be understood in a particular way. Although all law is supposed to be founded upon reason, it is obviously not identical to it. Coke used the phrase 'artificial reason' to characterize the reason of the law in order to indicate two things: 'the knowledge of legal reason by legal professionals is not spontaneous or innate [but rather learned through education and experience], and the reason itself is artificial in the sense that it is constructed by the art and professional skill of lawyers,'[15] in particular through legal rhetoric. Reason, in other words, is the product of legal processes, manufactured through the various artifices of the law and the system of legal education.

These two contemporary definitions of the common law – common erudition and common reason – clarify the epyllion's indebtedness to the cultural milieu out of which it emerges, especially in terms of its style of thought. Any rewriting of myth can of course be seen as depending upon a common erudition, and certainly Ovid was a key part of every Elizabethan schoolboy's education.[16] Writers engaged with the mass of mythological material just as the common law lawyers and judges dealt with previous interpretations of statutes and legal judgments; in both cases, the writers and the lawyers respect for the most part the dominant thinking of the tradition, but do not privilege any particular interpretation that has come before them. In the case of the law, some of this dominant thinking was crystallized in the form of the common law maxims, which John Rastell called 'the foundations of the law, and the conclusions of reason ... certain universal propositions so sure and perfect that they may not be at any time impeached or impugned.'[17] Common erudition's dependence upon these maxims is reflected in a playful way by the epyllion's use of sententiae, most often to express truisms about women. In spite of their dependence upon tradition, both common erudition and mythological writing allow for a great flexibility in thinking about the contemporary relevance of a law or a myth.

The characterization of the common law as common reason emphasizes that the law is a process through which reason and truth emerge. This mirrors the epyllion's interest both in developmental narratives and in the action of narrative itself. These narratives are not simply about the maturation of a youth, but rather about particular youths, whose lives achieve through the action of the narrative iconic significance. Through the action of the story of Venus and Adonis, the youth Adonis is turned into the cultural signifier 'Adonis.' The name comes to represent a common narrative, which expresses a cultural truth: the meaning or moral of the myth. Moreover, in these myths of metamorphoses, the transformation of the characters most usually represents a kind of justice, some kind of judgment upon their lives or recent actions. Important truths emerge through or are manufactured by the processes of mythological discourse, and the Elizabethans understood these truths to apply to their own culture.

But the most important connection between the philosophy of the common law and that of the epyllion is the central place occupied in both by rhetoric. The practitioner of the law or the writer of mythological narrative enters into a conversation with an established body of discourse, and the success of that intervention depends almost entirely upon a skilled use of rhetoric. Thomas Hedley in 1610 referred to the process of pleading used by lawyers and judges as a 'discourse of art or wit,' a description which could just as appropriately be applied to the epyllion.[18] This sense of the importance of rhetoric as a cultural skill would not, of course, have been limited to those who attended the Inns of Court, given the generally understood importance of rhetoric within humanistic culture. But then, as now, rhetoric was central to a legal career. In fact, Henrician-era humanists proposed various reforms to the common law, including, most ambitiously, a proposal written for Cromwell to establish a new law school in London to teach common lawyers according to humanist doctrine.[19] This proposal never came to fruition, but the change would later come; Louis A. Knafla argues that 'the development, thought and writing of the common law profession was transformed from 1580–1620 as the inns of court were drawn into the orbit of the education revolution of the Edwardian period.'[20] Chief among the changes was an increased interest in rhetoric. For those students who witnessed the moots or listened to the senior members of the profession disputing after the Readings, and then saw how these discussions became a part of the common erudition and thus of the common law, these exercises would have been an unusually potent demonstration of the potential power of effective rhetoric. It is thus not surprising that this genre of poems that emerged out of the Inns would frequently associate the maturation of the youth with the acquisition of rhetorical skills, especially since progress within the ranks of the profession depended largely upon a demonstration of those same skills.

Rhetoric is perhaps *the* central concern of the epyllion. Some of the poems share the humanist faith in rhetoric as both the foundation and the guarantee of civilization, whereas others see it more cynically as simply a powerful cultural tool that can be used for any purpose, moral or otherwise. All, however, are impressed with its power, and many epyllia seem on the surface to be little more than skilled debating jousts between various mythological characters. Some characters in the poems, particularly male youths, are seen acquiring a rhetorical education, or at the very least a better appreciation of the power of rhetoric. All the poems, however, can be seen as calculated displays of the poets' rhetorical skills. A. Leigh DeNeef argues, for example, that R.B.'s *Orpheus His Journey to Hell* functions as a catalogue of poetic and rhetorical forms, designed to show off the poet himself as a latter-day Orpheus.[21] One of the chief aims of the genre, as Elizabeth Donno writes, is to display the poets' ability to commandeer a well-known narrative and ring surprising changes on it; *inventio* was one of the key grounds on which a poet was judged.[22] In these poems *inventio* is at the forefront, as ninety lines of Ovid are spun out into nine hundred lines of rhetorical flash. Such display is to be expected in a culture in which advancement was increasingly dependent upon rhetorical ability.

More difficult to assess is the extent to which the genre's use of legal terms is a product of the Inns' culture. English literature in general in this period is unusually conscious of the law and prone to employing legal language. The English were in the second half of the century more than usually litigious, but they had been for some time a litigious nation.[23] Moreover, by this time a stay at the Inns was seen as an almost indispensable part of an English gentleman's education. That any genre of English literature, whether associated with the Inns of Court or not, should show a consciousness of legal language is not then surprising. And so although the genre originated in the Inns, with the young men of the Inns as its primary audience, other writers not associated with the Inns, most prominently Shakespeare and Marlowe, could pick up the conventions of the genre with ease (and in the case of these two writers, surpass the earlier examples of the genre quite considerably).

Although epyllia are often marked by legal language and an almost obsessive interest in rhetoric, this is not to say that characters in the poems explicitly reflect on legal issues. We do occasionally get satires on the legal profession, as in John Beaumont's *The Metamorphosis of Tobacco*, or the justice system, as in Francis Beaumont's *Salmacis and Hermaphroditus*. But for the most part the poems, on the surface, reflect their origin in Ovid. They are stories of gods and mortals, of youths changed to flowers, and nymphs transformed to rocks. The discourse of myth, however, is related to the discourse of law at a fundamental level. Law records or attempts to codify the expectations of the polis. It defines the basic conditions for membership in the community and, as we can see from even a cursory glance at legal history, the law is an ongoing process of interpretation. The law exists in a dynamic relation with other institutions (broadly understood) of a particular society; as the Marxist philosopher Louis Althusser might put it, the law is a relatively autonomous discourse that obeys its own discursive imperatives in the first instance, but which must of necessity respond to changes in other societal discourses. Indeed, it could be argued that this is precisely the law's function: to interpret or reflect on cultural change in light of societal consensus, and to codify that change.

Myth operates on a similar level as the law, but from a different perspective. Like the law, the impulse of myth is fundamentally interpretative. Leonard Barkan argues in his brilliant meditation on the history of the Ganymede myth, 'A narrative handed down from early times is not merely a random, arbitrary, or given set of signs for which later, more literate groups struggle to invent meanings. It is rather a hermeneutic exercise in itself, an attempt to interpret a reality which is itself as perplexing as any constructed symbols.'[24] He remarks elsewhere, 'The presence of a myth in a work of art testifies to a problem, a mystery, a complexity, even a self-contradiction. If we understand the myth, we can perceive at least the elements of the mystery.'[25] Barkan opposes the view that myths were ever believed in a simple or credulous way. On the contrary, myths from their origin are attempts to understand certain problems of existence. These problems, it could be argued, reside largely at the intersection of the self and the community. Following Claude Lévi-Strauss, Jacques Lacan argues that 'myth is always a signifying system or scheme, if you like, which is articulated so as to support the antinomies of certain psychic relations. And this occurs at a level which is not simply that of individual anguish and which is not exhausted either in a construction presupposing the collectivity, but which assumes its fullest possible dimension.'[26] Myth, according to Lacan, is not about the experience of individual subjects or about the collective group, but rather about a generalized subject within that group. As Arthur Golding writes in his 'Preface. Too the Reader':

Now when thou readst of God or man, in stone, or beast, or tree
It is a myrrour for thy self thyne owne estate too see.
For under feyned names of Goddes it was the Poets guyse,
The vice and faultes of all estates too taunt in covert wyse.

(81–4)

For Golding, Barkan, and Lacan, then, myth is an attempt to comprehend, within a fictional structure, certain contradictions or antinomies
of existence, contradictions that largely arise, we might note, from the
clash between individual desire and collective expectation. Or, to put it
another way, myth is a reflection on the problems of the law, from the
perspective of a generalized self.

Neither law nor myth is a static discourse. Both are attempts to understand or interpret the outlines or expectations of a particular society. As
Barkan argues, 'For those who believe ... that the history of a myth is not
only an effect of culture (like a sofa) but also a cause, then the history of
a myth becomes a history of how culture and myth constitute each
other.'[27] Barkan's cautions are important to bear in mind when dealing
with the epyllion. It is tempting to read these poems as simply literary
exercises, using the raw material of Ovidian myth as nothing more than a
platform for rhetorical flourish and self-display. To read them in this way
is, as Barkan would argue, to see the myth as having a stable meaning,
'Too often we establish the "facts" of a mythic narrative and then determine its conventional interpretations with the goal of setting the individual talent in the frame of tradition. Such a process implies that myth
making and myth exegesis are separate activities with a hierarchical
priority.'[28] This study follows Barkan's implied injunction by treating
epyllia as serious attempts to understand and reflect on the particular
cultural changes experienced by their writers.

Property and Subjectivity

In a scene very much interested in metamorphosis, bodily and otherwise, Hamlet comes across a lawyer's skull while bantering with the
gravedigger, 'This fellow might be in 's time a great buyer of land, with
his statutes, his recognizances, his fines, his double vouchers, his recoveries. [Is this the fine of his fines, the recovery of his recoveries,] to have
his fine pate full of dirt? ... The very conveyances of his lands will scarcely

lie in this box, and must th' inheritor himself have no more, ha?'
(5.1.103–12). The powerful lawyer, the sign of whose power was his
ownership of properties, now lies in a box too small to contain his deeds,
and the land that once defined him now occupies his head in a more
literal way, his 'fine pate full of dirt.' As Margreta de Grazia argues, this
scene's play with the relation between property, inheritance, and identity
is not surprising 'in a system in which property and proper names are
synonymous.'[29]

This section will explore some of the links between property and
identity, and the middle term between them, the body. Following Freud,
Lacan argues that the sense of the self is based first and foremost on the
subject's sense of his or her body. In a related manner, Radin is interested in the connections between rights, properties, and selfhood, especially in relation to legal dilemmas that highlight the surprisingly variable
limits of the body. Drawing upon these insights, we will look at how
shifting conceptions of property (which is becoming increasingly mobile
in the period), changing rights, and new conceptions of selfhood are all
related. It is safe to assume that the young men of the Inns would have
been aware of these legal and cultural developments, but even if they
were not, they would certainly not have been immune to their effects.
The metamorphoses of the epyllion give frequent testimony to the links
between selves, bodies, and properties, as bodies are turned into objects
and (less frequently) objects into bodies. Places are connected with acts
and dispositions (Thrace with pederasty, Panchaia with incest); bodies
are associated with landscapes, and sometimes, in the case of Scilla, even
become part of the landscape. More often, persons are transformed into
things that emblematize central properties of the self. All of these bodily
metamorphoses can be read as fables of subjectivity.

Although psychoanalysis has had, from Freud's reading of *Hamlet*
onwards, a strong connection to early modern literature, the rise of the
new historicism brought with it questions about the ability of psychoanalysis to comprehend historical and cultural difference. The *locus
classicus* for this objection was for a time Stephen Greenblatt's essay on
the trial of Martin Guerre, where he argued that 'psychoanalysis is the
historical outcome of certain characteristic Renaissance strategies' and
that its categories are therefore 'irrelevant to the point of being unthink-
able' for understanding early modern subjectivity.[30] The charges in this
essay have been answered in various ways by, among others, Meredith
Anne Skura, Elizabeth Bellamy, Tracey Sedinger, and Natalie Zemon
Davis,[31] but I want to go back to one of the central objections of the essay

for a moment. Greenblatt writes that psychoanalysis cannot understand what is at stake in the trial, because 'at issue is not Martin Guerre as subject but Martin Guerre as object, the placeholder in a complex system of possessions, kinship bonds, contractual relationships, customary rights and ethical obligations.'[32] Commenting on this, Davis responds that Greenblatt's argument 'goes too far, underestimating the ways in which people with a different sense of boundary from ours or Freud's – of property boundary and bodily boundary – understood a personal history and perceived the guarantee for some stability to the self.'[33] As de Grazia's psychoanalytic reading of *Hamlet* demonstrates, certain versions of psychoanalysis are well suited to explore the shifts in property boundaries and bodily boundaries, and the consequences these might have for subjectivity.

One key difficulty in this endeavour, argues historian Lyndal Roper, 'is to specify what precisely is historical about subjectivity.'[34] Bellamy, in her study of dynastic epic, draws attention to the ways in which new historicist studies foreclose on the notion of the unconscious, with the predictable result that they cannot imagine a subject who is not entirely conscripted to the interests of the state. This problem has to do with specifying the degree to which ideology informs subjectivity at the most fundamental levels. As Skura notes, 'The sequence of past efforts to reduce Freud to Marx or Marx to Freud have failed. Freudians have no way of talking about how culture affects the psyche except as superego and have no theory of group structure except as a projection of individual psychology. On the other hand ... Marxism has no theory of the subject, except as a product of ideology.'[35]

Kaja Silverman's concept of the 'dominant fiction' offers one avenue into this difficult task of identifying the historical dimensions of subjectivity, which at the same time exposes how ideology structures our most basic beliefs about what is real. According to Silverman, the dominant fiction is the agreed upon sense of reality that underwrites a certain society: it 'not only offers the representational system by means of which the subject typically assumes a sexual identity, and takes on the desires commensurate with that identity, but forms the stable core around which a nation's and a period's "reality" coheres.'[36] The dominant fiction thus encompasses a particular society's most basic and fundamental beliefs about the nature of reality. Silverman's analysis builds on the work of Althusser; in particular, she fleshes out the connections Althusser makes between his study of ideology and Lacanian psychoanalysis, in order to specify the connections between belief, subjectivity, and the shared sense of reality. It is the dominant fiction that blurs the difference between what is structural and what is contingent; it is the means through which what is only in fact historical or contingent in a particular culture attains the status of the eternal, the natural, or the normal.

The dominant fiction is thus related to what Althusser calls the dominant ideology. Silverman differentiates between them, however, by arguing that there is no necessary connection between the ruling class and the dominant fiction, but rather that ideologies gain legitimacy at least in part by mapping themselves onto the dominant fiction.[37] What this distinction allows us to see is that subjectivity is structured by a shared sense of the real, and thus determined by ideology to a far greater extent than might be apparent if we focus only on dominant or competing ideologies. We make a mistake, argues Silverman, when we assume that the subject precedes ideology: 'we will not be able to understand the full extent to which ideology permeates subjectivity as long as we conceptualize social agency only or even primarily as a carrier of competing class, racial or even gender values capable of being "grafted" on to an already-formed identity, or a previously articulated fantasmatic structure,' which is to say, we must explore 'the subjective bases of social consensus, and the ideological bases of conventional psychic reality.'[38] It is only when we begin to account for the ideological outlines of what constitutes reality for a particular culture that we can begin to fully historicize the subject. Such an exploration will overcome the problems that Bellamy argues beset most studies of early modern subjectivity, which do not account for the interpenetration of subjectivity and the shared construction of reality.

A clear shift in the early modern dominant fiction takes place in relation to property and law. In a provocative essay on the '"de-moralizing" of debt' in early modern England, Delloyd J. Guth opens with the observation, 'All law is based on property, and all legitimated rights and obligations find their roots in essentially proprietary concepts.'[39] This is true in a very direct way of the common law. To the modern mind, one of the more foreign aspects of medieval and early modern political culture is the buying and selling of what we would see as rights. Plucknett observes, 'Political rights and privileges, the powers of particular officers and the like were treated as if they were land – or at least incorporeal hereditaments, which mediaeval law hardly distinguished from land ... As long as the common law controlled political thought, this attitude of mind persisted.'[40] This property-based approach to rights seems perfectly suited for analysis by what Radin calls the 'personhood' perspective on property, a perspective which focuses attention on the relations between people and things, looking in particular at such questions as what is and is not property, and which kinds of property can and cannot be alienated. Such a perspective allows us to see a continuum between, for example, such early modern phenomena as the enclosure riots, which are clearly about property rights; social mobility, which is at least partially a matter of changing conceptions of property; and social status, which does not at least initially seem to have to do with property, but rather with properties of the self. In this light, a vast array of social and economic changes in the early modern period can be seen as challenges to earlier conceptions of property, and the value of Radin's approach is to show us that these changes necessarily must be accompanied by changes in the nature of the self.

In her essay 'Property and Personhood,' Radin discusses the relation between the two most common senses of the word 'property': things that are owned, and the qualities or attributes of a thing. She argues that these two senses cannot, in fact, be so easily separated: 'to say that property is a property of the self may be more than just wordplay.'[41] Property that is sufficiently treasured or intimate may well act as a part of the self, and properties of the self, such as rights, body parts, or body products, may well be sold. Liberal theories of property, however, tend to see these two things as distinct. Property that is regarded as essential to a sense of self is held to be inalienable and seems to be more protected than other kinds of property, at least in common opinion, if not actually in law. Property that is fungible or alienable, on the other hand, can be transferred without expense to the sense of self. One complication that immediately arises is the difficulty of distinguishing between the two kinds of property; this is further complicated when a property of the self becomes a property in the other sense. Radin cites the example of human organs, which don't seem to be owned until they leave the body, or artificial joints, which cease being property when they are put into the body, and become rather a part of the self. In a more recent book, *Contested Commodities*, she explores a range of contemporary issues that hinge to some degree on commodifying things whose commodification disturbs our notion of personhood, such as surrogate motherhood, baby-selling, prostitution, pornography, and the market in human organs.

Many of these issues concern not just the commodification of the body or body parts, but rather (or also) the commodification of rights, which also straddle the line between the two definitions of property. We might take as a corresponding sixteenth-century example the changes in rape law, which expose the boundary between selfhood and property. Rape occurs with some frequency in the epyllion; Lynn Enterline astutely observes that 'in the Ovidian tradition, rape is the call that interpellates the female subject.'[42] As Enterline's phrasing suggests, the ideological content of that interpellation can vary historically or culturally. Whereas in medieval law rape was considered a crime against property,[43] there were two significant changes in the law in the second half of the sixteenth century: rape and abduction came to be treated as separate crimes, and benefit of clergy was taken away for those convicted.[44] 'Once abduction was made a distinct felony ... the crime of rape came to be seen essentially as that of sexual ravishment, which in turn was viewed as the theft of chastity and virtue, rather than of body and chattels.'[45] Rape, in other words, changes from being a property crime against a woman's family to a crime against the woman's self. In her study of early modern rape trials, Garthine Walker cautions against the notion that 'the experience of rape is self-evidently similar to our own selves,' noting in particular how the law can structure experience: 'it is striking how the common law criteria for rape are present in its depiction even when stories were told in contexts other than *a priori* rape trials.'[46] The change in the legal definition of rape is accompanied by a change in the way rape is understood or experienced at the subjective level, and both are ultimately related to changing conceptions of property and bodily boundaries.

One question that Radin's work raises but does not explore is the psychic implications of social and legal change. What happens when, in a particular society, properties which were hitherto regarded as inalienable and thus essential parts of the self, become alienable or are alienated, when, for example, rights become commodities, or, in the case of the rape law, when what was extrinsic becomes intrinsic? How are these changes accommodated at the level of the self, and through what means? Under this rubric we might consider the shifts in property relations that accompanied the agrarian revolution of the early modern period, and which tended to be denounced as 'enclosure.' While actual enclosure was relatively minor, 'contemporaries used the term "enclosure" for a variety of agricultural practices that resulted in depopulation, the decay of tillage, engrossing, encroachment upon wastes or overcharging common practices, or the assertion of absolute rights of private property that led to the extinction of common use-rights.'[47] At the heart of the enclosure controversies is a conflict over properties and rights. The loss of common use-rights such as pasture, estovers, and turbary had dire economic effects for some, who were consequently forced to abandon rural life and move to urban centres to take up wage labour. Lost then were properties of the self, such as the right to graze animals on common land or to participate in communal decision making regarding land-use. This upheaval would occasion a large shift in the way in which the subject imagined him or herself: a whole set of properties (in the sense of material things) and activities that formerly defined the self would be lost. We can see one consequence of this in the huge increase in slander proceedings brought by women against women in the London courts, an echo of which we see in Francis Beaumont's *Salmacis and Hermaphroditus*, where Venus denounces Salmacis in court as a 'wanton strumpet and lascivious whore' (278). Laura Gowing argues that the slander suits bear witness to a redefinition of gender roles that was caused by large scale migration to the unfamiliar social spaces of London and the loss of the traditional structures of rural life.[48]

In a discussion of subjectivity and ideology, Slavoj Žižek draws attention to Marx's argument that the transition from feudalism to capitalism is characterized by a shift from a fetishization of intersubjective relations to a fetishization of commodities.[49] This shift can be imagined as moving from an emphasis on properties of the self (in relation to others) to properties owned by the self; or rather, from a self that is determined more by inalienable properties (essences) to a self largely constituted by alienable ones (commodities). Whereas in capitalist societies we believe we are free and equal individuals, in feudal societies the relations of submission and domination are both more visible and more determinant. These intersubjective relations come to be reified as status, which is experienced by the subject not as a relation, but rather as a property of the self or the ego. In such a society, social position is necessarily more determinant of identity. In feudal England, we can see this reification of relations in such material practices and social rituals as the status categories of the law, which governed people in different social categories with different laws, or, to take a more specific example, the sumptuary laws, which dictated what clothes could be worn or food consumed according to where one was located in the social order.

In such a system, the subject is encouraged to experience social position as a part of the ego, and social relations as constitutive of identity. This, presumably, is what Greenblatt is referring to when he encourages us to consider Martin Guerre 'as object, the placeholder in a complex system of possessions, kinship bonds, contractual relationships, customary rights and ethical obligations.'[50] Social position, along with all of its attendant rights, privileges, rituals, and obligations, becomes in Radin's terms personal property, or inalienable properties of the self. One of the most basic forms of personal property that Radin focuses on is the body. 'If it makes sense to say that one owns one's body, then in the embodiment theory of personhood the body is quintessentially personal property, because it is literally constitutive of one's personhood. If the body is property, then objectively it is property for personhood ... Certain external things, for example the shirt off my back, may also be considered personal property if they are closely enough connected with the body.'[51] Radin's discussion of the potentially variable limits of personal property and the body come interestingly close both to Davis's discussion of the different sense of property boundaries and bodily boundaries illustrated in the Martin Guerre case, and to Lacan's description of the bodily ego, the image of the body upon which one bases one's sense of self. Turning to Lacan's theory will allow us to explore the implications of Radin's argument at the level of the self.

Drawing attention to the historically variable nature of the subject, Lacan remarks on 'the growing dominance that the function of the *moi* has taken on in the lived experience of modern man, beginning from a set of sociotechnological and dialectical conjectures, whose cultural Gestalt is visibly constituted by the beginning of the seventeenth century.'[52] It is precisely this shift in the prominence of the ego or *moi*, and the various 'sociotechnological and dialectical conjectures' that prepare for the historical appearance of the individual that concern us here. At the heart of these, argues Žižek, are economic shifts, and in particular, the rise of the commodity. Following Alfred Sohn-Rethel, he writes that 'in the structure of the commodity-form it is possible to find the transcendental subject ... the apparatus of categories presupposed, implied by the scientific procedure (that, of course of the Newtonian science of nature), the network of notions by means of which it seizes nature, is already present in the social effectivity, already at work in the commodity exchange. Before thought could arrive at pure *abstraction*, the abstraction was already at work in the act of commodity exchange.'[53] The commodity form, in other words, is directly linked to certain styles of thought and being. The economic revolution of the period, most visible in the rise of the commodity, the contract, and wage labour is thus related to the emergence of new forms of subjectivity (the individual, the transcendental subject), new relations to the physical world (the scientific method, objectivity), and to new political and economic relations (the free and equal subjects of capitalist democracy). We will be tracing the connections between these categories in our discussions of individual epyllia, which can be seen as participating in this larger cultural revolution; the genre performs some of the metamorphoses that lead to the increased prominence of the ego, which Lacan sees characterizing the modern subject.

According to Lacan, the ego can be imagined as both a boundary and a container: 'the image of the body gives the subject the first form which allows him to locate what pertains to the ego and what does not.'[54] In *The Ego and the Id*, where Freud first fully elaborated his concept of the ego, he argues that 'the ego is first and foremost a bodily ego; it is not merely a surface entity, but is itself the projection of a surface.'[55] The ego's boundaries are modelled on the form of the surface of the body, although this surface is itself a projection, which is perhaps what leads Lacan to remark upon the 'ambiguous, uncertain character of the limits of the ego.'[56] This image of the body, which is further elaborated during the development of the subject, follows what Lacan calls an 'imaginary Anatomy' which 'varies with the ideas (clear or confused) about bodily functions which are prevalent in a given culture.'[57] As Lacan half-facetiously remarks, 'Surely false teeth are not a part of my ego, but to what extent are my real teeth?'[58] As Will Fisher shows, a similar question might be asked of the beard in early modern England.[59] What is to be emphasized here is the interrelation between the image of the body and the ego: what belongs to the ego and what does not is related to and dependant on what the subject believes is a part of the body and what is not. As both Lacan and Radin argue, the limits of the body are more variable than might be expected. This can be seen in the case of Robert, a child whose analysis is discussed in Lacan's first seminar. Robert believes for a time that his clothing is part of his body and thus a part of his self, and he fears he will cease to exist if he disrobes: 'his clothes were for him his container, and when he was stripped of them, it was certain death.'[60]

Recent studies in the early modern period have demonstrated how profoundly different scientific and cultural understandings of the early modern body are from our contemporary orthodoxies.[61] At the same time, however, these studies often imply that the outlines or the limits of the body are stable or self-evident, as when, for example, Bruce R. Smith refers to the 'shared fact of a human body.'[62] As historians of science have shown, facts are a matter of cultural agreement, part of what Silverman calls the dominant fiction. (The fact itself, it has been argued, is a product of the same social shift we are discussing and the concept may in fact have emerged out of the common law.)[63] Even the registers or discourses which structure the experience of the body are historically variable, as Janet Adelman points out: 'It's by no means clear in the twentieth century, let alone the sixteenth, that our notions of our bodies are more indebted to medicine and science than, say, to religious doctrine or to all the cultural and individual practices – and accompanying psychic fantasies – that teach us who we are in a bodily sense from birth onward.'[64] Which is to say, not just the social significance or experience of the body, but the 'fact' of the body itself, is a matter of social consensus, a part of the dominant fiction.

A different understanding of the boundaries of the early modern body is reflected in the medieval sumptuary laws, which are premised on another misrecognition of the connection between clothing and self, one which demonstrates the historically and culturally variable limits of the sense of the body.[65] This might account for why sartorial excess is such a frequent target of satirists and preachers, why it is often equated with physical deformity or monstrosity, and why it so frequently functions as a synecdoche for what is seen as a new and socially destructive form of individualism. Joseph Hall, for example, more than once attacks the farmer's social-climbing son, who encloses the fields to pay for his new-fangled clothes.[66] A similar conjunction is at work in the prominence of descriptions of torn or soiled clothing in the testimony of early modern rape victims: 'the sullying of her clothes is itself indicative of a personal violation, for clothes were so often the outward signifiers of individuality as well as status.'[67]

Paying attention to the cultural meaning of the body, which determines to some degree the very basic outlines of the ego, allows us to see, as Silverman argues, how ideology intrudes at the most fundamental levels of subjectivity. This awareness will be important in the readings of the poetry that follow, as both the epyllion and the *Metamorphoses* ceaselessly demonstrate the variable and unstable limits of the body. The bodily transformations with which the poems are concerned – 'shapes transformde to bodies straunge' (Golding) – can be read as a literalization or reification of the psychic shifts that are at the heart of the poetry and which haunt the poets' imaginations.

V.G. Kiernan notes that feudal 'western Europe had acquired a greater richness of forms of corporate life, a greater crystallization of habits into institutions, than any known elsewhere. It had a remarkable ability to forge societal ties, more tenacious than almost any others apart from those of the family and its extensions, clan or caste.' The 'fixity of personal relationships' that Kiernan notes in feudal Europe as the result of this 'crystallization of habits into institutions,' is precisely the reification of social relations through the codification of social rituals,[68] which is what Marx identifies as the fetishization of social status in the feudal economy. One major difference between the medieval subject and the modern subject is a misrecognition by the medieval subject of social position as essence, which is to say, social position is experienced as part of the ego, and thus related to the integrity of the self. This psychic economy is put into question when, in the early modern period, certain social practices change and begin to put an emphasis on the individual without respect to the social position which that person occupies, as, for example, William Holdsworth demonstrates happening in the legal system. In his monumental *History of English Law* he argues, 'All through this period the mediaeval common law was creating the idea of the normal person – the free and lawful man of English society.'[69] This 'normal person' is the contractual subject, who is also, as Christopher Pye points out, the commodified subject, the subject who can begin to imagine himself 'as a mere factor within a circuit of exchange.'[70]

Contract and Sovereignty

The decline of the status categories was intimately bound up with the development of contract law, and both, I will argue, coincide with England's experience with (almost) absolutist government.[71] As Guth's comment about law being founded upon property rights would indicate, shifts in the law are related to, or accompanied by, shifts in the notion of the self, most obviously the juridical self, but political, sexual, and social selves as well. Baker argues that the law changes partly according to its own internal logic, and partly in response to economic and social shifts. New situations arise and laws must then respond: 'the most immediate effect on the law of social change is that it compels lawyers to face questions never raised before; even a simple increase in the volume of litigation may encourage reconsideration of old ideas and the invention of new ones.'[72] The development of the contract is the most obvious example in this period of a profound rethinking of the social that can be seen reflected in the laws. Not only does the contract reflect the development of a new economy, it encourages or demands the rethinking of the borders of the self. In particular, the contract disengages the feudal subject from the status economy both by its insistence on the necessary fiction of the subject that owns itself and through the mirroring function it plays between similarly sovereign subjects.

Social historians since Max Weber have noted the connections between Renaissance individualism and the growth of capitalism, and more particularly, in terms of the law, a connection between these two and the rise of contract. Legal and economic historians point out that the development of some form of contract law was necessary for the kind of economy that was emerging, which saw both the growth of a labour market, and increasing trade beyond the borders of the community.[73] Contract law would not be fully developed in England until the seventeenth century, but its gradual development starts centuries earlier. Its appearance, argues legal historian Kevin M. Teeven, is connected to both a redefinition of property and a decline of status categories:

> During the Middle Ages, property was not 'owned' in the modern sense and so could not be freely contracted for. The economy of that time was not influenced to any significant degree by market forces, and experience shows that a market economy often plays a decisive role in the actionability of forward-looking contractual relations. In circumstances where an economy is not directed by market forces and where a society delineates a person's rights based on the status one was born into, there is little need of, or opportunity for, either freedom of contract or a flexible contractual device for planning. In the main, these early contractual relations did not involve obligations to be performed in the future but rather concerned present exchanges of feudal obligations without any money changing hands. The contract law of the Middle Ages was concerned with security and retention of the status quo rather than with novel trade agreements.[74]

Actions that would later fall under the category of contract were in the Middle Ages subject to actions under either debt or covenant, debt being the most common. One principal difference to note between debt and contract is a shift in temporal orientation: 'in modern legal theory a contract is an agreement to do something in the future, but in Debt the plaintiff was suing for the thing transferred to the debtor.'[75]

Contract law develops out of a rethinking of what does and does not constitute a legal obligation and how legal obligations are incurred: 'In the law it has been traditional to treat the basic distinction as that between obligations which are self-imposed, and obligations which are imposed on the citizen from outside. Broadly speaking, the law of contract is that part of the law which deals with obligations that are self-imposed.'[76] The increasing refinement of the Doctrine of Consideration in the sixteenth century, which was central to the theory of contract, is precisely the rethinking of obligation within early modern England.

Obligations that were previously dictated by custom and status are more and more replaced by obligations that were self-imposed: 'the concept of contract was, in short, replacing custom as a source of law – that is, as the regulator of social and political obligations – and as the source of individual rights and duties – that is, as the regulator of private obligations.'[77] Contracts spring up where feudal obligations previously existed. Obligations that had hitherto been regarded as a part of status, and thus a part of the self, were increasingly being replaced by obligations that were self-imposed and thus alienable or external to the self.

One of the most significant cases in the development of the contract was argued a series of times over the years 1597–1602, at precisely the same time that epyllia were being written. Slade's Case was 'remarkably widely reported'[78] at the time, and while Luke Wilson argues that the suddenness of the shift in thinking that it represents has been overstated, 'it nevertheless seems beyond dispute that the meaning of contractual relations was a matter of particular concern in the last decade of the sixteenth century and the first decades of the next.'[79] One of the key principles this complex case established was that implicit in a contract is a promise, and that the contract is made with intention to fulfil that promise. Legal historians have seen *Slade v. Morley* as a crucial turn in legal thinking about debt, obligation, and even legal processes (in particular, wager of law). But scholars have also argued that it 'has a place in the history of changing assumptions and habits of mind,'[80] in particular, a shift in thinking about intention and conscience, 'a reorientation of human interiority in terms of intentional action.'[81]

The development of contract law is thus at the same time a rethinking of subjectivity. Most obviously, we have the development of a subject that is free to contract for itself at present and for the future. This is clearly necessary for the development of a flexible labour pool composed of subjects who own their own labour power, rather than owing some or all of it to others. But the contract also implies a subject that owns itself, one that is relatively free of customary obligations or free enough at least to determine future action. The rise of contract thus involves a rethinking of the relations between the self and others, and the self and society, as the self comes less and less to be ruled, and therefore defined, by obligations to others based on social position.

Along with this freedom from customary obligation, notes Guth, comes the responsibility for self-management, a major concern of sixteenth-century humanists. The self must take upon it certain monitoring roles that were previously the responsibility of the community. This can be seen as a legal and economic parallel to the new role of the individual conscience in Protestantism. (This analogy would solidify in the seventeenth century with the development of Covenant Theology, which places God and Christian in contractual roles.) This is not to say, however, that with the appearance of the contract arrives the individual or the modern subject. As Mary Polito argues, Henry VIII and his humanist advisors developed a practice of sovereignty based on pastoral power.[82] The widely observed centralization of power that took place over the course of the sixteenth century was at the same time an extension of the monarch's power into the remotest parts of the kingdom and especially, the subject's conscience. Under the feudal system power is experienced in almost exclusively local terms, debt being paid to the overlord, or exacted from those immediately beneath. Absolutist rule inaugurates a new, more personal relation between the subject and the sovereign, where all power is now seen to radiate from and be invested in the body of the monarch. Power, then, is reconfigured and experienced by individual subjects along strictly Oedipal lines. The dyadic, mirroring function of the contract, which is undertaken between equals (or between those who are rendered as such in the moment of contracting) is thus the logical and in some ways necessary correlative of absolutism. This Oedipalization of political subjects in the early modern period would give way, as absolutism gives way, to the modern state, where the power of the state, as Jacqueline Rose observes, operates like the superego.[83] While absolutism may not then be a necessary step in the development of the modern state, it is a logical one (at least in the psychological dimension), and the model of the contract, which reconceives association along fraternal lines, would seem to be an integral part of that development. Both the contract and the oedipal crisis produce a new temporal orientation in the subject toward futurity, an orientation that has frequently been associated with the early modern subject and which accounts for the 'modern' in 'early modern.' Equally importantly, recognizing that the transitional political subject of the early modern state is produced through an Oedipal dynamic accounts for the masculine gendering of that subject, regardless of that subject's sex.

All of the changes in the common law, as reflected in statutes, legal decisions, and the common erudition, would have been explored at the Inns of Court through the Readings, disputations, and moots. Outside of this context, the ramifications of these changes, legal and extralegal, would also necessarily have surfaced in discussions and through nonlegal discourses such as literature and religion. The writers of the epyllion, then, would certainly have been exposed to the legal responses to these changes and, of course, would have experienced these changes in the culture at large.

Which returns us to myth. I argued earlier that myth is an attempt to comprehend certain contradictions at the level of the psyche, contradictions between the self and the social. Changes in the structure of the social will demand changes at the level of subjectivity; new contradictions will emerge that will need to be expressed, if not necessarily resolved. Myth performs that necessary function of interpretation, a parallel function to the law but from the perspective of the self rather than the social. These myths do not necessarily have to be rewritings of Greek and Roman myth, but within a dominant ideology – humanism – the very definition of which was its embrace of classical texts, it makes sense that this culture would return to classical myths. The epyllion's return is, however, an ironic one, and if the genre's aim was unconsciously serious, its tone suggests that it marks the end of this particular stage of humanism.

CHAPTER TWO

'Bold sharpe Sophister[s]': Rhetoric and Education

I prethee *Clodius*, tell me what's the reason,
Thou doost expect I should salute thee first,
I haue sized in Cambridge, and my friends a season
Some exhibition for me there disburst:
Since that, I have beene in Goad his weekly role,
And beene acquaint with *Mounsieur Littleton*,
I haue walkt in Poules, and duly din'd at noone,
And sometimes visited the dauncing schoole:
    Then how art thou my better, that I should
    Speake alwaies first, as I incroch faine would?
    But in a whore-house thou canst swagger too,
    Clodius good day; tis more then I can doo.

                       Everard Guilpin, 'To Clodius'

Everard Guilpin's epigram 'To Clodius' includes many of the popular stereotypes of the Inns of Court gentleman: university educated, under-read in the law (especially Littleton's *Tenures*), fashion conscious (parading his finery in St Paul's Cathedral), ostentatious, snobbish, and morally bankrupt. Guilpin, who studied at Cambridge and lived at Gray's Inn, presumably knew whereof he wrote.[1] This picture, or one very similar to it, shows up frequently in satires, epigrams, and Overburian characters, although Overbury himself disputes that an Inns of Court man would ever be found in a whorehouse. 'For his recreation, hee had rather go to a Citizens Wife, than a Bawdy house, onely to save charges: and he holds Fee-taile to bee absolutely the best tenure.'[2]

    The two poems discussed in this chapter, Thomas Peend's *The Pleasant fable of Hermaphroditus and Salmacis* and Thomas Lodge's *Scillaes Metamor-phosis*, were both produced by writers living at the Inns of Court and both direct themselves to (and in Lodge's case gently satirize) the young gentlemen who came to the Inns for their first taste of London life, and to pursue a career at the centre of the kingdom. These poems offer fables of the perils of London life for these young men desirous of metamorphoses, and in doing so, offer prescriptions for the formation of new sexual and political identities. That the writers would initially turn to Ovid for this purpose is not surprising, given the prominence of his works within the Elizabethan educational system. But as we noted earlier, there were many different versions of Ovidianism, correspond-ing to different cultural sites: the grammar school, the court, the theatre, and so on. Before turning to the poems, then, it will be useful to consider briefly those aspects of the Inns of Court educational system that are relevant to understanding the cultural underpinnings of the epyllion and the particular use it makes of Ovid.

The Inns of Court and the Performance of Rhetoric

As we have seen in the introductory chapter, epyllia were for the most part written by young poets pursuing an education (or simply connec-tions) at either the universities or, more often, the Inns of Court. Philip J. Finkelpearl, whose *John Marston of the Middle Temple* offers a far more comprehensive account of the Inns life than can be given here, charac-terizes the Inns of Court as 'a finishing school,' populated largely by 'an inbred milieu of young men, mostly wealthy, whose orthodox ideals and ambitions mingled easily with licentious conduct (or the pretense of it) and whose fashions in clothes and literature were picked up and dis-carded overnight.'[3] Young men on the rise engaged in mock combats, sparring over real and imagined points of law, just as the characters in the epyllion offer elaborate and legalistic disquisitions in support of their desire. Wilfred Prest argues that 'by the beginning of Elizabeth's reign, the law had virtually replaced the church as the career open to talents, the ladder on which able young men could climb to power and riches.'[4] In Joseph Hall's *Virgidemiarum* we see such a career, as the farmer Lolio 'drudges all he can / To make his eldest sonne a Gentle-man' by sending him to learn the law, 'At Ins of Court or of the Chancerie.'[5] After reading no more than a line of Littleton, and bank-rupting himself at his tailor's, Sartorio returns home to the farm to rack the rents and enclose the pastures. Another fictional example of such a career is that of Justice Shallow in *Henry IV, Part II*, who waxes nostalgic about his youthful days at Clement's Inn, having spent all of his time there drinking, fighting, and whoring. Nonetheless, as Falstaff bitterly observes, after sowing his wild oats in the city, Shallow returns to his country home: 'now is this Vice's dagger become a squire ... now has he land and beefs' (3.3.319–20, 327–8). Shallow's and Sartorio's experiences are presumably typical of a large number of country gentleman who attended the Inns of Court and went on to become Justices of the Peace or other local administrators.

The Inns of Court (Gray's Inn, Lincoln's Inn, Middle Temple, and Inner Temple), as well as the related Inns of Chancery, originated in the Middle Ages.[6] It would appear that from their origin until the seventeenth century, they served two major functions: providing London accommodations for lawyers, and providing an education in the common law. The seventeenth-century writer William Dugdale reports of medieval lawyers:

> they setled in certain Hostells or Inns, which were thenceforth called Inns of Court; because the Students in them, did there, not only study the Laws, but use such other exercises as might make them more serviceable to the King's Court, as Sir John Fortescue in the xlix Chapter of his Book, De Laudibus Legunt Angliae, observeth; where he saith; that the students in the University of the Laws (for so he calleth the Houses of Court and Chancery) did not only study the Laws, to serve the Courts of Justice, and profit their Country; but did further learn to dance, to sing, to play on Instruments on the ferial dayes; and to study Divinity on the Festival; using such exercises, as they did, who were brought up in the Kings Court.[7]

Attendance at the Inns, like attendance at the universities, underwent a phenomenal growth in the latter half of the sixteenth century.[8] By this time it was considered a part of a young gentleman's education to spend some time at the Inns, usually after having attended one of the universities or spent some time at one of the Inns of Chancery. This began to change around the time of the civil war, a change reflected in William Higford's advice in 1658 to his grandson, where he objects to the new fashion of sending young gentleman on the Grand Tour rather than to the Inns.[9] As Higford's opposition suggests, attendance at the Inns did not necessarily mean that one was going to become a lawyer. Many of the young gentlemen were there to acquire some passing knowledge of the law, which was considered both necessary and useful, both for future

involvement in lawsuits and for possible roles in adjudicating local squabbles. This thinking is reflected in Sir Humphrey Gilbert's plan for a new
school in London, Queen Elizabeth's Academy, written in the early years
of the reign (ca. 1570); he proposes that the curriculum include instruction in the law: 'it is necessary that noble men and gentlemen should
learne to be able to put their owne Case in law, and to haue some
Iudgment in the office of a Iustice of peace and Sheriffe; for thorough
the want thereof the best are oftentymes subiecte to the direction of
farre their Inferiors.' One of the reasons, moreover, that Gilbert advances for the foundation of such an academy is so that 'all those
gentlemen of the Innes of cowrte which shall not apply them selves to
the study of lawes, may then exercize them selves in this Achademy in
other qualities meet for a gentleman.'[10]

As Gilbert's comments indicate, in addition to providing young gentleman with the rudiments of the common law, the Inns served for many
as the point of introduction to life in London. They were ringed with
schools of fencing, dancing, and other gentlemanly arts, and were seen
as a prime site of access to the court. Moreover, they were also at the
centre of intellectual life; Barbara J. Shapiro notes that they were 'conveniently located near the Royal College of Physicians, the Society of
Apothecaries, and Gresham College – the centre of London scientific
activity. At Gresham College, scientific lectures could be heard during
the law terms. A fairly substantial portion of the upper classes who were
associated with the Inns of Court were exposed to the fashionable pur-
suits of the day.'[11] The Elizabethan College of Antiquaries, founded in
1572 largely by Inns of Court men, held its meetings during term time to
facilitate their attendance.[12]

For those who were there to become lawyers, a typical legal career
started with a couple of years at one of the Inns of Chancery, followed by
a long tenure at one of the Inns of Court, progressing through the ranks
of inner barrister, outer barrister, and then either Ancient, or Reader
and Bencher.[13] At the Inns of Chancery, the student would first 'become
acquainted with Littleton and the writs and would master the forms and
rudiments of pleading.'[14] George Buck offers a contemporary account
of the role of the Inns of Chancery (he notes that he himself attended
one of the Inns):

> In these houses or colledges the Tyrones and young Gentlemen, at their
> comming up are initiated to make first here an essay and a triall of the
> studie of the Law, which if they like and have a desire to proceed, then

remoue shortly after to one of the Innes of Court, whereunto that house of Chauncery belongeth: for he can take no degrees in an Inne of Chauncery ... twice euery yeere, in Lent and in August, a learned Gentleman is chosen out of the ranke and degree of counsellers, to come to heare the Mootes or disputations and exercise of the young Students, and to read a law lecture in euery of these houses of Chauncery, belonging to that Inne of court from which this Reader hath his mission.[15]

As Buck indicates, it was at the Inns of Chancery that the students would first encounter the moot, one of the major forms of legal education at both kinds of Inn. Students would then likely proceed to the Inn of Court that governed the Inn of Chancery he attended. (Gray's Inn, for example, governed Staple Inn and Barnard's.) Buck describes the rest of the process of education at the Inns of Court:

After some yeeres well imployed in the Studies of their professions viz. The municipall Law of Englande they obtaine the degree and title of Inner Barresters, and at the Seauen yeeres ende they proceede or become out-ward Barresters, and are then saide to bee called to the Barre, and shortly after they are allowed to make publik profession and practice of the Law in al courts and to giue counsell unto all Clients, and hereuppon they are also called councellors at the Law, and learned Councell. After some more yeeres and as they grow in Learning, and credit, they come to degrees of higher dignity, and reputation: and are allowed to read the Law publikely in their halls (which they perform with much magnificence, and solemnity) and are henceforth called readers ... Concerning the Scholler-like excercises which they haue in these houses: they haue conferences, and disputations which they call mootes, and pleadings, and putting cases, and Lectures, and readings uppon the Lawes and Statutes of England. But these ordinary Lectures, and readings are not performed with much magnificence, (as those more solemn readings are whereof I spake before) which are onely kept in the Lent, and in August, viz. twise a yeere. But all these readings, as well the greater as the lesser, serue much for the helpe and instruction of all professors there assembled, but chiefely of the younge Students, and Tyrones, who also if they be diligent, and desierous to attayne to the better knowledg of the Law, doe not only frequent these mootes, and lectures holden in their Houses, but also in the Tearme time resort to Westminster hall to heare the pleadings, & arguments, and iudgment of the best, and chiefest professors and Judges of the law.[16]

We can see contemporary evidence of these activities in the diary kept by John Manningham while in residence at the Middle Temple.[17] Manningham, in addition to attending, summarizing, and commenting on a remarkable number of sermons, reports on trials at the 'Kings benche' (81, 99), the county assises (53), a 'great Court of Merchant Adventurers' (75), Star Chamber (122), and the performance of *Twelfth Night* at the Inn as part of their Christmas celebrations (48). He participates in a moot on 16 December 1602 and another the following April: 'Mr Timo[thy] Wagstaffe and my self brought in a moote whereat Mr. Stevens, the next reader, and Mr. Curle sate' (224).

There were different kinds of moots but all involved the trial of a standard case from one of the moot-books.[18] J.H. Baker notes, 'these moots were practical exercises which mirrored the process of "tentative" oral pleading in the Common Pleas ... As in the real court, the main object was not to settle an abstract point of law but to frame an issue in a legally acceptable form.'[19] The moots were exercises that taught the practical use of both rhetoric and narrative, since every case would involve finding the appropriate narrative in the law for the presentation of the facts of the case. Advancement through the steps of the legal profession depended largely upon the participation in the moots, and thus upon the performance of rhetoric: 'As soon as a member of an inn was allowed to argue a moot at the bar, and did so, he thereby made himself a barrister; and as soon as he was allowed to sit on the bench at moots, and did so, he thereby made himself a bencher. Each step was doubtless regulated by customs and orders as to standing, but the process of graduation was inseparable from the performance of moots.'[20] This corresponds to a common pattern in the epyllion, where the line between immaturity and maturity is frequently marked by the acquisition and demonstration of rhetorical prowess.

The other major form of legal education undertaken at the Inns was the Reading, which took place during the vacations in Lent and in August. Benchers would lecture on one of the statutes, drawing out legal issues and expounding upon them. These would be accompanied by disputations, a string of legal cases that would be put by the Reader, which would then be disputed. Baker argues:

What was being taught was a method, and a cast of mind, rather than mere rules. Some of the questions were clearly designed more to stretch the mind than to establish any principles which might be of practical utility: for

instance, how to try bigamy in an appeal brought against a clerk by the
bishop and archbishop, whether a woman justice of the peace could send
her own husband to gaol, or how a person could be a villein every other day
of his life and a free man on alternate days.[21]

The process of exploration involved in the disputations is similar to that
involved in the epyllion, which plays with the logic of myths. Here we
might remember Lacan's comments about myth as a cultural logic. The
law is also a cultural logic of a more restricted kind: a codification of
expectations concerning, for the most part, the subject as citizen or the
juridical subject, rather than the sexual or religious subject. Therefore at
the centre of this educational system is rhetoric and logic. The lessons
learned in the disputations, particularly, as Baker notes, the exploratory
mindset, were useful training for the men who would take up positions at
the centre of early modern English society and government.

A final component of the Inns' education worth noting is more informal; it involves participation in various ceremonies and entertainments
that took place at the Inns. D.S. Bland, in fact, makes the argument that
participation in these entertainments was the most important part of the
Inns' education.[22] Although this overstates the case,[23] they were nonetheless a crucial part of it; one benefit cited in Nicholas Bacon's report to
Henry VIII on education was that it introduced the students to the
culture of court.[24] In a slightly different context, we see Thomas Heywood
arguing for the educational benefits of acting in *An Apology for Actors*.
The universities allow the performance of plays, writes Heywood, because it 'is held necessary for the emboldening of their Iunior schollers,
to arme them with audacity, against they come to bee imployed in any
publicke exercise ... It teacheth audacity to the bashful Grammarian ...
and makes him a bold Sophister, to argue pro et contra ... to reason and
frame a sufficient argument to proue his questions, or to defend any
axioma, to distinguish of any Dilemma, & be able to moderate in any
Argumentation whatsoeuer.'[25] He goes on to observe that '*Tully* in his
booke *ad Caium Herennium* requires five things in an Orator, *Invention*,
Disposition, *Eloquution memory*, and *Pronuntiation*, yet all are imperfect
without the sixt, which is *Action*.' Although Heywood is speaking from his
experience at Cambridge, his comments are, if anything, more applica-
ble to the Inns of Court education, and to the entertainments they
staged.

The most commented upon of the entertainments are the masques,
which were occasionally staged for visiting monarchs and dignitaries. As

with the masques at court, the Inns' entertainments were a chance both to gently comment upon current political affairs, and to showcase the talents of the performers. This could include the courtly arts that Dugdale refers to as a part of a gentleman's education, such as dancing, fencing, and so on, but would as well demonstrate the increasingly practical bureaucratic skill of rhetorical finesse. And as with the epyllion, a particularly skillful performance might, at the very least, bring one's talents to the attention of those who mattered. Legend had it that the dancing performance of Sir Christopher Hatton in the 1561 Inner Temple masque captured the attention of the queen and was the first step in a political career that took him all the way to the Privy Council and the most intimate circles of power.[26] The evidence suggests that the Inns' masques were very popular events.[27]

Louise Brown Osborne notes, 'The young men who were denizens of the Inns of Court were extraordinarily self-conscious students of literary expression ... Conscious attention to tricks of style was so assiduously and generally practised in the sixteenth century that the young [Middle] Templars could amuse themselves by devoting most of their Christmas revels in 1597–8 to elaborate literary parodies.'[28] Given that these particular revels took place during the same decade in which epyllia were written, it is perhaps not surprising that one of the chief targets of the parody is Petrarchan poetry. The Templars were warned that if 'any man swear his foul Mistris fair, his old Mistris young, or his crooked Mistress straight ... he shall be condemned as a forsworn Sorcerer for the one, and as a false seducer of the Innocent in the other.'[29] One of the participants in these revels was John Hoskyns, who later reproduced examples from his 'Tufftaffeta' speech in a guide to rhetoric written for a young man at the Middle Temple, *Directions for Speech and Style*. This speech was partly in response to the presence of Sir Walter Ralegh, and for this reason includes references to tobacco, that most fashionable commodity associated with the famous English adventurer. A few years later, while residing at the Inner Temple, John Beaumont would write an epyllion in honour of tobacco.

Understanding some of the Inns culture, their educational system, and their central position within Elizabethan political, intellectual and cultural life helps to put into context the concerns of the genre of the epyllion and what the young poets who wrote these poems may have been hoping to achieve. Whether or not they were consciously written as mere *jeux d'esprit*, the poems were written by and for young men who were training themselves to play roles at the centre of their nation's life.

If they are merely jokes, they are jokes that betray both the serious aims and the anxieties of their writers. For the rest of this chapter we will look at the first poem in the genre and one of its key precursors. While both of these poems offer very direct lessons for the young men of the Inns, we shall see that there are a number of less obvious lessons contained in them as well.

The Pleasant fable of Hermaphroditus and Salmacis

While Thomas Lodge's *Scillaes Metamorphosis* is usually recognized as the first example of the genre, Lodge clearly made use of Golding's translation of the *Metamorphoses*, and 'of even more importance, of a translation of the story of Salmacis-Hermaphroditus by Thomas Peend.'[30] In 1565 Peend published *The Pleasant fable of Hermaphroditus and Salmacis*, as a way of compensating, he says, for having had his translation of the *Metamorphoses* 'prevented' by the earlier publication of the first four books of Golding's (sig. Aii).[31] Peend's poem follows Ovid more or less faithfully, and in the tradition of the medieval Ovid, he appends the tale with a moral. In order 'that the unlearned myght the better understand these' verses, Peend also includes a glossary of mythological names and their significance.

The tale of Hermaphroditus and Salmacis would be the subject of a later epyllion by Francis Beaumont in 1602, but the poem's influence on the genre goes beyond this. James H. Runsdorf notes that one of Peend's innovations involves 'the extensive use of animal imagery to represent Salmacis's sexuality as predatory,'[32] which we will later see in Shakespeare; we might further note that in employing animals familiar to the English reader, Peend, like Golding, also anticipates one of the central strategies the epyllion uses to English Ovid.[33] More importantly, Peend introduces what will be the most common couple of the genre: the aggressive female wooer and the beautiful but reluctant youth. In discussing Shakespeare's innovation of portraying a 'chaste, resistant Adonis,' William Keach notes that 'Ovid himself provided the models for developing this conception in the tales of Hermaphroditus (*Metamorphoses* IV. 285–388), Narcissus (*Metamorphoses* III. 342–510), and Hippolytus (*Metamorphoses* XV. 492–546). Like Shakespeare's Adonis, all of these figures are supremely beautiful young men full of self-love and self-ignorance who come to tragic ends.'[34] Hermaphroditus, along with Adonis, Leander, Endymion, and Narcissus, acts out one of the most recurrent narratives of the genre: an attractive youth metamorphosed through desire.

In Peend's poem, Hermaphroditus is the child of Mercury and Venus,

'for beuty farre excellyng all / that erst before hym weare'(sig. A3),
surpassing, says the narrator, even the beauty of Ganymede, Narcissus,
and Adonis. At the age of fifteen he leaves home and wanders to the hot
land of Caria, where he is spied by the nymph Salmacis. She falls in love
immediately and attempts to woo him, but he 'blush[es] as red as blood'
(sig. A5v) at her advances and flees. Salmacis retreats, and then spies on
the youth from a bush. He strips, cavorts in the fields, and then slowly
enters the water. Overcome with desire, Salmacis stalks her prey, grabs him
in the water, and begs the gods to unite them. They do, but not in the way
she had in mind, and Hermaphroditus becomes a hermaphrodite:

> But now, when that *Hermaphrodite*
>   dyd see in water playne,
> He entred lyke a man therin,
>   and shulde come foorth agayne
> But halfe a man. Hym selfe he loste.
>   Hys fortune it was so.
>
> (sig. A8v)

Curiously, although the pair are united, Salmacis seems to have disappeared entirely; as with many epyllia, the poem is really only interested
in the fate of the youth. Resigned to his new status, Hermaphroditus asks
the gods to change the well so that it will have the same effect on
whoever else enters it. The gods answer his prayer.

At the conclusion of the story, Peend offers a justification for retelling
this 'tryflyng tale' of Ovid, saying that 'it shewes a worthy sence, / if it be
marked well' (sig. B1). He then shows the sense to us. For the person of
Hermaphroditus, 'understand, such Youthes as yet be greene' who, as
yet untouched by 'affection vyle,' go out in the world 'To lerne and see
the trades of men' (sig. B1r–v). The land Hermaphroditus travels to is
'the worlde / where all temptations be' (B1v). 'By *Salmacis*, intende eche
vyce that moveth one to ill' (B1v). When we surrender to such vices, 'We
chaunge our nature cleane, being made effemynat':

> And so it may now playne appere,
>   the Poet thus dyd tell.
> As many as hereafter shall
>   once enter in thys well
> Of vyce, he shalbe weakned so.
>   Hys nature sure he shall forgo.
>
> (sig. B2v)

Having expounded the meaning of the myth, Peend goes on to give notable examples of lustful women, including such Elizabethan favourites as Echo, Medea, Dido, Helen, Hero, and Juliet.

The moral of the story that Peend offers about worldliness (one which stretches back at least as far as the *Ovide moralisé*)[35] is interesting for a number of reasons. The moral itself is common enough; in surveying a number of early Ovidian poems, R.W. Maslen concludes, 'Evidently the Prodigal Son was alive and well at the beginning of Elizabeth's reign, and was closely connected in the Elizabethan imagination with Ovid's *Metamorphoses*.'[36] The need for a moral differentiates this poem from the epyllia of the 1590s; the later poems will either abandon this tendency or parody it, adopting a distinctly Ovidian amorality that becomes a hallmark of the genre. However, because the poems tend to tell the same story, that of a youth metamorphosed by desire, the moral of the earlier poem can perhaps tell us something about the interest that this particular story had for both the writers and readers of the genre, since the constituency of the poems is by and large the same. As Keach notes, 'Almost all the authors of the Elizabethan epyllia except Shakespeare were at one time or another formally connected either with one of the Universities or with the Inns of Court, or both.'[37] This is also true of Peend, who Wood says studied at Oxford and who was a barrister in London. Peend signs the dedication of *Hermaphroditus*, 'from my Chamber over agaynst Sergeants Inne in Chancery lane' and a later work is signed from the Middle Temple (*DNB*). Bearing in mind the Inns of Court milieu, the poem's moral becomes only too obvious and appropriate: Hermaphroditus is the naive youth from the country, newly arrived at the Inns to become a lawyer or a courtier, and in danger of being overwhelmed by the alluring vices of the great city, 'the world where all temptations be' (sig. B1v). This narrative is reminiscent of Francis Lenton's 1629 poem *The Young Gallants Whirligigg*, where the youth goes 'to the *Innes of Court*, / To study Lawes':

Now here the ruine of the Youth begins,
For when the Country cannot finde out sinnes
To fit his humour, *London* doth inuent
Millions of vices ...[38]

Like the young Inns of Court gallant, Hermaphroditus is insufficiently guarded against his own desires, and his masculinity becomes hopelessly compromised or metamorphosed.

The story of the 'green youth' from the country is a common enough narrative, but one which was frequently told about the young men of the Inns. Lenton, in his character study of 'A yong Innes a Court Gentleman,' observes, 'He is a youth very apt to bee wrought vpon at first entrance, and there are Fishers of purpose for such young fry.'[39] That this was not simply a literary invention is reflected in the courts. On 16 June 1596, Star Chamber heard a case against one Howe, a broker, and Easte, a solicitor, for 'coseninge diuers yonge gentlemen.' The Lord Treasurer 'gave good counsell to there Fathers, [that] when they sende there sonnes to th'innes of Cowrte to haue one or too superintendentes ouer them that maye looke ouer them, & certify there Freindes of there manner of lyuinge, as by experience he hathe knowne to be commonly used.' The Lord Keeper remarked that this kind of cozenage was 'a great and common offence; great because it concerns all the pillars of the land and commonwealth, noble and ignoble; common, because one Williamson has a "bedrolle" of all young gentlemen in the town.'[40] Thus while Peend's tale's moral is presented in general terms, it also contains a more specific lesson appropriate to both Peend's career and the role of the Inns as a notable place where young gentlemen were introduced to London.

Scillaes Metamorphosis

Lodge's *Scillaes Metamorphosis, Enterlaced with the unfortunate love of Glaucus* (1589) is even more explicitly directed to the young men of the Inns than Peend's poem. Lodge dedicates the work 'To his especiall good friend Master Rafe Crane, and the rest of his most entire well willers, the Gentlemen of the Inns of Court and Chauncerie' and signs himself 'Thomas Lodge of Lincolnes Inne, Gent.' This echoes the dedication of Lodge's *Alarum against Usurers* (1584), a pamphlet probably written around the same time to warn young gentlemen about various unscrupulous characters populating London. In particular, Lodge first addresses the same kind of commodity swindle at issue in the court case mentioned above, and there is every reason to believe that Lodge was himself a victim of just such a scam.[41] The victim's father in the *Alarum* bemoans, 'In the Universities thy wit was praised ... but beeing by mee brought to the Innes of Court, a place of abode for our English Gentrie, and the onely nurserie of true lerning, I finde thy nature quite altered, and where thou first shuldest have learnt law, thou art become lawless: Thy modest attire is become immodest braverie, thy shamefast seemelynes, to shamelesse impudencie: thy desire of lerning, to loitering love.'[42] Lodge's epyllion makes a similar pretence to counselling the young. The title page of *Scillaes Metamorphosis*, in a perhaps ironic nod to the tradition of moralizing Ovid, declares it 'Verie fit for young Courtiers to peruse, and coy Dames to remember.' The chance of coy dames reading it would have been remote, however: as Keach argues, 'Lodge's epyllion bears every mark of having originally been a private piece, probably written during the period 1584–1588 and circulated among his friends at Lincoln's Inn.'[43] This was the milieu, Ian Frederick Moulton writes, of most erotic verse of the period, which circulated 'in manuscript miscellanies complied mostly by well-to-do young men at the universities or the Inns of Court.'[44]

Unlike Peend's poem, *Scillaes Metamorphosis* diverges substantially from its source in Ovid. In the *Metamorphoses*, the story begins with Scilla, who is walking naked along the shore one day when Glaucus spies her from the water. Alarmed by his strange shape, she flees in terror, but he calls to her and tells her the story of his transformation. He was originally a human fisherman, he says, who one day landed his catch on a strange stretch of land, and all of his fish revived and 'too seeward took theyr flyght' (Golding 13.1096). Curious, he tasted the herb that they had been lying on, and it made him forsake the land forever. The sea gods received him, and asked Oceanus and Tethys[45] to make him immortal. As a result, his shape changed dramatically: he now has a great grisly beard and bushy hair, and a fish's tail. He concludes his tale by plaintively asking Scilla:

> But what avayleth mee
> This goodly shape, and of the Goddes of sea too loved bee,
> Or for too be a God my self, if they delyght not thee?
>
> (13.1124–6)

In spite of this explanation, Scilla flees without saying anything, and Glaucus is enraged. He asks Circe to make Scilla fall in love with him by means of herbs (transformation by herbs being one common thread of the stories in this section of Ovid). Circe refuses since she has fallen in love with Glaucus, who now flees her. Determined to seek revenge, Circe goes to the water where Scilla normally bathes, and puts some 'jewce of venymed weedes' (14.64) in the water. Scilla enters the water, and her lower parts are transformed into barking dogs: 'Nought else was there than cruell curres from belly downe too ground' (14.75). In this form she wreaks havoc for a while, until she is later turned to stone, becoming one half of the infamous marine hazard. For George Sandys, who as Leonard Barkan notes, 'summarizes and epitomizes, even plagiarizes a whole tradition of mythographic writings,'[46] the myth is about the perils of women:

> *Scylla* represents a Virgin; who as long as chast in thought, and in body unspotted, appears of an excellent beauty, attracting all eyes upon her, and wounding the Gods themselves with affection. But once polluted with the sorceries of *Circe*; that is, having rendred her maiden honour to bee deflowred by bewitching pleasure, she is transformed into an horrid monster. And not so only, but endeavours to shipwracke others (such is the envy of infamous women) upon those ruining rocks, and make them share in the same calamities.[47]

Sandys's moralization of Scilla comes very close to Peend's moralization of Salmacis. Both are 'infamous women' who seek to shipwreck the virtue of others.

In Lodge's poem, the transformation of Glaucus from human to sea god is never remarked upon, and in this version Thetis is his mother. If there is to be a metamorphosis of Glaucus, it will not therefore be of a merely physical nature. Circe is entirely removed from the tale: instead of Glaucus imploring Circe for aid, Glaucus's mother intervenes, pleading with Venus and Cupid to make Scilla fall in love with her son. This is accomplished, and now Glaucus is given the chance to reciprocate and rejects Scilla, having been cured of his love by Cupid. Scilla flees in anguish and, followed by a whole crowd of onlookers, seeks refuge on the shores of Sicillia. Allegorical figures of Furie, Rage, Wan-hope, Dispaire, and Woe appear by her side, and Scilla is metamorphosed into a rock. In short, the story told by Ovid (and by Golding in his translation) is nothing like that told by Lodge.

Another substantial change Lodge makes is the addition of an English narrator. The poem is set near Oxford, 'Within a thicket near to *Isis* floud' (1.2), which places the poem in an institutional setting mirroring that of the poem's circulation. The narrator is clearly a student, and so he acts as something of an identificatory relay between the young gentlemen of the Inns and the sea god who becomes his companion. This relay will become crucial for the metamorphosis that the poem, through its lessons, proposes for the reader. The poem begins with the narrator 'Walking alone (all onely full of griefe)' (1.1), when he is surprised by the appearance from the waves of the sea god Glaucus. At this point in the poem, then, the narrator fills the position of surprised auditor that was occupied in Ovid by Scilla. Like the narrator, Glaucus is mourning an unsuccessful love affair. The two sit down beneath a willow tree, the god's head on the poet's knee, and offer competing tales of woe. Glaucus notes the narrator's education and his seeming failure to profit by it: 'Thy bookes haue school'd thee from this fond repent, / And thou canst talke by proofe of wauering pelfe' (4.3–4). The reference to the education of the youth is a common feature of the genre, which again indicates its primary audience (those who fancy themselves just past immaturity). Glaucus goes on to point out the narrator's youthful naivete, in terms reminiscent of Peend's moral:

> Respect thy selfe, and thou shalt find it cleere,
> That infantlike thou art become a youth,
> And youth forespent a wretched age ensu'th.

(6.4–6)

Here as elsewhere, youth is figured as a potentially dangerous time of metamorphosis.

What are the models of transformation or metamorphosis offered by the poem? Since the original metamorphosis of Glaucus is left out, we are forced to look for other ways in which he (and possibly the narrator) are transformed. The most obvious answer is Glaucus's transformation from a spurned lover, bemoaning his rejection by his cruel mistress, to the disdainful and triumphant lover at the end, who cruelly delights in his former mistress's transformation. Like many of the epyllia that follow, the poem traces out a certain process, often figured as a maturation, whereby a youth who is initially associated with a Petrarchan script of desire triumphs over it. This is certainly the case with Glaucus. As Keach argues, Glaucus's initial posturing (and the narrator's) is in many ways a parody of contemporary Petrarchanisms: the young man besotted with the cruel mistress, moaning over love's losses, writing songs and blazons idolizing and idealizing her. The poems often suggest that such a relation to one's mistress is the product of immaturity, and part of the maturation process involves rejecting a fruitless enslavement to desire. The narrator of Marston's epyllion, *The Metamorphosis of Pigmalions Image*, for example, remarks that

I oft have smil'd to see the foolery
Of some sweet Youths, who seriously protest
That Loue respects not actuall Luxury,

...

And therefore Ladies thinke that they nere loue you
Who doe not vnto more then kissing moue you.

(19.1–3, 20.5–6)

We will see this transformation taking place in Glaucus, as he moves from one scheme of desire to another.

This contrast between Petrarchan and Ovidian eroticism is made early in the poem. The initial period of communal moaning and weeping between narrator and sea-god is interrupted by the 'sweet melodious noyse of musicke' that accompanies the arrival of the river nymphs (9.2). They too trade stories of love, but these stories are Ovidian rather than Petrarchan, tales of the cruelty of desire (rather than the cruelty of women) and full of punning stories about pricks in bushes and in 'Ladies bosomes' (15.6). The natural world responds in kind to their advance: 'The waterie world to touch their teates doo tremble' (10.6), and the flowers seem to recall their former human states and grow erect:

The flowres themselues when as the Nimphes gan bowe,
Gan vaile their crestes in honour of their names:
And smilde their sweete and woed with so much glee,
As if they said, sweet Nimph come gather mee.

(17.3–6)

Placing Ovidian eroticism in the poem in the natural world works, of course, to naturalize it, putting it in direct contrast to the bookish theories of love held by the narrator and Glaucus.

Petrarchan desire is characterized in the poem largely by disproportion. This is literalized in the physical comedy of the grotesque sea god posing as a melancholy youth, his head balanced on the narrator's knee, sighing, weeping, and, several times, fainting. Some version of the line 'so yong, so louely, fresh and faire' (75.4) is applied to him several times (35.4, 72.2), always inappropriately. Glaucus's rhetoric is marked by excess, and especially by water. He is forever weeping at the grandiloquence of his own rhetoric, which we might characterize as leaky. Hearing his tale 'The rockes will weepe whole springs to marke our losse' (19.3); 'The aire from Sea such streaming showres shall borrow / As earth to beare the brunt shall not be able' (29.3–4); his 'moanings are like water drops' (60.1); Glaucus weeps (8, 56, 60, 68, 78), Thetis weeps (2, 77, 80), shepherds weep (20), the nymphs weep (20, 35, 71, 80), the narrator weeps (1–3, 72, 73). All of the precedents that Glaucus gives for his situation are female (Venus [21–3], Angelica [24–6], and Lucina [27]), all of whom are pictured weeping.

Glaucus's Petrarchan rhetoric is thus implicitly connected with womanliness, especially as that is characterized in early modern rhetorical theory. Women, writes Patricia Parker, 'are figured in discussions of rhetoric in ways which evoke links with the "far-fetched," with uncontrollable and even indecent garrulity or speaking out, and with the "mooveable" transportability of certain tropes.' This last characteristic, argues Parker, is connected with the 'extravagantly "mooveable" and talkative harlot,' the woman who speaks in public and thus disrupts order and abandons modesty.[48] This applies more to Scilla in the poem than Glaucus, although as we will see there is a certain transferability between these characters. While Scilla's reputation is never impugned within the poem (although other nymphs comment on her un-nymph-like behaviour), Lodge in the 'Epistle Dedicatorie' personifies the poem as Scilla in ways that evoke the discourse of the common, public woman, passed from man to man: 'Ariued shee is [i.e., the poem], though in a contrary coast, but so wrackt, and weatherbeaten, through the vnskilfulnes of rough writers, that made their poast haste passage by night, as *Glaucus* would scarce know her, if he met her: yet my hope is Gentlemen, that you wil not so much imagine what shee is, as what shee was.' Scilla's punishment at the end of the poem, as well as the palpable relief of the other characters, seems attributable to her dangerous and disorderly mobility.

As we have noted, the removal of Circe from the poem means that it is Thetis, rather than Glaucus himself, who intervenes to effect Glaucus's liberation and transformation. The resolution involves two phases. First Glaucus is cured by Cupid:

> from his bowe a furious dart hee sent
> Into that wound which he had made before:
> That like *Achilles* sworde became the teint
> To cure the wound that it had caru'd before:
>   And sodeinly the Sea-god started vp:
>   Reuiude, relieud, and free from Fancies cup.
>
> (91.1–6)

Glaucus is thus cured by a generic drug, epic masculinity, that both infuses him with activity and quells his windy rhetoric. The cure is both sudden and hilariously phallic: 'all aloft he shakes his bushie creast' (92.4), evoking the Ovidian sexuality of the flowers who earlier tried to tempt the nymphs to take their crests in hand. The narrator feels a 'sodein ioy' (94.6) within his heart, suggesting that he too has been to some degree transformed. Aside from a new-found interest in sex with nymphs, the other major transformation in Glaucus is a shift in rhetorical method. Glaucus rarely speaks for the remainder of the poem, and when he does, he is short, pithy, and direct.

The second transformation is directed at Scilla. Soon after Glaucus's transformation, Scilla floats onto the scene and 'coilie vaunst hir creast in open sight' (95.3). Scilla's mobility, her phallic crest-vaunting, and her 'lawles heart' (97.6), all place her outside the realm of proper femininity. Cupid rectifies this by making her fall in love with Glaucus. In effect, what happens is the role of ridiculous Petrarchan lover is transferred from Glaucus to Scilla:

> Oh kisse no more kind Nimph, he likes no kindnes,
> Loue sleepes in him, to flame within thy brest,
> Cleer'd are his eies, where thine are clad with blindnes;
> Free'd be his thoughts, where thine must taste vnrest.
>
> (103.1–4)

It is Glaucus who now scorns and disdains, the two activities most frequently associated in the genre with the Petrarchan mistress, and Scilla becomes the wooer, the pursuer, the weeper, and the fainter. Woman as pursuer is, of course, inherently ridiculous, a continuation of the comedies of inappropriateness connected earlier with Glaucus's physical grotesqueness. At the same time, it makes plain what was perhaps only implicit earlier in the poem, that Petrarchan desire is inherently womanish.

Scilla's punishment does, in the end, return her to the role of Petrarchan mistress, if obliquely. She had been the subject of blazons earlier in the poem, first at length by Glaucus (stanzas 48–54) and later briefly by the assembled crowd (stanza 97). Nancy J. Vickers has argued that the impulse behind the figure of the blazon is to transfer the punishment of Acteon to Diana, to render the beloved silent rather than the lover.[49] This seems to be the end result here. Rather than having her lower half transformed to hounds, Scilla is beset by personifications of her own psychic disintegration. It is this psychic disintegration that finally renders her both immobile and silent. Diana thus becomes Acteon, but in a way that leaves her a permanent memorial to 'coy nymphs' everywhere. But Scilla's transformation is also, we should remember, a warning about rhetoric, and the appropriateness or inappropriateness of certain modes of eroticism. Scilla stands not just for coy Petrarchan mistresses, but for Petrarchan rhetoric in general, which is perhaps why the poem is 'very fit for young Courtiers to peruse' (as the title page says), young courtiers presumably being the most prone to Petrarchan rhetorical excess (as we learned in the 1597–8 Middle Temple revels).

Operating alongside this critique of Petrarchan love poetry is another story of rhetoric. Midway through the poem Glaucus tells of his rejection by Scilla, after which he wandered the rivers and oceans of the world until he ended up in 'A fruitefull Ile begirt with *Ocean* streames' (65.6):

> And heere consort I now with haplesse men,
> Yeelding them comfort, (though my wound be curelesse)
> Songs of remorse I warble now and then,
> Wherein I curse fond Loue and Fortune durelesse

(69.1–4)

The god's habit of singing to other hapless men his songs cursing Love and Fortune is reminiscent of another more important Ovidian singer, Orpheus. After losing Eurydice, Orpheus abandons the love of women, and dedicates himself to singing about love's disappointments. In R.B.'s *Orpheus His Journey to Hell*, for example, Orpheus similarly sings to the men of Thrace 'invective ditties' about 'unconstant Love' and the 'manie woes a womans beauty brings (110.1–3). Moreover, in Lodge's poem both the god and the narrator have Orphic abilities. Glaucus asserts that on hearing of their woes, 'the rockes will weepe whole springs to marke our losse' (19.3). Later he tells the nymphs that 'could my wit controule mine eyes offence: / You then should smile and I should tell such stories, / As woods, and waues should triumph in our glories' (39.4–6). Not only is Glaucus a singer in this version, he is also, like Orpheus, a musician: 'How haue the angrie windes growne calme for loue, / When as these fingers did my harpe strings moue?' (44.5–6).

The story of Orpheus is taken up at length in R.B.'s epyllion, but Orpheus had a far wider significance in the Middle Ages and the Renaissance than simply that of a character in the *Metamorphoses*. Orpheus was for early modern literary theorists the first poet, the originator of all poetic genres, and the model of the orator. The stories of Orpheus

charming rocks and trees with his song was a tribute to the power of
rhetoric that made him an obvious hero for an age that fetishized
rhetoric as one of the foundations of civilization. Thomas Cain argues
that the early modern humanists, 'find in Orpheus a convenient culture-
hero triumphantly symbolizing the goals of their rhetorical programme.'[50]
Given their own rhetorically based studies, the students of the Inns
would naturally see in Orpheus a model for their own aspirations as
poets, orators, and legislators. That the Inns were an all-male space also
resonates with Orpheus's career. Like Orpheus in the fields of Thrace,
or Glaucus and the narrator on the banks of Isis's flood, the young men
of the Inns to whom the poem is addressed inhabited a world of
homosocial conversation.

Scillaes Metamorphosis ends with a warning to women who might desire a
Petrarchan lover. The narrator writes:

> Ladies he left me, trust me I missay not,
> But so he left me, as he wild me tell you:
> That Nimphs must yeeld, when faithfull louers straie not,
> Least through contempt, almightie loue compell you
> > With *Scilla* in the rockes to make your biding
> > A cursed plague, for womens proud back-sliding.

(L'Envoy)

This, presumably, is the lesson fit for 'coy Dames to remember' that the
title page promises. In relaying this message from sea god to reader, the
narrator shows that he too has been hit by the arrow of disdain. Like
Glaucus, he has been transformed from a besotted Petrarchan lover in
the opening stanzas to a lover who lays down the law to proud ladies.

As we have noted, the poem was not meant at least initially for coy
Dames to read, so it is perhaps useful to isolate the lesson contained for
the 'young Courtiers' of the Inns. Unlike many of the central figures in
the genre, such as Adonis, Narcissus, and Hermaphroditus, Glaucus
does not come to a wretched end. Nor does he face an aggressive female
wooer, except when Scilla is shot with Cupid's arrow, and by this time he
is immune to her charms. Circe, the aggressive wooer in Ovid's version
and a far more threatening figure than Scilla, is omitted entirely. Unlike
the other male characters, Glaucus is not ultimately overcome by desire
or by a woman and therefore his transformation is enabling rather than
debilitating. Scilla has also changed in this version from the silent and

terrified maiden of the *Metamorphoses* to a proud and disdainful Petrarchan mistress: '*Scilla* a Saint in looke, no Saint in scorning' (31.5). It might be argued that in these poems the Ovidian aggressive female wooer is simply the flip side of the Petrarchan mistress. With the former, the youth is the helpless object of desire, with the latter, the youth is the slave to his own desire. In both cases, the youth, failing to escape, becomes like Hermaphroditus 'but halfe a man.' A whole man, argues the genre, is, like Glaucus or the narrator of *Pigmalions Image*, a desiring subject rather than the object of desire.

To point out that the aggressive female wooer and the disdainful mistress are two sides of the same coin is perhaps to question the usual generalizations about the difference between Petrarachan and Ovidian women. Finkelpearl, for example, argues, 'With respect to sexual fulfillment, Ovidian poetry is quite unlike – one might almost say, it is opposed to – the tendency of 1590s Petrarchanism. Petrarchan ladies refuse and rebuff; Ovidian ladies like Venus and Hero often pursue.'[51] Keach concurs with this, arguing that the 'aggressive female wooer' of the epyllion functions 'as an anti-type of the chaste, idealized, cruelly reluctant mistress so prominent in Renaissance lyric and pastoral poetry.'[52] While it is true that the Ovidian figures have more spunk than their Petrarchan counterparts, ultimately the epyllion is really only interested in the effect this has on the male figure. Generally speaking, the women are silenced, humiliated, or abandoned by the end of the poem, as is the case with Venus, Hero, Scilla, and, arguably, as we shall see, Pigmalion's former statue.

At one level, the poems show the dangers for a male of being the object of desire, whether this is the desire of a god or a goddess, man or woman, and they persistently attempt to reform him as the desiring subject. This we see in the narratives of the poems that feature the aggressive female, such as Shakespeare's *Venus and Adonis* or Thomas Edwards's *Cephalus and Procris*. It is at work in a different form in Marlowe's *Hero and Leander*, as Leander metamorphoses from a sexually ambiguous youth, desired by all, to a mature lover, possessing Hero instead of being possessed by her charms. The youth must reject the advances of the woman (or man or immortal) in order to become a man, or risk being trapped in an infantilizing, narcissistic relation, which is occasionally allegorized as a suspension of being. When we remember the importance in the genre of the rejection of Petrarchan erotics, we can see that at another level the poems are protesting a failure of the male subject to be in control of his own desire, which Dubrow argues in the Petrarchan scenario often involves a loss of agency or a blurring of the boundary between subject and object.[53] To be infatuated by the cruelly unresponsive woman is to be slave to one's own desire, which offends the integrity and autonomy of the self.

At still another level, this protest against subjection is enacted by the very choice of Ovidian erotics. In her discussion of Petrarch's use of Ovid, Lynn Enterline argues that 'Petrarch weaves a new, suffering "voice" by directing Ovidian irony against himself. In the *Canzoniere* a distance seems to surface *within* the poetic subject, pitting the self against itself, rather than, as in Ovid, *between* the narrating subject and his erotic stories.' Enterline argues that 'Petrarch's specifically autobiographical version of Ovidian stories paradoxically produces a discourse of the self in love that looks forward to the alienated linguistic subject, and the story of its desire.'[54] If Petrarchan erotics in some way acknowledges the alienated subject of language, the Ovidian poetry of the 1590s might be seen as an attempt to deny this alienation by asserting the subject's mastery over language, which it partially acts out in the genre's bravura displays of rhetorical skill. More importantly, however, Ovidian erotics install a distance between the subject and its desire, one that allows the subject to manage it. Or, put another way, Ovidian irony works to stave off any threat that desire might pose to the borders of the self. Here the role of the Ovidian narrator becomes crucial: the Ovidian narrator, much like Ovid himself in his poetry, is distanced, ironic, experienced. Heather Dubrow notes that the Petrarchan lover is often in a position of subordination, a subordination that troubles both the line between the sexes and the line between self and other. Whereas critics of Petrarchan poetry have argued that the Petrarchan poet achieves mastery through a repetition of defeat,[55] here the Ovidian narrator goes one better, implicitly retelling stories of his own erotic misadventures from a position of complete mastery, since they are displaced onto other bodies. The Ovidian narrator is thus also Orphic, looking back on lost desire and converting it into rhetorical mastery.

This position of mastery is emphasized by a more fundamental circuit of desire that the poems trace out, between narrator and reader, which often involves the narrator teasing the audience from a position of knowing: 'Who knowes not what ensues?' Marston's narrator coyly asks when Pigmalion and his statue consummate their passion, 'O pardon me, / Yee gaping eares that swallow vp my lines' (38.1–2). The reader is here implicitly feminized, as the narrator becomes the ultimate Lacanian Subject-who-is-presumed-to-know. A similar scenario is at work in *Scilla*, where the narrator becomes the knowing relay between erotic experience and poetic audience, and where the final lesson is delivered to 'ladies,' in spite of the fact that the initial audience was completely male. If these poems follow the Renaissance habit of presenting models of behaviour to the reader, it is not any particular character in the poems that is to be emulated, but rather the narrator's knowing voice that is the ultimate model for the reader, a position of unassailable mastery and masculinity.

Heterosexuality and Women

Although the poems tend to stage the rejection of Petrarchan erotics for Ovidian as a process of maturation and thus as a natural progression, we can see the amount of labour required for this maturation signalled in *Scillaes Metamorphosis*. The nymphs, Glaucus's mother Thetis, Venus, and Cupid all have to intervene to bring about this change. It might also be observed that the maturation or heterosexualization of desire is undercut by the homosocial scenario of the situation or telling of the poem. It is two men, rather than a heterosexual couple, who are united by the telling of the story (although not the story itself). Outside the poem this is mirrored in the dedication by Lodge 'To his especiall good friend Master Rafe Crane.' This brings up a rather obvious complication: if the poems are working to construct a heterosexual masculinity, what does it mean that half of the poem takes place with the god's head in the poet's lap? Why is the most eligible female spurned and chained to a rock? Doesn't this rather complicate the heterosexuality? I made the point earlier that rather too much was made about the differences between Ovidian and Petrarchan mistresses: both are props for the construction of differing forms of masculine subjects. What I want to argue for the rest of the chapter is a parallel point about heterosexuality: that heterosexuality has very little to do with women.

In her much-debated essay 'Women on the Market,' Luce Irigaray makes essentially this same point: 'reigning everywhere, although prohibited in practice, hom(m)o-sexuality is played out through the bodies of women, matter, or sign, and heterosexuality has been up to now just an alibi for the smooth working of man's relations with himself, of relations among men.'[56] Irigaray's argument about heterosexuality has unfortunately been overshadowed by her more provocative comments about what Eve Kosofsky Sedgwick would label 'homosociality.'[57] While theorists have focused on the homosocial, they have for the most part failed to investigate the nature and construction of heterosexuality. Irigaray's comments, however, parallel what Monique Wittig argues in *The Straight Mind*: 'straight society is based on the necessity of the different/other at every level. It cannot work economically, symbolically, linguistically or politically without this concept. This necessity of the different/other is an ontological one for the whole conglomerate of sciences and disciplines that I call the straight mind.' Wittig clarifies the import of the concept of the different/other by remarking that 'the concept of difference between the sexes ontologically constitutes women into different/others. Men are not different, whites are not different, nor are the masters. But the blacks, as well as the slaves, are.'[58] Judith Butler notes that for Wittig, 'the *relation* of heterosexuality ... is neither reciprocal nor binary in the usual sense; "sex" is always already female, and there is only one sex, the feminine.'[59]

Wittig's argument is valuable for pointing out the politics of difference, and showing the political nature of what is usually experienced as intensely personal: in particular, for showing that heterosexuality is not so much an experience of the passions as a mode of thought, that corresponds with modes of social organization and political subjection. Or, as Irigaray puts it more forcefully, 'Heterosexuality is nothing but the assignment of economic roles.'[60] Wittig's argument for a transhistorical heterosexuality is not an instance of biological essentialism; it does not necessarily contradict the social constructionist arguments that gender and sexuality are socially constructed phenomena, although it does qualify them in an interesting way. At the very least, it shows that the ubiquity of heterosexuality as an institution is not simply a coincidence. More importantly, it allows for a greater flexibility in identifying which practices and relations fall within the realm of the socially productive and thus within the realm of heterosexuality. For example, what has been called institutionalized homosexuality is not necessarily outside the sphere of heterosexuality; as Gerald Creet shows in his study of institutionalized homosexuality in Melanesia, practices generally designated homosexual can work entirely within the social order, to enforce the subordination of women and younger males.[61] Within the early modern period, this is particularly evident in the codes defining male friendship, which arguably differs from sodomy only insofar as it respects the dominant order – the difference, as Mario DiGangi has recently argued, between orderly and disorderly forms of desire.[62] Male friendship was bound up in a system of mutual advantage, and friends were assumed to be gentlemen. That is to say, early modern male friendship, however eroticized a relation, can hardly be seen as existing outside the dominant power structure of society and thus can usefully be labelled heterosexual. This is certainly the case with the two friends in *Scillaes Metamorphosis*, whose heterosexuality seems to comfortably coexist with, even depend upon, a circuit of desire between men.

When we remember Wittig's argument that heterosexuality is 'an ideological form that cannot be grasped in reality, except through its effects,' we can begin to see that every society, or every renegotiation of society, must also involve a renegotiation of heterosexuality, especially if, as Wittig argues, the 'social contract and heterosexuality are two superimposable notions.' And this, I would argue, is part of the project of the epyllion. Written in a period of societal change, by a group of writers who were arguably most attuned to these shifts, epyllia educate their gentlemen readers about desire. The morals of failure or success at becoming an autonomous subject of desire are at the same time aligned to stories of rhetorical mastery, which for the period meant cultural mastery. By aligning a particular mode of sexuality with cultural agency, the epyllion attempts to install a new version of normative male sexuality that Wittig would identify as heterosexual. While both Peend's and Lodge's poems are concerned with warning youths about the dangers of vice and especially of desire, we can see in the latter's rejection of Petrarchan erotics that they are at the same time establishing the conditions for a new heterosexuality.

CHAPTER THREE

'More lovely than a man': The Metamorphosis of the Youth

The previous chapter looked at a recurrent narrative told of the Inns of Court students, the country youth who is seduced by the temptations of the city, and how this narrative informs Lodge's retelling of the Glaucus myth. This chapter will take a more sustained psychoanalytical look at a concern at the heart of that narrative, that of the maturation of the young man. It will explore versions of this story in the three best-known epyllia, John Marston's *The Metamorphosis of Pigmalions Image*, Shakespeare's *Venus and Adonis*, and Marlowe's *Hero and Leander*. The latter poems by Shakespeare and Marlowe are the most successful and influential of the genre; there is a wealth of contemporary reference to these poems, both within the genre (spawning homages and imitations) and without. While the three poems differ in the kinds of narratives they offer – Shakespeare's story of the goddess and the young man is the most typical of the genre, Marston's, as might be expected, is the most anomalous – they all feature the transformation of a youth. As we saw in the discussion of Lodge's *Scillaes Metamorphosis* in chapter 2, this familiar narrative of maturation is being used to naturalize a number of more culturally specific narratives.

As their source would imply, epyllia are stories of change. I will argue in this chapter that there are often several stories of change that are being told simultaneously, and that these stories of change both reflect and produce a cultural change, specifically in the definition of the masculine subject. What can often be observed in these poems is a condemnation of those forms of desire that challenge the autonomy or integrity of the masculine subject, most notably, those involving either the beautiful youth or the cruel mistress. This is often accomplished by associating these scenarios of desire with what Lacan calls the Imaginary, the register of unregulated narcissistic relations and fascination by images. The stories often can be read as myths of the metamorphosis of the speaking subject, as it enters the symbolic register. Critics commenting on these poems have similarly noted this shift in scenarios of desire, but have usually accepted the ideology of these poems uncritically. Jonathan Bate, to cite a recent example, writes that 'Lodge and his successors show how love is; they don't moralize about how behaviour should be.'[1] This change in the conventions of love poetry is often seen as a shift towards a more 'realistic' portrayal of sexual desire, a reading that should raise some questions, given the violence and scopophilia that are typically the result of this metamorphosis.

The Metamorphosis of Pigmalions Image

On a first reading, the genre of the epyllion would seem to be predominantly concerned with those two countries of which Lacan wrote, Ladies and Gentlemen.[2] They are stories of sexual difference, sexual desire, and gender protocol. But while they are often concerned with aetiology, frequently providing fables of why things are the way they are, they do unwittingly show that gender protocol is essentially cultural, and therefore must be learned. Just as *Hero and Leander* tells us why half the world is black, the entire genre attempts to provide myths for why men and women act the way they do.

These poems, however, are not simply (actually only rarely) about men and women. More often they are concerned with a reluctant youth and a female wooer, often a goddess or a nymph. Adult males are noticeably absent, as is any figure of the law. The gods we might expect to play this role, Apollo or Jove, are usually figured as the Imaginary father, that 'obscene, ferocious figure in which we see the true signification of the superego,'[3] rather than the Symbolic father. Which is to say, the adult male gods are generally only present as anecdotal interruptions of the main narrative of the poem, and are almost always pictured in a tableau of 'headdie ryots, incest, rapes' (*Hero and Leander*, 144). It could be argued then that since they appear in the function of the Imaginary rather than Symbolic father, they represent a 'decline in the paternal metaphor,'[4] or a devaluation of the name-of-the-father. The only law in the universe of the epyllion is Love, which is generally hostile, pitiless, and capricious. The world of the epyllion thus resembles to a certain extent Žižek's description of the genre of *film noir*, which he says is characterized by a mutation in the role of the big Other. In this world, 'narrativization, integration into the symbolic order, into the big Other, opens up a mortal threat, far from leading to any kind of reconciliation.'[5] Death or a kind of death is generally the fate of the central characters in the epyllion: this is the only possible conclusion of their narratives, which are principally about integration into the symbolic order, or about how the characters come to be mythic signifiers. Žižek argues that the inevitable conclusion in the mutation of the role of the big Other is its loss as a guarantee of the sense of reality.

The evidence of a troubling of the sense of reality, what Silverman calls the dominant fiction, would suggest that epyllia are both a cause and effect of that troubling, and that they participate in the renegotiation of the social order in the Elizabethan world. One of the key ways they intervene, however, is in their investigation and reinvention of gender ideals, principally, of course, of masculinity. The most obvious parallel between *film noir* and the epyllion is the presence of some type of femme fatale, the irresistible and immoral woman who lures men to their deaths. The aggressive female wooer of the Ovidian universe plays a structurally similar role to the femme fatale, threatening the integrity (in both senses) of the male subject. Žižek's analysis is useful in pointing out that the femme fatale has really not much to do with women, and is instead an indicator of a disturbance in the field of the Other: 'the *femme fatale qua* embodiment of the universe's corruption is clearly a male fantasy, she materializes its inner antagonisms.'[6] In fact, argues Žižek, 'the *femme fatale* is nothing but a lure whose fascinating presence masks the true traumatic axis of the noir universe, the relationship to the obscene father, i.e., the default of the paternal metaphor.'[7] This is not to say, of course, that this fantasy has not been projected onto real women, but rather that it does not necessarily have real women as its origin.

I want to stress this point in order to counter such readings of the women in epyllia as that of Gordon Williams: 'The increasing assertiveness of women in Shakespeare's society was something of a male obsession. Contemporaries would have recognized Venus as embodying this new feminism, and qualified their attitudes accordingly.'[8] Heather Dubrow similarly argues of *Venus and Adonis* that 'in this epyllion, as in many others, ambivalence about an unsuccessfully manipulative heroine encodes ambivalence about a brilliantly manipulative queen.'[9] Regardless of the justice of Dubrow's or Williams's assessment of early modern gender relations, reading the epyllion in this way seems either too literal or not literal enough, especially when it leads to such ahistorical conclusions as Williams's: '[Venus's] vulnerability is that of the older woman, desperate to renew her youth in the arms of a young lover. The situation is a recurrent one in art as in life. It is memorably rendered in Mike Nichols's 1967 film *The Graduate.*[10] It is worth remembering that women in the epyllion are often not women at all, but rather nymphs or goddesses. They are quite patently fantasy formations, something to which Williams's use of the phrase 'male obsession' might point. Moreover, given that they often are immortal and in possession of superhuman power, and that the male characters in the poems are almost always human and often youths, they are structurally unsuitable for any 'realistic' depiction of gender relations. While the relations in these poems are structurally similar to the typical Petrarchan scenarios, the latter also do not correspond directly to social reality. Like the femme fatale, the female figures of the epyllion 'materialize [their society's] inner antagonisms,' embodying some threat or anxiety to the male subject; they function as symptoms, in other words, that point to general cultural disturbances but do not comprehend them directly.

In an attempt to identify one of the recurring fantasies of the epyllion, I will start with John Marston's *The Metamorphosis of Pigmalions Image*, which does not employ the usual cast of characters. Rather than discussing a youth and a goddess, Marston tells the story of a man and his statue, sculpted in the 'Image of a Womans feature' (2.2). In Ovid, this story is part of a linked group that Orpheus tells to his Thracian male admirers, dealing with 'prettie boyes / That were the derlings of the Gods: and of unlawfull joyes / That burned in the brests of Girles' (10.157–9). Other stories in this group include Phoebus and Hyacinthus, Cyniras and Myrrha, and Venus and Adonis. Pygmalion, who is neither pretty boy nor girl, fits into this group genealogically (he is grandfather to Cyniras), but we may wonder if his story is appropriate to this group for other reasons as well.

The story in Marston's poem is the familiar one: Pigmalion sculpts a beautiful statue and falls in love with it. He caresses the statue, takes it to bed, and pleads with Venus to intervene. Venus assents and changes the marble to flesh, and then sculptor and statue are wed. That Pigmalion should choose to sculpt a woman is, on the surface at least, somewhat odd, given that the opening stanza of the poem establishes his hatred for women:

Pigmalion, whose hie loue-hating minde
Disdain'd to yeeld seruile affection,
Or amorous sute to any woman-kinde,

Knowing their wants, and mens perfection
Yet Loue at length forc'd him to know his fate,
And loue the shade, whose substance he did hate.

(1.1–6)

Pigmalion shares with many other male and female characters in the epyllion a disdain for love: 'disdain' is a key warning sign in these poems for a subject who will be metamorphosed. The attitude it characterizes is either implicitly or explicitly linked to the figure of the Petrarchan mistress, and we will see that the conquering of disdain often implies the rejection of the Petrarchan code of love, in favour of another code. In this poem both Pigmalion and his statue will be educated or metamorphosed away from that attitude or position.

The opening stanza is interestingly clear on the transformation that Pigmalion will undergo: he will not actually learn to love women, but rather merely the 'shade' or image of women. To use Lacan's distinction, he might learn to love The Woman, but nothing will alter his perception of women as lacking, or not all, and men as whole. This is essentially the critique that Lacan makes of courtly love, that it employs a fantasy of The Woman to support a dream of male oneness, a critique that Irigaray subsequently develops at length in *Speculum of the Other Woman*. Lacan argues, 'There is no such thing as *The* woman, where the definite article stands for the universal. There is no such thing as *The* woman since of her essence ... she is not all.'[11] Lacan's editors gloss this by noting that '"The Woman" does not exist, in that phallic sexuality assigns her to a position of fantasy.' Woman, they argue, is 'a category constructed around the phallic term,'[12] by a phallic chisel perhaps.

The love of the ideal of The Woman, the fantasy creation of a man, is essentially what this poem is about, and in that regard it acts as a commentary on Petrarchan love conventions. As Finkelpearl argues, 'Pigmalion is a comic embodiment of the pseudo-Petrarchan wooer.'[13] This critique is signalled when the second stanza invokes the Petrarchan code. The narrator adopts at least temporarily the stance of the Petrachan poet when he writes that the beauty of the statue could have no rival, 'Vnlesse my Mistres all-excelling face, / Which giues to beautie, beauties onely grace' (2.5–6). The statue is made to stand as a parody of the Petrarchan mistress: she is made of stone, she refuses to respond to Pigmalion's blandishments, and she is patently a creation of the lover's imagination. This, indeed, seems to correspond to what George Sandys is thinking, when he tries to provide a historical justification for the myth: 'taken historically, this statue may be some Virgin on whom Pygmalion was enamoured, who long as obdurat as the matter whereof she was made, was mollified at length by his obsequiousnesse.'[14] Marston plays with the overwrought praises of the mistress proffered by the (in this case literally) idolatrous Petrarchan lover when he notes that 'Her breasts, like polisht Iuory appeare' (8.1): if they look like ivory, it is because they are made of ivory. The lover's frustration is satirized later in the poem when Pigmalion exclaims:

> why were these women made
> O sacred Gods, and with such beauties graced?
> Haue they not power as well to coole, and shade,
> As for to heate mens harts? or is there none
> Or are they all like mine? relentlesse stone.
>
> (21.2–6)

This richly ironic condemnation of the relation the misogynist poet has with the fantasy of The Woman is perhaps a satire of the sixteenth-century version of the question, 'what does woman want?' Marston is clear on the sculptor's misrecognition of the sculpture for a woman, rather than an image of The Woman. As such, Marston shows, Pigmalion is sculpting not a woman but rather his own desire, which has little to do with women.

Marston's literary satire extends to the blazon of the mistress, a stand-ard feature of both the epyllion and the Petrarchan love poem, which Marston shows to be a disingenuous masturbation fantasy rather than an exalted praise of the beloved. Marston makes the hypocrisy of the poet clear in his comparison of Pigmalion to the 'subtile Citty-dame / In sacred church' (10.1–2) who hides her eyes at a shameful sight, but peeks through her fingers: 'So would he view, and winke, and view againe, / A chaster thought could not his eyes retaine' (10.5–6). As Pigmalion progressively works downwards, he is continually delighted by what he finds he has sculpted. His scopophilic desires are fully indulged:

> He wondred that she blusht not when his eye
> Saluted those same parts of secrecie:
> Conceiting not it was imagerie
> That kindly yeelded that large libertie.
> O that my Mistres were an Image too,
> That I might blameles her perfections view.
>
> (11.1–6)

Marston satirizes the poet who is lost in his own fantasy creation, by taking on to a certain extent the persona of the Petrarchan poet in order to make clear the parallel between sculptor and poet. He rejects the idealizing intent of this poetry later, however, when he laughs at the 'sweet Youths, who seriously protest / That Loue respects not actuall Luxury' (19.2–3). Marston insists that an 'adult' male love inevitably leads to sex, not to poetry of praise. The joke of this poem, perhaps, is that few statues, or poetic personas, ever come to life, and thus the Petrarchan lover is simply indulging his own youthful fantasies, which have little to do with the mature interactions of men and women. The true metamorphosis of the poem, then, is not conversion of ivory to flesh, but Pigmalion's transformation from youth to man, from an idealistic, ultimately narcissistic lover to an adult lover of women.

Marston's criticism of the sterile, un(re)productive and immature nature of Pigmalion's infatuation with an image is linked to the warnings frequently given in other epyllia about the dangers of narcissism. As Lacan points out of another genre, 'The element of idealizing exaltation that is expressly sought out in the ideology of courtly love ... is fundamentally narcissistic in character.'[15] Marston's characterization of Pigmalion's desire is similar to Elizabeth Grosz's brief summary of the Lacanian Imaginary: 'The imaginary is the order of identification with images. It is the order of dual, narcissistic relations with others, of libidinal pleasure unregulated by law, and indistinguishably intra- and interpsychical aggression.'[16] Pigmalion's libidinal pleasure is certainly narcissistic, and certainly unregulated. Insofar as Marston insists that Pigmalion's desire is unreproductive, it is outside of the law, a point made both by the reference to the church-goer's hypocrisy and the recognition that his own mistress would not countenance Pigmalion's scopophilia. The poem suggests that the sculptor must break out of this narcissistic circuit in order 'to know his fate' (1.5), which will include both marriage and the birth of a child at the conclusion of the poem (stanza 39).

But if the poem is ultimately about the maturation of the subject into heterosexuality, it also shows that it is not exactly an untroubled or unproblematic trajectory. If the poem is not about a woman (a class at least initially despised by Pigmalion), but rather The Woman, then perhaps the gender of the statue is not as stable as it appears. Given Marston's insistence that the sculptor is deluded by the image of his own desire and not by an other, it may be that the statue is something of a mirror image or alter-ego. This is hinted at in the account of Pigmalion's reaction to the transformation of the statue:

Doe but conceiue a Mothers passing gladnes,
(After that death her onely sonne hath seazed
And ouerwhelm'd her soule with endlesse sadnes)
When that she sees him gin for to be raised
From out his deadly swoune to life againe:
Such ioy *Pigmalion* feeles in euery vaine.

(30.1–6)

The strangeness in the gender reversal effected by this metaphor is
worth noting here; Pigmalion is compared to a mother, and the statue to
a dead boy. All of a sudden we are in the more familiar terrain of the
epyllion, which is littered with phallic women and dead youths. This is
not the first time, however, that Pigmalion has been compared to a
woman; earlier, we saw him compared to the hypocritical city dame.
More importantly, he is linked to Venus by his rhetoric. Douglas Bush
argues that there is a 'fairly clear' echo in Pigmalion's wooing to Shakespeare's *Venus and Adonis*: 'Art thou obdurate, flinty, hard as steel? / Nay,
more than flint, for stone at rain relenteth' (199–200).[17] The poem thus
contains not one but two of the epyllion's central narratives: the maturation of the foolish Petrarchan youth (Pigmalion) into an adult lover of
women (the statue), and the aggressive female wooer (Pigmalion) who
pursues the youth (the statue). This also, of course, points to the connections between these narratives, both of which encode anxieties about
male wholeness.

In one sense the gender reversal shows the truth of male poetic and
artistic ambition: as Mieke Bal notes, 'One performance is inaccessible
to men. childbirth. *The* phantasma, the ideal hidden behind so much
ambition, is man giving birth to a child.'[18] One can see this desire for
immortality through childbirth played out in Plato's *Symposium*, in the
glorification of pederastic desire: 'there are some whose creative desire
is of the soul, and who long to beget spiritually, not physically, the
progeny which it is the nature of the soul to create and bring to birth.'[19]
The adult male's immortalization through the education of the youth is
echoed in Pigmalion's wish for his creation that 'his soule might part in
sunder / So that one halfe in her had residence' (15.1–2). If the statue is
in fact a male youth, we can see that its transformation into a woman
complements the progress of Pigmalion's desire from a sterile narcissistic love to a heterosexual one.

The narrator's pretensions to being outside the narcissistic circuit of
desire occupied by Pigmalion collapse by the conclusion of the poem,

where the narrator reproduces the sculptor's scopophilia. He teases the reader by not showing the scene of sex that follows, reserving it for his own view: 'Let him [the reader] conceit but what himselfe would doe / When that he had obtayned such a fauour' (34.1–2). The irony of the first part of the poem all but vanishes as the statue becomes the masturbation fantasy of the poet rather than the sculptor. The woman remains an unnamed, unspeaking artistic artefact, but now the narrator rather than the sculptor occupies the position of lover/creator, revelling in the 'arms, eyes, hands, tong, lips, & wanton thigh' (37.6) of The Woman. As Lynda E. Boose argues, Marston here 'experiments with masturbatory strategies of inhibited desire destined to stimulate the reader's desire by creating a friction with it.'[20] The narrator's continual teasing of the reader, insistently gendered male, points to another more fundamental circuit of desire: 'Who knows not what ensues? O pardon me / Yee gaping eares that swallow vp my lines' (38.1–2). The fantasy of The Woman is merely a conduit for the now more overtly sexualized relation between reader and writer, in which the poet's 'lines' are swallowed by the 'gaping eares' of other men, a replay of the pederastic/pedagogic ethos signalled earlier. The narrator becomes Venus to the reader's Adonis and this sexual 'feminization' of the reader echoes the gender instability that epyllia both evoke and try, ultimately unsuccessfully, to control. Women in the epyllion often function as stand-ins for men, however much the poems attempt to institute a heterosexualization of desire. Thus the poet could be said, like the sculptor, to have learned to 'love the shade, whose substance he did hate' (1.6), although this is possible in this satiric version because the shade of the woman seems to cover the substance of a youth. The homoerotic and homosocial circuit alluded to here answers to the original production of the poem in the Inns of Court: an erotic performance exclusively for men, and ultimately about men.

What Marston's poem attempts, then, is to write a new narrative of desire for men. The older Petrarchan script is rejected as immature, and a new model for the relations between men and women is proposed: one in which the man is no longer at the mercy of his beloved, who is no longer, or at least differently, idealized. The lover in the epyllion rejects the notion that 'Loue is a child, contented with a toy, / A busk-point, or some fauour still's the boy' (19.5–6). This is essentially the same narrative that is played out in different terms in Lodge's *Scillaes Metamorphosis*. Glaucus's victory over desire parallels to a certain extent Marston's confident advice to women that 'Ladies, thinke they nere loue you, /

Who doe not vnto more then kissing moue you' (20.5–6). These two poems agree that enslavement by Petrarchan idealism is infantile: what a real man wants is sex. In both poems, however, the maturation or heterosexualization of desire is founded on the homosocial scenario of the situation or telling of the poem.

What I want to suggest about the genre of the epyllion is that the poems often contain several developmental narratives, some of which are used to naturalize others. The stories that tell of the maturation of desire and associate this with a rejection of Petrarchan values are overlaid onto a more universal story of the development of the speaking subject and the price of entry into the symbolic. None of these narratives is naturally or necessarily related to the others: becoming a speaking subject does not necessarily involve becoming a heterosexual, or rejecting Petrarchan values. It is, however, the function of the epyllion to join these three stories, to use the universal story of the speaking subject to naturalize the cultural story of the institution of a new version of heterosexuality.

As we have already observed, the poems often portray a youth developing an increasing ability for rhetoric while at the same time acquiring an appreciation for the power of rhetoric, as we will see again in both Shakespeare's and Marlowe's poems. At the same time, these poems explain how subjects become signifiers, illustrating this in a literal fashion as boys are turned into flowers and nymphs into echoes. Related to this is their demonstration of how subjects enter the symbolic by occupying the place of their proper name. Thus the youth Adonis becomes the mythic signifier 'Adonis,' the iconic signifier of his own narrative, and the price of this is a death (of sorts). The poems take what are already mythic signifiers, and provide an ontology for them. Desire in these poems ends in death and a story; they tell how subjects come to be sites for rhetorical invention.

In that regard, we could argue that the epyllion shows how subjects are spoken by culture. Lacan argued that subjects do not speak, but rather language speaks through them. This, presumably, is something the humanists understood at least implicitly, given their emphasis on learning the rules of rhetoric. According to humanist teaching, the purest speech is that which comes closest to the accepted model of discourse. This is not just a matter of conscious imitation of the rhetorical models, but rather an unconscious introjection of the laws of speech. Speech is for the humanists connected with civilization and order, as it is, in a sense, for Lacan: he argues that the third term in the triad nature, society, and culture 'could well be reduced to language, or that which essentially distinguishes human society from natural societies'[21] This is not so far from Thomas Wilson's portrayal of rhetoric in the *Arte of Rhetorike* as the civilizing force par excellence, that which restored law to human society. Before God gave rhetoric to the world, says Wilson, 'none remembred the true observation of wedlocke, none tendered the educations of their chyldren, lawes were not regarded, true dealinge was not once used.'[22] In short, it was rather like the world of the gods in the epyllion, who delight in disguising themselves and 'Committing headdie ryots, incest, rapes' (*Hero and Leander*, 144).

The difference between Lacan's view of language and the humanists' of rhetoric is that the humanists have a nominalist or referential theory of language, and they believe that one can master discourse, or that language is instrumental. Indeed, in John Hoskins's *Directions for Speech and Style*, written for a young man at the Inns of Court, the preface suggests that one must master rhetoric *because* language is referential because the laws of language correspond to the God's law in nature: 'the order of God's creatures in themselves is not only admirable and glorious, but eloquent; then he that could apprehend the consequence of things, in their truth, and utter his apprehensions as truly were a right orator.' Thus, concludes Hoskins, to disobey the laws of rhetoric is to disobey the laws of order: 'disordered speech is not so much injury to the lips which give it forth or the thoughts which put it forth as to the right proportion and coherence of things in themselves, so wrongfully expressed.'[23] Disordered, chaotic speech is an affront to the eloquence of the order of nature. The most artificial speech is thus the most natural speech, a paradox that is reflected in Hoskins's discussion of plainness of speech, which is 'both in method and word to use, as ladies use in their attire, a kind of diligent negligence.'[24] Plainness is a verbal *sprezzatura* that shares with Castiglione's courtier the goal of naturalizing a highly technical and practised performance. Much of humanist teaching from Erasmus on constitutes a shift away from the medieval emphasis on laborious memorizing and theorizing towards a graceful practice learned through imitating the example of the ancients, with less of an explicit emphasis on the rules. It is arguably in the seventeenth century that the ideology of plain speech becomes fully naturalized, and the plain speaker begins to believe him or herself to be speaking unrhetorically. One can argue, then, that the humanist theories of rhetoric contribute to or participate in the emergence of the Cartesian ego, which will be theorized as the origin of speech and thought, a position which, of course,

Lacan rejects. He draws attention 'to the growing dominance that the function of the *moi* has taken on in the lived experience of modern man, beginning from a set of sociotechnological and dialectical conjectures, whose cultural *Gestalt* is visibly constituted by the beginning of the seventeenth century.'[25] It is perhaps useful to remember exactly what Lacan means by the modern *moi* or ego: 'We call ego that nucleus given to consciousness but opaque to reflection, marked by all the ambiguities which, from self-satisfaction to "bad faith" (*mauvais foi*) structure the experience of the passions in the subject; this "I" who, in order to admit its facticity to existential criticism, opposes its irreducible inertia of pretences and meconnaissances to the concrete problematic of the realization of the subject.'[26] Lacan does not argue that the pre-Cartesian subject had no ego, but rather that it played a less dominant function in the subject than it comes to after the sixteenth century. To say this, however, is to recognize that the ego must have been differently constituted in order to play this different role. If the structure of the 'experience of the passions' somehow changes, a change in which I am arguing the epyllion participates, then this implies as well a change in the agency through which those passions are experienced. How this agency comes to occupy a new function in the subject is through the intervention of a whole array of 'sociotechnological and dialectical conjectures,' among which are those of love poetry and humanist rhetorical theory. We can perhaps see evidence of this development in Hoskins's manual. Hoskins argues that by speaking according to the laws of order, one will give the illusion of speaking freely. The Cartesian ego will come to believe in this illusion.

What has all this to do with the epyllion? Hoskins's comment on plain speaking suggests the link: there is a connection between speech and women. One of Lacan's most prominent interventions into Freudian psychoanalysis is to introduce a structuralist theory of language and connect that with the order of the unconscious (although he is always careful to say that this was implicit in the work of Freud). He draws upon the structuralist anthropology of Lévi-Strauss to discuss the relation between kinship and language: 'It is essentially on sexual relations – by ordering them according to the law of preferential marriage alliances and forbidden relations – that the first combinatory for the exchanges of women between nominal lineages is based, in order to develop in an exchange of gifts and in an exchange of master-words the fundamental commerce and concrete discourse on which human societes are based.'[27] Feminist scholars such as Gayle Rubin and Luce Irigaray have further developed Lévi-Strauss's theory of kinship, the latter remarking that 'women, signs, commodities, and currency always pass from one man to another; if it were otherwise, we are told, the social order would fall back upon incestuous and exclusively endogamous ties that would paralyze all commerce.'[28] Irigaray's formulation echoes both Lacan's and, interestingly, Wilson's view of civilization (although Irigaray and Wilson certainly differ in their attitudes towards this civilization). Jacqueline Rose has drawn attention to an apparent shift in Lacan's treatment of femininity: 'Lacan moved away ... from the idea of a problematic but socially assured process of exchange (women as objects) to the construction of woman as category within language (woman as *the* object, the fantasy of her definition).'[29] This latter view, for example, allows Lacan to speak in the seminar on femininity of 'all those beings who take on the status of women,'[30] rather than of biological women (although Judith Butler might point out that this is not an unproblematic category either). The one view does not necessarily preclude the other, however, and may work to de-essentialize it. In fact, integrating the latter view into the former, that is discussing the exchange of those who take on the status of women, makes sense in a period or a literary genre in which youths and women are to some degree interchangeable.

Bearing in mind, then, Lacan's earlier statement on the foundations of discourse, we can see that it is not merely coincidental that these poems that are primarily concerned with sexual relations are at the same time concerned with the uses of rhetoric. More specifically, these stories are concerned with rewriting narratives of desire so that men are taught to be less subjected in their relation to women (or, in the pederastic script, to men), and in a sense, to be more economically astute. This we saw in Marston's condemnation of the Petrarchan script as sterile and unproductive. This is often complemented by the characters' increasing prowess in rhetoric. It should be noted that this mastery over desire is based as much on misrecognition as is the presumed independence of the Cartesian ego: individual men are no less determined by the kinship system, or by desire, than they are by language, but cultural fictions such as epyllia often work to encourage the subject to misrecognize his or her relation to the symbolic order in particular ways. The subject always misrecognizes its relation to the symbolic order; what is important to notice is which form that misrecognition takes. At the same time that these poems promote this particular misrecognition, they teach the danger for men of being the objects of desire: they show the potential dangers to the economic system, as Irigaray might put it, of men becoming commodities. In so doing, they are involved in the heterosexualization (or again, as Irigaray would call it, a hom(m)-osexualization) of desire.

If these poets show how subjects become signifiers, they also show how mythical signifiers come into being. They show how subjects become sites for rhetorical invention. By speaking again on the various topoi of the *Metamorphoses*, epyllia rewrite cultural memory: they can be viewed as a sort of cultural *Nachträglichkeit*, that effect a meta-metamorphosis. Arthur Golding's 1567 translation of Ovid makes explicit that these stories are morality tales for English consumption. He is thus involved in both a righting and a rewriting of cultural memory. Golding is generally seen to be less moralistic than the medieval tradition of *Ovide moralisé*, which sought to rewrite the *Metamorphoses* in terms of Christian doctrine. The Ovidian poets in turn are read as less moralistic than Golding: more playful and ambiguous, and less condemnatory of the machinations of desire. William Keach singles out as one of the most important influences of Ovid on these poets Ovid's view of erotic experience, which he says is characterized by ambivalence: 'a constantly active and poised awareness that sexual love can be humorous, grotesque, and animal-like in its savagery as well as beautiful, emotionally compelling, and an essential part of what it means to be human.'[31] As I noted above, modern critics of these poems often see these poems' portrayal of sexual relations as more realistic than their predecessors. While it is certainly true that the Ovidians are less concerned with Christian doctrine, it is probably a mistake to read these poems as less 'serious' than Golding about rewriting Ovid, or about providing a reforming mirror for their own world. Their concerns have merely shifted, and they use Ovid to discuss gender relations.

Venus and Adonis

In one of his more famous marginal notations, Gabriel Harvey recorded sometime in 1599 that 'the younger sort takes much delight in Shakespeares Venus, & Adonis.'[32] Katherine Duncan-Jones suggests that among the 'younger sort' thus entranced were Thomas Edwards, author of *Cephalus and Procris* and *Narcissus*; Michael Drayton, author of *Piers Gaveston*; and Thomas Heywood, author of *Oenone and Paris*; all of them wrote poems indebted to Shakespeare's.[33] Beyond newly emerging writers, however, there is another group of readers that may also have taken delight in the poem: the younger sort who attended the Inns of Court. While Shakespeare did not himself attend the Inns (as far as we know), he was certainly acquainted with that world and its literary tastes. For example, his friend and 'cousin,' Thomas Greene, transferred to the Middle Temple in 1595 after a stay at Staple Inn, one of the Inns of Chancery (this stay would normally last about two years).[34] In 1594, a year after the publication of the poem, *The Comedy of Errors* would be performed at Gray's Inn. Most relevant to the present discussion, however, is the fact that Shakespeare's poem is dedicated to Henry Wriothesley, the earl of Southampton, who was admitted to Gray's Inn on 29 February 1588; G.P.V. Akrigg argues that it was likely in the company of Inns of Court men that Shakespeare first met his patron.[35]

This was not, in fact, the first poem of this sort dedicated to Southampton. Two years earlier John Clapham, a secretary to Lord Burghley, dedicated his neo-Latin poem *Narcissus* to Southampton, and scholars have identified a number of similarities between Clapham's and Shakespeare's poem.[36] Clapham's poem, in turn, seems to have been influenced by early epyllia written in English; Charles Martindale and Colin Burrow argue that the poem makes a nod towards Marlowe's epyllion in the ecphrasis,[37] and in its relocation of the mythological action to England Clapham's poem follows Lodge's *Scillaes Metamorphosis* (and in this it will be followed to some degree by Shakespeare). And like almost all examples of the genre, the poem is most interested in youths.

Clapham's poem starts with a description of the palace of Love, to which many young men flock (57). Among them is Narcissus, accompanied by Liberty and Youth (65), who is embraced by Venus on his arrival. Narcissus is subsequently shot by Cupid and then instructed on the finer points of love and the psychology of women. He gallops off on a horse named Libido (151), falls in love with his reflection, and drowns himself in the pond at dusk when his image disappears. Akrigg argues of Shakespeare's and Clapham's poems that 'the basic pattern is the same: the meeting with Venus, the departure of the young man, Venus's lamentation, and the final metamorphosis';[38] Martindale and Burrow similarly note, 'There are signs that Shakespeare, rather than just taking allegorical or mythographic materials from *Narcissus* (as earlier commentators believed), absorbed the poem's shape and, especially in the early part of *Venus and Adonis*, filled the stiffly allegorical forms of Clapham with luxurious vitality.'[39]

While it is important to note the similarities between Clapham's and Shakespeare's poems, particularly the ways in which Adonis is indebted to the portrayal of Narcissus, it is equally important to note how both poems participate in a particular literary and cultural milieu, one centred around the Inns of Court. Whereas the earliest epyllia are admonitory tales directed towards the young men of the Inns, these poems offer warnings to a particular young man, Wriosthesley.[40] Considering Shakespeare's poem within the context of the epyllion brings certain aspects of the poem, such as the interest in Venus's rhetoric, the rhetorical education of Adonis, and the poem's use of Petrarchanisms, into sharper focus. It also helps us to see in a different light Shakespeare's innovation of having a resistant Adonis, whose resistance may have less to do with morality than it does with a dangerous narcissism. As we have already noted, while the genre has a number of different candidates for positive exempla of masculine subjectivity, it is virtually unanimous in holding up Narcissus as the chief example of failure. As we shall see in more detail in our reading of Edwards's *Narcissus*, the beauty of youths is perceived both by the genre and arguably by the culture at large as somehow dangerous. While the story of Adonis traditionally figures the fleeting nature of beauty, within the genre Adonis represents not so much beauty as more specifically the beauty of the youth. Indeed, in its parade of surpassingly beautiful young men such as Leander, Cephalus, and Narcissus, the genre suggests that youth *is* beauty, an attitude reflected in the Sonnets as well, where the beloved is both Narcissus and Adonis. But the beauty of youths is at the same time dangerous, both to themselves and to those around them. This is a particular concern of the genre, and negotiating this perilous transitional phase becomes a recurrent theme.

In *Venus and Adonis*, the dangers posed by the beauty of the youth are told though the genre's most popular narrative, that of the reluctant youth and the ardent female wooer. Bearing in mind the other poems' reactions against Petrarchanisms and their sometimes ambiguous gender coding, it is not too extreme to read the reluctant youth as the Petrarchan mistress and the ardent goddess as the frustrated lover. Reading the gender of the goddess as male could be supported by noting the similarities between the Petrarchan code and Platonic pederasty. In both, sex is nominally disallowed, and in the latter, the youth is bound by honour to resist, or at least not to enjoy, the advances of his adult lover. This scenario can be seen in play in *Hero and Leander* in the various references to Ganymede, in the relation of the poet to Leander, and most clearly in the encounter between Neptune and Leander. The very category of 'youth' or 'boy' must be considered in relation to the more capacious category of 'not-man,' which at least in classical cultures and arguably in early modern England, denoted a proper or at least possible object of desire. Indeed, Will Fisher argues that boys 'were quite literally a different gender from men during the early modern period.'[41] At the same time, youths are a very special subset of the category 'not-man,' in that they will possibly become men. It is precisely this possibility that provides much of the erotic interest in a number of the poems, and it is certainly at the heart of the most central metamorphoses of the genre.

If the youths of the epyllion are not men, it is worth noting that the goddesses are generally not women either. They frequently insist that they are not mortal, and that their powers are far greater than their beloveds'. Structurally speaking, they could be read as phallic mothers, or more simply as men. This confusion of genders is supported within the poems by the ambiguous gender coding of the characters. Venus, for example, when she first sees Adonis, woos him in the following manner:

'Thrice fairer than myself,' thus she began,
'The field's chief flower, sweet above compare,
Stain to all nymphs, more lovely than a man,
More white and red than doves or roses are ...'

(7–10)

As Lucy Gent observes, Venus 'out-Petrarchs the most Petrarchan sonneteer.'[42] Adonis, for his part, 'burns with bashful shame, she with her tears / Doth quench the maiden burning of his cheeks' (49–50). Venus, in a move that would no doubt please Marston, plucks Adonis from his horse: 'Over one arm the lusty courser's rein, / Under her other was the tender boy' (31–2). She sets him down, and then 'Backward she push'd him, as she would be thrust, / And govern'd him in strength, though not in lust' (41–2). Superior in strength and driven by lust, Venus plays the man when Adonis will not and pushes him into the position she wishes to occupy. Adonis, by being so thrust, is thrown into the position of the female.[43] Venus brags to Adonis of her sexual conquests, saying that she has led 'the stern and direful god of war ... prisoner in a red rose chain' (98, 110), thus presenting herself as the erotic version of Hercules and his golden chain of rhetoric. Through the early part of the poem Adonis continues to play the role of the reluctant mistress, leading to Venus's exasperation:

'Fie, liveless picture, cold and senseless stone,
Well-painted idol, image dull and dead,
Statue contenting but the eye alone,

Thing like a man, but of no woman bred!
Thou art no man, though of a man's complexion,
For men will kiss even by their own direction.'

(211–16)

Adonis, in a manner similar to Pygmalion's statue, is the shade but not
the substance of man. If Venus is temporarily acting the part of Pygmalion
in this scenario, showing the ridiculous side of Petrarchan desire, Adonis
shows the 'danger' to the beloved youth that Marston only hinted at.

The comparisons between Adonis and Pygmalion's statue make sense
within a critique of Petrarchan verse, but they also make sense within the
Ovidian universe, as Adonis is the descendent of Pygmalion and his
statue, and his tale is part of the linked series of stories told by Orpheus
in Book 10. It is thus appropriate that Adonis not only resembles the
statue but also its creator; significantly, both he and Pygmalion begin
their tales by scorning love and women. More to the point, as Lynn
Enterline points out in her discussions of both Petrarch's and Marston's
treatments of the myth, Pygmalion's attachment to his statue is fundamentally narcissistic.[44] In both Shakespeare's and Marston's poems, then,
we see a strange potential for reversability in the central character: from
subject to object, and male to female. This instability is also a characteristic both of the position of the Petrarchan author and of the youth.

Because Adonis is a male youth, he is at least literarily an acceptable
object of desire in the early modern world. What these poems stress,
however, is the danger for the male of being the object of (male) desire,
even if this warning is refracted through the figure of the female wooer.
The heterosexualization of desire is here partially accomplished through
an incomplete heterosexualization of the pederastic couple. It is clear
enough in these poems that this form of coupling is not acceptably
heterosexual, even if it is nominally so. One of the ways by which this
condemnation is accomplished is similar to the way in which Marston
condemns Petrarchan love: by associating this scenario with the Imaginary, and by condemning it as sterile, immature, or infantile.

This regressive fantasy scene is clear in Venus's erotic proposal to
Adonis:

'Fondling,' she saith, 'since I have hemmed thee here
Within the circuit of this ivory pale,
I'll be a park, and thou shalt be my deer:
Feed where thou wilt, on mountain or in dale;

Graze on my lips, and if those hills be dry,
Stray lower, where the pleasant fountains lie.

'Within this limit is relief enough,
Sweet bottom-grass and high delightful plain,
Round rising hillocks, brakes obscure and rough,
To shelter thee from tempest and from rain;
Then be my deer, since I am such a park,
No dog shall rouse thee, though a thousand bark.'

(229–40)

Venus's body threatens to swallow Adonis's being, trapping him in an infantilizing dyadic relation. The metaphor clearly evokes the relation of mother and child, hinted at occasionally throughout the poem. This relation is made explicit later in the poem when Venus frantically searches for Adonis, 'Like a milch doe, whose swelling dugs do ache, / Hasting to feed her fawn hid in some brake' (875–6). She later recaptures this relation when she plucks the flower that springs up from Adonis's blood, knowing full well that it will 'wither in [her] breast' (1182):

'Here was thy father's bed, here in my breast;
Thou art the next of blood, and 'tis thy right.
Lo in this hollow cradle take thy rest,
My throbbing heart shall rock thee day and night ...'

(1183–6)

The relation of mother and child is posited within the poem as a smothering one, something which the youth must escape in order to become a man. C.S. Lewis responds to this presentation when he comments, 'I have never read [the poem] through without feeling that I am being suffocated.'[45] But this mother is also persistently figured as vampiric: 'Panting he lies, and breatheth in her face. / She feedeth on the steam, as on a prey' (62–3); 'Look how a bird lies tangled in a net, / So fast'ned in her arms Adonis lies' (67–8); 'Now quick desire hath caught the yielding prey, / And glutton-like she feeds, yet never filleth' (547–8).

The course of the seduction runs through the various possibilities that Grosz sees in the Lacanian Imaginary:

The unmediated two-person structure of imaginary identifications leaves only two possibilities for the child, between which it vacillates but cannot definitively choose: being overwhelmed by the other, crowded out, taken over (the fantasy of the devouring mother/ voracious child); and the wretched isolation and abandonment of all self-worth by the other's absence or neglect (the fantasy of the bad or selfish mother/child).[46]

The vacillations between subject and object and male and female that we have noted in the poem are clearly characteristic of the register of the Imaginary. Further, the scenarios Grosz mentions of isolation and abandonment are acted out in the deaths, imagined and real, of Venus and Adonis. The former scenarios are far more central: in the genre, for a male to be the object of desire is to be trapped in the arms of the mother. In Michael Drayton's *Endimion and Phoebe*, Endimion gives in to the desire of his goddess, and is condemned to a form of suspended animation. Phoebe

> layd Endimion on a grassy bed,
> With sommers Arras ritchly over-spred
> Where from her sacred Mantion next above,
> She might descend and sport her with her love,
> Which thirty yeeres the Sheepheards safely kept,
> Who in her bosom soft and soundly slept.
>
> (983–8)

Adonis says of love, 'I have heard it is a life in death' (413), which seems a fairly accurate description of Endimion's fate. This suspended state is enacted by the poem itself, which is curiously static until Adonis breaks away from Venus's arms. Lewis notes that even 'the stanza of *Venus and Adonis* is unprogressive.'[47] Linked to this unproductive scenario of desire is the similarly unproductive position of narcissism, against which Adonis is warned (157–62).

Part of Adonis's education, both sexual and rhetorical, comes from the poem's two digressions. In the first, Adonis (and the reader) are witness to a 'natural' example of proper gender relations when Adonis's horse is spied by a 'breeding jennet, lusty, young, and proud' (260) and desire causes him to break free of his reins:

> He looks upon his love, and neighs unto her,
> She answers him, as if she knew his mind;
> Being proud as females are, to see him woo her,
> She puts on outward strangeness, seems unkind,

Spurns at his love, and scorns the heat he feels,
Beating his kind embracements with her heels.

Then like a melancholy malcontent,
He vails his tail that like a falling plume
Cool shadow to his melting buttock lent;
He stamps, and bites the poor flies in his fume.
His love, perceiving how he was enrag'd,
Grew kinder, and his fury was assuag'd.

(307–18)

The lessons offered here by the natural world are remarkably similar to the gender ideologies of the other epyllia. The female horse only ever reacts, and her brief attempt at playing the disdainful Petrarchan mistress is only meant to excite her lover into more masculine shows of force. Venus urges Adonis to read the horses as an example: 'learn of him, I heartily beseech thee, / To take advantage on presented joy' (404–5). Her reading of the parallels is only a partial one, however, as the mare's actions amount to nothing more than simply presenting herself to view, certainly far less than Venus herself does. Nonetheless, the poem, like Venus, sees the horse as an example to be followed, and promotes this by persistently pairing horse and man, as when Venus initially abducts them both: 'Over one arm the lusty courser's rein, / Under her other was the tender boy' (31–2). Venus's praise of Adonis's beauty is paralleled by the narrator's longer blazon of the horse; both for their beauty are compared to works of art, but whereas the metaphor is used to accuse Adonis of being less than a man ('Fie, liveless picture, cold and senseless stone' [211]), the horse becomes the ideal horse ('So did this horse excel a common one' [293]). The horse is, in short, an equine equivalent of Adonis, and stands as an example of a more proper masculinity, a piece of natural rhetoric that Adonis should aim to emulate.

The other major foray into the rhetoric of the natural world is Venus's tale of Wat the hare (679–708). This replaces the story in Ovid of Atalanta and Hippomenes, which Venus tells for similar reasons, namely, to warn Adonis from the hunt.[48] In Ovid, Hippomenes and Atalanta are ungrateful to Venus for her assistance and ignore the clear warnings of the gods; as a consequence they are turned into lions. Both failings – ingratitude and inattention – are also characteristic of Adonis. Venus pleads with Adonis not to pursue the boar, and to hunt the hare or the fox or the roe instead. This segues into a story of the hare trying to elude the hunters and the hounds. The story is distinctly Ovidian in its interest in the darker side of desire: the hare relentlessly pursued and the cruel fate that awaits it provide a contrast to the previous lightness of the poem but foreshadow Adonis's end a little later. But the Hippomenes myth is not the only one invoked here. Through the tale of Wat, Adonis also becomes Acteon: 'And now his grief may be compared well / To one sore sick that hears the passing bell' (701–2). Even more so than Hippomenes, Acteon is an appropriate model for Adonis, particularly because of the reversal that occurs as the hunter becomes the hunted, which is, of course, the central narrative of the poem. While Venus's hunting of Adonis is comic, it will be perversely reprised in the boar's turning of the tables at the end of the poem. But the Acteon myth has a further significance in that it is also a tale of rhetoric, which is why Acteon becomes for so many poets a compelling model for their own vocation.

The story of the hare breaks off before it reaches its conclusion, when Venus loses her place: '"Where did I leave?" "No matter where," quoth he, / "Leave me, and then the story aptly ends"' (715–16). Is Adonis's death partly attributable to his failure to listen well to this story? He has had more obvious warnings, of course, but is this a test of the reception of rhetoric? Venus does mention that she is uncharacteristically inter- ested in morals at this moment – 'Unlike myself thou hear'st me moral- ize / Applying this to that, and so to so' (712–13) – but he refuses to listen to her explication of the tale. While his own rhetoric may have improved over the course of the poem, we can see that he is not yet skilled in attending to the rhetoric of others, which includes, in Hoskyns's terms, the rhetoric of the natural world.

Hallet Smith, in his introduction to the poem in the *Riverside Shake- speare*, argues that 'the celebrated description of the horse, the account of the coursing of the hare, and the images of the dive-dapper, the snail, and the lark ... [are] difficult to harmonize with the elements of classical myth.'[49] In fact, as we have seen, the digressions are very much of a piece with the rest of the poem, and this disjuncture between the mythological material and Shakespeare's 'country taste and outlook' may also be working as part of the genre's rejection of the Petrarchan code as sterile literary cliché. The poem's counterposing of a 'natural' narrative of desire (that is at the same time heavily cultural), works precisely to make the central narrative of Venus's seduction and Adonis's rejection of her seem unnatural. At the same time, the use of the English countryside as

backdrop is similar to Lodge's Oxford setting, Clapham's lightly allegorized English setting for the Narcissus myth, or Edwards's Spenserian
additions to his poems. All of these participate in what might be called
an Englishing of the muse, part of an attempt, as we shall see in later
chapters, to claim a classical heritage for England, while at the same time
rewriting the script of normative desire.

As with the youths in other epyllia, if Adonis is to become a man, he
must reject the position of object of desire. What might have enabled
him to do this is the education in rhetoric he receives over the course of
the poem. As a number of critics have observed, Shakespeare's major
change to the myth is 'the creation of an Adonis who resists [Venus's
attractions] ... Shakespeare compensates for the myth's lack of action by
turning the poem into a debate, thus restoring rhetoric to its primary
function.'[50] Initially Adonis is as silent as Pigmalion's statue, confining
himself to mostly struggling against Venus and blushing. When he finally
does speak, 185 lines into the poem, he blurts out a mere line and a half:
'Fie, no more of love! / The sun doth burn my face, I must remove'
(185–6). Venus slyly notes the insufficiency of this immature ejaculation,
remarking: 'young and so unkind, / What bare excuses mak'st thou to
be gone!' (187–8). He speaks again almost two hundred lines later,
offering only slightly more plausible excuses to be gone. We are over
four hundred lines into the poem before Adonis offers any substantial
speech (409–26), or attempts to counter any of Venus's logic, at which
point she mutters, 'What, canst thou talk? ... hast thou a tongue?' (427).
He offers his lengthiest speech, lasting thirty-nine lines, just before he
leaves both the poem and Venus for the last time, and by this point he
has become something of an orator:

> What have you urg'd that I cannot reprove?
> The path is smooth that leadeth on to danger.
> I hate not love but your device in love,
> That lends embracements unto every stranger.
> You do it for increase: O strange excuse!
> When reason is the bawd to lust's abuse.
>
> (787–92)

It is only when Adonis has begun to learn rhetoric that he can break out
of Venus's arms, and reject the form of desire that she represents. At the
same time he shows himself to be resistant to her rhetoric: 'know, my
heart stands armed in mine ear, / And will not let a false sound enter

there' (779–80). He declares that he will no more be the object of rhetorical persuasion than he will be the object of desire, and he makes it clear that the one often involves the other. But while his rhetorical ability may have improved (even if it consists largely of clichés), we have seen in the Wat episode that he is far from sensitive to the rhetoric of others and is completely unable to recognize even the simplest of allegories.

In spite of his rhetorical shortcomings ('the text is old, the orator too green' [806], as he himself recognizes), it is worth looking at the arguments that Adonis makes against Venus. Not surprisingly, given the connections between language and the exchange of women, and given that this poem is by Shakespeare, the thematics of their discussions turn out to be principally economic. Venus's arguments often echo those made by the sonneteer to the young man, especially when the conversation turns to begetting. This leads Nona Fienberg to remark, 'So often in *Venus and Adonis* does Venus employ the language of the marketplace as language of seduction, that she seems to have come to earth to learn to speak commercial jargon.'[51] It is as a commodity, in turn, that Adonis speaks of himself, a dangerous position in the sexual economy, as Irigaray points out, for a man to be in:

> 'Fair queen,' quoth he, 'if any love you owe me,
> Measure my strangeness with my unripe years;
> Before I know myself, seek not to know me,
> No fisher but the ungrown fry forbears;
> The mellow plum doth fall, the green sticks fast,
> Or being early pluck'd, is sour to taste.'
>
> (523–8)

Adonis is perhaps being a little dishonest here: given that he is a youth he is ripe for the picking, according to both Venus and the Platonic theory of desire. In fact, if Venus waits too long, the fry will develop not into a fish but a fisher, not a commodity but an exchanger of commodities. The anxiety underlying Adonis's argument seems to be that if he allows himself to become the object of desire he will be forever condemned to that position. While this particular plum might be sour, we can see in *Hero and Leander* and in other poems that invoke the Ganymede myth that youths were not, at least in some contemporary literary works, forbidden fruit. However, Adonis's reluctance to be a commodity is not unusual. It is, as I have suggested, the most typical narrative in the epyllia. It is only his disingenuous argument that is out of place, the protest that he was never a suitable object of desire.

How does the boar figure in this scenario? This has been a problem
for critics, especially because of Shakespeare's decision to make Adonis
reject Venus in favour of the hunt. In older versions of the story, such as
Robert Greene's retelling of the myth in *Perimedes the Blacke-Smithe* (1588),
Adonis gives in to Venus, and his killing by the boar can then be read as a
punishment for succumbing to lust: 'So Long he followed flattering
Venus lore, / Till seely Lad, he perisht by a bore.'[52] Venus's recognition
that she would have killed Adonis in a similar way is perhaps an indication that Shakespeare knew well this tradition, and was specifically avoiding it. Shakespeare's alteration of the poem spoils the moral reading of
the poem, so that whatever the meaning of the boar is, argues A.C.
Hamilton, 'it cannot be simply "moral." Since Adonis does not yield to
Venus, the poem's center becomes a mystery.'[53] Although he grapples
with the issue, Hamilton does not get any closer to pinning down the
boar than to argue that it 'expresses all those forces which seek to pluck
the flower of Beauty.'[54] William Sheidley points out that it is difficult to
read the boar as punishment for anything, as is the tradition, but then
goes on to suggest that Adonis is somehow being punished for being
imperfectly or incompletely phallic: 'The dislocation of phallic potency
predicates the frustration of Venus and brings about the destruction of
Adonis. Properly placed, in Adonis, if that were possible, it might have
rendered all well. How can Adonis deal with the suffocations of Venus's
advances and free himself from her constricting embrace? Slice through
them with the phallic tusk.'[55] Sheidley's interpretation of the boar is to a
certain extent persuasive, but unfortunately he does not pursue his own
arguments to their conclusion. Why does Adonis choose the boar over
Venus? That is to say, what if, as Gordon Williams argues, 'Adonis's
death, far from being a punishment, is a consummation devoutly to be
wished'?[56] What does the boar's goring of Adonis say about 'phallic
energy'? One conclusion, writes Sheidley, is that 'the properly ordered
male must accept and realize his phallic potential.'[57] What exactly does
this say about Adonis then? And what precisely is an improperly ordered
male? Further, argues Sheidley, 'Shakespeare's Boar is ugly and destructive, and, by extension, the phallic energy he embodies may be ungentle,
violent, and even painful, but it is also clearly necessary and productive.'[58] Necessary for and productive of what? Heterosexuality? Phallic
masculinity? I do not want to suggest that these are not conclusions one
can draw from the poem: indeed, part of the argument of this chapter is
that epyllia work to install precisely that version of phallic masculinity
that Sheidley finds there. We must, however, be careful not to confuse
the imperatives or norms of a particular cultural order with universal

prescriptions. In other words, Shakespeare's poem might be participating in the inauguration of a new mode of phallic masculinity, a shift in the dominant fiction, rather than simply showing how Adonis falls short of a timeless masculine ideal.

Venus is clearly terrified by the boar, fainting when Adonis mentions it. She describes it as an avatar of death, correctly predicting the outcome of the hunt: 'I prophesy thy death, my living sorrow, / If thou encounter with the boar to-morrow' (671–2). Heather Asals argues that 'to the reader familiar with the most basic elements of Neoplatonism, it would have been clear that the blindness of the boar identified him as unadulterated lust.'[59] Reading the boar this way would make him something of a counterpart to Venus, which could account for the appearance of Jealousy at this point in the poem (649). Jealousy presents to Venus 'The picture of an angry chafing boar, / Under whose sharp fangs, on his back doth lie / An image like [Adonis]' (662–4). This reproduces the positions that Venus and Adonis occupy earlier in the poem, and which at this point in the poem is being parodied with Adonis ineffectually on top: 'He will not manage her, although he mount her' (598). Venus does not fear the boar for her own sake but rather for its potential to take Adonis away from her. This reading of the rivalry between Venus and the boar could be supported by Adonis's earlier pronouncement: '"I know not love," quoth he, "nor will not know it, / Unless it be a boar, and then I chase it"' (409–10). Finally, when Venus sees Adonis dead she draws something of a parallel between herself and the boar, and rewrites the killing in a specifically erotic way:

> He ran upon the boar with his sharp spear,
> Who did not whet his teeth at him again,
> But by a kiss thought to persuade him there;
> And nousling in his flank, the loving swine
> Sheath'd unaware the tusk in his soft groin.
> 'Had I been tooth'd like him, I must confess,
> With kissing him I should have kill'd him first.'
>
> (1112–18)

Although these parallels do exist between Venus and the boar, clearly the boar has got something that Venus has not, something which, moreover, Adonis apparently wants. If the desires of Venus and the boar are both figured in the poem as dangerous, clearly they are dangerous in different ways. Hunting and the boar are both persistently gendered masculine in the poem: Adonis chooses this world of vigour and hardness over the soft, effeminizing arms of Venus, or, as tradition has it, he chooses between the soft hunt and the hard hunt, erotics and hero-ics.[60] In that regard, the boar is more of a stand-in for Mars than Venus: 'On his bow-back he hath a battle set / Of bristly pikes that ever threat his foes' (619–20).

The boar's connections with Mars should prompt us as well to see him as in some way a reflection of Adonis, which would help to clarify why Venus seems to equate Adonis's interest in the hunt with a dangerous narcissism. Certainly the exchange of roles between hunter and hunted, a literalization of the figure of chiasmus that persistently accompanies Adonis, would suggest some kind of reciprocity or reversibility between the two characters. The association of the hunt with narcissism is one of the chief consequences of Shakespeare's innovation of a resistant Adonis, a consequence that is perhaps attributable to the poem's precursor, Clapham's *Narcissus*. The equation between narcissism and the hunt is suggested early on in the opening chiasmus – 'Hunting he lov'd, but love he laugh'd to scorn' (4) – and in Adonis's later objection to Venus – '"I know not love," quoth he, "nor will not know it, / Unless it be a boar, and then I chase it"' (409–10). His later objections to Venus, especially his banal, priggishly idealistic opposition of love and lust, are attributable more to his literary origins as Petrarchan mistress, and to the narcissism of Petrarchanisms in general, than they are to any interest in morality. This is, after all, an Ovidian poem at heart.

If the ending of the poem has been a puzzle to critics, it is probably because Adonis seems to be embracing vigorous, masculine activity over Venus's effeminizing charms. That is, the hunt is typically seen as pro-ductive rather than sterile and narcissistic. However, the horse episode, the poem's chief example of an Ovidian, adult masculinity, should steer us away from such a reading. Moreover, the boar in this version is, quite unusually, portrayed as a lover, and it is not only Venus who characterizes it as a figure of desire. The one fleeting image we have of the boar that is not mediated through Venus is of his 'frothy mouth bepainted all with red, / Like milk and blood being mingled both together' (901–2). Because of the poem's very careful use of colour, the mingling of red and white, and in particular on his mouth, makes the boar a perverse figure of Petrarchanisms, and thus some kind of reflection of Adonis ('More white and red than doves or roses are' [10]) and of Venus as Petrarchan poet. Seen in this light, Adonis's death is an ironically appro-priate Ovidian punishment. Because he scorns love and rejects her counsel, preferring instead to play the Petrachan mistress, Adonis meets death in the form of a monstrous Petrarchan lover, the boar. As with other versions of the myth, Adonis's death can still be read as a punishment, but in this case for the opposite reason, for rejecting Venus rather than for embracing sexual pleasure. And further, for rejecting Ovidian desire in favour of perverse Petrarchanisms.

An anonymous poem published in 1597, *The Legend of Orpheus and Euridice*, characterizes the boar in a similar fashion.[61] The poem is written using the *Venus and Adonis* stanza, devoting six of them to outrage over Orpheus's introduction of pederasty to Thrace. It culminates by characterizing Orpheus's sin as:

> The *Calidonian* Boare which Gods have sent
> For to destroy the gardens of the blest,
> Whose bloody tuskes in shivering pieces rent
> The daintie young brought up in beauties nest,
>   Virginities defrauder, Autumnes cold,
>   which hurts the bud ere it the leaves unfold.
>
> (sig. E7)

The can be little doubt here that the poet is thinking of Shakespeare's poem, objecting to Orpheus's seduction of youths in much the same terms that Adonis objects to Venus. If we read Shakespeare's boar in a similar light, as the poem encourages us to do, we see the connection between Petrarchan poetry and sodomy that surfaces frequently in the genre, a connection I will explore in greater detail in the following chapter.

While Venus does not avenge the insults to herself in as direct a fashion as she does in the Atalanta and Hippomenes story, she does not hesitate to kill Adonis a second time, metaphorically, when she plucks the flower that grows after his death. It is significant that in this version Venus does not cause Adonis's transformation. In Ovid, Venus decides that 'From yeere to yeere shall growe / A thing that of my heavinesse and of thy death shall showe / The lively likenesse. In a flowre thy blood I will bestowe' (10. 849–51). In Shakespeare's version it is much less clear how Adonis is transformed, or even whether he is transformed, except in Venus's rhetoric:

> By this the boy that by her side lay kill'd
> Was melted like a vapor from her sight,

And in his blood that on the ground lay spill'd,
A purple flow'r sprung up, check'red with white,
Resembling well his pale cheeks and the blood
Which in round drops upon their whiteness stood.

She bows her head, the new-sprung flow'r to smell,
Comparing it to her Adonis' breath ...

(1165–72)

The flower's origins are ambiguous, and Venus transforms it into Adonis only through a series of comparisons, most of which return him to the position of Petrarchan mistress.

Venus's early aggression towards Adonis is reprised by her plucking of the flower, demonstrating for at least the second time in the poem the fleeting nature of beauty. She of course recognizes this, but as is her wont, rationalizes it away:

'Poor flow'r,' quoth she, 'this was thy father's guise –
Sweet issue of a more sweet-smelling sire –
For every little grief to wet his eyes;
To grow unto himself was his desire,
And so 'tis thine, but know it is as good
To wither in my breast as in his blood.

(1177–82)

Venus's final words on Adonis, made to the flower, evoke both common satires of Petrarchan poets ('For every little grief to wet his eyes') and narcissism ('To grow unto himself was his desire'). At the same time they reprise Venus's economic complaints about Adonis's narcissism, arguing that the flower might as well be plucked, since Adonis's blood is not a source of life.

It is important to note that Adonis's transformation takes place only in the sphere of Venus's rhetoric. In the poem, rhetoric is connected with creation and vitality. As Richard Lanham observes, 'To talk well is to be alive, to see, hear, feel. To all of these, serious, inarticulate Adonis is insensitive. Venus really creates with her own praise the Adonis who can represent beauty. She creates herself with her own praise. She creates the significance of Adonis's death by her descriptive sorrow. Only she can give meaning, not only to her desire for Adonis, but to his for the boar.'[62] Adonis's failure to 'take advantage on presented joy' (405) is linked to both his rhetorical shortcomings and his inability to apprehend in a sophisticated way either Venus's rhetoric or the rhetoric of the natural world. Adonis does not even understand the implications of his own rhetoric – 'Hunting he lov'd, but love he laugh'd to scorn' (4) – and Venus attempts throughout the poem to teach him both the truth of the metaphor – love is a hunt – and the force of chiasmus in order to coax him into becoming an adult masculine subject rather than a narcissistic Petrarchan youth. While Adonis recognizes the dangers of being the object of desire, he nonetheless cannot break out of the circuit of narcissism to become a desiring subject. Tone-deaf to the last, Adonis is felled by his own metaphor.

Adonis's transformation changes irrevocably the script of desire. Venus announces that sorrow will hereafter always wait on love (1136), that love will be untimely, unsuitable, and unseemly, and that desire 'shall be fickle, false, and full of fraud' (1141). Venus's catalogue of unsuitable lovers is reminiscent of Freud's comment that heterosexual love is always one generation out of sync. One of the more interesting of Venus's prophecies is that desire 'shall be cause of war and dire events, / And set dissension 'twixt the son and sire' (1159–60). Adonis's encounter with the boar can thus be said to institute the Oedipus complex, the very story of heterosexuality itself, the means by which sons are separated from mothers, and homosexuality is disallowed.[63] If the poem does end with the institution of heterosexuality, it is on rather unstable ground. As with the earlier poems, the homoerotic desire that underwrites the encounter of the boar and Adonis certainly troubles the narrative, and it is by no means certain how long Venus will remain immured.

Hero and Leander

The last example of the genre I will consider in this chapter is Christopher Marlowe's *Hero and Leander*. Although Marlowe was, like the other young poets who wrote epyllia, educated and ambitious, he was also more seriously invested in shocking or challenging orthodoxy than were either Shakespeare or the young men at the Inns of Court. In looking at *Hero and Leander* I want to show how Marlowe is clearer than the others about what is at stake in these rewritten narratives from Ovid. For Marlowe, as for the others, the poems are principally about rhetoric: stories of how subjects become places or sites for rhetorical invention, which are at the same time extravagant rhetorical performances on these places. Marlowe's poem differs from the others by openly displaying the homoerotic desire that informs all of these poems, at the level of both story and narration. He is also interested in how rhetoric is not always used, *pace* the humanist rhetorical theorists, for the sake of goodness and civilization, but rather that it is quite often to be found in the service of cruelty and conquest.

If the typical narrative strategy of the epyllion is to start with a mythic signifier and tell the story of how the subject became a signifier by bringing it to its death or transformation, this would account for some of the necessity of calling Marlowe's poem unfinished, as is the tradition. Certainly Marlowe does not, like most of the writers in this genre, tell the tale to its conclusion, but given that Marlowe does not appear to have been particularly concerned with conformity for its own sake, this should hardly be surprising, much less an argument for the poem's status as finished or unfinished. As Marion Campbell notes in her summary of the debate, much of the argument for considering the poem as unfinished is based either on the thinnest of speculation, or on the fact that Chapman decided to pick up the tale where Marlowe left off.[64] In any case, given the poem as we have it, it makes more sense to consider how its lack of resolution, or its unfaithfulness to its source (a hallmark of the genre, we might recall), may work with its other unconventional elements.

Let us begin a somewhat selective reading at the beginning:

On *Hellespont* guiltie of True-loves blood,
In view and opposit two citties stood,
Seaborders, disjoin'd by *Neptunes* might:
The one *Abydos*, the other *Sestos* hight.
At *Sestos*, *Hero* dwelt ...

(1–5)

As Patrick Cheney observes, in these opening lines Marlowe 'introduces the central principle of his Ovidian-based poetics of desire: separation – rendered here in physiological, political, theological, and metadiscursive forms.'[65] We start with two sites of desire, Abydos and Sestos, which may stand for those two countries, Ladies and Gentlemen. Actually we have three sites of desire, if we include the Hellespont as a place.[66] How does the Hellespont figure in this poem? Outside the poem, it is already a rhetorical site of invention, having acquired an iconic relation to the poem's story: 'hence, in allusion to the story of Leander, something that separates lovers' (*OED*). Is it curious that the dictionary fails to mention Hero? Or is *Hero and Leander* in some way only the story of Leander? The narrator would seem to agree with the dictionary when he remarks in his introduction to the characters that it is Leander 'whose tragedie divine Musaeus soong' (52), which tragedy is the source of Marlowe's poem (in addition to the two letters in Ovid's *Heroides* [XVIII and XIX]). But perhaps the dictionary meaning is more subtle, and the Hellespont in some way separates lovers from themselves: perhaps it acts as a divide or marking point between two different stages of the character. Is it a different Leander that arrives, breathless and naked, at Hero's door?

Whatever the vicissitudes of the *OED*'s definition, it is clear enough that the Hellespont divides something from something else (but thereby also joins them), and that it acts as both a passage and a bar to desire. One of the more obscure connections it makes is perhaps between the source of the poem and the poem itself. It acts, as I have suggested the characters in the epyllion act, as an iconic signifier of the story about to be told. It is also the first site of the poem, the true site of invention we might call it, to use rhetorical terminology. But water, Wilson warns us, is an unstable site for memory (and hence writing): 'Who hath seen a print made in water of any yerthly thing?'[67] he says in his section on memory. This poem, then, is built on shaky foundations, taking place, as it does, 'On *Hellespont*.' The word 'Hellespont' is something of a *mise-en-abyme*, conjuring up the story before the story takes place, telling (or acting as a site of memory for) the poem from within the poem itself. But if it joins the poem to its story, it will also be the poem's divide, acting as one of the prime sites of narrative interruption in the Neptune episode. Moreover, although its iconic status is signalled in the poem's opening line, where it is already 'guiltie of True-loves blood,' this poem will not bring us to the point where the iconicity is established. Hero and Leander will not die in this Hellespont, and thus a gap opens between the source and the poem.

The initial divide that the Hellespont marks is the one between Abydos and Sestos. These two places will function as two different sites of (different) desire that are disjoined by a third: the province of Neptune's might and desire. The two cities stand in a relation of mutual reflection, 'in view and opposite,' each seemingly defining the other, but separated by the bar. The gap that stands between them is mirrored by another gap that opens in the fourth line. The first half of this line, 'The one *Abydos*,' reads as a copula, i.e., 'the one [was] *Abydos*,' but the second clause disrupts this. We are forced to read back and rewrite this when we learn that 'the other *Sestos* hight.' The city then is not Abydos, but is rather called by that name, a subtle yet important distinction. 'Sestos' is not the city, but rather the signifier of the city. This gap between thing and name mirrors the gap between subject and mythic signifier that is central to the action of the typical epyllion, a gap which the poems attempt to close by enacting the closure of the narrative. As Judith Haber notes, the poem is forever playfully but pointedly forestalling closure;[68] Georgia E. Brown further argues that the poem highlights its failure to bring the poem to its possible conclusion in order to focus attention on the telling of the tale, rather than on the tale itself.[69] Because for the genre this passage to iconic destiny is at the same time the story of the emergence of heterosexual desire, Marlowe's refusal to bring the poem to its proper end is at the same time a refusal to participate in the heterosexualizing of the subject.[70]

Both Abydos and Sestos can function as memory places, with the images that correspond to them being Hero and Leander. In rhetorical handbooks the student was instructed to envision the speech as a mansion with rooms or 'places,' filled by 'images,' which are generally mythological or historical figures who would remind the orator of each subtopic. The description of Hero fits perfectly the criteria given in the *ad Herennium* for an active image, which calls for a figure of 'exceptional beauty,' ornamented with such things as 'crowns or purple cloaks' or other fabulous attire to make them more distinct, perhaps smeared with blood, or given 'certain comic effects to our images.'[71] Hero is presented as a figure of wondrous beauty and attire: green garments with 'lining, purple silk' (10), 'Her kirtle blew, whereon was many a staine, / Made with the blood of wretched Lovers slaine' (15–16), crowned with a 'myrtle wreath' (17), and other accoutrements too numerous to mention. She is even assigned comic effects, from bees which buzz about her mouth (23–4) to the gold and pearl sparrows filled with water that adorn her buskins, 'Which as shee went would cherupe through the bils' (36). The narrator's description is largely devoted to her clothing and their high-mimetic effects, such as her veil of 'artificiall flowers and leaves, / Whose workmanship both man and beast deceaves' (19–20). As Nancy J. Vickers similarly observes of Petrarch's Laura, 'Her textures are those of metals and stones; her image is that of a collection of exquisitely beautiful disassociated objects.'[72] Hero is a wondrous automaton, a simulacra of perfect workmanship and beauty that confounds all, another more complicated version of Pigmalion's statue. At the festival, her beauty 'stole away th'inchaunted gazers mind' (104), just as the statue enchants Pigmalion's gaze. Some of the festival-goers, giving up hope after seeing great princes turned away, 'Pyn'd as they went, and thinking on her died'

(130). As the quotations indicate, Hero functions as a hyperbolic parody of the Petrarchan mistress, the object of fetishism and idolatry, an innocent yet dangerous femme fatale.

If the narrative of the epyllion typically takes the characters to the point where they become their names, or become fully iconic, Hero is already there. She seems to already embody the principle of metamorphosis; her beauty, for example, can change pebbles to diamonds. Her fantastical garments, moreover, combine to give the impression of a walking tree, with her veil of flowers and leaves, and her buskins with birds and branches. In the world of the metamorphoses, then, it would appear that she is already post-transformation, which perhaps accounts for the collapse of metaphor all around her. Sestos, the place this wondrous image inhabits, is the site of mimesis gone wild, where the thing represented mingles with the representation, where the signifiers have overtaken the signifieds. Sestos appears as the place of the Imaginary, of excess, chaos, and lethal, enchanting images.

Things are different in Abydos. In order to fulfil his destiny of becoming an image or icon, Leander must cross the Hellespont and so we might wonder whether mimesis functions differently in Abydos. 'Unlike the portrait of Hero,' which W.L. Godshalk says represents a triumph of art over nature, 'the portrait of Leander does not seem to reveal a preference for art or nature.'[73] The metaphors applied to Leander do not share the uncanny habit of becoming literal as they do in Sestos, where tears are really pearls and bees are really confused, nor are they death-dealing. Whereas in Hero's case, Apollo really has courted her for her hair, in Abydos the narrator employs the conditional: '*Jove* might have sipt out *Nectar* from his hand' (62); 'Had wilde *Hippolitus, Leander* seene ...' (77). Language is somehow inadequate here: 'I could tell ye ...' (65), the narrator says when beginning his description of Leander, but then falters in his task: 'but my rude pen, / Can hardly blazon foorth the loves of men / Much lesse of powerfull gods' (69–71). The blazon that he can manage will have to 'suffise' (71) he says, aware in this particular place of language's insufficiency. Whereas Hero is the sign made flesh, or rather the flesh made sign, Leander in Abydos is the seductively mobile signifier that evades description and closure: 'Some swore he was a maid in mans attire, / For in his lookes were all that men desire' (83–4), and those that know otherwise say that he is 'made for amorous play' (88). Leander is all amorous play, the play of the signifier that eludes the narrator and all of the other awestruck pursuers.

If desire is more fluid in Abydos, so is gender. As in epyllia that chart or suggest a course towards heterosexuality, this poem opens with the youth who is the object of desire. Unlike the other poems, however, here this is not associated with sterility or immaturity. To be sure, both Hero and Leander are initially portrayed as immature for comic effect, but this immaturity is not necessarily associated with being the object of desire. Nor is being the object of desire associated with a suffocating danger, except when that very assumption is being parodied in the Neptune digression. More importantly, this desire for the youth is not played out through a goddess, but rather more clearly located in adult admirers, foremost among them the narrator, whose disingenuous claim about his inability to blazon forth the loves of men comes in the middle of one of the most homoerotic passages in English poetry. Marlowe is of course being ironic here about his abilities, and the target of the irony could be precisely the heterosexualization of desire that can be seen in such poems as *Scillaes Metamorphosis* or *Venus and Adonis*. This unwillingness to contemplate homoerotic desire is gently satirized in the figures of those who 'swore he was a maid in mans attire' (83). The narrator's disingenuousness suggests that these men may also be less than honest about their own desire, and that their swearing may be simply for warding off the spectre of sodomy. In any case, with the exception of the goddess Cinthia (59), all of Leander's many admirers seem to be male, from the 'rudest paisant' (79) to the 'barbarous *Thratian* soldier' (81) and few of them seem to be disturbed by the fact of his gender.[74] We might also note that the festival where all of this starts is held by 'The men of wealthie *Sestos*' in honour of 'Rose-cheekt *Adonis*' (91, 93), rather than Venus, whom Hero serves.

The most prominent of Leander's admirers is Neptune, whose dalliance with Leander is the subject of the second digression (639–710). After Hero and Leander arrange to meet, Leander swims the Hellespont at night to be with her; Neptune mistakes Leander for Ganymede and attempts to pull him under the water. While we are here, we might as well ourselves digress to consider the implication of digressions. If a digression is a lapse from the proper order, it might well be considered dire, for as Wilson writes in his section on disposition, 'without order nothying can be. For by an order wee are borne, by an order wee lyve, and by an order wee make our end.'[75] Freud notes in the *Three Essays* that any excessive attention to foreplay, which takes one away from the main narrative of sexual intercourse, amounts to perversion:[76] this digression would seem to fall into this category. Certainly modern critics have read its content as perverse. Haber argues that Leander's objection 'vocalizes the conventional reader's concern (saying, in effect, "Oh no, not *another* story"),'[77] but she does not identify what precisely a 'conventional reader' might be, or why this reader would choose to identify with the hopelessly naive Leander, the butt of many of the poem's jokes. In a similar vein, J.B. Steane writes that 'Leander is aghast at this monstrous irrelevance to his purposes with its infuriatingly gratuitous addition to his already considerable difficulties,'[78] but this better describes the critic struggling with a homoerotic text than Leander's struggle with Neptune. It is not as if Leander has never encountered this sort of attention before. Rosamund Tuve attempts to remove all taint from the passage by reading anything suspicious in it as metaphor: 'remembering that the substitution of *the physical ocean* for *Neptune* was as natural as breathing to any Elizabethan, we can re-read the images as convincing and accurate description of the caressing flow of the water.'[79] Doubtless the Elizabethans were unsurprised if, holding shells up to their ears, they heard homoerotic fables like the one Neptune tells Leander.

In discussing this passage, Clark Hulse notes that 'as in Shakespeare and Fletcher, the pubescent male is the middle term between male and female, between desire and its object.'[80] This is contradicted to some degree by his later claim that 'Marlowe never makes any distinction between the nature of the desire directed toward Hero and that toward Leander,'[81] unless we are to assume that Hero is also a 'pubescent male.' In any case, it is difficult to imagine what 'the middle term between ... desire and its object' might be. Presumably what Hulse means is that the narrative of sexual development for a man would proceed from his being an object of desire, a youth, to being a desiring subject. The digression from this particular narrative seems to be what bothers Leander, rather than 'the nightmare intrusion of a homosexual into a normal man's life' as J.B. Steane puts it.[82] Leander has left Abydos, the place of his youth and thus of being an object of desire, and is adamant about reaching Sestos and becoming a subject. Hulse argues that 'Marlowe's fear is that Leander will play the Narcissus, that, like the passive Hero or the proud Adonis, he will consent only to be the object and not the actor of desire.'[83] But this seems an inaccurate description of Narcissus (who is both object and subject of desire), Hero (who is by no means uniformly passive), and of Marlowe, who appears to be parodying the sort of anxiety Hulse describes with Leander's response. In any case, the lines from which Hulse picks up the warning about narcissicism are attributed by the poem to some of Leander's admirers (87–90), and there is no reason to believe that the narrator agrees with them.

In the narrator's blazon of Leander, he alludes to the Ganymede myth in discussing Leander's physical beauty: '*Jove* might have sipt out *Nectar* from his hand' (62). In the digression Neptune initially believes Leander to be Ganymede, and in a reversal of the myth pulls him down into the water rather than up into the heavens:

> But when he knew it was not Ganimed,
> For under water he was almost dead,
> He heav'd him up.

(653–5)

Neptune does not, however, stop pursuing Leander. Leander responds to him saying 'You are deceav'd, I am no woman I. / Thereat smilde *Neptune*, and then told a tale' (676–7). The narrator is presumably smiling along with Neptune, given his own obvious desire for Leander in the blazon. In fact, the ribald fragment of the tale that Neptune goes on to tell – of an unidentified beautiful youth who is desired by all but especially by men and who is in constant danger of being pulled into the water – is remarkably similar to the narrator's introduction of Leander. Just as Adonis cuts off Venus's telling of the story of Wat the hare, Leander interrupts the telling of this tale; in both cases the inattentiveness to rhetoric is of a piece with their sexual unworldliness. Leander's protest to Neptune is similar to Adonis's claims of unripeness, but whereas Adonis's claims are left unchallenged (and thus, perhaps, implicitly endorsed), both Neptune and the narrator, older and wiser, know better.

If Marlowe's purpose is to mock humanism, this digression could well be central to his purposes. Leander has earlier in the poem displayed both a rhetorical training and a lack of worldly sophistication, which would probably characterize the average humanist pupil or Inns of Court scholar. When Leander first attempts to seduce Hero, the narrator compares him to a 'bold sharpe Sophister' (197), and Hero asks, 'Who taught thee Rhetoricke to deceive a maid?' (338). Clifford Leech notes that '"Sophister" was a Cambridge term for a second- or third-year undergraduate.'[84] Could Marlowe in the Neptune digression, and indeed throughout the poem, be playing with the long established connection between pederasty and humanism? In his study of the deployment of the Ganymede myth in humanist writings, Leonard Barkan writes that in the humanist world the two terms form a hermeneutic circle, each term summoning up the other:

In the High Middle Ages the fanciful rhetorical activities connected with high-flown pedagogy, with Platonism, and with the imaginative recuperation of pagan culture came to be associated with the practice of homosexuality. Not only is the student-teacher relationship reinvestigated (and perhaps re-experienced) in its potential for Socratic pederasty, but homosexuality is itself understood as homologous to new practices of rhetoric, grammar and poetic innovation.[85]

Evidence for the continuation of these associations into Elizabethan England can perhaps be seen in E.K.'s gloss on the January eclogue of Spenser's 'Shepheardes Calendar,' where E.K. denies that the friendship between Hobbinol and Colin contains any 'savour of disorderly love, which the learned call paederastice.'[86] There is something of a hint in there that the learned know whereof they speak. In any case, the situation is complicated when we learn in a gloss of the September eclogue that Hobbinol is the learned 'Mayster Gabriel Haruey: of whose speciall commendation, aswell in Poetrye as Rhetorike and other choyce learning, we have lately had a sufficient tryall.'[87] If Barkan is correct in his reading of humanist desire, the scandal of Marlowe's digression is not (just) in its explicit homoeroticism, but rather in its making explicit the homosocial, pederastic basis of humanism. This is exactly the scandalousness that Luce Irigaray locates in 'masculine' homosexual relations: '*Because they openly interpret the law according to which society operates*, they threaten in fact to shift the horizon of that law. Besides, they challenge the nature, status, and "exogamic" necessity of the product of exchange.'[88] At the same time it should be noted that Marlowe's openly displayed homoeroticism would have been less outrageous then than now. However, it was precisely at this time, argue Alan Bray and other historians of sexuality such as Philippe Ariès and Michel Foucault, that homoeroticism, even in the sanctioned form of male friendship, is becoming more scandalous.[89]

The first digression, while less scandalous, is generally seen to be a little less successful than the second. Hulse dismisses it as a 'shaggy god story': 'however much we may sympathize with the sentiment, we must admit that it has next to nothing to do with the rest of the poem, and pointedly ignores the obvious parallel between the fates of Mercury and Leander, which is presumably the point of the story.'[90] The digression (385–484) consists of an inset narrative discussing the amorous adventures of Hermes and a country maid, as well as the tale of the Destinies' love for Mercury. Rhetoric and desire are, as in the rest of the poem, central elements. Mercury falls in love with a maid, immobilizes her by charming her feet and begins to have his way with her. She resists, he lets her go, and then attempts to charm her mind with a tale. The narrator approves: 'Maids are not woon by brutish force and might, / But speeches full of pleasure and delight' (419–20). We are not given the tale that he tells her. The situation is similar to Venus's candid admission in Shakespeare's poem that she is merely spinning out a tale, 'Applying this to that, and so to so / For love can comment upon every woe' (713–14). Interrupted by Adonis, she cannot remember what she was saying; the only purpose of her 'moraliz[ing]' (712) was to keep Adonis by her side. In this digression, the country maid is almost won, but she demands immortality in exchange for her virginity, and much negotiation among the gods ensues. We will see the same sort of negotiations later in Beaumont's *Salmacis and Hermaphroditus*; for the wise maid, the commodification of chastity should be countered with a contract.[91]

The moral of the narrative is a little unexpected. After the deceits are untangled, Hermes is sent to hell by the Destinies:

> And but that Learning, in despight of Fate,
> Will mount aloft, and enter heaven gate,
> And to the seat of *Jove* it selfe advaunce,
> *Hermes* had slept in hell with Ignoraunce
> Yet as a punishment they added this,
> That he and *Povertie* should alwaies kis.
> And to this day is everie scholler poore ...
>
> (465–71)

How did scholars enter into this? Given that this poem is as much a display of rhetorical finesse as anything else, and given that the audience for these poems was the young men at the universities and Inns of Court, it perhaps makes sense that a fable of learning should be included. The three Parnassus plays, for example, written by students at Cambridge, have as their central theme the poor financial prospects of humanists.[92] It may also be relevant that Marlowe was identified and identified himself publicly as a scholar.[93] But what then does the fable tell us? If we read the tale again, knowing that the Hermes/Mercury figure is a representative of scholars, we see rhetoric in the service of desire and deceit. This, of course, characterizes much of the poem, from Leander's rhetorical seduction of Hero, to Neptune's attempts at Leander, to the narrator's caressing of Leander's body in the blazon. Like the digression with

Neptune, it makes explicit the erotics of rhetoric, in this case by directly signalling the place of the production of rhetoric. In doing so it shows how desire interrupts narratives, and in the process interrupts and disrupts the poem.

If desire and rhetoric are persistently coupled in the poem, it is in the ending where we begin to see the consequences of the heterosexualization of desire. Leander there persuades Hero to admit him to her bed, where the seduction becomes ever more insistent:

> And now she lets him whisper in her eare,
> Flatter, intreat, promise, protest and sweare,
> Yet ever as he greedily assayd
> To touch those dainties, she the *Harpey* playd,
> And every lim did as a soldier stout,
> Defend the fort, and keep the foe-man out.
>
> (751–6)

Henry Peacham's characterization of rhetoric as a conquest of the listener's bodies (the orator's 'words pearce into their inward partes') is here enacted, except that rhetoric is not seen to be in the service of innocence and goodness, as Peacham believed it inevitably must be.[94] Instead, Marlowe continues his account of the seduction by insisting that 'Love is not full of pittie (as men say) / But deaffe and cruell, where he meanes to pray' (771–2). Marlowe thus puts the lie to a commonplace of poetry; the men who say that love is 'full of pittie' are perhaps using poetry or rhetoric to rewrite the scene of seduction. Moreover, as John Leonard suggests, it now seems that Hero's resistance is precisely what is stimulating Leander's desire.[95] The common poetic conceit of love or courting as a seige or battle is replaced by a more brutal image:

> Even as a bird, which in our hands we wring,
> Foorthe plungeth, and oft flutters with her wing
> She trembling strove ...
>
> (773–5)

The violence that is alluded to but written away in the battle metaphor becomes explicit and immediate, although this rapidly metamorphoses into a metaphor for Hero's pleasure. This is in turn replaced by the description of Hero's humiliation at the break of day. The poem ends with the implicit comparison between Hero's shame and that of 'ougly night' (816), who is mocked by the sun, 'Til she o'recome with anguish, shame, and rage, / Dang'd downe to hell her loathsome carriage' (817–18).

We become aware at the end of the poem that certain transformations have taken place, which might supply the poem, at least partially, with a conclusion proper to an epyllion. Leander, for example, has been transformed from the sexually ambiguous youth who was the object of everyone's desire at the beginning of the poem. In his rejection of Neptune, his apparently violent seduction of Hero, and his scopophilic pleasure in the naked Hero – 'Whence his admiring eyes more pleasure tooke, / Than Dis, on heapes of gold fixing his looke' (809–10) – he is obviously a man, a desiring subject. Hero too has undergone a transformation worthy of the *Metamorphoses*, when 'Meremaid-like unto the floore she slid / One half appear'd, the other halfe was hid' (799–800). But another more subtle transformation has occurred. Whereas earlier in the poem Hero was noticeable primarily for her wondrous clothes, she is now naked and blushing, and seems more fully alive than ever before. John Klause notes that *Hero and Leander* is characterized by hard, metallic surfaces, and that even the bodies seem to be carved out of stone.[96] Although this certainly applies earlier in the poem, the somewhat pathetic image of Hero slipping naked out of bed onto the floor is different from that of the automaton introduced by the blazon. She is now no longer the perfect image for memory, no longer a triumph of art over nature, or the flesh made sign. Hero is first introduced with an epithet, 'Hero the faire, / whom young Apollo courted for her haire' (5–6). Where the metaphor was there made literal, the narrator undoes this at the end of the poem:

And from her countenance behold ye might,
A kind of twilight breake, which through the heare,
As from an orient cloud, glymse here and there.

(802–4)

The metaphor is again the sun, Apollo, courting her hair, although it is more distant, and certainly less literal. Hero has undergone a process opposite to the one expected. Rather than transforming a person into a *topos* or image, Marlowe has transformed an image into a person. The process is similar to one Lynn Enterline identifies in Shakespeare's *Lucrece*, a movement 'from the rhetoric of the Petrarchan *blason* to that of Ovidian animation.'[97]

This transformation of Hero from image to person is similar to the transformation of Pigmalion's statue, or indeed, of the nymph Scilla from disdainful Petrarchan mistress to humiliated and spurned wretch. As in these poems, we see that the transformation of the woman into a less powerful and perhaps pathetic figure is the necessary accompaniment to the maturation of the youth into a fully phallic masculinity. Where Marlowe's poem differs from these others is the extent to which we are forced to contemplate how 'ungentle, violent, and even painful,'[98] to use Sheidley's words, this phallic energy can be, or towards whom it is generally directed. Hulse ignores this imbalance when he writes, 'If Hero and Leander seemed, like Mercury and his maid, to be innocent of the sexual violence practiced by Jove and Mars, they are revealed in their moment of consummation to be no different after all.'[99] This elides the fact that Mercury tries to rape the maid, and by parallelling the former couples with the couple 'Jove and Mars,' the comparison neatly removes the objects of the latter couple's violence. A similar flattening gesture occurs when, as Hulse notes, 'The poem breaks off as it began, with scopophilia; the universal gaze linking human beings to the spheres amid the contrary movements of adoration and laughter.'[100] What is lost again in Hulse's equation is who is doing what to whom. At the beginning of the poem both Hero and Leander were the objects of this 'universal [masculine] gaze' but this has now changed. Leander, who has become a man, now does the gazing, while Hero remains the object of the 'adoration and laughter.' It is no doubt significant, as David Lee Miller observes, that 'the action does not, in fact, climax with the long-delayed penetration of Hero, but with the complete exposure of Hero's body to her lover's gaze.'[101] The gender divide and the consequences of this divide are made perfectly clear by Marlowe: the couple to which they are implicitly compared are a male Hesperus mocking an ugly female Night.

Critics commenting on the end of the poem often remark on how difficult it would have been for Marlowe to finish it; this comment rests on the assumption, of course, that the poem is somehow unfinished. The printer's comment at the end of the poem, *desunt nonnulla* or 'something is missing,' might give this assumption some credibility, although Godshalk argues that this is nothing more than 'an early critical opinion' on the printer's part.[102] What is certainly missing in this poem is death, or more specifically the deaths of Hero and Leander, as C.S. Lewis points out: 'A story cannot properly end with the two chief characters dancing on the edge of the cliff: it must go on to tell us either how, by some miracle, they were preserved, or how, far more probably, they fell over.'[103] Lewis is no doubt correct in seeing this as a matter of 'propriety,' as he puts it a little later,[104] and one can read a faint desire for punishment in his wish to see the characters go off the cliff. The poem does not take the characters to their proper places, but perhaps because (as the critics implicitly suggest) this would undo everything the poem has been doing up until the end. It would mean, for example, erasing the desire that Marlowe was interested in exploring: the desire that informs rhetoric and the production of rhetoric.

In his argument for considering Marlowe's poem and Chapman's continuation as one poem, C.S. Lewis paradoxically draws attention to 'that change in English poetry with which Chapman's succession to Marlowe coincides. The old love for a poetry of pure deliciousness was, indeed, losing its edge. Honey began to pall. That is why a movement either to the more violent and knotty poetry of Donne or to the harder and severer poetry of Milton was necessary ... The English Muse loses her innocence in the process of telling how Hero lost hers.'[105] As we will see later, the genre of the epyllion is to a large degree premised on the ruin of maids. But one need not go as far as Chapman's poem to see a turn to more violent poetry, which Lewis here naturalizes as a simple change in taste, figuring violence as, presumably, the meat of poetry. Marlowe is quite explicit about the violence directed towards Hero at the end of the poem, which Lewis employs in an oddly cheery way to discuss changing fashions in love poetry. There is a consciousness of this change of fashion in the final lines of *Hero and Leander*, which might explain why Marlowe chose to go no further with the story.

Marlowe's consciousness of this change, which is readable as the end of Renaissance humanism in England, can be seen earlier in the poem in his openly homoerotic portrayal of Leander and Neptune. It may be functioning analogously to the way in which Barkan sees Caravaggio's *Amor Vincit Omnia* working, given that in both 'the erotic/humanistic tradition is made manifest.'[106] Barkan argues that the sublimation of homoeroticism was fundamental to the erotics of humanism:

For this 'Renaissance' (of whatever date) to take place, there needs to be a kind of mediated naivete: cultural self-consciousness but not meta-self-consciousness; homoeroticism but not unsublimated homoeroticism. In the *Amor Vincit Omnia*, the laying bare of culture's material trappings is of a piece with the nude boy's frank invitation to the viewer. Neither culture nor eros is an elusive goal that the self desires to approach through the tortuous path of figura.[107]

Like Caravaggio's painting (executed around 1600), *Hero and Leander* is shocking in its explicitness: not necessarily its sexual explicitness, although that has given more than one critic cause for alarm. The explicitness that is truly scandalous is that which lays bare a culture's desire. This is what Marlowe's poem does for both the culture that is passing away and the one that is gaining ascendence: showing the homoerotic basis of Renaissance humanism, and the violence implicit in the emergent heterosexuality.

CHAPTER FOUR

'Yon's one Italionate': Sodomy and Literary History

Having considered the most famous examples of the genre, Shakespeare's and Marlowe's, in this chapter we will look at some of the more obscure examples, concentrating principally on two by Thomas Edwards and one by John Weever, all of which are heavily indebted to their predecessors. For instance, Adonis is invoked in two of the three poems, and in both cases he is recognizably Shakespeare's Adonis. All three of the poems have as their main narrative the story of a young man, and in all three cases, rhetoric plays a central role. But these poems are of interest not so much because they testify to their models' popularity and influence, or even for showing the use that can be made of the resources of the genre by less singular or original geniuses. Rather, they are interesting because they take the concerns of the genre into the social realm; the three poems, for example, all show an interest in English literary culture and English nationalist sentiment, singling out and praising English writers, and damning their Italian contemporaries.

Whereas Weever's poem engages in the controversy over English satires, Edwards's poems participate in the establishment of an English literary canon, which is founded upon a rejection of Italian poetry. For both poets these are matters not merely of literary taste but of national importance. We can see in the poems a desire to claim Ovid for the English literary tradition, to make England, not Italy, the rightful heir of the golden age. The poets share with their generation of writers an interest in national canon formation and the role that literature can play in constructing a sense of nationhood. This is not to say that these poems leave behind the questions of selfhood and sexuality that elsewhere concern the genre; on the contrary, they testify to the degree to which these concerns are implicated in larger societal questions.

Narcissus

> Is thine own heart to thine own face affected?
> Can thy right hand seize love upon thy left?
> Then woo thyself, be of thyself rejected;
> Steal thine own freedom, and complain on theft.
> > Narcissus so himself himself forsook,
> > And died to kiss his shadow in the brook.
>
> > > (*Venus and Adonis*, 157–62)

Of the many early modern versions of the Narcissus myth, Edwards's *Narcissus* is surely the strangest, combining (among other things) cross-dressing, sonnetteering and overseas trade. Narcissus is the epyllion's favourite example of failed masculinity. For other characters in the genre, Narcissus is an example of how not to behave, and what not to become. In Edwards's version, as in other epyllia, this failure is to some degree connected with Petrarchan verse. At the same time, because of the connections between narcissism and male friendship, one of the key humanist models of political subjectivity, the poem gestures towards the broader connections between the literary and the social worlds.

Little is known about Thomas Edwards beyond what can be surmised from his sole surviving publication, which includes both *Narcissus* and *Cephalus and Procris*. It was entered in the Stationer's Register on 22 October 1593 and was published by John Wolfe in 1595. The poems themselves went missing until 1882, when a copy was found in the Cathedral Library of Peterborough. W.E. Buckley subsequently edited the text, and attempted to pin down the identity of Edwards. He puts forward a number of possible candidates, none definitive. A further effort by Charlotte Carmichael Stopes was similarly unsuccessful in providing conclusive evidence.

Cephalus and Procris is mentioned in W[illiam] C[ovell]'s *Polimanteia* (1595), in a section where Covell discusses writers from the two universities and the Inns of Court. The placement of the poem's mention suggests that its author belongs to the latter; in any case, it suggests that a student wrote the poem. The dedicatee of Edwards's volume, Thomas Argall, came from a family connected to the law. His father, Richard Argall, attended the Inner Temple, as did his brother Richard and his grandson Thomas;[1] Buckley writes, 'There is no evidence to show that he carried on the family business as a notary, but he may have done so, and Thomas Edwards, the author of the Poems, may have been one of his clerks; at all events, he seems to have been in some way dependent on, or indebted to him.'[2] Edwards describes himself as a 'young beginner' and a 'scholar,' and he is certainly up-to-date with literary fashion.[3] Mark Eccles has subsequently noted that Argall entered Lincoln's Inn in 1584/5, and that a Thomas Edwards, born about 1567 in Shropshire, was specially admitted to Lincoln's Inn on 16 June 1587, after having attended Furnival's Inn. This Edwards was a chamber-fellow of Christopher Brooke, friend of John Donne. A court document shows him in March 1592/3 to be a servant to Sir John Wolley, Latin secretary to the queen, and thus as an aspiring bureaucrat and humanist.[4] This fits with the hints in the dedication that Edwards is at court at the time of publication. Given the usual profile of most writers of epyllia, it is likely that this is the Thomas Edwards who registered the poems in 1592/3 and published them in 1595.

In Ovid, the tale of Narcissus is part of a series concerning Tiresias, and one of the unifying links of the series is a concern with gender transformations and gender differences. Ovid stresses that Narcissus is poised between youth and manhood, a perilous place according to the epyllion: 'Cephisus' child had reached his sixteenth year, and could be counted as at once boy and man. Many lads and many girls fell in love with him, but his soft young body housed a pride so unyielding that none of those boys or girls dared touch him' (83). Narcissus, like Tiresias, seems to exist in state of gender flux. This is noticeable not so much in the various desires directed at him – other youths in Ovid are admired by lads and girls – but in his carefully specified age, which puts him on the cusp of the two genders of youth and man, the same place in which we find youths such as Adonis and Leander. This flux will be Narcissus's punishment at the end of the tale, which he himself recognizes. 'It is I who kindle the flames which I must endure. What should I do? Woo or be wooed? But what then shall I seek by my own wooing? ... How I wish I could separate myself from my own body' (86). Narcissus's dilemma, at least as he sees it, is that in love there must be some distinction between wooer and wooed, on the basis of either gender or something else. Whether this is between a man and a youth, or a youth and a maid, is perhaps immaterial.

In Arthur Golding's translation of Ovid, Narcissus similarly stands 'beetwene the state of man and Lad' (3.438). In this version, we can see the influence of early modern male friendship discourses on the story, and thus Narcissus's dilemma becomes rather different than it is in Ovid:

O pierlesse piece, why dost thou mee thy lover thus delude?
Or whither fliste thou of thy friende thus earnestly pursude?

Iwis I neyther am so fowle nor yet so growne in yeares,
That in this wise thou shouldst me shoon. To have me to their Feeres
The Nymphes themselves have sude ere this. And yet (as should appeere)
Thou dost pretende some kinde of hope of friendship by the cheere.

(3.570–5)

Golding plays here with the eroticism that is a familiar current in male
friendship discourse, as well as the narcissistic dimensions of that relation. According to the tradition, which stretched from Aristotle's *Ethics*
to Montaigne's *Essais* and had Cicero's *De Amicitia* as its centrepiece, the
friends are mirrors for each other. As Sir John Harrington translates
Cicero, 'He surely is a freend, that is an other I.'[5] In the most usual
version of the story, the friends are raised together, educated together,
and even look alike. In Shakespeare and Fletcher's *Two Noble Kinsmen*,
which builds on Chaucer's *Knight's Tale*, the male friends Palamon and
Arcite engage in heavily eroticized exchanges in their prison cell:

Here being thus together,
We are an endless mine to one another;
We are one another's wife, ever begetting
New births of love; we are father, friends, acquaintance;
We are, in one another, families:
I am your heir, and you are mine ...

(2.2.78–83)

The narcissistic dimensions of this relation are clearly recognized in the
play. Directly after this speech, Emilia and her waiting woman wander
through the garden just beneath their prison window, and remark upon
the narcissus that grows there: 'That was a fair boy certain, but a fool /
To love himself. Were there not maids enough?' (2.2.120–1). Later,
looking on their pictures, Emilia compares Arcite to Ganymede and
Palamon to Narcissus (4.2.15, 32). Friends, it would seem, occupy the
same space of potential gender flux as Narcissus. By introducing the
discourse of friendship, Golding changes the dynamic of Narcissus's
dilemma. The problem is no longer the lack of a power differential
between the lovers (friendship insists upon equality) and Narcissus's
desire is perhaps more than just sexual. At the same time, Golding may
be making a point about the erotic dimensions of contemporary friendship discourses. As we shall see in our discussion of Orpheus in the
following chapter, the story of the male friends almost always combined

both an erotic and a political dimension, the latter seen in the frequent opposition between the idealism of the friends and the political tyranny in which they find themselves.

As Louise Vinge notes in her compendious survey of the Narcissus theme, Thomas Edwards's *Narcissus* departs quite radically from the dominant version of the myth.[6] As with Lodge's *Scillaes Metamorphosis*, the poem is linked to the complaint genre, although its content signals its affinity to the epyllion. The poem is full of references to Marlowe's *Hero and Leander* and to Shakespeare's *Venus and Adonis*.[7] Both Leander and Adonis are in fact summoned up by Narcissus to commiserate with him – they will be 'haplesse boies together' (25.3) – and in both cases they are recognizably the well-known literary versions. Reference is made, for example, to Hero's 'vale of lawne' (26.5) and her 'buskins all of shels ysiluered ore' (26.6); Adonis is 'thrice faire' (24.2), echoing Venus's 'thrice fairer than myself' (7). Edwards's narrator, a ghostly Narcissus returned from his watery grave, is modelled on Marlowe's rather than Shakespeare's narrator, offering knowing (if occasionally clunky) asides to the reader: 'Come sing with me, and if these noates be lowe, / You shall haue some prickt higher ere ye goe' (1.6–7). In the Envoy, Edwards salutes what he sees as the English canon, giving Spenser and Sidney pride of place, but then turning to poets associated with the epyllion: Watson, Marlowe, and Shakespeare.

For a poet so clearly enamoured of Marlowe's *Hero and Leander*, the Narcissus myth would seem an obvious choice, which makes Edwards's alterations all the more puzzling. As usual, Narcissus is a supremely beautiful youth who scorns his many admirers, but here the admirers seem without exception to be women: 'looke how Gnats soft singing swarme together, / So did faire Ladies round about me houer' (6.6–7). That Narcissus might also be desired by men is hinted at in only the most delicate ways, as we shall see below. Narcissus's problem in this version is as much sexual ignorance as it is pride:

> Aie me, I not respected dalliance then,
> Though many did incyte me to disport,
> I knew not I what ioyes they gaue to men.

> (7.1–3)

'Respect[ing] dalliance' is a key part of the Ovidian sensibility, which the narrator, the ghostly Narcissus, seems to have acquired. Later, reflecting on the 'many times' he had 'been luld a sleepe / In Ladies bowers' he complains: 'Had *Priapus Narcissus* place enioy'd, / He would a little more haue done then toy'd' (14.1–2, 6–7). The older Narcissus thus has much in common with Marlowe's narrator and other adult males in the genre, in that he is principally interested in sex. He seems at the same time, however, to have remained a youth, re-imagining himself as a sexually-aware Ganymede as he calls on the 'sable winged messenger of Ioue': 'Wide ope thy wings, I'le houer twixt thy armes, / And like the cock when morne comes sound alarme' (31.6–7). If the ghostly Narcissus is Ovidian, we might expect that the youthful Narcissus, as he is already coded naive, will also be coded as Petrarchan. This we can see most obviously in the references to his 'scorning' (36.7) and 'coie disdaines' (37.4), the favourite activities of Petrarchan mistresses. And in spite of the poem's appeal to Leander, it is Hero that Narcissus most resembles when his beauty causes near-riots among the townsfolk (stanza 12).

This leads us to the most dramatic innovation that Edwards makes in the story. Midway through the poem, Narcissus's female admirers send him jewels:

> I tooke the Iewels which faire Ladies sent me,
> And manie pretie toies, which to aduance
> My future bane, vnwillingly they meant me,
> Their whole attire and choice suites not content me;
> But like a louer glad of each new toy,
> So I a woman turned from a boy.
>
> (44.2–7)

While unexpected, this transformation of the story does echo its placement in the Tiresias section of Ovid, as well as the gender confusion implicit in Narcissus's suspension between the categories of youth and man.[8] The next stanza ambiguously suggests that the cross-dressed Narcissus now seeks the attention of male admirers:

> how farre did I exceed
> Those stately dames, in gesture, modest action,
> Coy lookes, deep smiles, faining heroique deeds,
> To bring them all vnder my owne subiection.
>
> (45.1–4)

Narcissus's transformation into the Petrarchan mistress is perhaps the true metamorphosis in this version of the story, and it has the same appropriateness of many of the transformations in Ovid: if you act the Petrarchan mistress, you will become one. Narcissus's story would at this point seem to be a confirmation of the worst fears of the Elizabethan antitheatricalists: dressing in women's clothing can addle a youth's mind, and his perversion will inevitably lead to the seduction, subjection, and perversion of others.[9] And in fact later in the poem, in his lengthy attempted seduction of his image, Narcissus and his reflection are compared to actors, and the action between them to a play.

Wandering about in women's clothing one day, chanting 'soueraigne sweet Sonetto's to loues mother' (46.4), Narcissus happens upon a shallow spring. It is not his reflection, however, that initially attracts him, but rather his own voice: 'Oh what diuine Saint is it that doth sing!' (49.3). Led by his 'attractiue Syren-singing selfe' (50.1) he sees his own reflection in the clear water, and falls in love. Echo's part in the story is thereby absorbed into Narcissus's narrative, although she does make a vestigial appearance later in the poem to appeal to the gods for justice (stanzas 89–92), thereby replacing the male lover in Ovid who calls upon Nemesis. Narcissus still falls in love with his own image, but in this version it is the image of a woman rather than a man. Presumably this is done to remove the potential taint of sodomy from the myth, although it has to be said that the result is something far stranger. That the poem is interested in removing the homoerotic elements of the myth is indicated in one of the many stanzas devoted to Narcissus's wooing of his image:

> Oh why doth Neptune closet vp my deere?
> She is no Mermaid, nor accounted so,
> Yet she is faire, and that doth touch him neere,
> But she's a votarie, then let her go,
> What beautie but with wordes men can vndo?
>   Oh *Neptune* she's a *Syren*, therefore nay,
>   *Syrens* are fittest to adorne the sea.

(70.1–7)

Edwards here reprises, in a revised form, the famous Neptune digression from Marlowe's *Hero and Leander*. As Leander is swimming the Hellespont, he is mistaken for Ganymede by Neptune, who hauls him under the waves. Leander protests, 'You are deceav'd, I am no woman I. / Thereat Neptune smiled' (675–6). Here, it is Narcissus's image that is held prisoner by the lustful Neptune. Because of the cross-dressing, the protest of mistaken gender identity will not work here (as long as Edwards wants to keep the poem out of the realm of the homoerotic), so Narcissus is forced to make the more feeble complaint that the Syren is a saltwater, rather than a freshwater, deity. The multi-layered comedy of misapprehensions in Marlowe's poem is here oddly transformed. In Marlowe's poem, Leander is either unaware that men desire youths or that he still is one, and Neptune is mistaken about either Leander's availability or his identity. The narrator, while sympathetic with Neptune's position, sees all desire as inherently comic. Here the joke is also on the youth in question, but it is either far simpler (he does not remember that he is in drag), or far more complicated (he does not realize that all gender identity is to some degree drag).

In spite of at least forty stanzas spent wooing his image, and in spite of direct addresses to the character by his older and wiser self, Narcissus never seems to realize that he has fallen in love with his own reflection. In the penultimate stanza, he leaps into the spring seeking 'the fauour of my shaddowed mistres' (93.5) and dies. Removing the final realization dramatically changes the moral of the story. It can no longer function as a fable of pride or self-love, but becomes instead an admonitory tale about the dangers of cross-dressing, or the warping effects older women may have on younger men. The incredibly long wooing scene should, however, alert us to another story that is going on at the same time. Debates between lovers (one-sided as they usually are) are one of the most common elements of the epyllion, and certainly present in the poems that serve as Edwards's model. These debates typically involve the exposure of Petrarchan rhetoric as naive, deluded, ethically suspicious, or all of the above. When we remember that it is Narcissus's voice that draws him rather than the vision of a beautiful youth, even a beautiful cross-dressed youth, we might begin to see that this is another satiric attack on Petrarchan poetry, which would answer Vinge's question as to 'whether Edwards' poem can possibly be a literary poetical pamphlet, directed especially against contemporary love lyrics.'[10]

The poem, in fact, directs itself to Petrarchans, in particular, it would seem, Petrarchan ladies, the same 'coy dames' to whom Lodge writes. In spite of the fact that the initial readership of the poems would have been almost exclusively male, the first stanza of the poem addresses

> You that are faire, and scorne th'effectes of loue,
> You that are chaste, and stand on nice conceites,
> You *Delians* that the Muses artes can moue,
> You that for one poore thing make thousands treate,

You that on beauties honor do curuate;
    Come sing with me, and if these noates be lowe,
    You shall haue some prickt higher ere ye goe.

(1.1–7)

Although on first glance these lines seem directed towards women, the narrative of the poem suggests that they could equally be directed towards youths; the principal moral example, after all, concerns Narcissus, not Echo. Bearing that in mind, the lewd final couplet echoes Marston's effeminizing of the (male) reader in his poem: 'O pardon me / Yee gaping eares that swallow vp my lines' (38.1–2). The tone, of course, recalls Marston as well. The mock seriousness of the first five lines is quickly pricked by the rudeness of the last two; the comedy of the poem will depend upon a juxtaposition of these two erotic ideologies, Petrarchan and Ovidian, represented most prominently in the poem by the young Narcissus and his ghostly self. The relation between these two figures is essentially the same as that between Marlowe's narrator and Leander, which prompts us towards the consideration of a key dynamic in the genre upon which we have already touched. The Ovidian narrator converts loss to triumph by projecting his desire into the past, replaying his erotic defeats through the bodies of others. This crucial temporal distance allows for the detachment necessary to see all desire as comic, and Petrarchan desire in particular as immature.

Edwards uses the Narcissus story to make a sophisticated and compelling critique of the gender dynamics of Petrarchan poetry. That borrowed jewels start everything in motion is appropriate, given the central role that jewels often play in Petrarchan compliment. Narcissus has been led by his 'Syren-singing selfe' (50.1), which is to say, by his own rhetoric. Like the typical Petrarchan poet, Narcissus has fallen under the spell of his own words: 'His owne conceit with that of his did fire him' (49.6). The woman he falls in love with, much like Pigmalion's statue, is one of his own creation: a woman constructed out of bits and pieces of other women's clothing, recreated in his own image, and wooed with 'out of date' clichés:

I scorn'd loue, yet lou'd one of my owne name,
My selfe complaining of my face too faire,
And telling how my griefes procured teares:
    Confused arguments, vaine, out of date ...

(86.3–6)

118   Sexuality and Citizenship

We have then in Narcissus's attempted seduction of his own cross-dressed self, the familiar Ovidian story about the Petrarchan poet: an immature, narcissistic poet who is in love with a fantasy woman of his own creation, rather than the sexual pleasures offered by flesh-and-blood women. As the narrator puts it in the Envoy, 'Such a fauour's nothing worth, / To touch not to taste the treasure' (2.5–6). Youthful poets who are drawn to the rhetorical perversions of Petrarchanisms will remain forever youths, trapped in the ambiguous space between youth and man, oscillating helplessly between object of desire and desiring subject. Here we see the sophisticated use that Edwards's poem, with its doubled mirroring structure, makes of the theory behind the mirror literature of the period (which was largely in the complaint mode). The youthful Narcissus offers us the negative exemplum of a youth seduced by Petrarchan rhetoric, while the older Narcissus, like the genre itself, invites us to reform ourselves, or at least our rhetoric, according to the example of the disembodied Ovidian voice.

Sodomy and Nationalism

In the Envoy to *Narcissus*, Edwards launches into a flurry of archaic language, presumably in homage to the 'mighty swaine' Collyn (5.1), Edmund Spenser. Spenser, writes Edwards, 'vnlockt *Albions* glorie, / He twas tolde of *Sidneys* honor' (6.1–2). Edwards then mentions other worthy poets using the names of their creations (Rosamund, Amintas, Leander, Adon), perhaps, again, in homage to Spenser's pastoral mode. After calling the roll, he comes to the point:

What remaines peerelesse men,
That in *Albions* confines are,
But eterniz'd with the pen,
    In sacred Poems and sweet laies,
Should be sent to Nations farre,
    The greatnes of faire *Albions* praise.

(12.1–6)

Edwards is interested in the promulgation of Albion's poetic reputation, with the specific and recognizably humanist interest in Albion becoming the inheritor of Rome: 'Then thus faire *Albion* flourish so, / As *Thames* may nourish as did *Pô*' (15.5–6).

Other poems in the genre have a similar interest in national canon formation. In *Cephalus and Procris*, Edwards pays homage to an almost identical set of poets; the final stanza of William Barksted's *Mirrha the Mother of Adonis* is an homage to Shakespeare. Moreover, we frequently see an Englishing of the muse taking place: poems are set in Oxford (*Scillaes Metamorphosis*); English deities are introduced (*Cephalus and Procris*); the English countryside or country customs are added to the background (*Venus and Adonis, Faunus and Melliflora*). In this poem, Edwards uses English history as a source of mythical referent, summoning up Drake and Edward III in stanza 57. Richard Helgerson has written of how a generation of writers in the late sixteenth century had a shared project of writing the idea of the English nation into being: 'in chivalric romance, historical narrative, and topographical description, these poets sought to articulate a national community whose existence and eminence would then justify their desire to become its literary spokesmen.'[11] Edwards's Envoy, along with his repeated invocations throughout the poem, signals his allegiance to this generational project.

This raises the question of the relation between the three elements of the poem we have looked at: the poem's interest in the formation of a national(ist) poetic canon; its rejection of Petrarchanisms; and its removal of homoeroticism from the myth. The last of these is related to what might be seen as a fear in the poem of the beauty of youths, a fear that we see represented in the antitheatrical tracts as well. In an educational culture suspicious about the links between pedagogy and pederasty, in the context of a general societal redefinition of relations between men, the tension of which seems to surface in accusations of sodomy, this fear of the attractiveness of male youth is understandable.[12] In bemoaning his fate early in the poem, Narcissus blames neither pride nor self-love for his downfall, but rather his beauty and his insufficiently persuasive female wooers: 'O had I bene lesse faire, or they more wittie, / Then had I not thus playn'd in tragicke song' (11.1–2). One of his wooers later remarks that beauty 'Is ruinous and quite without content,' concluding, 'Then youth and beautie hold not hands together, / For youth is best, where beautie hath another' (21.5, 6–7). The narrator responds, somewhat cryptically, that 'Beautie and youth are baites without a lure' (22.5). This fear of the beauty of youths is most evident in an extraordinary outburst by the ghostly Narcissus:

Would some good man had massacred my face,
Blinde stroke my eies, as was my hart thereto,

Dasht in my throate, my teeth, done some disgrace,
For with my tounge some say they were vndoe,
Or me foredone to shame, ere they did woe.
  I am perswaded then, I had not beene,
  What now I am, nor halfe these griefes had seene.

(12.1–7)

The violence of this passage is completely out of keeping with the rest of
the poem and remarkable in that the narrator is contemplating the
disfiguration of his younger self. It suggests that the beauty of youths is so
irresistible, so likely to lead to tragedy, that the only recourse is for 'some
good man' to destroy it. This would seem to confirm Stephen Orgel's
point concerning the anxieties about the uncontrollability of male desire which lurk in the antitheatrical tracts.[13]

But what is the danger posed by the beauty of youth? For Narcissus,
the danger rebounds for the most part upon himself. The stanza above
suggests that the desire directed at Narcissus was more dangerous and
more deforming than a literal deforming of his face would have been.
Whereas the poem suggests that this desire is directed at youths by
women, other moments in the poem – the massacre stanza, the Ganymede
reference, Narcissus as cross-dressed seductress, and the Neptune episode – all suggest that it is at least as likely that this desire comes from an
older man. This might link up to the economic objections that Adonis
makes to Venus, which we have quoted elsewhere. Adonis objects that he
will be deformed by Venus's attention, and fail to develop to maturity. As
such, he will be a useless commodity:

Who wears a garment shapeless and unfinish'd?
Who plucks the bud before one leaf put forth?
If springing things be any jot diminish'd,
They wither in their prime, prove nothing worth;
  The colt that's back'd and burthen'd being young,
  Loseth his pride, and never waxeth strong.

(415–20)

He makes a similar argument about small fry and unripe plums about a
hundred lines later. Whether or not Shakespeare's narrator agrees with
this particular line of argument – Marlowe's, we can be certain, does
not – it is certainly in accordance with Narcissus's views.

But is it true that 'the colt that's back'd and burthen'd being young, /

Loseth his pride, and never waxeth strong' (419–20)? That is, are youths such as Leander really damaged by these encounters, or is it the 'good man' of Edwards's poem, so concerned with the welfare of youths that he seeks to bash their teeth down their throats, that is at risk? Venus's desire, whether we see her as cross-dressed or not, could be classified as sodomitical. Alan Stewart argues, following Jonathan Goldberg, that 'sodomy is by definition a disturbance of alliance/marriage arrangements.'[14] Stewart shows how accusations of sodomy frequently arise when the new social relations between men fostered by humanism challenge or disrupt this older system.[15] The Narcissus/Adonis problem is slightly different: it is not just that present reproductive capacity is being misdirected; future reproductive capacity is also being jeopardized. This is clearly related to the problem in, for example, the Sonnets, where the beautiful young man is urged to overcome his narcissism and marry: 'From fairest creatures we desire increase ... But thou, contracted to thine own bright eyes, / Feed'st thy light's flame with self-substantial fuel' (1.1, 5–6). Venus similarly warns Adonis not to bury his talents: 'Foul cank'ring rust the hidden treasure frets, / But gold that's put to use more gold begets' (767–8). The language of gold, commodities, and investment reminds us that there are more economies at stake in sodomy than simply the sexual one.

This begins to explain the link between the poem's disavowal of homoeroticism on the one hand, and its interest in a national poetic canon on the other. The link between the two is Petrarchan poetry. Petrarchan poetry, the genre that places the youth at risk, is revealed to be in some sense sodomitical. It celebrates an emasculating rhetoric that compromises the subject, rendering him a slave to his own desire, or what amounts to the same thing, to that of a woman. Poets that engage in such effeminizing rhetoric run the risk, like Narcissus, of turning into women. This rhetoric leads youths away from a poetry that celebrates or promotes a reproductive sexual and national economy, and renders them instead self-regarding, self-consuming, and ultimately deformed. Whereas in other poems that we have looked at, Petrarchan poetry figured only as a danger to the youth himself, here it represents a broader danger, presumably because of the role that literature plays in sustaining a national identity. Petrarchan poetry is, quite literally, a drag on the national poetic economy, seducing English youth with cheap Italian imports. Good poetry, on the other hand, sends 'to Nations farre, / The greatnes of faire *Albions* praise' (Envoy, 12.5–6), sailing back, no doubt, with a good return on this literary investment.

Cephalus and Procris

If *Narcissus* is Thomas Edwards's homage to Marlowe, *Cephalus and Procris* is his tribute to Shakespeare. Certainly Aurora's wooing of the youthful, beautiful, boar-hunting Cephalus owes much to *Venus and Adonis*:

> Anone with smiles, she threates his chast conceites,
> And (looking on his eies) him she entreates,
> With kisses, sighes, and teares reuying them,
> As though their sexe of duetie should woe men,
> He striuing to be gone, she prest him downe:
> She striuing to kisse him, he kist the growne.

(211–16)

In spite of the fact that Cephalus is a married man, he is nonetheless portrayed as a fresh-faced youth with a 'down-soft breast' (234), and the gender-reversed wooing is played for the same kinds of comedic effects as in Shakespeare's poem. As we shall see, there are other similarities as well, principally concerned with the uses and abuses of rhetoric. But there are also a number of continuities with *Narcissus*, in particular a concern with a national canon, Petrarchan poetry, and the rhetoric appropriate to the public sphere. What most obviously unites Edwards's poems, however, is their startlingly cavalier use of their source material.

In Ovid, the Cephalus and Procris story demonstrates the destructive power of jealousy. Aurora, goddess of the dawn, falls for Cephalus, who is married to the beautiful Procris. He resists her, but on his way back home he begins to doubt Procris, and Aurora aids this by disguising him. He tests her devotion to him, she finally hesitates, he pounces, she flees in shame and devotes herself to Diana. This sojourn with Diana works to establish or at least imply Procris's chastity. Cephalus persuades her to come back and she gives him as a present a spear that never misses its target; they live together happily for a number of years. One hot day while hunting, Cephalus calls to the wind to cool him. A rube hears him calling to Zephyr and reports this to Procris, who, inflamed with jealousy, determines to catch Cephalus in the act. She hides in the bushes, he hears a rustling and hurls his spear, mortally wounding her. Procris tells him of her fears about Zephyr taking her place; he clears up the misunderstanding but she nonetheless dies.

George Sandys reads it as a story about the psychological mechanisms of jealousy:

For jealousy springs from the abundance of love, which makes the lover under-value him-selfe, and over-value the affected; imagining that no eye but must of necessity looke with the like admiration & desire; envious of every mans worth, and prone to beleeve what he feareth. In so much, that the felicity of life, consisting in the fruition of beauty and noble endowments, by a melancholy and groundlesse suspition, converts to the deadliest of diseases; in the blood a continuall fevor, and in the mind a Fury. (*Ovid's Metamorphosis Englished*, 348)

The goundlessness of the jealousy, and the parallels between the two lovers' situations are made more clear in Sandys's translation of Zephyr as 'Ayre.' Both lovers are caught up in foolish suspicions, although Procris is the one who pays with her life.

George Pettie offers a version of the tale in his *Petite Pallace of Pettie his Pleasure*, which some have argued is a source for the love test in Shakespeare's *Cymbeline*. Pettie sets the tale in Venice. The lovers have an over-rapid courtship, which leads Cephalus to just as rapidly grow tired of his wife. (This hastiness, according to the male friendship discourse, is one of the key problems of heterosexual unions.) Procris nonetheless remains passionately devoted to her husband. He sets in motion a plan to get rid of her by going away on business and then coming back before his scheduled return. Disguised, he tells her that he met her husband abroad, who inflamed his desire by telling him of her great beauty, but who also told him how he had become sick of her. She refuses to believe it. When this doesn't work, he seduces her with gold and merchandise. This works, but Cephalus forgives her:

Cephalus knowing women to be weak to withstand the sight of money, and thinking that her very nature violently drew her to him, whom being her husband, though to her unknown, she loved entirely, he thought best for his own quiet, and to avoid infamy, to put up with this presumption of this evil in his wife patiently, and to pardon her offence; and so they lived quietly together awhile. But within short time she, partly for want of government, and partly thinking her husband would revenge the wrong which she had done to him, fell into such a furious jealousy over him, that it wrought her own destruction and his desolation.[16]

Procris becomes the very avatar of jealousy, with the predictable results. Cephalus woos the 'gentle Air,' and Procris, hiding in the bushes to witness the illicit liason, is mistakenly hit with a dart. He comes to her and the mistake is cleared up: 'and so joining her lips to his, she yielded up her breath into his mouth, and died. And he with care consumed, tarried not long behind her, to bewail either his own deed, or her death.' The lesson is clear: 'Now Gentlewomen, let the casual end of this gentlewoman be a caveat to keep you from such wary watching of your husbands! ... the chiefest way to keep your husbands continent, it is to keep yourselves continent.'[17] In Pettie, the story is no longer about mutual jealousy, although it is, like Sandys's version, to some degree a tale about the management of the self, of desire, and ultimately, of the wife. Cephalus has allowed himself to be managed by his desire, and thus ends up with an unsuitable wife. Procris's problem is identified by Pettie as a 'want of government' although it is not clear whether what is lacking is self-governance, or government by her husband. In either case, it is clear that what is not appropriate is the wife attempting to govern the husband. The most she should strive for, says the narrator, is to govern herself.

Edwards's version of the tale shares some of this interest in governance in the household, although this is bound up with other issues that are common to the genre, such as gender and rhetoric. Edwards starts his tale with a wilfully ungoverned Aurora, who 'Rapt with a suddaine extasie of minde' (47), goes out into the world. She comes across Cephalus, 'a man of some compare' (147), who is taking a respite from hunting. She falls in love, and in attempting to kiss him, drags him off his horse. Unlike Adonis, Cephalus manages successfully to avoid his ardent admirer, and he successfully kills the boar. Aurora catches up and attempts to woo him again, and when this is unsuccessful, she plants the seeds of jealousy in his head:

> Drown'd in a sea of ouerswelling hate,
> As one that lies before his enimie prostrate,
> Willing to liue, yet scorning to beg life,
> So feares he now (as twere) with his false wife;
> Sometimes he cals her faire, chast, wise, and graue,
> Anon with too too wrathfull tauntes he raues.

(391–6)

Here we see the psychological imbalance that Sandys identifies in jealousy, and a notable failure on the part of Cephalus to manage his passions by his reason. It is for this reason that as in Ovid, Cephalus returns home in disguise to tempt his wife. One slight difference to note is that in Ovid, the idea of the love-test comes to him on his own; here the deception is suggested by the wilful Aurora.

Procris, suggests the narrator, puts up only token resistance to his seduction: 'She (as some say, all woemen stricktly do,) / Faintly deni'd what she was willing too' (435–6). Cephalus, encouraged by this, 'heape[s] flax on the fire' (438) and she 'At least gaue notice of her willing minde / (*Æsopian* snakes will alwaies proue vnkind)' (445–6). The parenthetical gnome and the Aesopian moral are, as we have seen, completely characteristic of the genre; here they are used to naturalize a view of women's will in order to suggest that there was only ever one possible outcome for Cephalus's actions:

> Vnhappy woman, she the dull night spent
> In sad complaintes, and giddie merrymentes,
> Sometimes intending to excuse her crime ...
>
> (461–3)

Procris's capitulation represents another change in the story. In Ovid, when Procris hesitates, Cephalus pounces and denounces. Here, Cephalus presses further and seems to get what he wants.

As in Ovid, Procris flees, but this time she ends up not in the company of Diana, but rather in that of a simultaneously English and Ovidian goddess, the 'Good Faierie Lady' Lamie (488). Lamie avers that everything was Cephalus's fault:

> Wast not inough for *Læda's* Swanly scape,
> That *Iupiter* was author of the rape?
> What can be more for *Cephalus* than this,
> That *Cephalus* was author of thy misse?
>
> (529–32)

In light of the narrator's position on women and temptation, we are forced to agree with Lamie here that Cephalus is indeed the author of Procris's 'misse.' What is perhaps more pointed is Lamie's earlier comment: 'Aie me, who can (quoth *Lamie*) be so cruell, / As to convert the building Oake to fuell? (525–6). This suggests both that Cephalus has destroyed his home ('the building Oake') by succumbing to burning jealousy and moreover that he has mismanaged a resource that should have been under his control, his wife.

In spite of her English origins, Lamie is definitely Ovidian in attitude: 'I pray thee tell me, who would not consent, /Amorously boorded, and in merriment?' (535–6). She proposes that Procris simply reverse the situation, and return home in disguise to seduce Cephalus. Procris decides instead to collapse beside a river for a 'season liuelesse' (591), where she is encountered by an 'vnciuill Swaine' (611) who seems to have wandered in from *The Faerie Queene*. (This sense is strengthened by the unexpected reference to Procris as '*Amoretta*' [613].) After unsuccessfully wooing her, the base Clown tells her of Cephalus's affair with Aurora, and shades of Spenser,

> Like some pernitious hegg surpriz'd with sin,
> Cutting the aire with braine-sick shreekes and cries,
> Like a swift arrow with the winde she highes.
>
> (658–60)

The result is the traditional one. Although it is unclear what Cephalus is actually up to in the bushes (it appears he might be conducting an affair with nymphs), Procris receives the fatal dart, and dies. What is striking in this account is that she dies without knowing that her jealousy was groundless. This change removes the symmetry of the story, and thus changes the meaning of the story entirely. It is difficult to see the story as being simply about jealousy anymore, since Procris does seem to be guilty to some degree, even if it was her own husband she slept with. Nor is it clear that Procris's jealousy is groundless, although Cephalus does end the poem with a lament to the 'saffron God' of marriage.

If the story is not about jealousy, then what is it about? We might profitably return to one of Edwards's models for a moment, Shakespeare's *Venus and Adonis*. Critics have noticed that one of the narratives of the poem is the rhetorical education of Adonis. It is also, by extension, a test of the reader's rhetorical sophistication. Venus is an able and amoral rhetorician. We are warned in the opening lines of the poem that she is 'Sick-thoughted' (5), so that the poem then may well function, as Stanley Fish argues of *Paradise Lost*, as an education in reading.[18] Adonis over the course of the poem becomes an able rhetorician, but he does not necessarily become a sophisticated audience for rhetoric. This we can see most clearly in the Wat digression, where, if Adonis were listening, he would have learned of his own fate and how to avoid it.

Much the same could be argued of Cephalus. Aurora tells him 'A thousand prettie tales ... Of *Pan* his *Sirinx*, of *Ioues Io*, / Of *Semelè*'

(225–7), and offers up 'meny sad laments, / And Madrigals with dolefull tunes' (259–60). Aurora, like Venus, is a Petrarchan wooer, her 'kisses, sighs, and tears' (213) echoed later in the narrator's reference to Dante's *dolce style nuovo* as filtered through Petrarch: 'That still *Styll* musicke sighing teares together' (681). As with all Petrarchans, Aurora will do or say anything in support of her immoral desire, even when reminded that Cephalus is married. She tries a number of arguments before planting the idea of unfaithfulness in Cephalus's head. That he should succumb so quickly and fully to this ruse makes Procris's later timid hold-out to his deception seem positively heroic by comparison. Bearing in mind the example of Narcissus, we may see this element of the narrative as another comment on the warping (and antisocial) effect that Petrarchan poetry can have on a youth. Whether the fault is Aurora's or Cephalus's, his failure of self-management leads very directly to a failure to manage his wife. Here we return to Pettie's version of the story, where one of the problems is Procris's 'want of government.'[19]

In *The Usurer's Daughter*, Lorna Hutson explores the humanist interest in Xenophon's *Oeconomicus*, a treatise concerned with managing the household. Hutson sees the interest in this text as part of the humanists' ongoing attempts in the sixteenth century both to define and to advocate for their role in governance. In the Xenophon-inspired treatises, 'The woman, as good wife, is merely the example of his ability to govern':

> The cultural significance of this natural history concerns men: its function in the sixteenth century was not to legitimate a new version of femininity, but a new version of masculinity. The point of it was not, primarily, to guarantee in reality the husband's governance of his wife, but to prove, through a persuasive fiction of the well-governed wife, the legitimate and responsible contribution of a Christian humanist education to the secular and practical spheres of masculine activity.[20]

A similar set of concerns can be seen at the heart of *Cephalus and Procris*. We have already noted that Procris dies without knowing that her jealousy was groundless. This may be, following Pettie, because it is not up to wives to attempt to govern their husbands, except by the example of their own constancy, and so whether or not Cephalus is guilty is immaterial, at least from the perspective of the wife. Indeed, her death may be seen as the logical consequence of pursuing her husband into the realm of the social, and thereby implicitly confirming her own sexual incon-

stancy. The Envoy suggests that Procris's motives were far from pure, that
Cephalus was innocent, and that Procris was responsible for her own
demise:

> Oft hits the same,
> For who the innocent,
> To catch in secret snares,
>   (And laughes at their false shame,)
> Doth couertly inuent,
> Themselues not throughly ware,
>   Are oft beguil'd thereby,
>   Woemen especially.

(stanza 9)

Much as in Pettie's story, here in the Envoy Procris is seen as the
meddling wife who gets what she deserves. But the removal of Procris's
final moment of realization might also indicate that the poem is simply
not interested in Procris except as an example of Cephalus's ability to
govern his wife. Although the representation of her actions constitutes a
significant part of the poem, we only ever get her reported speech, never
her speech itself. Procris, rather than being a rhetorician, becomes
simply rhetoric: the rhetoric of her husband, and of the narrator.

Patricia Parker notes the connections between women and rhetoric in
humanist discourse: 'it is not necessary to read far in the handbooks of
rhetoric or discussions of language in the English Renaissance ... to
perceive an intimate and ideologically motivated link between the need
to control the movement of tropes and contemporary exigencies of
social control, including, though not limited to, the governance of the
household or oikos.'[21] Certainly we can see this connection between
women and rhetoric in the portrayal of the errant Aurora, as she wreaks
havoc upon the social institution of marriage through her immoral use
of rhetoric. Procris also is an errant woman, which is underscored by the
narrator's reference to her as Amoretta, the perennially chased heroine
of Spenser's Book III. Although Procris never speaks, her wandering
from the house constitutes a kind of speech, or at least demonstrates the
parallels between women and rhetoric: 'Behind this concern for woman's "wandering," errancy, or "mooveable" ways lie anxieties about female sexuality, but, even more specifically, about its relation to property,
to the threat of the violation of this private place if it were to become a
"common" place.'[22] Cephalus's failure to prevent Procris's wandering is

thus linked to his own faulty rhetoric, which causes her to emulate, in her wandering, his errant discourse.

As Lamie suggests, Procris is not to be blamed for her inconstancy. As the narrator implies more than once, it is in woman's nature to give in to temptation, especially of a sexual or material nature. Writers in the tradition of the *Oeconomicus* would seem to agree. Lupset, for example, writes that 'the very trouth is, that there is noo yvelle housewyfe but for her fautes the good man is to be blamed. For I am vtterly of the opinion, that the man may make, shape and forme the woman as he will.'[23] Cephalus's failure to govern himself well is mirrored by the example he provides of how not to 'make, shape and forme the woman'; his rhetorical seduction of his wife teaches her to be unfaithful. While it is to some degree a testament to the power of his rhetoric, it is more an example of a bad governor. His failure to govern himself, his (perhaps youthful) inability to resist Aurora's (Petrarchan) rhetoric, his own badly motivated rhetoric, and his poor governance of his wife all exist on a continuum.

The link between management of the household, and the humanists' role in the management of the nation is not immediately clear in the poem. We might remember, however, that the good rhetorician in the poem, the one who offers successful fictions about women, is the poet himself. And as we can see from both the prefatory matter and various interjections in the poem, Edwards is very much concerned with the social role of what he calls scholars. In the prefatory matter to the volume that includes both *Cephalus and Procris* and *Narcissus*, Edwards remarks in his dedication 'To the Honorable Gentlemen & true fauourites of Poetrie' that 'Base necessitie, which schollers hate as ignorance, hath beene Englanddes shame, and made many liue in bastardy a long time.' The poverty of humanist scholars, a frequent refrain from Erasmus to the present day, is a national issue, argues Edwards. Echoing Sidney in the *Defense of Poesy*, he talks about the reciprocal and nationally necessary relation between poets and soldiers: 'Well could Homer paint on Vlysses shield, for that Vlysses fauour made Homer paint' (sig. A2v). This, sadly, is not the case in England: 'But why temporize I thus, on the intemperature of this our clymate? wherein liue to themselves, Schollers and Emperours' (sig. A3r). The problem is not just, he argues, that emperors see poetic fame as merely ornamental, but that scholars talk only to each other, and fail to see the role they must play in the nation. Through their petty and self-interested squabbling, they 'quench honor with fames winges, and burne maiestie with the title of ingratitude' (sig. A3r). Edwards assures his reader that he makes this critique because 'I honour learning with my heart. And thus benigne gentlemen, as I began, so in duety I end, euer prest to do you all seruice' (sig. A3r).

Within the poem, Edwards continues the poverty-of-scholars refrain, alluding to Marlowe's inset narrative about Mercury and the maid in *Hero and Leander*, which concludes with the lines, 'And to this day is everie scholler poore / Grosse gold, from them runs headlong to the boore' (471–2). In a slightly different vein, Edwards remarks of Apollo's golden tree:

> Hence twas that *Hermes* stole from heauen the power,
> To soueranize on schollers idle howres,
> And had not *Ioue* bene fauourable then,
> They never should haue bene accounted men,
> But liu'd as pesants, shaddowes, imagies,
> And nere haue had the princes *similies*.
>
> (123–8)

As with the dedication, princes and poets are linked; poets are accounted men, and princes are given similes (presumably of themselves) as a result. A second mention of the poverty of scholars leads into a digression on Spenser and Sidney (and perhaps Marlowe; he seems to refer to the closing lines of *Hero and Leander*, which he certainly knows well). He apostrophizes to Spenser: 'Where is that vertuous Muse of thine become? / It will awake, for sleepe not prooues it dumme' (189–90). Spenser here and elsewhere in Edwards is celebrated for being the English epic poet; Sidney's nationalism in the *Defense* and elsewhere no doubt contributes to his mention here. Edwards implores the readers, presumably the 'Honorable Gentlemen & true fauourites of Poetrie' to whom the dedication was addressed, to 'tread the pathes' of the '*Arcadian knight*' (192) so that their deeds will become the subjects of English poets: 'Be your soules agentes in our tragicke song ... Then shall our quill, lift honor to your name' (194, 198). As in the dedication, Edwards argues for the need for poets and leaders to support each other within this new nation. The digression, unusually pointless even by the loose standards of this genre, seems to have no connection to the story other than to argue for the importance of a national canon of poets.

The second digression is of a similar theme, and similarly irrelevant to the narrative of the poem. It opens with what seems to be a comment on the portrayal of fury in revenge tragedy, which presumably has some relation to Procris's jealous rage:

> The staring massacres, blood-dronken plots,
> Hot riotous hell-quickeners, *Italian-nots*:
> That tup their wits with snaky *Nemesis*,
> Teat-sucking on the poyson of her mis,
> With ougly fiendes ytasked let them bee,
> A milder fury to enrich seeke wee.
>
> (667–72)

The unusual phrase '*Italian-nots*' serves to accent revenge tragedy's common identification with Italy. After rehearsing the example of Homer and Ulysses, Edwards moves on to reject Petrarchan verse:

> Gladly would our *Cephalian* muse have sung
> All of white loue, enamored with a tounge,
> That still *Styll* musicke sighing teares together,
> Could one conceite haue made beget an other,
> And so haue ransackt this rich age of that,
> The muses wanton fauourites haue got.
>
> (679–84)

Petrarchans, the wanton favourites of the muses, are masters of pastiche rather than poets. Their poetry is rejected, predictably if paradoxically, in favour of Spenser's and Sidney's poetry:

> Thy stately verse was Lordly borne,
> Through all *Arcadia*, and the *Fayerie* land,
> And hauing smale true grace in *Albion*,
> Thy natiue soyle, as thou of right deserued'st,
> Rightly adornes one now, that's richly serued.
>
> (692–6)

Digression over, Edwards returns to the story.

Attempting to piece together exactly what this digression is doing is difficult. It could be read in the context of a larger attempt in the poem, and in *Narcissus* as well, to claim Ovid as part of the English humanist heritage, while at the same time rejecting Petrarch as a baneful Italian influence on sturdy English verse. This Englishing of the Ovidian muse is accomplished both through the introduction of Lamie, but also through the suggestion that the poem is in fact set in England. The poem opens with an extended metaphor of the dawn coming slowly across the earth. Towards the end Aurora stops and looks at

> The golden Sonne-beames of *Apolloes* tree:
> Where valorous warlike Knightes, for feates ydone
> Are registred, yclept Knightes of the Sonne:
> Knights of the Garter, aunceint knightes of Rhodes,
> She mainely postes, and there a time abodes.

> (114–18)

(Here as elsewhere, when Edwards turns nationalistic, his vocabulary turns Spenserian.) As in Book II of the *Faerie Queene*, we see here a writing of English history into myth, or rather the suggestion of a continuity between the golden age and the English present. Aurora's journey finally ends at an unnamed island:

> Hence post we foorth vnto an *Ocean*
> That beats against the bankes of *Helycon*,
> Whereon if so the ruler of the East,
> But cast an eie, we are not meanely blest,
> No more but so, for more were ouer much,
> Gold is approu'd but by a slender touch.

> (129–34)

In Aurora's travels from the Hesperides to England, the poem suggests there is both a geographical and literary continuity from classical literature to English verse, from Homer and Ovid to Spenser.

Edwards's arguments for the national importance of poetry, and for a canon of English poets, are related to the main narrative of rhetorical mastery. As in his *Narcissus*, there are positive and negative exempla on offer. Cephalus is a poor manager of his wife, and hence likely to be a poor humanist. He is thus unsuitable for participation in the administration of the nation. Edwards, however, servant to the queen's Latin Secretary, demonstrates his fitness for further service both through his rhetorical ability, his knowing rehearsal of favourite humanist themes, and his promotion of English poetry. The spirits of Spenser and Sidney live on in him, and just as those two proved able and willing (if not entirely successful) servants of the nation, so too will Edwards.

Faunus and Melliflora

John Weever's *Faunus and Melliflora, Or, the Original of our English Satyres* (1600) contains many of the familiar elements of the epyllion. Like Edwards's poems (among others) it shows the influence of Shakespeare and Marlowe; Venus and Adonis actually appear in the poem, and Venus plays a substantial role. As Arnold Davenport shows in his edition of the poem, it also is heavily indebted to Sidney's *Arcadia*,[24] the text that John Hoskyns recommended as a source of rhetorical inspiration for his young Inns of Court protégé. It is not known, however, where Weever spent the years immediately following his graduation from Cambridge in May 1598. The *DNB* entry reports that he returned to his home in Lancashire and had little knowledge of London; Keach uses this biographical information to differentiate the poetical careers of Weever and his fellow satirist Marston.[25] In his brief biography of Weever, however, E.A.J. Honigmann argues that 'it is much more likely that he moved from Cambridge to London, where he seems to have been a well-known figure in literary circles until 1601.'[26] Indeed, even internal evidence in the volume – the satires on London figures that appear in 'A Prophesie of this present yeare, 1600,' which is appended to the poem – suggests that Weever had some direct experience of London life beyond simply reading Marston's *Scourge of Villanie*.

The story of the poem is, as both the dedicatory poem and the poem itself signal, an invention of Weever's, but the poem is resolutely an epyllion. There are, for example, some Ovidian metamorphoses, as Faunus's father Pycus is turned into a magpie, and Faunus and Melliflora's son into a satyr. More importantly, however, the poem is suffused with Ovidian desire. As Keach argues, the central unifying theme is the opposition between Diana and Venus, and the poem sides heavily with Venus. The poem is replete with Marlovian observations on the comedy of desire: 'boyes loue is foolish, Loue to youth brings wit' (436); 'In womens mouths, No is no negatiue' (310); 'God or man thinkes he the Cushion misses, / That wooes all day, and winnes nought else but kisses (145–6); 'old men do no good, / Yet will be fumbling' (807–8). There are the usual sententiae – 'A dogge tied vp in golden chaines will rage' (664) – and aetiological myths; as a result of Cupid's appearance at a Parliament of the Destinies (where the Destinies, in a manner reminiscent of the English parliament, sit on 'wooll-packe[s]' [598]), the Destinies decree 'That man for his vnmanlike treacherie, / Should be tormented with vile iealousie' (653–4). There are also playful corrections of myth: '*Ouid's* beguilde, it was not *Phaeton*' (150) that scorched the earth, but rather the sun, trying to get a closer look at Melliflora; the boar didn't kill Adonis, Adonis was slain by Cupid after Melliflora ran by: 'Whilst narrowly vpon her lookes he spide, / Strooke with loues arrow, he fell downe and dide' (477–8). Weever even includes the portrait gallery that occasionally appears in one form or another in these poems, in this case offering up a picture of Acteon and Diana (274–8).

The poem has an action-packed narrative. It begins with 'Some higher power' (5) creating for Saturn a beautiful youth, Pycus, who is averse to women and love, but who nonetheless falls in love with Canens. They, in turn, have a beautiful son named Faunus. Faunus is the by-now familiar naive youth, who shares with Thomas Edwards's Narcissus a passion for fine clothing and jewels, the latter given by female admirers. Unlike Narcissus, Faunus does not scorn women. Wandering through the Latian mountains, Faunus comes across a band of nymphs playing English country games, 'Barlibreake' being their favourite. Faunus immediately falls in love with the nymph Melliflora, and joins Diana's troop for seven days of games. They are finally interrupted by the appearance of Shakespeare's boar, which is killed by a well-aimed knife thrust by Faunus. Nonetheless, the two lovers are separated: Melliflora becomes the cause of Adonis's death, and Venus, mistaking Faunus for Adonis, begins to woo him before giving up and flying home.

Faunus returns to his father's court, where he receives a long diatribe against women and love by Pycus. Love is horrified by this, and turns to the Parliament of Fates for a judgment against Pycus. Faunus, after agonizing over 'What garment best might please his faire Nimphs eies' (682), flees his father's court, and collapses in the woods. Melliflora coming upon him thinks he is Adonis (726), realizes her mistake, and showers his sleeping body with kisses and speeches. Faunus wakes up, mistakes Melliflora for Venus (804), and temporarily flees. They are then reunited, Faunus delivers a long speech against virginity, and they resolve to marry. The nymph Deiopeia, who has long been in love with Faunus, tells of Melliflora's treachery to Diana, and she curses their child, who becomes a satyr. In an abrupt transition, in which the poem switches from the pastoral to the epic mode, we are told that Faunus's descendent is Brutus, who brought with him to Troynovaunt satyrs and fairies. The latter spawn the knights of *The Faerie Queene*, and the former are responsible for the satires currently being written in England. Best among these, says the narrator, are those of Marston and Hall, although he does not approve of satires in general. To illustrate some of what 'Brutus left behind in Italie' (1088), translations of three satires by Horace, Persius, and Juvenal follow, before Venus breaks into the poem and the main narrative resumes. Venus comes to England, and, seeing the slanders being perpetrated against her in satires, orders them all burned. A new Satyr will rise from the cinders, she says, to satirize the satyrs. The book concludes with the satiric 'Prophesie of this present yeare, 1600,' which makes good on Venus's promise.

Davenport suggests that the volume may have been the product of an over-hasty combination of an epyllion and the classical translations, rushed into print because of the ban on satires issued by the bishop of London and the archbishop of Canterbury on 1 June 1599.[27] (Marlowe's translation of *Ovid's Elegies* and Marston's *Pigmalion* were burned as a result of this ban.) Keach convincingly argues that whether or not this was the case, the volume shows an overall unity and that the inclusion of the satires was well prepared for. For example, he notes, 'We are told at the beginning of the poem that Pycus was the offspring of Saturn (ll. 5– 8), a figure whose traditional associations include strong ties to satire and to a hatred of love and women.'[28] Moreover, the entire poem is structured around an opposition between Diana and Venus, 'to provide a mythological basis for the enmity between satire and erotic poetry.'[29] This replaces the usual opposition in the genre between Ovidian and Petrarchan eroticism, which was present even in Marston's more satiric *Pigmalion*. As in Marston's poem, the hypocrisy of those who condemn or vilify desire is exposed, only in this instance it is satirists, rather than 'subtle Citty-dame[s]' (10.1) who are the subject of criticism. There are other elements of the poem, however, that suggest a number of unifying narratives reminiscent of those in Thomas Edwards's poems. In particular, it is worth examining what Weever does with the central narrative of the maturation of the youth, and how that might be connected with the interest in satire and the English literary scene, the inclusion of English elements, and the rewriting of Shakespeare and Marlowe.

Unlike most other examples of the genre, *Faunus and Melliflora* has at its centre a successful heterosexual love affair. Although the youthful Faunus is occasionally shaky on the protocols of courtship (much like Leander), he nonetheless falls in love as he is supposed to, pursues his love and wins her, and ends the poem married with children and ruler of Rome. This, as Keach observes, is in marked contrast to the two main models for the poem. The narrator's early description of Faunus, in which the narrator objects that 'my Muse yet hardly can / Emblazon forth the beutie of a man' (45–6), suggests 'that perhaps masculine physical beauty is going to be praised in the extravagant homoerotic terms of Marlowe's Leander portrait ... [however] Weever's narrator suppresses the Marlovian emphasis on masculine sensuality and focuses instead on Faunus's ornate costume.'[30] The citation is direct, in other words, but the redirection of the description of Faunus is equally pointed, as if Weever is correcting Marlowe. The same might be said of the even more direct allusions to Adonis: 'unlike Shakespeare's Adonis, Faunus's masculinity is not undermined by an excessive aversion to women or to love. It is merely swathed in the foppish elegance of youthful dandyism.'[31] An equivalence between Faunus and Adonis is insisted upon, as both Venus and Melliflora mistake the one for the other. Faunus enters the poem just as Adonis exits this life. Moreover, Faunus successfully slays the boar, and although he does not sleep with Venus, neither does he contemptuously reject her advances: 'The shamefac't Faunus thereat something smiled, / Venus lookt on him, knew shee was beguiled' (505–6). The echo to the Neptune digression in Marlowe's poem ('thereat Neptune smiled') in the context of another case of mistaken identity perhaps indicates that Faunus is not hostile to Venus's advances, but merely that he has someone else in mind. Indeed, in Faunus's speeches to Melliflora (which echo Leander's to Hero), he is clearly of Venus's camp, arguing against virginity and service to Diana. Even more directly than with Marlowe, Weever seems to be straightening out Shakespeare: in this revision, Adonis's rejection of love is seen to be merely a youthful phase, as witnessed by his fatal attraction to Melliflora. Moreover, Faunus picks up Adonis's story where it broke off, and carries it to its proper conclusion.

Faunus, then, is the successful version of Adonis, Leander, Narcissus, and all the other youths in the genre who fail to metamorphose into adult (heterosexual) men. In most other examples of the genre, Petrarchan poetry was directly or indirectly implicated in the failure, as the youth failed to mature into an Ovidian understanding of desire. In this poem, as in Shakespeare's, Ovidian desire is implicitly connected with rural England, as the nymphs spend their time playing English country games. As Keach notes, 'English country games were notoriously lustful' and these games become highly sexualized in the poem's lengthy account of a game of 'Barlibreake' (356–82) and another unnamed one involving dropping a napkin (385–416).[32] The threat to the maturation of the youth in this poem is not Petrarchan verse, as it usually is in the genre, but rather satiric poetry, first embodied in the poem by

Faunus's father Pycus. When he learns of the love affair, Pycus rails against women in terms reminiscent both of Juvenal and of Weever's contemporaries like Marston and Nashe:

And what are women? painted weathercocks,
Natures ouersight, wayward glittring blocks:
True, true-bred cowards, proude if they be coide,
A seruile sex, of wit and reason voide:
Shall women moue thee, whom so many loathes,
In gaudie plumes trickte, and new-fangled cloathes?

(529–34)

(The last charge against women is ironic, given Faunus's predilection for sartorial display.) Pycus, we should remember, was also once a beautiful youth. After Jove deposed his father,

Some higher power for aged *Saturne* stroue,
Gaue him a gift, which angred lust-stung *Ioue*:
A louely boy, whose beautie at his birth,
Made poore the heau'ns to enrich the earth.
...
His name was *Pycus*, yet surnam'd the Faire,
Whom *Circe* chaunted in her scorne-gold haire,
Whom Ladies lou'd, and loued of so many,
The wood-Nymphs woo'd him, yet not won of any.

(5–8, 17–20)

Pycus seems to have been created as something of a Ganymede, and although he does end up marrying Canens, his tendency towards satire is perhaps connected to his pederastic origins. The connection between satire and pederasty would make then a further parallel between satire and Petrarchan verse, a parallel made more directly in William Barksted's *Mirrha*, where the satyr Poplar spouts Petrarchan compliment. The link between satire and pederasty in Weever's poem parallels the connections Edwards suggests between sodomy and Italian poetry.

The sexually suspect nature of satire is made clear later in the poem. After the three translations, Venus bursts back into the poem to remedy the introduction of satire into England from Italy. First, however, she takes revenge on Italy for being the birthplace of satire:

I know not whether, that (for Satyres spight)
Italians should in fond loues take delight.
In stranger sinnes, sinnes which she was ashamed,
Among th'Italians rightly should be named.
Sinnes, scarlet sinnes, sinnes who delights to vse,
In other regions thus we him abuse
(For through the world her wrath's inueterate)
In odious termes, Yon's one Italionate:
And (to be breefe) that lustfull venerie,
Should be the downfall of all *Italie*:
This is the cause Italians to this day,
Are euer readie, apt, and prone that way.

(1614–25)

Weever here partakes of a widespread English condemnation of things Italian. Ascham's *Scholemaster*, for example, rails against the 'enchantments of Circes, brought out of Italy, to mar men's manners in England; much by example of ill life, but more by precepts of fond books, of late translated out of Italian into English, sold in every shop in London; commended by honest titles, the sooner to corrupt honest manners ... [and] beguile simple and innocent wits.'[33] Lynda E. Boose argues that these condemnations greatly increased in the 1590s with the importation of the pornographic works of Pietro Aretino[34] or 'lustfull *Aretine*' (Weever, 'A Prophesie,' 50), and that the 1599 bishops' ban had as much to do with pornography as it did with satire. Weever also has a more specific point to make, however. It seems relatively clear that although the attack here is more generally on 'lustfull venerie,' Weever is not so secretly alluding to sodomy and/or pederasty, which the Elizabethans frequently associated with Italy and not infrequently with Aretino.[35] This is made clear by a warning in the prophecy appended to the poem:

O Wakefull prophet that so farre away,
Could spie the dawning of this New yeares day!
And in thy true authentique prophesie,
Foretell that brutish sensuality,
Leopard-skind, soule-polluting Sodomy,
Dogges appetite, and damn'd impiety,
Should be transported into *Italie*
From England, this same year of Iubile.

('A Prophesie,' 61–8)

Transporting sodomy into Italy, implies the poem, is like carrying coals to Newcastle.

The problem with satire is two-fold. Not only does it hypocritically and pruriently excoriate vice, and thus needlessly pillory Venus, it also teaches vice to those who would otherwise be left innocent. Rather than eliminate vice, the rhetoric of satire perversely encourages it, as the poem makes clear with an example that again connects satire and sodomy:

> Not long agoe (by chance) these eares of mine,
> Ore-heard yong *Tusco* reade a Satyres line,
> And grauel'd (as it seem'd) stood censuring,
> His eies fixt on a weather-cocke, misconstruing
> The gloomie sense, and sembled thereupon,
> Of fryes and puisnes a conuocation:
> Slubbering the margent with their greasie thumbs,
> They found no means, till court-boy *Brisco* comes.
> This agent patient in a moment spide
> Light in this darke line. *Tusco* then replide:
> I'me glad of this, I thought there had not bin
> Such nouell pastimes, such a new found sinne:
> And since in *Paules* (I walking) *Tusco* met,
> And at his heeles I saw yong *Brisco* iet.
> But by the sprightly essence of my soule,
> My retchlesse lines shall *Brisco* not controule:
> Nor rubbe the botch sore on his ridden side,
> Nor gird the galled blisters on his hide:
> That would but more his griefe exasperate,
> And all the world by him exulcerate.
> Sinne's like a puddle or a mattery sincke,
> The more we stirre them, stil the more they stincke.

('A Prophesie,' 86–107)

As La Rochefoucauld says about love in general, Tusco would never have experienced sodomy had he not read about it first. Tusco initially does not understand the 'dark line' of either satire or sodomy, misconstruing the poem to refer to a weather-cock. The line being read is perhaps from a satire appended to Marston's *Pigmalion*, which asks, 'But ho, what *Ganimede* is that doth grace / The gallants heeles.' It is only when court-boy Brisco struts by that Tusco sees the light, and learns 'a new found sinne,' so that when next seen, Brisco graces Tusco's heels. It does no good, argues the narrator somewhat salaciously, for the satirist to ride the already galled Brisco poetically; the only possible effect is the further corruption of youth.

On that note, we should recall that 'Fryes' and 'puisnes' are both terms for students, the latter term most usually applied to those of the Inns of Court. We have here, then, the same sort of admonitory lesson that we saw in the very earliest examples of the genre. Students, for satirists such as Marston and for humanist culture generally, are inevitably associated with pederasty, at least via their tutors:[36]

> Had I some faire brats, they should indure
> The new found Castilian callenture:
> Before some pedant-Tutor in his bed
> Should vse my frie, like Phrigian Ganimede.
>
> (*Scourge of Villanie*, III.75–8)

In the same volume Marston speaks of 'each odd puisne of the Lawyers Inne,' and 'some span-new come fry / Of Inns a-court.'[37] When we note as well that Tusco is none too clever and obsessed with fashion (as witnessed by his stroll in Paul's), it seems clear that Weever is invoking the contemporary satiric portraits of the Inns of Court gentleman. Other examples of the vices of London follow this portrait, but none of them directly link the reading of satire with learning the vice, focusing instead on the hypocritical nature of contemporary satirists. Satire, in other words, is inherently sodomitical and Italy is ultimately to blame.

Weever does not entirely reject satire, merely the practices of contemporary satirists. This, as Keach suggests, seems to be the impulse behind the inclusion of the satire by Horace, which doesn't display the sexual prurience and moral outrage of the other examples. Thus we can see a narrative in Weever's poem similar to the one identified in Edwards's. Edwards redraws literary history by excising Italy and Petrarch, making England the rightful heir of classical Latin verse. Weever draws a fanciful genealogy via Brutus that avoids the intervening continental history, and that warns against the 'Leopard-skind, soule-polluting Sodomy' ('A Prophesie,' 65) that is part and parcel of Italian literature produced since the classical age and which has infected contemporary English satire. The vices attached to Petrarchan poetry and to satire are the same: they are puritanical and hypocritical, and they stand in the way of a healthy Ovidian sexuality. Youths seduced by them end up dead like Adonis, or jetting about in Paul's with court-boy Brisco at their heels. Either way, the youth is lost. Whether the chief carrier is satire or

Petrarchan verse, England must avoid the baneful effect of contemporary Italian poetry because of the danger it poses to the health of the nation. By avoiding these dangers, England can at the same time claim for itself the imperial heritage of classical Rome, at least in the realm of literary history.

Marlowe's Wake

In addition to the poems discussed in detail in this chapter, there are a number of other epyllia produced in the 1590s and early 1600s that follow Marlowe more or less directly, often signalling as well their devotion to Shakespeare, Lodge, and others. As a group, they are interesting for what they say about the reception of Marlowe and his poem, and about the perception of the poems as a recognizable genre.

Most obviously indebted to Marlowe's poem are the two continuations of it by Henry Petowe and George Chapman. Petowe's *The Second Part of Hero and Leander* (1598) is an enthusiastic tribute to 'that admired Poet *Marloe*' (sig. Asv), employing somewhat imperfectly Marlowe's heroic couplets to furnish the lovers with a happy ending. By contrast, Chapman's *Hero and Leander* (1598) adds four sestiads to the original poem's two to bring the lovers to their unhappy deaths. Chapman's continuation picks up on the final lines of Marlowe's poem to significantly darken the tone and offer the moralizing comment on the lovers that Marlowe refused to make.

Written slightly earlier than these two poems, Dunstan Gale's *Pyramis and Thisbe* recounts the tale from the fourth book of the *Metamorphoses*; the only known edition of this poem was published in 1617, but its dedication is dated 1596. In spite of its source, the poem finds its primary inspiration in Marlowe, Shakespeare, and Lodge rather than Arthur Golding or Ovid. Gale's tragic couple is clearly based on Marlowe's (Pyramis and Thisbe are both extravagantly beautiful; the description of Thisbe's garments recalls that of Hero's; the lovers dwell not 'On Hellespont,' [Marlowe 1] but 'Neere to the place where *Nilus* channels runne' [1.1]), and much of the comedy in the early half of the poem is similarly at the expense of the immature lovers. The tragicomic story and the modulations in tone recall *Venus and Adonis*, a debt made clearer by references to Shakespeare's characters.[38] Oddly, Venus is the source of metaphors not for Thisbe but for Pyramis, who, after discovering Thisbe's bloodied scarf and imagining her to be dead, is described as 'sicke thoughted' (21.11) and is compared to a 'mournefull Doe lament[ing] / For her young kid' (22.1–2). Lodge's poem is signalled in the natural world's attraction to Thisbe (recalling similar moments with Scilla) and in the poem's moments of hyperbolic excess, seen, for example, in the lengthy comic descriptions of the blood gushing out of Pyramis's body and Thisbe's nose.

The most unexpected debt in the poem, however, is to Shakespeare's other narrative poem, *The Rape of Lucrece*. In a later chapter we will encounter other borrowings from *Lucrece*, which occur almost exclusively in poems about rape. The borrowings here do not seem to be as meaningful or systematic: Pyramus's hand, 'like a trembling executioner' (26.9), does not want to participate in the suicide and has to be talked to, much like Lucrece's: 'Poor hand, why quiver'st at this decree?' (1020). When Thisbe kills herself, her blood encircles Pyramus's body, just as Lucrece's circles her own. In both cases, the blood appears to guard the encircled corpse. Stylistically, certain turns of phrase recall *Lucrece*'s fascination with repetition and inversion, particularly at the moment of Thisbe's death: 'With that same blade, her selfe, her selfe did murther' (39.12) echoes lines like 'Himself himself seek every hour to kill' (998) and 'My self thy friend will kill myself thy foe' (1196) from Shakespeare's poem. While the borrowings are not particularly meaningful or systematic, they are interesting because they indicate that Gale was imitating what he saw as a group of similar poems, a group that for him included *Lucrece*.

Probably written when the vogue for the genre was over, the anonymous *Philos and Licia* (published 1624 but entered into the Stationer's Register 2 October 1606 to W. Aspely) is indebted to Marlowe's poem and, to a lesser degree, Shakespeare's and Drayton's. The very slight narrative is likely an invention of the author. Philos goes to Licia's room one morning, they discuss their love for each other, they are betrothed, and after a delay of two days, are married. There are no significant bars to their union, and no metamorphoses take place. The narrative largely serves as the occasion for a series of erotic descriptions: Licia naked in bed, blazons of the two lovers, Helen undressing for Paris, and Licia bathing naked in a river. The poem shows many of the standard rhetorical interests of the genre, including hyperbole, blazon, ecphrasis, epic simile, and digression, along with other common thematic elements, such as the beauty of youth, debates about love (and, in particular, virginity), and the power of rhetoric.

In an otherwise unremarkable example of the genre, two things stand out. One is an orgy of ecphrasis: the poem starts by having Philos climb the stairs to Licia's room. He encounters paintings on the wall, then tapestry, and then more paintings on Licia's ceiling. Later in the poem,

Licia puts on a scarf decorated with episodes from the *Metamorphoses*. Finally, killing time before her marriage, she embroiders yet more episodes on a dress and on another scarf. The multiple instances of ecphrasis do not have an obvious point beyond introducing mythological referents and allowing for the inclusion of more erotic episodes. They do, however, indicate the importance of the device for the genre.

The second point of interest is that the protagonist, for at least part of the poem, is described as 'blacke' (8), 'swarthie,' and 'tawnie' (9). He pleads to Licia, 'Though I am blacke, yet do not me despise, / Love looks as sweet in blacke as faire mens eies' (8). This gives rise to several common images, such as 'An orient pearle hung in an Indians eare' (8), and offers occasion for a series of black and white contrasts. In spite of Philos's anxieties about his own attractiveness, he is soon after described as 'a perfect well shap't man' (11). Licia never responds to Philos's concerns about his blackness, which leads to the suspicion that the poet subsequently forgets his colour, especially when later Licia 'stroaks his [Philos's] alabaster skin' (26). Since Philos's colour never figures as a complication in the narrative, it would seem that it is largely there because of the genre's interest in fashion and novelty.

A couple of points can be made about these and other poems following in Marlowe's wake. The first is the evidence they give of a confidence in an English poetic tradition. Inserted in one of *Philos and Licia*'s many tableaux, for example, is the figure of 'Fame / Bearing a lawrell, on which *Sydneys* name' (3) can be read. In all of the poems it is clear that their most immediate inspiration is English rather than classical poetry; these poets are not so much imitating Ovid or even Golding's Ovid as they are imitating Marlowe or Shakespeare, and this is especially evident in those poems that depart from Ovidian subject matter. As tributes to Marlowe, they position him as an English Ovid, without even bothering to make that claim explicitly. This is clearest in Henry Petowe's lengthy tribute to Marlowe in his poem, which concludes with the sentiment:

Marlo must frame to *Orpheus* melodie,
Himnes all diuine to make heauen harmonie,
There ever liue the Prince of Poetrie
Liue with the liuing in eternitie.

(sig. B2v)

The imagined collaboration between Orpheus and Marlowe echoes Petowe's earlier characterization in the dedication of Marlowe's unfinished poem as a (presumably singing) head with a body.

Ironically, the other connection between Marlowe and Orpheus is their promotion of pederasty. In spite of the fact that these poems are to greater and lesser degrees tributes to Marlowe's, none follow his interest in homoeroticism. Two of the poems end happily and the other two tragically, but all have age-appropriate heterosexual unions at the centre of their narrative. Unlike Edwards and Weever, these poets deal with the anxieties surrounding sodomy and a national poetic canon by simply ignoring them (if they are infected by them all); this is possible because they see themselves as unproblematically inhabiting an existent national tradition. The poems' distance from an Ovidian sexuality, and even a Shakespearean or Marlovian one, can be seen as evidence of the cultural shift regarding sexuality in which the poems participate. Devoid of the anxieties that animate their predecessors, the poems are peculiarly flat, even when written by reasonably talented poets.

CHAPTER FIVE

'The *Thracian* fields and company of men': The Erotics of Political Fraternity

This chapter will look at two examples of the genre that explore, in unexpected ways, new models of political relations. This subject is perhaps not entirely surprising in the case of R.B.'s *Orpheus His Journey to Hell*, since Orpheus was a frequently cited model for humanist orators. In R.B.'s version of the story, Orpheus's journey becomes the occasion for the formation of a new political community, based on affectionate bonds between adult men. Orpheus's company of men thus functions as a precursor to the imagined community of the modern nation, which, as Benedict Anderson writes, 'is always conceived as a deep, horizontal comradeship.'[1]

The story of Francis Beaumont's *Salmacis and Hermaphroditus* does not seem initially to lend itself to political readings, but as with many epyllia, the digressions from the main narrative take the poem in directions that reveal the interest that the main narrative holds for the writer. There, in his satire of the Elizabethan justice system and his imagining of a world essentially ruled by bargains, he prefigures in a comic way the social contract. My reading of this poem will be interrupted by a digression that considers the political economy of vision, and the means by which ideology is incorporated by the subject through its experience of space. I will consider how the new technology of perspectivism in painting is supportive of the new political relations explored in the poems, which in turn helps to explain the genre's interest in the figure of ecphrasis.

Salmacis and Hermaphroditus

'My wanton lines doe treate of amorous love,' begins the narrator in Francis Beaumont's *Salmacis and Hermaphroditus*, asking Venus's blessing on his poem, so that 'as I write, one line may draw the tother, / And every word skip nimbly o're another' (1, 11–12). Wantonness is something of a narrative principle in this poem, which early on veers from its principal story into a series of digressions and linked stories in a manner that is reminiscent of Ovidian narrative design in general and Marlowe's *Hero and Leander* in particular. Marlowe is clearly a model for the poem, as seen in the tone, in the numerous aetiological asides, in the verse form (heroic couplets), and in its invocation of Mercury rather than Orpheus as its exemplar of rhetoric. And as with Marlowe's poem, the digressiveness, the indirection, and the frustration of the reader's expectations are crucial elements of the poem, which uses the myth for the most part as occasion for rhetorical play. Hermaphroditus can be seen as emblematic of the genre not just because he is a beautiful youth, but also because he is the child of Mercury and Venus, or rhetoric and desire. Hermaphroditus is the embodiment of wanton lines, in other words, and a demonstration of the potential effects of rhetoric upon its audience.

The poem is prefaced by the usual crowd of dedicatory poems, praising the author and recommending the poem. Beaumont dedicates the undertaking to Calliope, the muse of poetry, and asks her forgiveness for presuming her 'Mayden-cheeke to stayne' (10), by addressing his efforts to her. This staining of the muse's cheeks is a more benign version of what we have seen in other dedicatory poems, which often involve the ruin of a maid. The mock courtesy fades, however, in the final couplet: 'I vse thee as a woman ought to bee: / I consecrate my idle howres to thee' (13–14). Calliope, much like Hiren and Scilla, becomes a common woman at the hands of the poet and his circle. At least one of these poets, A.F., sees the poem as evidence of a rebirth of poetry in English, and he establishes this in terms similar to those of Thomas Edwards:

> The matchlesse Lustre of faire poesie,
> Which erst was bury'd in old Romes decayes,
> Now 'gins with height of rising maiesty,
> Her dust-wrapt head from rotten tombes to rayse.
>
> (1–4)

England thus becomes the direct inheritor of Rome through the rewriting of 'wanton Ouid' (7). At the same time, the rewriting of Ovid is the avenue for further metamorphoses in England, as Beaumont concludes in 'The Author to the Reader': 'I hope my Poeme is so liuely writ, / That thou wilt turne halfe-mayd with reading it' (9–10). The combination of rhetoric and desire in these wanton lines turns the poem itself into either Salmacis or the enchanted well, threatening to replicate in the reader the fate of Hermaphroditus.

The main narrative of *Salmacis and Hermaphroditus* is a story close to the heart of the genre: the bashful youth who is the universal object of desire. As we saw in chapter 1, an early Ovidian narrative poem employing the same myth, Peend's *The Pleasant fable of Hermaphroditus and Salmacis*, was a major influence on the first example of the genre, Lodge's *Scillaes Metamorphosis*, and it started off what would be a recurring narrative. As with the early poems, this narrative is directed in the first instance towards the Inns of Court. Beaumont, like his older brothers Henry and John, attended the Inner Temple, John and Henry enrolling in 1597, and the younger brother a few years later in 1600. Their father, Sir Francis Beaumont, was a judge of Common Pleas who had also been a member of the Inner Temple and their grandfather John was Master of the Rolls. In spite of this family background it would appear that none of the sons were there to actually become barristers, although the writings of the two younger brothers certainly show an awareness of legal matters.

Beaumont's Hermaphroditus resembles Peend's, and is a combination of all of the usual traits of the youth in the genre: he is bashful, generally silent, and irresistibly attractive. Like the majority of these figures, his beauty leads him to an unfortunate end. The characteristics of the narrator's voice are also very much staples of the genre: cool, aloof, and bemused by the absurdities of desire. And, as with a number of the other poems, therein lies a central irony: one of the prefatory poems announces this to be the work of a young poet, and if, as most critics agree, the poet is Beaumont, the author would be all of eighteen at the time of publication.[2]

Beaumont's Hermaphroditus, like Ovid's, is fifteen. Like many of the other recurring figures in the genre such as Narcissus, Adonis, and Leander, he is described as surpassingly beautiful:

When first this wel-shapt boy, beauties chiefe king,
Had seene the labour of the fifteenth spring,
How curiously it paynted all the earth,
He 'gan to travaile from his place of birth.

(79–82)

As in most versions of the story, he travels to the land of Caria, where he comes upon a fountain. In this version, it is the same stream by which Narcissus met his fate. After two lengthy digressions involving the nymph Salmacis, we get a brief wooing scene, in which Salmacis, in the tradition of Ovidian women, does all the talking. She then retreats, Hermaphroditus strips off and dives into the water, and she, inflamed with desire, dives in after him. As Ann Thompson points out, in this version the embrace appears to be a killing one,[3] and Hermaphroditus's final wish is that

> Who e're heated by Phoebus beames
> Shall come to coole him in these silver streames,
> May nevermore a manly shape retaine,
> But halfe a virgine may returne againe.
>
> (915–18)

The reference to the 'manly shape' is perhaps telling; hermaphroditism is here viewed as a deformation rather than a doubling.[4] Beaumont's phrasing echoes Golding's translation to some degree: 'whoso bathes him there, commes thence a perfect man no more' (4.349). As a number of critics and historians have shown, the early modern period was fascinated with the figure of the hermaphrodite, which seemed to embody for that culture some of their anxieties about the body and especially the instability of gender.[5] Stephen Greenblatt argues that the anxieties about the body are fundamentally anxieties about selfhood, and thus the cultural fascination with the hermaphrodite can be read as a product of a general redefinition of subjectivity.[6] Hermaphroditus's failure to metamorphose into a 'perfect man' mirrors the stories of other youths in the genre, stories that can similarly be read as fables of subjectivity.

As Thompson notes, the poem draws frequent parallels between Hermaphroditus and Narcissus, the latter of whom makes appearances in a number of epyllia. In one of only two speeches by Hermaphroditus in the entire poem, the parallel becomes explicit when Hermaphroditus sees his own reflection in the nymph's eyes:

> How should I love thee, when I doe espie
> A farre more beauteous Nymph hid in thy eye?
> When thou doost love, let not that Nymph be nie thee;
> Nor when thou woo'st, let that same Nymph be by thee:
> Or quite obscure her from thy lovers face,
> Or hide her beauty in a darker place.
>
> (691–6)

Here Hermaphroditus repeats the error of Narcissus in Thomas Edwards's version of the myth, mistaking a reflection of himself for that of a beautiful nymph. Narcissus, however, was cross-dressing at the time, which might lead us to think that no metamorphosis was necessary for Hermaphroditus to embody his own name. Keach observes that this is 'the central irony of Beaumont's handling of Hermaphroditus – he is androgynous and effeminate long before his identity merges with that of Salmacis.'[7] But although Salmacis's pond is the same as that beside which Narcissus pined, it is the nymph's eyes, rather than the crystal waters, in which Hermaphroditus sees himself reflected. The persistent allusions to Narcissus would suggest that if the two principal characters are not (yet) the same person, they are to a large degree mirror images of each other.

As we might expect from the Narcissus motif, Hermaphroditus and Salmacis consistently mirror each other, most prominently in their virtually irresistible beauty. The poem starts with a series of tributes to Hermaphroditus's charms, which turn out to have alarming powers. In the first of these tributes Diana falls in love with the youth, but 'the boy ran: for (some say) had he stayd, / Diana had no longer bene a mayd' (33–4). Next we hear that

> Phoebus so doted on this rosiat face,
> That he hath oft stole closely from his place,
> Where he did lie by fayre Leucothoes side,
> To dally with him in the vales of Ide.
>
> (35–8)

The rose, originally only white, was dyed red when, Hermaphroditus lying upon it, it blushed. Finally, and grotesquely, we learn that Venus, thinking Hermaphroditus's eyes a little dull in comparison with the rest of his face, plucked out Cupid's 'sparkling eyes' and gave them to the boy (70). The force of these anecdotes is to suggest that Hermaphroditus's beauty is a perverse, occasionally deforming force, with the power to make the beholder radically change its nature, from virgin to ravisher or from white to red. Hermaphroditus, we observe, already has in some form the power that he will later ask his parents to bestow upon the waters. It is here that we see the most crucial parallel with Edwards's poem, in its testament to the irresistible power of the beauty of youths and the danger that that beauty poses to its beholders, especially men.

The praise of Hermaphroditus's beauty ends with a little blazon:

For his white hand each goddesse did him woo:
For it was whiter then the driven snow:
His legge was straighter then the thigh of Jove:
And he farre fairer then the god of love.

(75–8)

Salmacis is introduced with a longer blazon that nonetheless establishes
a parallel with the youth:

So faire she was, of such a pleasing grace,
So straight a body, and so sweet a face,
So soft a belly, such a lustie thigh,
So large a forehead, such a cristall eye,
So soft and moyst a hand, so smooth a brest,
So faire a cheeke, so well in all the rest,
That Jupiter would revell in her bowre,
Where he to spend againe his golden showre.

(105–12)

Hermaphroditus, we are told, seeks out fountains because he 'did love to
wash his ivory skin' (88); Salmacis, the laziest of nymphs, does not hunt
with Diana, 'But in her cristall fountaine oft she swimmes, / And oft she
washes o're her snowy limmes' (375–6). Hermaphroditus is compared to
Narcissus (703–6); Salmacis is similarly drawn:

Oft in the water did she looke her face,
And oft she us'd to practise what quaint grace
Might well become her, and what comely feature
Might be best fitting so divine a creature.

(383–6)

Both youth and maiden have golden hair, and both have it torn out over
the course of the poem: the youth's by other nymphs, and Salmacis by
her own hand.

As with Hermaphroditus's, Salmacis's beauty leaves no end of disrup-
tion in its wake. In the first digression, Jove falls in love and vows to make
her a star, which Venus opposes because of its potentially disruptive
effect in the heavens. In the second digression, Bacchus falls in love with
Salmacis and he is on the verge of ravishing her (with her consent) when
Apollo intervenes. In revenge, Bacchus has Mercury steal the wheels off

Apollo's chariot. Apollo, in an unexplained move, asks Salmacis to get them back for him, and in return he will show her the most beautiful youth ever. Although some critics have complained about the irrelevance of these digressions,[8] the digressions do feature similar narratives about the disruptive power of the nymph's beauty, and, interestingly, they each feature one of Hermaphroditus's parents: Mercury and Venus (Hermes and Aphrodite). These are the two that will eventually transform the waters of the pool, after the two curiously doubled central figures are merged.

This seeming interchangeability of Salmacis and Hermaphroditus is directly acted out in the wooing scene, when Salmacis takes command: 'Wert thou a mayd, and I a man, Ile show thee, / With what a manly boldnesse I could wooe thee' (715–16). The rather obvious irony is that she lacks no manly boldness at all, and the hypothetical wooing is an actual one, or rather would be, if its object were not now hiding in the bushes. Having lost her prey, Salmacis reflects, once again with irony, 'Why wert thou bashfull, boy? Thou hast no part / Shewes thee to be of such a female heart' (747–8). In fact, the boy has already mistaken himself for a nymph, and Salmacis's female heart is anything but bashful. Salmacis as wooer, however, is reminiscent less of Venus than of Leander. Rather than the expert and amoral rhetorician in Shakespeare's poem, Salmacis speaks like the 'bold sharp sophister' Leander, when we see her forensic rhetoric at work in lines 747–8, attempting to isolate the cause (in the Aristotelian sense) of Hermaphroditus's bashfulness. Salmacis, like Hermaphroditus, is both youth and maiden, which perhaps accounts for the relative colourlessness of the Hermaphroditus character, and for the insistent parallels. When Salmacis is overtaken by desire at the sight of the naked Hermaphroditus bathing, this repeats an earlier scene where Jove fell in love with a naked Salmacis bathing. When Salmacis falls in love with Hermaphroditus, then, it is as if she is falling in love with herself, or as if Narcissus is being wooed by his own image.

What might the poem be suggesting by combining so forcefully the myth of Narcissus and that of Hermaphroditus? At the very least, the parallel between youth and nymph should make us question what has been said about the inversion of gender in the poems. It would appear that the reverse of a youth in the poem is a youth, or rather, that the category of youth is one that cannot be easily resolved into male or female. This finds parallels in the changing ideas about hermaphrodites in the medical literature of the period: 'once the hermaphrodite came to be seen primarily as a being of intermediate (rather than doubled) sex, it also became emblematic of all kinds of sexual ambiguity, and associated with all practices that appeared to blur or erase the lines between the sexes,' such as sodomy, transvestism, and sexual transformation.[9] Some of these connections can be seen in Thomas Middleton's *Micro-Cynicon* (1599), where 'ingling' Pyander, a 'pale chequer'd black hermaphrodite,' seems to be a transvestite prostitute and a youth.[10] This is in line with the way Sandys views the tale: 'The *Carians* therefore addicted to sloath and vice were called *Hermaphrodites*; not in that of both sexes, but for defiling themselves with either.'[11] Hermaphroditus, like many other youths in the genre, is already in some way both male and female; the metamorphosis that the genre is always aiming towards is one that rids itself of the female side, becoming fully masculine. The youth, as we have seen in this and in other poems, is a potential object of desire for virtually everyone: gods, goddesses, nymphs, and so on. The youth's own desire is rather narrower, either absent or directed towards himself or a mirror of himself. This, for the other characters in the poem, makes the ages of fifteen and sixteen a dangerous time. If the youth remains fixated on himself or his double and does not direct his desire outwards, he will pine away by the side of a real or metaphorical river. This accounts for the necessity of goddesses, or in this poem nymphs, teaching gender protocol to youths. However, if the youth does not also avoid desire improperly directed at him, he will be deformed, just as his beauty causes deformation in others. We have seen this in Adonis's protests against Venus (415–20) and Adonis could well point to the conclusion of the Hermaphroditus myth as proof of his objection.

As poem after poem tells us, to be the object of another's desire is the same as to be unduly subject to one's own desires, a point this poem makes by having Hermaphroditus desire himself in the eyes of another; either of these positions causes effeminization. We can see this in Golding's translation of Ovid where, in the 'Epistle' prefacing his translation, he glosses the myth in this way:

> Hermaphrodite and Salmacis declare that idlenesse
> Is cheefest nurce and cherisher of all volupteousnesse,
> And that voluptuous lyfe breedes sin: which linking all toogither
> Make men too bee effeminate, unweeldy, weake and lither.
>
> (113–16)

In a similar vein, Sandys tartly observes: 'Sensuall love is the deformed issue of sloth and delicacy: and seldome survives his inglorious parents.'[12] This is similar to Peend's reading of the poem as the tale of the youth leaving home who is subsequently overwhelmed by vice. But what Beaumont's combination of the two myths shows us is that Hermaphroditus's union is not so much a transformation as merely a stasis. If the pool will henceforth cause 'a mayden smoothnesse' (922) to seize the limbs of whoever swims in it, it will not thereby change the outward appearance of any youths from the epyllion who happen to dive in. That is, the youth will not become maiden-like, but merely remain maiden-like. The metamorphosis is in fact only an apparent one; instead, he will suffer the fate of not metamorphosing into a man (which in the genre is the most miraculous of transformations) and secondarily, his beauty will remain a potential danger to all those around him, effeminizing any adult males who stray within his vicinity.

What does the poem see as the salient characteristics of adult masculinity, to which the youth must aspire? The poem offers us a couple of substantial portraits of adult gods, Jove and Apollo. Both of these play the figure of the law to some degree, although neither fulfils the position of the Law, in Lacanian terms, because of the limits that are set on their actions. Whereas Jove figures largely in the first digression, Apollo makes a number of appearances over the course of the poem. Thompson suggests that the love narrative of Apollo and Thetis acts as a counterbalance to the main narrative: 'by balancing the sadness of the Narcissus story against the optimism of the Phoebus/Thetis story, the poet of Salmacis and Hermaphroditus gives us a finely modulated and satisfactory ending.'[13] This overstates the case, as Apollo's appearances are not restricted to his connection to Thetis. He is first seen, as we have noted, abandoning Leucothoe to look on Hermaphroditus. He rescues Salmacis from Bacchus 'for an old affection that he bore / Unto this lovely Nymph long time before' (463–4). Later Salmacis notes that 'He nightly kisseth Thætis in the sea: / All know the story of Leucothoë' (769–70). Apollo may nonetheless provide one model of adult male sexuality that serves as a positive example to Hermaphroditus's negative one. Indeed, this is precisely how Salmacis sees it, and monogamy does not appear to be the attraction for her.

As Teresa M. Krier notes, 'One of the large subjects of Beaumont's poem is the pleasure of sexual watching.'[14] This is not entirely unusual in the genre. Marston's poem is, if anything, even more invested in the exploration of scopophilia, as Pigmalion's eyes devour his statue. Marston's narrator in sympathy moans, 'O that my Mistres were an Image too, / That I might blameles her perfections view' (11.5–6). In Marlowe's poem, which seems to be the other major influence on

Beaumont, the culmination of Hero and Leander's bliss is not coupling but rather seeing:

> So *Heroes* ruddie cheeke, *Hero* betrayd,
> And her all naked to his sight displayd.
> Whence his admiring eyes more pleasure tooke,
> Than *Dis*, on heapes of gold fixing his looke.
>
> (807–10)

Sexualized looking is one of the pleasures of the genre itself, on evidence not just in its love of the blazon and ecphrasis, but in its languid descriptions of bodies at rest and in motion. Marlowe's description of the waves caressing Leander's body is a prime example of this, but Marston again lays out the underlying psychology for us:

> And now me thinks some wanton itching eare
> With lustfull thoughts, and ill attention,
> List's to my Muse, expecting for to heare
> The amorous discription of that action
> Which *Venus* seekes, and euer doth require,
> When fitnes graunts a place to please desire.
>
> (33.1–6)

While Marston is apparently satirizing the reader's scopophilia, he is also satirizing those who do not admit that sexual desire is part of the pleasure of reading; the hypocrisy of the 'subtile Citty-dame' (10.1), after all, is not so much that she has desire, but that she cannot admit to it.

In Beaumont's poem, as Krier observes, sexual watching of various kinds is omnipresent. There is, for example, the narcissistic pleasure that both Salmacis and Hermaphroditus take in their own reflection. This has to be differentiated from the pleasure of looking on others, which is, for the most part, associated with a healthy Ovidian sexuality. Every act of looking or being looked at is sexualized. In one of the aetiological myths the poem offers – why the dawn is red – Aurora blushes, 'Lothing of ev'ry mortall to be seene' (604). The nymphs, less bashful, steal Hermaphroditus's clothes, 'Because the wanton wenches would so fayne / See him come nak'd to aske his clothes againe' (91–2). Apollo is the supreme example of this general scopophilia, 'the fierie and all-seeing light / Of Phoebus' (763–4) overseeing much of the action of the poem.

An explanation for the genre's erotic investment in the field of the visual can be found by looking at its similar interest in ecphrasis, the verbal description of pictorial representation. The most extended example of this occurs in Shakespeare's *The Rape of Lucrece*, where Lucrece stands in front of a painting of the Fall of Troy and expounds on it at some length. While other poems do not engage in this pursuit to quite the same degree, we can see examples of it in Marlowe, Weever, Barksted, and most of the other poems. In the following chapter, we shall see that Lucrece uses the painting of Troy to build up a new identity for herself through serial acts of identification. Having had her identity as good wife destroyed by the rape, she turns to the painting, isolating various figures for examination and briefly identifying with them. By the end of the passage, she seems to have acquired both a new sense of self that allows her to act within the social, as well as a keener appreciation of the possible duplicity of representation. What the passage demonstrates is how the self is to a large degree constituted through the visual field, or as Beaumont puts it, that 'mortals still are subject to their eye' (139), the central point of Lacan's theory of the mirror stage. What has to be remembered, however, is that the parameters of the visual world are both socially and historically determined, and so the genre's keen interest in its own visual economy may be linked to its interest in subjectivity.

In Beaumont's poem, sexualized looking and political subjectivity are oddly intermixed in its one example of ecphrasis. The description of the painting above the throne of Astraea, the goddess of Justice, occurs as a digression within the first digression, which suggests that it functions as a *mise-en-abyme* for the poem, rather like the description of Aeneas's shield in the *Aeneid*. We will discuss the ecphrasis in a different context a little later, but it is worth quoting the entire passage here:

> Then [Astraea] descended from her stately throne,
> Which seat was builded all of Jasper stone,
> And o're the seat was paynted all above,
> The wanton unseene stealths of amorous Jove;
> There might a man behold the naked pride
> Of lovely Venus in the vale of Ide,
> When Pallas, and Joves beauteous wife and she
> Strove for the prise of beauties raritie:
> And there lame Vulcan and his Cyclops strove
> To make the thunderbolts for mighty Jove ...

(211–20)

There are a number of seeming incongruities at work here, not the least of which is that this erotic painting hangs in a courtroom. The jasper throne recalls a more famous instance of ecphrasis in similarly incongruous circumstances, the carvings on the jasper walls of Venus's temple in *Hero and Leander*. The description of the painting juxtaposes at least four instances of viewing: Jove's unseen seeing in his 'wanton unseene stealths' (214); Paris's judgment of the goddesses; the viewer of the painting's pleasurable assumption of Paris's position: 'There might a man behold the naked pride / Of lovely Venus' (216–17); and finally, the outward gaze of the law, which in this case is sorting out the marital squabbles of Venus and Vulcan. Sexualized looking, in the form of Jove's pleasure, is linked to aesthetic pleasure, in the painting's viewer. These are further folded into the pleasures of judging, those of Paris and further, by implication, those of Astraea, so that scopophilia is located at the heart of civilized order. Equally interesting is the arrangement's suggestion that aesthetic pleasure is based to some degree on identification with a pre-existing position (in this case, that of Paris) and that this identification takes place within the regime of the law. This particular aspect of the ecphrasis thus offers an allegory of the ideological manoeuver Graham L. Hammill identifies in perspective painting, which operates by 'promising the mastery of the visual field by positioning the subject at a point that the system has already, objectively thought.'[15] What the combination of these instances of seeing forces upon us is a recognition of the mutual interpenetration of the erotic economy, the visual economy, and what we might designate as the political economy of the poem. If the painting is a *mise-en-abyme*, it shows the link between the poem's key concerns, pointing to the centrality of the visual economy in the formation of the subject.

On Perspective

Given the poem's characterization of its central figure, it is interesting that Leon Battista Alberti identifies Narcissus as the origin of painting: 'I used to tell my friends that the inventor of painting, according to the poets, was Narcissus, who was turned into a flower; for as painting is the flower of all arts, so the tale of Narcissus fits our purpose perfectly. What is painting but the act of embracing the surface of the pool?'[16] The development of perspective in painting in the Renaissance has been seen as one of the period's defining features, and Alberti's *On Painting*, which first theorized the technology of perspective, is generally regarded as one of the key texts of Western culture.[17] Erwin Panofsky's classic essay, *Perspective as Symbolic Form*, links the development of perspective in the visual arts to broader social change, especially with regard to the subject:

> Perspective subjects the artistic phenomenon to stable and even mathematically exact rules, but on the other hand, makes that phenomenon contingent upon human beings, indeed upon the individual: for these rules refer to the psychological and physical conditions of the visual impression, and the way they take effect is determined by the freely chosen position of a subjective 'point of view.' Thus the history of perspective may be understood with equal justice as a triumph of the distancing and objectifying sense of the real, and as a triumph of the distance-denying human struggle for control; it is as much a consolidation and systematization of the external world, as an extension of the domain of the self. [18]

Panofsky links the triumph of perspective to a triumph of objectivity over subjectivity, in particular, replacing what Ernst Cassirer calls 'psychophysiological space' with mathematical space: 'Exact perspectival construction is a systematic abstraction from the structure of this psychophysiological space. For it is not only the effect of perspectival construction, but indeed its intended purpose, to realize in the representation of space precisely that homogeneity and boundlessness foreign to the direct experience of that space. In a sense, perspective transforms psychophysiological space into mathematical space.'[19] Alternatively, we might argue that perspective attempts to inaugurate a new regime of psychophysiological space, one in which the viewer functions to some degree as object: his or her social relations are derealized, and bodies are made equivalent, as in a mathematical formula. That is, perspectivism institutes a radical realm of equality in space, although this equality also extends to the object itself. This informs one of the traditional objections to perspectivism, that it seems to refuse any commentary on what it portrays, or what Martin Jay identifies as 'the increasing autonomy of the image from any extrinsic purpose, religious or otherwise.'[20] At the same time that it makes the subject interchangeable with other subjects (or indeed, other objects), it paradoxically allows the colonizing the visual field by the ego, making the world, as Panofsky writes, 'an extension of the domain of the self.'[21]

Perspectivism, which offers the illusion of looking through the plane of representation rather than at it (not at the surface of the pool but at what is reflected in it), is obviously a style of representation, and as such, has no greater claims on truth than any of the styles which preceded or succeeded it. It may be seen as the pictorial equivalent of the plain style in rhetoric, which claims a similar objectivity in attempting to draw attention away from its own representational schemes. While perspectivism is only a style, as the dominant style of visual representation in the early modern period, it may, as Panofsky argues, tell us something about the period's visual economy. This is not to say that the style of painting shows us, in a direct way, how the early modern subject viewed the world (which would be as simplistic as claiming, on the basis of medieval painting, that medieval subjects saw the world in two dimensions) but rather that this new way of organizing space and bodies within the painting may in some way correspond to changes in the way in which the early modern subject experienced its body as it moved through social space. Christopher Pye, in discussing the first instance of perspectivism in English literature, takes this argument even further:

> While *King Lear* suggests the linguistic and erotic underpinnings of the
> perspective effect and the emergent empirical subject associated with it, the
> play also reveals a phantasmatic structuring space beyond such effects, and
> thus beyond the negational subject, its reverse face as it were. That space –
> or, rather, the entire, articulating opposition between empiricism and fan-
> tasy, the vanishing point and its beyond – coincides with the emergence of a
> radically distinct sociality and a distinctly political subjectivity.[22]

Pye does not discuss in any direct way the emergence or the outlines of this 'distinctly political subjectivity,' and so we will turn once again to the work of Kaja Silverman, whose discussion of the ideological foundations of the bodily ego helps to explore the links between social space and subjectivity.

In *The Threshold of the Visible World*, a title taken from a phrase in Lacan's essay on the mirror stage, Silverman revisits the psychoanalytic notion of the bodily ego. The bodily ego, as I argued in chapter 1, is the foundation of the subject's sense of self. Freud theorized that the bodily ego is in the first instance a projection of the form of the body, which has been interpreted by Lacan in almost exclusively visual terms. Silverman argues, however, that the sense of the body is not purely visual: 'it would seem that one's apprehension of self is keyed both to a visual image or constellation of visual images, and to certain bodily feelings, whose determinant is less physiological than social.'[23] Most obvious among these bodily feelings are those originating from the surface of the body, 'cutaneous sensation,' which, like the visual image, 'is conferred on the subject from outside ... the body is not the simple product of physical contact ... it is also profoundly shaped by the desires which are addressed to it, and by the values which are imprinted on it through touch.' The other major form of physical sensation is postural, which, like cutaneous sensation, is also profoundly social, 'the deployment of the body's muscles for the purpose of fitting it smoothly within an imagined spatial envelope.'[24] Thus the sense perceptions that derive from the surface of the body and from the physical movement of the muscles and skeleton through space are not ideologically neutral but rather are historically specific. As Teresa Brennan argues, 'The spatial perceptions of people in given historical periods will vary along with their body images and perceptions of the other.'[25]

Silverman's discussion of the bodily ego is valuable both for showing how the sense of self is not purely visually derived, and for showing that the physical experience of the body, upon which the sense of self is partially based, is to a large degree the product of a society's spatial relations, experienced at the level of the body. The two experiences of the body (visual and physical) are, however, linked, and they are most clearly linked in painting, which is directly expressive of a particular society's spatial regimes. In the early modern period, we can also see the link between posture and ideology made very clearly in the conduct books which, as George Vigarello shows, attempted to use the new rules of perspective to arrange the body in space, in accordance with 'the sixteenth century's enthusiastic belief in proportion.'[26] The conduct books' regulation of the body is one means through which, argues Hammill, 'the civilizing process conscripts the body within civic modes of discipline.'[27] Regulation of posture is supplemented by proxemic codes, styles of movement, and other prescriptions for physical decorum. Thus the subject's skin and muscles are avenues through which the subject quite literally incorporates ideology, as it moves through space. This means that spatial relations are not just experienced or understood visually, and that the relations between bodies in space will be expressive of historically specific social forms. Nonetheless, it is through visual representation (particularly of bodies) that these social forms are most clearly expressed.

This should lead us to see some of the ideological work being performed by perspectivism, as it moves from a psychophysiological to a mathematical sense of space. Perspectivism does not allow for the portrayal *at the level of form* of social relations that are anything other than equal, however these relations might be rendered at the level of content. This mathematical sense of space implies equality or exchangeability between the subjects and objects portrayed; we might link this to the positions implied by the contract, which, as we have argued, commodifies the contracting subjects, at least insofar as it depends upon two parties who are equal in the abstract or rendered as such in the moment of contracting. In a similar fashion, perspective painting renders all subjects equal and thus exchangeable. This commodification arguably occurs in the viewing of the painting as well: the painting flatters the viewer who occupies the central viewing position, but this prescripted position is occupied serially by innumerable interchangeable subjects.

Spatialization, especially in painting, is linked both to temporality and to forms of narrative. This is most obvious in the contrast between early modern painting and its medieval precursors. Medieval painting is notable for its ability to represent sequences of events, in accordance with its theological, and therefore nonlinear, sense of time. Perspectivism is just as notable for its inability to portray anything more than a single instant in time, which is the time of the subject's viewing. The perspective painting, as Panofsky argues, is oriented towards the viewing subject, and this is true both spatially and temporally. The mathematical sense of space is thus matched by a mathematical sense of time, where the succession of historical moments is linked by nothing other than strict order, and the subject thereby occupies an eternal present. This particular sense of time, argues Benedict Anderson, is a necessary component of the modern experience of national belonging.[28] As with the contract, there is no debt to the past, and the self becomes commodifiable and exchangeable. What Silverman's analysis of the bodily ego enables us to see is how these new relations of space and time, as well as the political relations that they support, are constitutive of our most basic experience of selfhood.

We have seen before in the epyllion a protest against this commodification of the self, most notably in Adonis. Beaumont plays with the interchangeability of the subject in *Salmacis and Hermaphroditus*, where the central characters are virtually identical, so that their final merging seems a natural development rather than a miraculous metamorphosis. Their interchangeability is most on display in the Narcissus scene, where Hermaphroditus falls in love with his own reflection in Salmacis's eyes. But this scene also illustrates succinctly Panofsky's point about the logic of perspective painting, where the imagined world seen through the plane of representation is merely an extension of the colonizing self. It is in the two digressions of the poem, however, where we can begin to intuit the connections in the poem between vision and contract.

In the second digression, Phoebus (mistakenly) saves Salmacis from Bacchus in memory of the pleasure of looking at her:

> This saw bright Phoebus: for his glittering eye
> Sees all that lies below the starry skye;
> And for an old affection that he bore
> Unto this lovely Nymph long time before,
> (For he would ofttimes in his circle stand,
> To sport himselfe upon her snowy hand)
> He kept her from the sweets of Bacchus bed
> And, 'gainst her wil, he sav'd her maiden-head.

> (461–8)

Phoebus, scopophilic like the rest of the gods, nonetheless upholds the law. This is a characteristic of Jove as well, which is the point of the first digression. That narrative begins when Jove falls in love with Salmacis after seeing her naked. Rather than deceive her by disguising himself, as he normally would do, he deals with her honestly, telling her

> that if he would,
> He could deceive her in a showre of gold,
> Or like a Swanne come to her naked bed,
> And so deceive her of her maiden-head:
> But yet, because he thought that pleasure best,
> Where each consenting joynes each loving brest,
> He would put off that all-commaunding crowne ...

> (121–7)

The episode of Leda and the Swan is here rewritten: the outrage, the poem implies, did not so much lie in the ravishment, but rather in the disguise. The pleasure consists not just in the having or the viewing, but in the mutual recognition, as reflected by consent. By attempting to enter into this pleasurable relation of mutuality, however, Jove ends up entering into a contract with her. She will give up her maidenhead if he makes her a star in heaven. Salmacis, who has perhaps read the nymph's equivalent of *The Lawes Resolution of Womens Rights*, insists that the bargain be notarized by an official:

But yet Astraea first should plight her troth,
For the performance of Joves sacred oth.
(Just times decline, and all good dayes are dead,
When heavenly othes had need be warranted:)

(145–8)

This is a typical Ovidian joke about the gradual decline of the world, but it is also a comment on the changing legal climate in England, especially the ongoing definition of contract law, which is lightly reflected on here. There are, in fact, a surprising number of contracts undertaken over the course of the poem: Venus bargains with Vulcan to stop the stellification of Salmacis, and then Vulcan bargains with Jove over the same matter. He will continue to make thunderbolts for Jove, if Jove will give up Salmacis. The contract, not desire, is the fundamental force in this universe.

Jove's attempt to have his contract notarized by Astraea leads into a satire of the legal profession. Critics have read the episode in court as a satire of Elizabeth, who was frequently allegorized as Astraea. Clark Hulse, for example, writes that 'the attack on the Court of Elizabeth is so clear that it seems probable that Beaumont's play on the *Judgment of Paris* [painted above Astraea's throne] is yet another travesty of the official iconography of Elizabeth, another hint that beneath the thick paint of Court puritanism, all is not sound.'[29] It is clear that the justice system in general is being satirized when Jove beholds Astraea's tower:

from the palace side there did distill
A little water, through a little quill,
The dewe of justice, which did seldome fall,
And when it dropt, the drops were very small.

(161–4)

Before he makes it to Astraea's court, Jove must push his way through a crowd, 'some serving men, and some promooters' (169), all of whom demand bribes. Then he passes through a hall 'full of darke angels and of hidden wayes, / Crooked Maeanders, infinite delayes' (177–8) until he reaches an aged porter, who relieves him of his remaining cash, for 'None must see Justice but with an emptie purse' (186). Keach notes that 'the parody of legal procedure ... would have had a special appeal for Beaumont's fellow students at the Inns of Court.'[30]

The court that Astraea presides over could be either Chancery or

Requests, prerogative courts which provided recourse for cases for which no appropriate common law writ existed.[31] In these courts women could and frequently did present grievances against their husbands or others, as Venus does here. This would tie in well with Salmacis's insistence that the bargain she makes with Jove, which seems to be an Ovidian version of marriage, be notarized. According to the common law, married women in sixteenth-century England had the status of feme covert, a legal fiction through which their rights were subsumed by their husbands' (and which meant they could not own property). Chancery, which existed to ameliorate the harshness of common law, became one chief place of recourse for women. Legal historian Maria L. Cioni writes, 'During this period, Chancery laid the foundations for married women's property rights, gave security to women who held real and personal estates by means of future equitable interests not recognized at the common law, granted protection to the estate of the jointress and accorded a right to separated or divorced women to take a share of their husband's estate commensurate with the portion they brought into the marriage; that is, they were allowed "equity of settlement."'[32] Significantly, given the number of bargains that are struck in this poem, Chancery was also involved in the gradual refinement of contract theory.[33] Venus's objections to Salmacis's stellification, her argument that Jove should 'place in heaven no more / Eche wanton strumpet and lascivious whore' (277–8) would also be familiar to students of law. In her study of the consistory courts of London, Laura Gowing draws attention to the formidable number of lawsuits brought by women against other women for sexual slander. Gowing argues that this explosion of litigation attests to anxieties about changing sexual and social roles and, most immediately, to a change in social space, as people moved into unfamiliar urban environments with entirely new spatial economies.[34] The slander suits, then, are to some degree the result of a demand to integrate these changes at the level of the ego or the sense of self.

The painting above Astraea's throne in the court of law, the poem's nod to the genre's interest in ecphrasis, has already been discussed. Keach argues of the painting that 'the Goddess of Justice in *Salmacis and Hermaphroditus* is shown to be inextricably linked with the disorder and irrationality inherent in erotic power, with Jove's "wanton unseene stealths" and with Venus's "naked pride."'[35] This interpretation ignores the last of the three parts, Vulcan's workshop. Hulse, as we have seen, focuses on the middle panel, the Judgment of Paris. If we look at all three panels together, however, we see that it is an inset miniature of the digression as a whole: Jove's seduction of Salmacis; Venus's objections to Salmacis's stellification, 'fearing now she should not first be seene / Of all the glittring starres as shee had beene' (269–70); and the final outcome, Vulcan back making thunderbolts because Jove has agreed to give up his erotic plans in order to keep his throne. If we use the painting as a gloss on the digression, we come to a quite different conclusion than Keach does regarding the ways in which the 'disorder and irrationality inherent in erotic power' rules the world of the gods. The key thing to note is, of course, the conclusion to the tale. Rather than have 'mortall men ... plucke him from his throne' (338), Jove must 'forgoe the pleasure of the mayd' (340). Far from being ruled by irrationality and disorder, the world of the gods here is startlingly legalistic and rational. Jove will forego pleasure in the name of the public good (or at least his own political power): 'Therefore the god no more did woo or prove her, / But left to seeke her love, though not to love her' (351–2). Jove still loves the maid, but no longer seeks her love. The qualification is important here: unlike Salmacis at the end of the poem, Jove can master his desire. Moreover, like Orpheus in *Mirrha* or the good humanist ruler in general, he puts public good ahead of private pleasure.

The second digression illustrates similar themes with a similar series of plot elements. Bacchus bargains with Salmacis for her virginity, Apollo intervenes to save her, Bacchus bargains with Hermes to steal Apollo's chariot wheels, and Apollo bargains with Salmacis to get them back. While desire might be an irrational and disorderly force, it is nonetheless mastered in both narratives. Salmacis's virtue remains intact, Apollo's wheels are returned, bargains made are kept. The erotic economy in this poem functions in precisely the same way as a more literal economy, founded on the equalizing power of the contract.

As with many of these poems, it is in the digressions where we see much of the real interest in the themes of the myth appear. Whereas the main narrative supplies the negative exemplum for the development of the youth, the digressions give us the outlines of successful adult masculinity. This is to a large degree bound up in the new visual and spatial economy, which finds its best expression in perspective painting. There, the field of vision is colonized by the observing eye. Moreover, as Martin Jay observes, 'The moment of erotic projection in vision ... was lost as the bodies of the painter and viewer were forgotten in the name of an allegedly disincarnated, absolute eye. Although such a gaze could, of course, still fall on objects of desire ... it did so largely in the service of a reifying male look that turned its targets to stone.'[36] Thus the separation from and mastery over objects in perspective painting is complemented by the subject's mastery over his own desire. In the epyllion, this is a mastery realized above all else by the narrator, whose position within (or distance from) the narrative most closely approximates the Lacanian gaze.

At the same time, while the ecphrasis suggests that scopophilia is located at the heart of civilized order, emblematized to some degree by the way in which the 'all-seeing light / Of Phoebus' (764–5) pervades the poem, the visual economy in the poem has a regulating function for the subject. The poem parallels contract and vision, most tellingly in Jove's interest in the erotic appeal of mutual recognition, 'Where each consenting joynes each loving brest' (126). The visual economy of perspective painting, founded upon a mathematical equality of objects (and hence subjects) in space, parallels the political economy of the poem, which is ruled by the contract.

The digressions, then, tell an interesting story about the role of law in the universe. Whereas other poems in the genre have suggested that the law of the universe is desire, these poems show there is a greater force than Cupid. But this greater force is not, as we might expect, the adult male gods like Jove or Phoebus, but rather the law of contract. This is an important point to observe, since this law in effect flattens the political relations between gods and mortals: all are rendered equal by the (erotic) contract. While the first digression may give us a parody of the bureaucratic tangles of the Elizabethan justice system, it does not challenge the fundamental principles of that law. Whereas in previous poems rhetoric has been seen as the foundation of civilization, here contract and the legal system play that role. Given the common link of the Inns of Court, this is not as profound a difference as it might appear. What is important to remark, however, is the new configuration of the political realm that the digressions envision, one which is premised not on the absolutism of Mount Olympus, but rather on the contract. These are essentially the same relations that we see worked out in *Orpheus His Journey to Hell*, although we arrive at them not through heterosexual dalliances, but rather through homosocial bonding that is premised for the most part on the rejection of women.

Orpheus His Journey to Hell

As with many other examples of the genre, R.B.'s *Orpheus His Journey to Hell* is less than faithful to its origins. The length of the poem is entirely out of proportion to its various sources, and thus we can see that the story is to some degree only a pretext for other explorations. What does the poet, increasingly identified as Richard Barnfield,[37] find in the career of Orpheus that resonates with the lives of the 'Gentlemen Readers' he addresses? In his commentary on the poem, A. Leigh DeNeef writes, 'As he follows Orpheus through the narrative, R.B. re-enacts his protagonist's life: he re-creates Orpheus' original creations, he becomes Orpheus, and his poem becomes the Orpheus myth.'[38] There were, however, a number of different versions of the Orpheus legend, taking their cues from the three principal classical sources in Virgil's *Georgics*, Ovid's *Metamorphoses*, and Boethius's *Consolation of Philosophy*, as well as the many medieval renderings in the tradition of the *Ovide moralisé* and the Neoplatonic appropriations of the story. Thus, while DeNeef is undoubtedly correct to note the identification of the poet R.B. with the original poet Orpheus, it is nonetheless necessary to specify which Orpheus R.B. is attempting to become. The different versions of the Orpheus legend had, by the time R.B. came to write his poem, been used to tell any number of different stories, although for the Renaissance, it was most frequently a story of the power and civilizing force of rhetoric. What precisely are the dimensions of this particular Orpheus, and what might the portrait of the first poet and founder of civil society tell us about changing conceptions of the speaking subject and of political community in Elizabethan England?

R.B.'s *Orpheus His Journey to Hell* is in many ways a typical epyllion, and there is other circumstantial evidence which suggests that, like most other examples of the genre, it was written for an Inns of Court audience. It is often assumed that Barnfield attended Gray's Inn, although his name does not appear on the register. However, Andrew Worrall argues that like his father, Barnfield may have attended Barnard's Inn, one of the Inns of Chancery associated with Gray's.[39] In the title page's identification of the author as simply 'R.B. Gent' we can see a desire for relative anonymity (which signals the aristocratic disdain of publishing) colliding with an insistence on the rank of this anonymous author. This reflects what Prest calls the students' 'aggressive insistence on their own gentility,'[40] which is consistent with more general Elizabethan anxieties about status and social mobility. However, since the Inns of Court were at this time one of the prime sites of social advancement in the city where class boundaries were most fluid, these anxieties would no doubt be more pronounced. The preface's address 'To the Gentlemen Readers' (and the preface's repeated references to its audience as 'Gentlemen') as well as its printer suggest an Inns of Court audience. The printer of *Orpheus*, Richard Jones, who entered the poem in the Stationer's Register on 26 August 1595, had previously printed Thomas Lodge's *Scillaes Metamorphoses* (1589). Lodge is identified on the title page of that poem as 'Thomas Lodge of Lincolnes Inne, Gentleman' and he dedicates the poem 'To his Especiall good friend Master Rafe Crane, and the rest of his most entire well willers, the Gentlemen of the Innes of Court and Chauncerie.' Around the time that *Orpheus* appears, Jones also printed T[homas] H[eywood]'s *Oenone and Paris*, which was entered in the Stationer's Register on 17 May 1594; a neo-Latin poem, *Raptus Helenae*, was entered on 16 May 1595.

Jones seems to have marketed himself to the members of the Inns of Court and Chancery, perhaps taking advantage of the close proximity of his shop, which the title page notes is 'neere Holburne bridge, at the signe of the Rose and Crowne,' to the Inns. (Both Lincoln's Inn and Gray's Inn were in Holborne, and the latter was the most aristocratic and literary of the Inns of Court.) In 1597, for example, Jones printed 'The Arbor of amorous Deuises. Wherin, young Gentlemen may reade many plesant fancies, and fine deuises,' by N[icholas]. B[reton]., Gent.[41] Jones writes the preface to this volume, addressing it 'To the Gentlemen readers,' and alludes to a relation that either existed or that he wished to create by the mentioning of it: 'Right curteous Gentlemen, your absense, this long time of vacation hindered my poore Presse from publishing any pleasing Pamphlet, to recreate your minds, as it was wont: yet now, to give you notice that your old Printer forgetteth not his best friends, he hath thought it meet to remember his duetifull good wil he beareth to you all, publishing this pleasant *Arbor for Gentlemen*' (Breton, sig. A2). Jones continues in this vein at the end of the preface: 'such as are in the countrey, God send them a happy and speedy returne to *London*, to the pleasure of God, their harts content, and to the reioycing of all Cittizins, and specially to the comfort of all poore men of Trades.'[42] This sort of complaint about the economic effect of the Inns' vacations on the surrounding merchants of Westminster seems to have been common; in Thomas Dekker's 1608 dialogue *The Dead Tearme*, a personified Westminster complains to London that 'These Vacations are to mine owne body, like long and wasting consumptions.'[43]

R.B., in his prefatory address 'To the Gentlemen Readers,' mentions that the poem is 'The infant muse of an imboldened pen,' which fits the profile of the typical writer of this genre. As DeNeef shows, *Orpheus* is in some ways a poem about rhetoric itself, in its catalogue of various poetic and oratorical genres. 'R.B. consistently directs his reader's attention to a general theory of literary genres, ' writes DeNeef, and thus the poem itself is 'a narrative exploration of the powers such genres have to reflect, shape, alter, teach, and transform experience.'[44] For early modern literary theorists, Orpheus was the first poet and rhetorician, as well as the originator of all poetic genres. Moreover, his ability to persuade even rocks and trees with his song is a tribute to the power of rhetoric that could not fail to impress a humanistic culture that fetishized rhetoric as the civilizing force *par excellence*:

> It is the Renaissance humanists who bring Orpheus to his fullest development as prototype of the compellingly articulate man, the glorified orator or poet. It is the humanists who promote the idea of a primarily literary culture; who shift the emphasis in the trivium from logic to rhetoric; who make the formal oration the goal of education; who equate eloquence and civilization. And it is the humanists who quite naturally find in Orpheus a convenient culture-hero triumphantly symbolizing the goals of their rhetorical programme.[45]

For George Puttenham, as for others, the story of Orpheus was the story of civilization. In a chapter entitled 'How Poets were the first priests, the first prophets, the first Legislators and polititians in the world,' Puttenham argues that the story of Orpheus charming nature is an allegory showing 'how by his discreete and wholsome lessons uttered in harmonie and with melodious instruments, he brought the rude and savage people to a more civill and orderly life.'[46] In England, in the eyes of Sir Thomas Elyot at least, it was at the Inns of Court where one could witness a contemporary vision of this Orphic rhetorician. 'It is to be remembered that in the lernyng of the lawes of this realme, there is at this daye an exercise, wherin is a maner, a shadowe, or figure of the auncient rhetorike. I meane the pleadynge used in courte and Chauncery called motes [moots].'[47] This connection between the Inns of Court, where one learned the common law, and civilization is not merely accidental. As we noted in the introductory chapter, the common law tradition had, over the course of the century, become increasingly central to English self-definition. For English writers, then, Orpheus is not just a poet but also a lawyer, a legislator and a politician, and one who was trained, moreover, at the Inns of Court.

Orpheus is not only the symbolic originator of all poetry. It might also be argued, ahistorically, that Orpheus was more specifically the originator of the epyllion. In Ovid, Orpheus changes his song after returning from Hell, backsliding on the *gradus Virgilianus* from epic to something lighter: 'Often ere now I have told of Jove's power; in loftier strains I have sung of giants and those victorious thunderbolts which were hurled down upon the plain of Phlegra, but now I need a lighter refrain to tell of boys whom the gods have loved, and of girls who, seized with lawful passion, have paid the penalty for their amorous desires' (X. 228–9). What in effect Orpheus describes here is the typical amatory subject matter of the Elizabethan epyllion, and indeed, some of the stories he recounts – Venus and Adonis, Pygmalion, and Myrrha – are the narrative matter of the more famous examples of the genre. It is arguable, then, that the epyllion is one of the most Orphic of poetic genres, in spite of the fact that it postdates Orpheus considerably. This is, however, consistent with the poet's attempt to become Orpheus. The poet thus becomes belatedly the originator of the genre in which he writes.

R.B.'s poem uses many of the elements of the narrative as it is recounted in Ovid's *Metamorphoses*, although, like other epyllia, it embellishes the story greatly, using the narrative as an occasion to ostentatiously display poetic ability. DeNeef catalogues the many genres that R.B. either writes or alludes to over the course of the poem, a display which is appropriate given that for the humanists, Orpheus was the originator of all poetry. More importantly, however, this display also serves to showcase R.B.'s Orphic ability. In a culture that fetishized rhetoric, and at an institution that was the centre for its study, this kind of self-display or self-advertisement is to be expected.

Although Kenneth Gros Louis asserts that R.B. uses essentially the same story as Ovid,[48] there are, in fact, significant differences to be noted between the poem and its source. In this version, Orpheus charms the rocks and trees before he loses Eurydice (rather than after, as with Boethius) and before he descends into Hades (rather than after, as with Ovid and Virgil), rendering the journey and his loss of Eurydice rather more incidental to the acquisition of poetic ability than in other versions of the myth.[49] On returning, he does not institute pederasty among the Thracians, as both Ovid and his Elizabethan translator Arthur Golding have it. Instead, his songs against women draw to his company married men, and it is the wives of these men who kill him. After his death, the gods reward Orpheus with poetic immortality, but they do not reunite him with Eurydice in the afterworld.

In addition to these innovations, which will be discussed below, R.B. also adds a frame to the story, in the form of the address 'To the

Gentlemen Readers.' There, in the tradition of both the *Ovide moralisé* and Arthur Golding's 'Preface. Too the Reader,' R.B. offers something of an allegorical interpretation of the story. The readers are invited to accompany Orpheus and 'aduenture for a woman' down into 'Plutoes den' (3, 4). In the preface's summary of the story, Orpheus's backward look is not due to jealousy or desire (as in the poem itself), but suggests instead a peculiar self-involvement: 'with a retrograde aspect, / Orpheus reflected on the helles hee past' (13–14). This story, says the poem, is a 'president to Louers in their Loues pursuit, / Not to regard or grudge the paine that longs vnto it' (17–18). The conclusion drawn here seems a curious rewriting of the loss of Eurydice, who is lost here more because she fails to hold Orpheus's attention, than through an excessive claim on it. This sense is reinforced in the next stanza, which argues that the principal lesson of the narrative is 'To shew that Musicke can all hels remooue, / From out the mind, though neere so maine and manifold' (22–3). Here we seem less in the realm of *Ovide moralisé* than in that of Boethius's *Consolation of Philosophy*, in which the Orpheus story was about cultivating a detached attitude towards the world, and fixing one's atten-tion on God or the good.[50] Music, rather than philosophy, offers the consolation here, but given the quasi-religious nature of Orpheus's songs in Neoplatonist thought, this is perhaps an appropriate substitution.[51] Nonetheless, as a reading of the poem in question, the moral is clearly inadequate. In most readings of the poem Orpheus fails to find consola-tion, which failure leads invariably to his death.

The moral drawn by the preface makes sense only if we decide that the poem was never about the loss of Eurydice, or that the loss of Eurydice was only the pretext for the story of another metamorphosis. That is to say, rather than being lost, Eurydice may be expelled in favour of a different kind of community constructed within the poem. While Eurydice can hardly be removed from the story, Orpheus's grief at her loss is substantially undercut both by the changes the poet makes to the story and, as we shall see below, by the way Orpheus sings of his loss. Orpheus's rather equivocal relation to the loss of Eurydice is further underscored by the Thracian men's completely unequivocal abandoning of their wives, as they (like the gentlemen of the Inns) follow Orpheus's example without hesitation. The resultant community in the fields of Thrace is mirrored in the relation the poem attempts to establish with its reader-ship, especially here in the preface. The prefatory poem ends with another invitation to R.B.'s audience, 'Now read it (Gentlemen) if you please' (24), so that the narrative of Orpheus is enclosed within a circuit of male poet and male readers. This in itself is hardly unusual, but here it significantly corresponds to a pattern of pastoral male conversation that recurs through the poem. Like Orpheus in this poem, then, the poet gathers around him a coterie of male auditors.

The main body of the poem starts with an account of the golden age, the divine origins of Orpheus, and a comment on his ability to charm the forces of nature through song. His charmed life is interrupted by a Boethian-style Fortune, which 'oreturne[s] him' (9.6) through 'The pleasing poyson of self-killing Loue' which 'at last made entrance to his mayden-heart' (10.1–2). The play here on 'maiden-head' implies both Orpheus's youthfulness and the sexual ambiguity of youths in the world of the epyllion: Adonis, Narcissus, Leander, are all in their own epyllia described in feminine terms, and as objects, rather than subjects, of desire. Here the mention of 'self-killing Loue' (10.1) suggests the danger that desire poses to the male subject and the integrity of the self. Moreover, the love of Orpheus for Eurydice is characterized as immature and therefore doomed to failure:

> But as it is in things being soonest growne,
>> whose flowered blossoms euery blast decayes:
> And neuer stayes the Autumne to be mowne,
>> but floorishes and falles within few dayes:
> So is't in loue, which being quicklie sproong,
>> Dies oftentimes when as it is but yoong.

(11.1–7)

There is a strong implication here that, snake or not, the coupling was not destined to last. The poem's insistence on the immaturity of Orpheus and his love for Eurydice is again consistent with the narratives of maturation that recur throughout the genre, and the narrator's warning about immature love more specifically echoes Adonis's protest to Venus regarding his 'unripe years': 'The mellow plum doth fall, the green sticks fast, / Or being early pluck'd, is sour to taste' (Shakespeare, 524, 527–8). In a genre that was written for the amusement of young men, and in a culture that saw one of the main purposes of literature as didactic, these admonitory narratives, while light-hearted, are perhaps not as innocent as they seem. That the stories of becoming a rhetorician (and thus a lawyer, legislator, humanist) are overlaid onto stories of erotic transformations suggests that the poems are involved in policing or renegotiating the boundaries of desire within their culture.

There is a further explanation for the poet's insistence on the immaturity of the love of Orpheus and Eurydice. Laurens J. Mills shows that Renaissance friendship literature frequently opposed friendship and courtly love. One of the typical distinctions made (since at least Cicero's *De Amicitia*) is that friendship develops over a long period of time, whereas heterosexual love grows and fades rapidly, a distinction we have already seen in Pettie's rewriting of the Cephalus and Procris story. On the title page of Robert Greene's extremely popular *Ciceronius Amor, or Tullies Love* (1587), this opposition is established in terms strikingly similar to R.B.'s characterization of Orpheus and Eurydice's love: 'young Gentlemen that ayme at honour should leuell the end of their affections, holding the loue of countrie and friends in more esteeme than those fading blossomes of beauty that onely feede the curious suruey of the eye.'[52] Given the poem's repeated use of male friendship literature conventions, it is likely that this particular convention is at least partly responsible for the narrator's unusual interjection at this point.

After the introductory stanzas, Orpheus and Eurydice meet, fall in love, and are married. The day of the marriage is rendered over eight stanzas, giving the poem some opportunity to range on themes more usual in the epyllion: desire and the anticipation of its consummation. The subsequent loss of Eurydice to a snake bite occasions some grief and substantial amounts of song, as in Boethius's version of the myth. It is remarkable how legalistic Orpheus manages to be in his sorrow, protesting to the gods the 'vniust diuorcing' (26.6) and 'injurious rape' (27.4) of Eurydice, and offering precedents in support of his argument that she be returned to him. His singing draws a diverse crowd of 'beasts and birds, fish, foule, and other thinges' (24.4), the same sort of audience that we have seen earlier in the golden age section of the poem (stanzas 7–8). This staging of rhetoric will be repeated several times, although for the most part with groups of men as Orpheus's auditors. The next scene of rhetoric is a group of 'sillie ghostes' on the 'Stygian bankes' (35.6, 5), to whom Orpheus relates his woes: 'Thus (quoth he) for my Loue have I forsooke / the *Thracian* fieldes and company of men' (37.1–2). His song finished, he persuades Charon to let him cross, and, once over, he must charm the porter of the gates of hell, and the Furies. This he does through a song which once again recounts his woes.

Orpheus's song to the Furies is remarkable for its interpretation of Eurydice's death:

Vnconstant Lasse to him that lou'd thee well,
   made thee Commander of his liues estate:
To leaue him so, and choose the Prince of Hell,
   and thus reward his loue with thankles hate.
Thy folly makes me now with sorrow sing,
The effect of Loue to be a fickle thing.

(54.1–7)

This is a moment which demonstrates Gros Louis's claim that the poem 'illustrates how completely Orpheus has been adapted to popular Elizabethan poetic and dramatic themes,'[53] in this case, themes which are almost entirely inappropriate to the narrative. They do, nonetheless, coincide with other narratives in the genre, particularly those concerning rape; in particular, reinterpreting the ravishment as desertion is consistent with anxieties addressed by the law in its attempts to guard against the rape victim's consent after the fact, anxieties which were exacerbated by the possibility of consenting against one's will. Although reading Eurydice's death by snake bite as a wilful abandonment of Orpheus, and thus as yet another example of women's fickleness, is something of a stretch, it is congruent with Orpheus's later songs. The casual rewriting of Eurydice's 'vniust diuorcing' (26.6) as an unjust divorce is consistent with Orpheus's and the poem's lack of interest in Eurydice or her sufferings. Eurydice becomes, as do Lucrece and Helen in their narratives, the occasion for speech and the foundation of male political communities.[54]

Orpheus's next song in hell stills the torture of various mythical figures, including Tantalus, Prometheus, and Sisyphus. This scenario is a feature of all three main versions of the story; what is original here is the colloquy that ensues. The ghosts of hell

followed *Orpheus* to the Cypres trees,
   vnder whose shades the wearie Souldiours rest:
Who sorting there themselues in companies,
   with euerlasting quietnes are blest.
And in their conference there again reuiue
Th'exploytes they did, when as they were aliue.

(68.1–6)

This scene of conversation under the cypress trees is very clearly pastoral, as 'gins the Poet once againe relate / the waightie cause that drew him to that place' (70.1–2). The song that follows is an example of judicial rhetoric. As DeNeef notes, Orpheus's songs 'invoke all three of the rhetorical types' of speeches, epidiectic, judicial, and deliberative.[55] In this case, the oration argues that because the men have similarly been tried by 'Loues hard euent, / and the vnconstant kind of womens sect' (71.1–2), they should aid him in his attempt to win back Eurydice. Here we see that the poem's presentation of Eurydice is partly the heritage of homosocial traditions of pastoral, which the poem repeatedly invokes.[56] The rhetoric is successful, and 'towards *Pluto* all of them doe goe' (76.5).

Once again, Eurydice's death has been interpreted as an example of the fickleness of women and once again, like Lucrece, her death provides the occasion for the formation of a male community. But although the setting of this particular scene is pastoral, the heritage of Orpheus's audience is of a different genre:

> There was old *Priam* and his fiftie sonnes,
>   that for their countries honour were supprest:
> The Greeks, whose name in euery Poem runs,
>   there spend their quiet dayes in peace and rest.
> And he whose loue did win the *Carthage* Queene,
> Venterous *Aeneas* rest vpon that greene.
>
> (69.1–6)

Orpheus's journey here takes on epic significance, by putting him in the company of the epic heroes of the *Iliad* and the *Aeneid*. Epics are, of course, foundational narratives, and the community established here proleptically signals the community that Orpheus will found at the end of his own epic journey. The modulation between the pastoral and epic at the same time signals a movement from the private realm of emotion to the public sphere. This is a transition that both Orpheus and the poem make in moving from Eurydice to the men of Thrace and a social community based on affectionate bonds between men.

After persuading Pluto, and then gaining and losing Eurydice, Orpheus returns to Thrace. Boethius and Virgil both say that Orpheus avoids the company of women. Ovid says that as a result of his loss, 'Orpheus preferred to centre his affections on boys of tender years, and to enjoy the brief spring and early flowering of their youth: he was the first to introduce this custom among the people of Thrace' (227). Arthur Golding elaborates on this:

Orphye (were it that his ill successe hee still did rew,
Or that he vowed so too doo) did utterly eschew
The womankynd. Yit many a one desyrous were too match
With him, but he them with repulse did all alike dispatch.
He also taught the *Thracian* folke a stewes of Males too make
And of the flowring pryme of boayes the pleasure for too take.

(X. 87–92)

Golding's innovations make a clear moral point about pederasty: by
mentioning the 'stewes' or brothels, he removes the pederasty from its
pastoral context and places it in an urban one. In R.B.'s version, after
Orpheus returns he begins to sing 'inuectiue Ditties' about 'vnconstant
Loue' and the 'manie woes a womans beautie bringes' (110.1–3). Echoing his songs in hell on Eurydice's unfaithfulness, he sets himself up as
an 'instance' of 'One that had suffred all this pleasing woe' (111.5–6).
Orpheus's invective becomes an irresistible lure to married men:

[Orpheus's] songes did sort vnto such deepe effect,
    as draw mens fancies from thir former wiues:
Womens vaine loue beginning to neglect,
    and in the fieldes with *Orpheus* spend their liues:
With which sweet life they seem'd so well content,
    As made them curse the former time they spent.

(112.1–6)

It might be noted that the Inns of Court were, like R.B.'s Thracian fields,
an all-male space and a place of homosocial refuge: 'it was said that one
Ulveston got himself made steward of the Middle Temple in 1451, and
one Isley steward of the Inner Temple, "for excuse for dwelling this time
from their wives."'[57] Peter Goodrich discusses at length the '"homosociality" of eating rites' at the Inns as well as the Inns' structuring of a
communal identity around attendance at the Inns' commons: 'All the
ceremonies of investiture or inception into the various ranks of the
profession take place via the commons and so, too, all rituals of collective membership of the community of the Law, feasts, banquets, revels
and games, are held in commons.'[58] Orpheus's pastoral coterie of dis-
gruntled husbands resembles to some degree Duke Senior's band of
merry men in *As You Like It*, as well as scenes of male conviviality in
Milton's pastoral verse.[59] The rejection of the wives by the men of Thrace

follows or rewrites Orpheus's loss of Eurydice and subsequent rejection of all women. By moving away from the pederastic version of Ovid and Golding, R.B. rewrites Orpheus's relations with men according to the terms of Renaissance male friendship. R.B. thus brings Orpheus's homoeroticism back into the realm of the licit and indeed, the socially validated, a move that Kenneth Borris, in a felicitous phrase, calls R.B.'s 'homosocial engineering.'[60]

The homosocial dimensions of pastoral have been frequently commented upon, as has the political nature of pastoral, although the connection between these two has generally gone unnoticed. Louis Adrian Montrose has identified 'a dialectic between Elizabethan *pastoral forms* and Elizabethan *social categories*. Elizabethan pastoral forms may have worked to mediate differential relationships of power, prestige, and wealth in a variety of social situations.'[61] The principal distinction that pastoral both depends upon and effaces is that distinction between gentleman and non-gentleman, or between those who work and those who do not. The 'sweet life' of Orpheus's followers suggests that they fall into the category of those who do not work, and are therefore gentlemen. If as Montrose argues, pastoral verse is often used to mediate social categories, in this instance the pastoral is being used as a space to negotiate new social roles and new political relations. In particular, the homosocial gatherings in the fields of Thrace, where the first orator and legislator gathers about him companies of men, mirror the homosocial world of the Inns of Court, where the changing dimensions of political subjectivity were most keenly felt. The crucial change that R.B. makes in the narrative at this point, from youths to married men, means that the gathering is essentially among social equals, a form of sociality increasingly being theorized in England. Moreover, in the House of Commons's increasingly bold infringements on Elizabeth's prerogative in the latter part of the reign, as well as in the members' assertions of their autonomy and free speech, we can see, argues Wallace MacCaffrey, a growing sense of the importance of an egalitarian body in the affairs of the state.[62]

In R.B.'s version of the tale, it is the abandoned wives of the Thracian men who are incensed about Orpheus, rather than women who have been spurned by him in favour of beautiful youths. Unlike the hot-headed Bacchantes of the *Metamorphoses*, these women are unusually rational, at least when deciding on what course of action to take in the face of their defecting husbands:

They gin deuise how best they might relieue,
   their fading glorie being almost worne.
Which by no meanes they hope for to atchieue,
As long as *Orpheus* doth remaine aliue.

Which to preuent in solemne wise they cite,
their companie together all in one:
Where euerie busie head will needs indite,
a meanes how they might get poore *Orpheus* gone,
Mongst whome at length the case was thus deriued,
That *Orpheus* of his life should be depriued.

(113.3–6; 114.1–6)

The congregation of the Ciconian women sounds rather like a meeting of a debating society in a law school, putting forth a series of resolutions. This is reflective of a general tendency in the epyllion for characters to offer up lengthy legalistic disquisitions, usually in support of their own desire, and is reflective as well of the genre's usual audience of lawyers and law students. The women's apparent rationality is perhaps linked to the fact that they are now, in some sense, the defenders of civilization, rather than the forces of irrationality, if the commonly made link between rhetoric, rationality, and civilization is remembered. Before God gave man rhetoric, states Thomas Wilson in *The Arte of Rhetorike*, 'None remembered the true observation of wedlocke, none tendered the educations of their chyldren, lawes were not regarded, true dealinge was not once used.'[63] By defending marriage, the women are defending civilization, laws, contracts, rhetoric. The justice of their execution of Orpheus seems to be reluctantly recognized in the poem by the gods:

     though heauens frowne,
       yet they [i.e., the women] defend their quarrell to be good,
And for their massacre this reason render,
He was an enemie vnto their gender.

(116.3–6)

Whether or not the gods approve (they frown but do not intervene), the women at least argue the legality of their actions, in what is a strict departure from the legend. Rendering reasons has never been part of Bacchic culture. If the women are read as defenders of civilization, the ending may show, as DeNeef argues, the price of the misuse of rhetoric. This, again, would find resonance with a London audience; copies of satires, Marston's *Metamorphosis of Pigmalions Image*, and Marlowe's translations of Ovid would all be burned in London a few years after the writing of *Orpheus His Journey*. The Ciconian women, like the officials of London, are merely policing the boundaries of acceptable speech.

The wives' actions also throw into relief the sodomitical nature of Orpheus's community. The punishment that they settle on, execution, is in line with the Elizabethan legal system. To say that this city of the plains is sodomitical is not necessarily to identify any sexual activity among its inhabitants. As a number of critics have argued, it is the disturbance of marriage, and not any particular activity, that becomes identifiable as sodomitical and antisocial. Bray has shown that the signs of male friendship are by and large the same as those of sodomy, which means that there is always a possibility that the exalted relation can be identified or misidentified as the abhorred one. It is this dangerous ambivalence that the poem seems to be highlighting at this point. The wives are, after all, only apparently rational. They can muster apparently legal arguments, but their actions are described as nonrational, and hence, antisocial in themselves. This might be taken as a commentary on the accusations of sodomy that misunderstand (in the poem's terms) the relation they are seeing. If R.B. is in fact Richard Barnfield, this could be taken as an indignant if oblique commentary on the hostile (and in the poem's terms, irrational and uncivil) reception to his earlier, more explicitly homoerotic work.

Since Orpheus is ultimately immortalized by the gods, it may be that they are not so concerned with the misuse of rhetoric, or the maintenance of heterosexual bonds as DeNeef thinks. The 'faire heauens,'

> pittying his end that so had spent his dayes:
> In justice thus his merits do reward,
>   vnto their euer memorable praise.
> Thus they determin'd all with one consent,
> For to draw vp his heauenlie Instrument.

(118.2–6)

Orpheus's end is a triumph, and he gains immortality in 'the euerliuing registrie of fame' (119.2). There is no apparent condemnation of his satire and no indication that his anti-feminine invective is not in fact one of the merits for which he is being rewarded. Indeed, the poem itself may be satirizing the women, and their attempts at rhetoric. That the women are themselves misusing rhetoric is signaled by the distance between the apparently calm deliberations of the women and their frenzied murder of Orpheus; the poem uses this distance for comic effect. This satire of women's rhetoric would find precedent in Venus's lengthy arguments in Shakespeare's poem, which even the naive Adonis can see through: 'What have you urg'd that I cannot reprove?' (787), he priggishly objects. Satire and the epyllion were at times closely related genres, argues William Keach: 'both types of poetry spring from the same immediate literary background, from sophisticated writers with University backgrounds ... and with close ties either to one of the Inns of Court or to a literary coterie like that of Southampton.'[64] Both were interested in contemporary sexual mores, although from different perspectives owing to their differing origins in Ovid and Juvenal. Many of the epyllia were in fact satiric to some degree, from Marston's hard-edged *Metamorphosis of Pigmalions Image* to Marlowe's more genial *Hero and Leander*. The epyllion generally affected a tone of worldly wise licentiousness, satirizing older Petrarchan pruderies, whereas satire excoriated any examples of licentiousness it could find. In spite of these obvious divergences, it could be argued that both are involved in a project of redefining normative sexuality for their culture. Focusing strictly on sexuality, however, narrows the scope of *Orpheus*'s intervention into its cultural milieu. Its interest in a particular version of homosociality corresponds to a mode of political subjectivity that was emerging in England, a form of sociality that was modeled to some degree on Renaissance male friendship.

Orpheus and Citizenship

The poem's interest in friendship and pastoral male conversation reflects the all-male educational setting in which these poems generally circulated. For Francis Bacon, one of the most prominent of the Inns of Court writers, the Orpheus legend was really the story of philosophy, and of the two principal kinds of philosophy. Orpheus charming the dead allegorizes natural philosophy, which aspired to such feats, whereas Orpheus charming the rocks and beasts allegorizes civil and moral philosophy. It is in discussing the latter that Bacon alludes to Orpheus's life after Eurydice: 'it is wisely added in the story that Orpheus was averse from women and from marriage; for the sweets of marriage and the dearness of children commonly draw men away from performing great and lofty services to the commonwealth; being content to be perpetuated in their race and stock and not in their deeds.'[65] (It might be noted that Bacon was later accused by Simonds D'Ewes of following Orpheus's example too closely: D'Ewes writes of that 'unnatural crime which he had practised many years; deserting the bed of his lady, which he accounted as the italians and turks do.')[66] Bacon is speaking of precisely the sort of career that the Inns of Court were preparing their students for, 'great and lofty services to the commonwealth,' rather than a retired life of philosophical contemplation. Even more so than in R.B.'s version, Bacon's Orpheus is blameless, and his death here is wholly unjustified. For Bacon, Orpheus's destruction shows how civilization may succumb to barbarism, and philosophy consequently be lost. Bacon neglects to gloss the part of the story that mentions Orpheus's institution of pederasty, which would perhaps not have been so easy to moralize; as Alan Stewart, Leonard Barkan, and other writers have shown, pederasty and humanism became in the early modern imagination suspiciously intertwined.[67]

Bacon's glossing of the Orpheus legend should be read in relation to his essay 'On Friendship,' which perhaps provides the theory for the practice in R.B.'s Thracian fields. In that essay, written at the Inns of Court, Bacon says, 'A principal fruit of friendship is the ease and discharge of the fulness and swellings of the heart, which passions of all kinds do cause and induce.' He concludes that if a man 'have not a friend, he may quit the stage.'[68] The stage in question seems again to be the public one, since the essay considers at length the cases of those in positions of high authority: kings, generals, caesars. Friends, who must be equals (hence the problem for princes), can be perfectly honest with each other: the relation is remarkable for the homogeneity or equality that cannot be found in any other relation. 'A man cannot speak to his son but as a father; to his wife but as a husband; to his enemy but upon terms: whereas a friend may speak as the case requires, and not as it sorteth with the person.'[69] Here we can see part of the reason why it is specifically wives that are rejected in *Orpheus*. The relation between man and wife, like that between philosopher and pupil, is structurally unequal, and cannot provide the kind of mirroring function that is necessary for the development of this particular subjectivity. A friend, says Bacon, following the traditions of writing on male friendship, is both 'another himself' and 'far more than himself':

Men have their time, and die many times in desire of some things which they principally take to heart; the bestowing of a child, the finishing of a work, or the like. If a man have a true friend, he may rest almost secure that the care of those things will continue after him. So that a man hath as it were two lives in his desires. A man hath a body, and that body is confined to a place; but where friendship is, all offices of life are as it were granted to him and his deputy.[70]

The relation between a man and his friend is thus like Narcissus's dream realized, but with the crucial difference that this relation is played out at least partially in the public sphere: it is as much a political relation as an erotic one. Jeffrey Masten argues that 'the sanctioned homoeroticism of male friendship ... is not only sanctioned but also *constitutive* of power relations in the period ... it figures importantly in the construction and reproduction of the entitled English gentleman.'[71] There had always been a political dimension to the friendship tradition, in the assertion that friendships could not or would not flourish in political tyrannies. Jacques Derrida, however, identifies a key contradiction in this political dimension: 'on the one hand, friendship seems to be essentially foreign or unamenable to the *res publica* and thus could not found a politics. But, on the other hand, as one knows, from Plato to Montaigne, from Aristotle to Kant, from Cicero to Hegel, the great philosophical and canonical discourses on friendship ... will have linked friendship explicitly to virtue and justice, to moral reason and to political reason.'[72] Because of the utopian, narcissistic dimension of much of the tradition of writing on male friendship, the relation tends to figure more as the matrix or precondition for its political realization rather than its foundation. In Bacon, however, the friendship itself becomes an avenue to political action.

We can see both in Bacon's glossing of the Orpheus legend and in his discussion of friendship elements of Platonic pederasty being rewritten.[73] Both dream of an immortality achieved through means other than biological reproduction. In the former Bacon echoes Plato's description of immortal ideas born through the intercourse of philosopher and pupil, although, like R.B., he drops any mention of pederasty. In the latter, we see a modified version of this Platonic reproduction, only now between equals rather than with the structural inequality of the pederastic contract (or indeed, the marriage contract). In his study of the collaboration of Beaumont and Fletcher, Jeffrey Masten notes the common tendency in male friendship texts to differentiate friendship from Platonic pederasty, a differentiation that has occurred in R.B.'s rewriting of the myth.

In discussions of both Platonic pederasty and Renaissance male friend-ship, the model for male relations is generally put forward as the founda-tion of sociality, the highest possible human relation. What precisely are the implications of this negotiated shift from a relation based on in-equality to one based on equality? We may want to recall at this point Lacan's insistence on the role of narcissism in the formation of the ego: the famous mirror stage is a story of narcissism, as the infant moves from a sense of a body in fragments, to a visually available sense of bodily coherence. We can see in Bacon's discussion that the friend works precisely in this way, providing a mirror of the self. A relation that was structurally unequal would compromise this mirror function, but more crucially, it would also compromise the borders of the self, as the part-ners in the pederastic couple play more or less fixed roles of subject and object of desire. In the narcissistic ideal of Renaissance male friendship, no such distinction is possible. To what extent is this rewriting of male sociality a necessary part of the development of the Cartesian or even the Hobbesian self? Must democratic culture itself have a mirror stage, in this case in the form of male friendship, before moving on to theorizing an egoistic self-sufficiency?

It could be objected that the Orpheus story is in fact the very opposite of the mirror stage. After his return to Thrace, Orpheus becomes narcis-sistically self-absorbed, for which reason he winds up as the Lacanian body-in-pieces. In fact, however, the continuation of the story traces out the reverse: from the body-in-pieces, Orpheus becomes immortalized, the disembodied singer, the legendary orator. Orpheus achieves the Renaissance goal of literary immortality, which R.B. then takes upon himself, in yet another act of self-creation that is achieved through mirroring. In Ovid, Orpheus is re-united with Eurydice in the Elysian fields, but for reasons which are perhaps clear by now, R.B. chooses not to incorporate that part of the story into his poem. Eurydice is more rejected than lost in this poem, and her rejection is necessary both for the formation of a community of male equals, and for the autonomous speaking subject that can be constructed through that community. Through the action of the poem, Orpheus becomes the immortal orator, the very image for the Renaissance of the rhetorician, which for the humanists is the noblest and most honourable form of political and cultural being.

The rejection of Platonic pederasty in favour of male friendship may then have less to do with erotic scenarios than with political enfranchise-ment. The image of the male couple (who were, it should be remem-

bered, presumed to be gentlemen) provides both the model of citizenship and, in Bacon's essay, the technology for its production. That this
discussion should surface at the Inns of Court, or in genres associated
with the Inns of Court, is not to be wondered at. As one of the prime sites
of social advancement in Renaissance England, the school where virtually every gentleman spent at least some of his educational career, the
Inns would naturally be the site of debate about the nature of political
subjectivity and the social contract. It was also, to a greater extent than
the universities, a site of social mobility, a phenomenon which contrib-
uted to the obsolescence of the status categories in England.

More immediately, however, the Inns would have been the site where
the ongoing changes in English law would have been debated, and their
shifts most keenly observed. As we have noted in an earlier chapter, one
of the ongoing developments in law that had begun in the Middle Ages
was the gradual erosion of status categories in law, and the emergence of
the 'normal person' – the 'free and lawful man of English society,' whose
rights are essentially the same as those of anyone else. William Holdsworth
argues that the emergence of this normal person is largely due to the
'growing supremacy of the common law,' at the centre of which movement were the Inns of Court.[74] The development of the concept of the
normal person in law is clearly an important cultural shift, one which
contributes to the emergence of what has been called the individual,
whose rights are also essentially the same as those of anyone else. The
individual and the friend and the normal person are all related in that
they are not (at least in theory) bound up in relations of submission and
domination, but are rather predicated upon a relation of equality. This
can also be related to the increasing importance of the contract, which
also presupposes a certain equality, as well as a subject free to contract
for itself at present and in the future: a subject, in other words, that owns
itself.[75]

In 'New English Sodom,' Michael Warner traces out a similar conjunction of forces in seventeenth-century New England. Warner argues that
in re-imagining social relations, Puritan leaders drew upon such discourses as male friendship and contract theory. John Winthrop, for
example, in his *Arbella* sermon, makes 'the theoretical claim that affectionate male-male bonds can sustain a disciplined public body.'[76] The
model of sociality provided by male friendship worked well within Covenant theology, the basis of Puritan political theory, especially when
combined with the erotics of Christian charity: 'implicitly male contractual relations – for that is what covenant theology was modeled on – were

becoming paradigmatic of God's own behavior. At least in part, mutuality and interest were becoming the principles of the social bond, not hierarchy and divine command.'[77] Like the relations traced out in Orpheus, then, Puritan society was informed by, and in some sense founded upon, erotic bonds between male social equals.

R.B.'s poem apparently participates in negotiating an earlier shift in political subjectivity, through its rewriting of the Orpheus legend. What is the true metamorphosis in the poem then? Through its rejection of Eurydice and its emphasis on pastoral male conversation, the poem employs the pastoral mode in a very particular way. The rewriting of an erotic scenario becomes at the same time the rewriting of a political one, much as we see in Beaumont's poem, where Jove's desire for erotic mutuality leads to a vision of a universe ruled by the contract. Like Sidney or Milton, R.B. uses the pastoral as a space in which to renegotiate models of political being, in this case, a political subject relatively free of the relations of submission and domination inscribed in the status categories. This subject, which is increasingly being theorized by the common law, will figure in Hobbes's theory of sovereignty, as well as, on a more practical level, the political projects of many Civil War groups. For Bacon at least, Orpheus as poet is secondary to Orpheus as rhetorician, lawyer, politician, legislator. The narrative of the birth of the poet becomes the narrative of the birth of the early modern individual. What the poem demonstrates, however, is the particular homosocial matrix and the homoerotic circuit of desire that subtends this subjectivity. For both Bacon and R.B., the highest form of political and social being can only be produced through an erotic bond between gentlemen.

CHAPTER SIX

'Riot, revelling and rapes': Sexual Violence and the Nation

The previous chapter looked at the connection between erotic scenarios and political subjectivities. In this chapter I will widen the focus by considering sexual violence and sexual perversity in the epyllion; in particular, I will look at the ways in which the 'headdie ryots, incest, rapes' (*Hero and Leander*, 144) of the genre function in the creation of male communities and the subjectivities that correspond to these communities. One particular concern will be rape, which is often figured as the sexual equivalent of tyranny. Classical tyrants are frequently associated with rape, and both rape and tyranny can be read as violations of the bonds between men, especially male equals. In the literature of male friendship, tyranny often serves as the paradoxical precondition or matrix out of which male friendship arises and against which it inevitably struggles. In a parallel fashion, rape in classical literature, especially epic literature, often marks a foundational moment, particularly for a state that defines itself against tyranny. Bearing in mind the different aims of the two genres – the epic and the epyllion – this chapter will explore the ways in which rape functions as a foundational moment or marker in developmental narratives of male subjectivity.

The approach of this chapter, looking at the effect of rape on men rather than women, may itself seem perverse. To the early modern mindset, it would have seemed less so, if the legal system is any indication. As we noted in the introductory chapter, while the laws were increasingly considering rape as a crime against the person, it was nonetheless still a property crime against the woman's family. Norman Bryson argues that prior to the nineteenth century, rape and other sexual crimes had not yet been fully interiorized and thus were still implicated in a number of discourses that looked beyond the individual. This is not to say, of course, that victims of rape did not experience their violation fully, but rather to point out that we cannot assume that the experience of the body is historically invariable or transparent to our modern eyes. As Garthine Walker argues, 'To interpret the narrative framework of early modern accounts of rape as if the experience is self-evidently similar to our own serves, unhelpfully, to reproduce rape as a natural- ised, ahistorical category.'[1] We should also remember that epyllia, like myth or the law, are concerned with generalized subjects rather than particular ones. It is the cultural meaning of rape and the uses to which rape as a metaphor is put, then, that concern the genre, rather than the phenomenon of rape itself.

The changes in the rape laws in the sixteenth century testify both to a shift in the meaning of rape, and to a more general redefinition of the body and its relation to the self. They also testify, as we shall see below, to ongoing anxieties in the period about women and property, which were exacerbated by Henry VIII's Statutes of Uses and Wills. These questions surface most obviously in the question of consent, a key factor in deter- mining whether rape had taken place. But consent, like the body itself, is not an ahistorical phenomenon. The poems that we shall look at in this chapter, William Barksted's *Mirrha the Mother of Adonis*, Thomas Heywood's *Oenone and Paris*, Shakespeare's *The Rape of Lucrece*, and Barksted's *Hiren, the Faire Greeke*, all hinge to some degree upon the problematic question of the woman's consent. At the same time, rape in these poems brings with it questions beyond the self, allowing the poets to look at the emergence of a particular version of political subjectivity, one which allows the subject to manage contradiction in the self in order to act in the world. This will allow us see the connection between the changing rape laws and, for example, England's complicated relations with the Turkish empire in Barksted's poem *Hiren*. We start, however, with a poem that deals not with rape but rather with incest.

Mirrha the Mother of Adonis: Or, Lustes Prodegies

As with many stories retold in the epyllion, that of Myrrha[2] carries with it whole traditions of interpretation, and Myrrha herself comes to signify such divergent possibilities as evil, in Dante's *Inferno*, and the Virgin Mary, in the *Ovide moralisé*.[3] (This latter interpretation is most surprising when we remember that this is a tale of incest, initiated by the daughter.) William Barksted's *Mirrha the Mother of Adonis: Or, Lustes Prodegies* (1607) follows in more than one sense Marston's *Metamorphosis of Pigmalions*

Image. In Ovid, the two stories are part of a linked series of tales in Book X sung by Orpheus after the rape of Eurydice, boys whom the gods have loved, and … girls who, seized with unlawful passion, have paid the penalty for their amorous desires' (229). In this group are the stories of Ganymede, Hyacinthus, Pygmalion, Myrrha, and Adonis. These last three stories are genealogically linked: Cyniras, Myrrha's father, is the grandson of Pygmalion and his transformed statue; Adonis is the product of the incestuous union between Cyniras and Myrrha. In addition to following from Marston's storyline, Barksted to some degree emulates his tone as well. While he lacks Marston's crisp lasciviousness, he is certainly not averse to reproducing some of Marston's salacious moments of scopophilia. Particularly memorable is Mirrha's suicide scene, which Barksted renders in mildly pornographic terms. As with a number of epyllia, and Marston's in particular, there is a critique of Petrarchan verse. Whereas in Marston, Petrarchism is disdained as the stuff of youths, here it is condemned more as a hypocritical discourse of seduction. What is particularly interesting in this poem is the way in which this critique is bound up with a tale of incest. The ban on incest is the most ubiquitous of societal laws, and thus myths of incest must to some degree engage with or expose the fault lines of a particular culture.

Barksted's poem reflects its story's placement in Ovid by starting with Cupid's journey to Thrace to hear Orpheus singing. As with any mention of Orpheus in the genre, the opening stanzas here seem to be making a point about the role of rhetoric:

Tis saide when *Orpheus* dyed, he did descend
    To the infernall, so the *Furies* boast:
Where now they giue him leaue his eies to bend,
    without all feare, on her whome he once lost,
By a regardant looke, but tis not so:
Ioue not reseru'd such musicke for belowe,
    But placed him amongst celestiall stars,
    To keep the Scorpion, Lyon, Beare from Iars.

(3.1–8)

Rather than looking on Eurydice in the underworld (and the poem places an emphasis on looking rather than speaking), Orpheus is rescued by Jove to occupy a position in the heavens. The proper place of rhetoric, the poem seems to be arguing, is not the private sphere of emotion, but rather the public sphere of masculine activity. Rhetoric's role is to keep the peace, in this case on a universal, or at least celestial, scale. Although Orpheus is separated from Eurydice, he nonetheless sings of her loss, and a crowd of figures from the *Metamorphoses* are struck by his song: Daphne mourns 'Apollo's wrong'; Hermaphrodite weeps for himself and Salmacis; Clitie grieves Leucothoes's wrong; Cicnus (Cygnus) mourns for Phaeton. Orpheus becomes a stand-in here for Ovid as well as for the author, who has begun the poem with the line, 'I Sing the ruine of a beautious Maide' (1.1). Loss in the private sphere can be converted to success in the public, and indeed, such loss is often the enabling condition for masculine reproduction, as the narrator demonstrates in the opening stanza: 'Great is my quill, to bring foorth such a birth, / as shall abash the Virgins of our earth' (1.5–6). The ruin of maids is for Ovid, Orpheus, and the narrator the fertile occasion for public rhetorical performance.

The song of Orpheus sets the context for Cupid's wooing of Mirrha, who has come, 'Amongst the rest of Vesta-vowed Girles' (8.1) to hear Orpheus sing. 'A bright diamond circled with pearls' (8.3), Mirrha's beauty is such that it 'made Love, love' (8.6); Cupid removes his wings and turns Petrarchan:

> Giue eare eternall wonder to a swaine,
>> Twas writ in starres that I should see that face:
> And seeing loue, and in that loue be slaine,
>> if beautie pittie not my wretched case.
> Fortune and loue, the starres and powers diuine,
> Haue all betraide me to those eyes of thine.
>> O proue not then more crueller the[n] they,
>> Loues shaftes & fates wheeles, who hath power to stay.

(16.1–8)

Mirrha rejects Cupid's rhetoric, reminding him she is dedicated to Vesta:

> Leaue gentle youth, do not thus snare a maid
> I came to *Orpheus* Song, good then forbeare,
> It is his tune, not yours can charme mine eare.

(12.6–8)

Orpheus's rhetoric and Cupid's are thus explicitly opposed in the poem. This opposition echoes and reinforces the earlier one between Orpheus languishing in his own private hell and Orpheus providing a socially useful function in the heavens with his songs of loss. We might note here that this long opening section, roughly one quarter of the poem, is largely an invention of Barksted's and so we can assume that this set of oppositions will provide the structuring principle of the tale.

Another quite crucial innovation in the opening section occurs when Cupid and Mirrha part. He begs a kiss, which 'did inspire, / her brest with an infernall and vnnam'd desire' (24.7–8). In Ovid, Cupid denies that he caused Myrrha's incestuous desires: 'Cupid denies that it was his bow which wounded Myrrha, and defends his torches against so grievous a charge. One of the three sisters, armed with firebrands from the Styx and swollen snakes, breathed a blight upon her' (233). Later in the poem Barksted picks up on this, but modifies it to some degree: 'shall I say *Cupid* with his brand did fire thee? / Accuse the Fates or thee shall I accuse?' (27.4–5). Barksted's equivocations here – is it Cupid, Fate, or Mirrha that is responsible? – are partially resolved at the end of the stanza: 'wise destinie, true loue, and mortall thought, / would nere confirme this, this the furies brought' (27.7–8). This agrees with Ovid, but because it is so circuitously phrased and because this action is not narrated in the poem, ultimately we fall back on the conclusion to the Petrarchan dialogue that opens the poem; Cupid's kiss, tainted with its Petrarchan discourse, stands in as the infectious cause of Mirrha's 'infernall and vnnam'd desire' (24.8). Venus at the end of the poem concurs with this saying that it was 'the spight / which from my accurst Sons bow did fowly light' (111.5–6) that caused all of the commotion.

Cupid's transformation from Ovidian deity to Petrarchan swain is paralleled by another interpolated incident late in the poem. After Mirrha flees Cyniras's incestuous embrace, she comes upon a satyr named Poplar. Like Cupid, Poplar is physically transformed by Mirrha's beauty – 'so fell his rudenesse from him, and her shine, / Made all his earthie parts pure and diuine' (75.5–6) – and like him he is metamorphosed into a Petrarchan poet:

Thus he begins, fairer then Venus farre,
    If Venus be, or if she be tis thee:
Louelie as Lillies, brighter then the starre,
    that is to earth the mornings Mercurie:
Softer then Roses, sweeter breath'd then they,
blusht boue Aurora, better cloath'd then May
    lipt like a cherrie, but of rarer taste,
    Deuine as Dian, and as fully chaste.

                                                            (76.1–8)

Poplar's rhetoric is hilariously inappropriate given Mirrha's current situation (miserable, pregnant, and on the run), which provides a comment on the relation of Petrarchan compliment to reality, a common enough observation even in Petrarchan verse ('My mistress' eyes are nothing like the sun'). Being a satyr, Poplar is in any case, like Cupid, an unlikely candidate for Petrarchan poet, both because of the legendary appetites of the satyrs and because of the common early modern association between satyrs and satire; even Mirrha is surprised at his conversation, 'Wondering that such a shape had such a tongue' (78.2). (We have, nonetheless, seen the same connection made in Weever's *Faunus and Melliflora.*) This incongruity is forcefully demonstrated when, after his rhetoric fails to woo her, he 'on sudden like a subtill snake, / rould in a heape, shootes foorth himself at le[n]gth' (79.1–2) and grabs her. This is much the same comedy of disproportion that was present in Lodge's poem, when the shaggy sea-god turns into a swooning, lovesick swain.

Mirrha is saved, or only perhaps interrupted (it appears she might be yielding) by the appearance of Diana, who changes Poplar into a poplar. The incident recalls in a number of ways the Acteon story: Poplar stumbles upon Mirrha while she is by a stream, and mistakes her for a nymph. He compares her to Diana, and Diana converts him to a tree using the same method – enchanted water – that converted Acteon to a stag. She declares the ground to be 'accursed' (84.1), which in the poem seems to be a judgment not just on the seduction, but also on the discourse of seduction. Acteon, after all, was metamorphosed to keep him from talking about Diana: 'Now, if you can, you may tell how you saw me when I was undressed' (79). Poplar is similarly prevented from any further poetic offerings; he will become instead a mute 'Trophey ... of *Dians* power' (85.2). Having the central scene of incest bracketed by these two scenes of incongruous Petrarchan wooing once again suggests that Petrarchan verse is implicated in the incest itself.

For Freud, the dissolution of the Oedipus complex depends upon the acceptance of the laws of civilization: 'the catastrophe to the Oedipus complex (the abandonment of incest and the institution of conscience and morality) may be regarded as a victory of the race over the individual.'[4] That is, the individual accepts certain restrictions on its desires as the price of belonging to the group. A similar understanding of incest is clear in Ovid's introduction to the tale, when Orpheus 'congratulate[s] the people of Ismarus and our part of the world, and count[s] this country happy to be so far from regions which produced such wickedness ... It is a crime to hate one's father, but Myrrha's love was a crime worse than any hate' (233). Building on Freud, Claude Lévi-Strauss argues that the incest taboo marks the line between nature and culture. Again, this insight is clearly present in Ovid, when Myrrha struggles with her desires: 'No fault can be found with this kind of love on the grounds that such affection is unnatural, for other animals mate without any discrimination; there is no shame for a heifer in having her father mount her, a horse takes his own daughter to wife, goats mate with the she-goats they have sired, and birds conceive from one who was himself their father. Happy creatures, who are permitted such conduct! Human interference has imposed spiteful laws, so that jealous regulations forbid what nature itself allows' (233). Except for a fleeting and cryptic remark on the part of Mirrha – 'O sinne (saies she) thou must be Natures slaue' (38.5) – Barksted leaves this nature versus culture debate out.

In place of the nature/culture dichotomy, we have the division between Orpheus and Cupid that is established in the opening stanzas of the poem. This in itself is an unsurprising opposition. Orpheus, as the representative of rhetoric, is frequently associated in humanist literature with civilization. Cupid, just as frequently, is associated with the anarchic force of desire. What is unusual is the opposition that gets mapped onto these two characters: humanist rhetoric versus Petrarchan verse. From the more benign opposition that opens the poem – Orpheus in hell with Euridice versus Orpheus keeping the peace in the heavens – we move to a more radical split: chastity versus chaos. Other oppositions in the poem line up with this one, most notably the female gods' reaction to the incest itself: '*Venus* [doth] smile, but frowning *Iuno* checks / their stolne delight' (64.4–5). Petrarchan verse is thus paradoxically associated with nature, lawlessness, hypocrisy, and uncontrolled desire.

After the kiss from Cupid, Mirrha seems quite literally possessed by the spirit of Petrarchan verse. In Ovid, Myrrha's nurse promises to use witchcraft to cure her; here the witchcraft is associated with the disease itself. Mirrha complains:

> if there be sorceries,
>   Philters, inchauntments, any furie new
> That can inspire with irrelegious fire,
> The brest of mortall, that vntam'd desire
>   Possesseth me, and all my bodies merit,
> Shewes like a faire house, haunted with a spirit.

(46.3–8)

Whereas in Ovid the nurse believes her charge to be possessed, in this version it is Mirrha herself who suggests it. Barksted offers a portrait here not of a desiring woman, or even a woman struggling with forbidden desire, but rather a female character who is pulled along by some force beyond her control, participating in a narrative that seems to have been imposed on her. In the early debate with Cupid, she resists being scripted into the role of Petrarchan mistress. When Cupid waxes lyrical about the powers of her beauty, she insists, 'Stay there ... giue backe those powers their owne / or not impose their powerfull force on me' (17.1–2). This kind of anti-Petrachan objection is not entirely outside the realm of the Petrarchan universe. But Mirrha's rejection of that role makes Cupid impose another on her: the role of Petrarchan lover. Unlike the situation in *Scillaes Metamorphosis*, however, where Scilla's transformation is played, at least initially, for comedy, here it is consistently told as tragedy. Mirrha never seems to enthusiastically put on the role of Petrarchan lover. Although she is possessed with incestuous desire, it seems to hold no attractions for her. Bowing to some kind of inevitability, she simply wishes it were over, 'wishing euen in that griefe the lustfull feate, / Were now perform'd (woemen ofte longings lacke)' (36.3–4). She does nothing to seduce her father and tries to avoid it by killing herself. Even the idea of committing suicide comes as something other than a conscious decision: 'A strange conceite, had now possest her braine, / nie equall to her lust, thought innocent' (37.1–2). It is the nurse who saves her from suicide, worms the secret out of her, and arranges the seduction of Cyniras.

The metaphors leading up to the consummation reinforce the suggestion that Mirrha is being propelled by forces beyond her control. She goes to her father

> as a poore bird long time in a snare,
> Ready for fammine and her woe to die,
>   whom an unskilful fouler vnaware
> hath guiuen freedome, to her foode doth hast.

> (59.2–5)

The bird metaphor is followed up in the next stanza when Mirrha, ascending 'those staires to lust' hears her father's voice and dives to the ground: 'nere lay patridge closer to the dust, / at sound o' the Faulccons bell' (60.1, 3–4). (This echoes Lucrece's fear at Tarquin's voice in Shakespeare's poem: 'Harmless Lucretia, marking what he tells / With trembling fear, as fowl hear falcons' bells' [510–11].) Finally, in bed with her father, Mirrha lies 'like [a] silly doue within the Eagles grip' (63.2), prior to being graphically deflowered. This last bird metaphor is reminiscent of the final encounter between Hero and Leander:

> Love is not full of pittie (as men say)
> But deaffe and cruell, where he meanes to pray.
> Even as a bird, which in our hands we wring,
> Foorthe plungeth, and oft flutters with her wing,
> She trembling strove ...
>
> (771–5)

Mirrha has already been warned about the cruelties of love, of course, by Love himself: 'Though he be king of sportes he neuer sports, / when as he wounds, but playes the Tirants part' (21.3–4). The force of the bird metaphors is to make Mirrha seem quite helpless in the face of her own desire: she is possessed by an overpowering hunger, she is the partridge trembling at the sound of her impending executioner, she is a dove in the grip of an eagle.

Responsibility is not exactly in question here; in the Ovidian universe, crimes committed unwillingly or even unwittingly are still crimes. It could well be argued that Mirrha has already committed the crime, in the realm of rhetoric. In another of Barksted's innovations, Mirrha stumbles into a portrait gallery before she retires to her bedroom to commit suicide. There, she comes across pictures of her father, mother, and a number of her suitors. This is a typical moment in the epyllion, which as we have seen is much given to ecphrasis. Most relevant here, however, is Lucrece's long monologue in front of the painting of the seige of Troy (1464–1568). Mirrha begins a dialogue with her father's picture, ventriloquizing his questions to her. This scene replaces an incident in Ovid in which Myrrha actually talks to her father. In the person of her father, Mirrha says to herself:

> Let her that needs and is not faire at all,
>   Repine at fortune, loue shall be thy thrall,
>   wing'd as he is, and armed thou shalt see
> (I haue the power to giue) and giue him thee.
>
> (32.5–8)

Cyniras's ventriloquized words are ambiguous: will love be Mirrha's slave, or will she be his? Does Cyniras give love to Mirrha, or Mirrha to love? In Mirrha's eyes, he has the power to give love to her, but he also has the power to give Mirrha away. Mirrha responds in an equally equivocal manner by saying, 'Nature hath made me yours, yours I must be: / You choose my choice, for in you lies my choice' (33.2–3). Mirrha has learned the language of seduction from Cupid, and in this poem, such language is Petrarchan. And just as with Cupid's discourse, Mirrha's here is ethically slippery. The scene could be taken as a commentary on the centrality of the figure of prosopopeia in the genre of the epyllion; the poems frequently consist of nothing more than ventriloquized dialogues between iconic personas. As such, the scene comments on the ethics and motives of the figure.

But we might also see the portrait scene as a commentary on the narcissism inherent in Petrarchan verse. The parallel between Pygmalion and his statue and Mirrha and the portrait is significant, as both seduce an aesthetic artifact. We might also think of Narcissus and the image in the water. In all of these cases we see a figure who has rejected desire falling in love with (quite literally) an unsuitable object. We should remember too the role that the echo of Narcissus's voice plays in his own self-seduction. In the epyllion, this kind of narcissistic self-absorption is regularly associated with Petrarchanisms and the fate of such a person is generally a punishing metamorphosis. This should make us modify our judgment of Mirrha's appearance early in the poem. In the genre of the epyllion, being a beautiful young woman dedicated to virginity is unnatural or, at the very least, as incongruous as Hero's position as 'Venus nun' (Hero and Leander, 45). Her dedication to her 'cold fruitelesse Virginitie' (20.5) could thus constitute the crime in the poem, rather than the incest. Echoing both Hero and Adonis, Mirrha pleads, 'I know not loue, sure tis a subtle thing' (18.1). Cupid's warning is true of the genre of the epyllion as a whole, where 'loue and chastitie, were euer foes' (20.8) and love will always win. In spite of her protestations to the contrary, Mirrha, like Hero, is the Petrarchan mistress who will be metamorphosed by love. Unlike Hero's, however, her education will be harsh. In the portrait scene we see her transformation into Petrarchan lover, condemned to act out a parody of Petrarchan desire. Everything after this – the suicide attempt, incest, flight, attempted rape – is all part of the fallout, which accounts for Mirrha's seeming lack of will. Her final metamorphosis into a tree is thus a respite rather than a judgment. This explains the gods's mercy in transforming her: the incest was the punishment rather than the crime.

After Diana transforms her into a tree, Mirrha weeps myrrh. This is not without precedent in the poem. When Mirrha flees Cyniras, she comes to 'odorous Panchaia' (71.4). At this point in the narrative we have an aetiological digression, concerning the origin of the land's perfumes:

> *Hebae* now banish'd from the *Aetherian* boule
>   vppon a feast day mongst the Gods aboue,
> Where twas made lawfull, all without controule
> might freely drinke it chanc'd the Queen of loue
> Whether she long'd, or enuied *Hebaes* starre,
> Women are enuious, where they long for nectar)
>   forc'd her to skinke so much, the iuice ran ore,
>   so that Ioues drinke washt the defiled flore.
>
> With this he storm'd, that's Priests from altars flie
> Streight banish'd *Hebae*, & the world did thinke
> To a second Chaos they should turned be,
>   the clouds for feare wept out th'imortal drinke
> and on *Panchaia* there this nectar fell,
>   Made rich th'adiacent lands with odorous smell,
>   and such rare spices to the shoares were giuen,
> As Ioue would think no nectar were in heauen.

(stanzas 72–3)

Mirrha's tears were earlier compared to '*Hebaes* Nectar ... spilt on heauens flore' (41.6), and in this digression, we see many of the same themes in the larger narrative. Venus causes Hebe to defile her father's house by spilling his nectar, a description that brings out the sexual nature of the offence. (In Barksted's version, the seduction of Cyniras is accomplished by wine, which further reinforces the parallel.) Hebe, like Mirrha, seems strangely incidental to the crime itself, even though she is the one punished for it. She is banished, and the crime, like incest, is of such magnitude as to threaten general chaos. The final result of the crime is fortuitous: the clouds weep out the spilled nectar, and the land below becomes the source of prized commodities.

Mirrha's crime also results in a number of good things. First, of course, is the sap, the tree's tears of repentance: 'These *Pius* drops, made

densive by the sunne, / Are kept for holy vses' (101.6–7). Next is her
'misbegotton babie' (102.1), the beautiful Adonis. Venus observes that
Adonis's rejection of her completes a circular narrative that began in the
opening section of the poem:

> Wel, wel (quoth she) thou hast reueng'd the spight
> which from my accurst Sons bow did fowly light
>   On thy faire Mother, O immortall boy.

> (111.5–7)

More importantly, the birth of Adonis enables the art of Shakespeare,
and the poem closes with a modestly (and accurately) unfavourable
comparison between Barksted's muse and Shakespeare:

> His Song was worthie merrit (*Shakespeare* hee)
> sung the faire blossome, thou the withered tree
>   *Laurell* is due to him, his art and wit
>   hath purchast it, *Cypres* thy brow will fit.

> (112.5–8)

The final product of Mirrha's crime is of course this poem. The dedicatory poems draw attention to the parallel between Mirrha's metamorphosis, and the power of Barksted's art. One of the writers of these
poems, William Bagnall, commends Barksted, saying:

> thou doost chaunt incestuous *Myrrha* forth,
>   with such delight,
> And with such goulde[n] phrase gild'st ore her crime
> That what's moste diabolicall, seemes deuine
> ...
> Then since he best deserues the Palme to weare,
>   Who wins the same:
> Doe thou alone inioy those sweets, which beare
>   thy Mirrhas name.
> And euer weare in memorie of her,
> An anademe of odoriferous *Mirrhe*,
> And let *Apollo*, thinke it no dispraise,
> To weare thy *Mirrhe*, & ioyne it with his bayes.

> (*The Poems of William Barksted*, 7–8)

Through Barksted's transformative art, Mirrha becomes a precious commodity, which in turn becomes a testament to the art itself. Crime is rendered productive, as Bagnall's poem records in a potentially equivocal way: Barksted 'with such delight ... gild'st ore her crime.' The uneasy combination of Barksted's pleasure and Mirrha's shame is evoked as well in Robert Glover's dedicatory poem, which remarks in a series of crude double entendres, 'happie Mirrha that he rips thy shame, / Since he so queintly doth expresse thy sin' (*Barksted*, 5). As the reference to Shakespeare and the crowd of dedicatory poems make clear, Mirrha's ruin enables Barksted to enter into the public world of rhetoric.

Rape and Incest

Having suggested that the incest in the poem is a punishment rather than a crime, I want to consider further whether the incest might be better considered as a rape. There are a number of things in the poem that might push us towards this way of looking at it: the central scene, for example, is bracketed by two seduction scenes that both carry more or less explicit threats of rape. The story that begins the story is also a rape narrative: the abduction of Eurydice, which occasions the transformation of Orpheus from lover to orator, the prototype of Barksted's transformation. The incest scene itself, as we have seen, is accompanied by a series of metaphors that suggest an unwillingness on Mirrha's part, metaphors that in other poems, such as *The Rape of Lucrece* and *Hero and Leander*, are suggestive of sexual violence, not internal struggle. The notion of volition was one of the recurring problems around rape trials, especially given the widespread belief that consent was necessary for conception, so that if a woman conceived, she could not have been raped.[5] We see this, for example, in Weever's *Faunus and Melliflora*, connected, moreover, with an opposition between Petrarchan and Ovidian masculinity:

> Blushing and sighing Theseus never strove,
> To woe and winne Antiope his love.
> Nor would hee have his time so spent and lavisht,
> But laid her downe, and some say she was ravisht,
> And so she was, but ravisht with content,
> And got with childe, belike both did consent.

> (321–6)

Caught up in this connection between rape and conception is the notion that the body may consent when the mind does not, which certainly seems to be the case with Mirrha. Mirrha's desire, we have noted, is more like a demonic possession, which brings us back to her initial encounter with Cupid, which was rendered in phallic terms: 'Shall I say *Cupid* with his brand did fire thee?' (27.4).

Rape is a fairly common occurrence in the Ovidian universe, especially between immortals and maids, and often hard to distinguish from seduction.[6] It is, in fact, a frequent cause or accompaniment of metamorphosis, whether this is the gods changing shape to approach the object of their lust, or whether it is the mortal herself who is transformed, through grief, mercy, gratitude, or revenge. Indeed, Lynn Enterline argues that 'in the Ovidian tradition, rape is the call that interpellates the female subject.'[7] Rape often marks the border and the difference between the worlds of the human and the immortal; the 'headdie ryots, incest, rapes' of the gods distinguish them from human society, and metamorphosis is the visible sign of any such border crossings.

Norman Bryson's discussion of the meaning or function of rape in the paintings of Lucretia and of the Sabine women prompts us to think about the representation of rape in complex ways.[8] In particular, Bryson argues that with the advent of sexual psychopathology and its attendant identity categories (e.g., rapist, homosexual, pedophile), rape has become to a large degree unrepresentable because of a privileging of interiority. In earlier representational regimes, the meaning of rape was not entirely private and psychological but was implicated in other discourses, involving family, class, politics, and so on. This is especially the case with narratives that are exemplary or epic or explanatory, such as the rape of Lucretia, which is less about the violation of a Roman matron than it is about family, honour, class, and especially, the foundation of the Roman republic. It is important, then, to be attentive both to the imperatives of the genre in which the rape narrative appears and to the discourses evoked by rape in the historical period which produces the narrative. In the case of the epyllion, this means remembering both the functions of mythological narratives (concerned primarily with the group and the generalized individual rather than particular individuals) and the corresponding concerns of the era in which such narratives are produced.

Rape and incest, in the economic scheme of things, are both violations of the most basic laws of culture. Incest, we have noted, is often figured as one of the barriers between the human and the nonhuman, but the incest ban is also necessary for exogamy and thus the basic structure of society. As Claude Lévi-Strauss argues, human society is founded on the exchange of women, money, and signs; incest violates this by taking a woman out of circulation. Hence the logic of Cupid's punishment of Mirrha, since she has already taken herself out of circulation through her dedication to chastity. Rape is similarly a crime against the economic order, either through the theft of a woman (abduction) or of her exchange value (in early modern terms, her chastity). Whereas the exchange of women establishes ties between families or groups of men, rape sets up divisions or distinctions between these groups (although it may well consolidate bonds within the offended or offending group).[9] Such a theft is at the heart of the *Iliad*, where the rape or theft of Helen is the cause of the Trojan war. Similarly, the rape of Lucretia is the occasion for the overthrow of tyranny in Rome and the birth of the Republic; Stephanie H. Jed notes 'how many incidents of sexual offense registered in ancient historiography are necessary markers of change in a legal and political system.'[10] Incest in the Myrrha story functions in a parallel fashion, as a marker of the borders of communities. In Ovid, Orpheus begins this tale by reassuring the Thracians that such things occurred elsewhere; Barksted updates this sentiment, noting the events are 'As farre as Trace from vs, so farre from hence ... such songs as these more fit the Tartars eares' (26.3, 7).

In her discussion of the use of the Lucretia story in humanist thinking, Jed shows how the story becomes the foundation for what she calls 'chaste thinking,' a kind of thinking that she argues is characteristically humanist. She draws attention to Brutus's role in the tale as both castigator of tears and opponent of tyranny:

> To castigate means to make chaste. In Livy's narrative, the passage from Lucretia's chastity to Tarquin's violation of this chastity to Brutus' castigation of the Romans for their tears forms a lexical chain which embodies a logic of chaste thinking: the rape of Lucretia is transformed into an injury against the honor of her male survivors by virtue of this chain; and Brutus takes over from Lucretia the function of preserving chastity by castigating the Romans for their tears.[11]

Brutus is able, writes Jed, to separate himself from his emotions and to think in a particular way about the rape, one which allows him to use it politically. In the epic narrative, then, chaste thinking allows for political action; in the case of the Lucretia story, republicanism. By contrast, in the ironic or erotic epic, i.e., the epyllion, chaste thinking allows both for a particular kind of thinking about desire, one that renders it inherently comic, and for a subjectivity that corresponds to that desire. This would account, for example, for the seeming incongruity between the comic attitude taken towards Mirrha's crime, and the exalted claims for the public rhetoric of the poem.

In the story of Lucretia and in other rape narratives with political inflections, rape tends to stand for or epitomize tyranny; Tarquin's rape is an outrageous extension of his family's political tyranny.[12] It is thus, we might note, the symbolic opposite of male friendship, which in the classical tradition is antithetical to tyranny. Because the epyllion is not in the first instance concerned with political systems, the tyranny will surface in other ways. If Brutus is castigator of tears and opponent of tyranny, for the Ovidian poet tears and tyranny are to be found most often in Petrarchan poetry. Tears, for satirists and Ovidians alike, are the scornful and effeminate mark of the Petrarchan poet. In these poems tyranny surfaces in two guises. One is the tyranny of the woman over the poet, the cruel mistress who torments her lover. The other is the virgin's tyranny over desire itself, the tyranny of the woman who chooses to follow Diana's cruel regime. If, for Brutus, chaste thinking involves primarily a political victory and secondarily a psychological operation, for the Ovidians it is the reverse. Rape in the poems functions as a dividing line or an occasion that allows or encourages the distance from desire that we have identified as a key characteristic of the Ovidian speaker, the occasion for a metamorphosis through which the speaker sees desire from the perspective of the immortals. At the same time, this metamorphosis implies for the speaker a political position, which, if not strictly speaking republican, nonetheless allows him, like Brutus, to speak as a man to other men. This political position, we might note, is essentially the contractual subject that will develop in seventeenth-century political theory, and which we saw in the previous chapter's discussion of R.B.'s *Orpheus His Journey to Hell*. Before considering Shakespeare's version of the Lucretia story, which in fact veers to some degree from this political pattern, we shall consider one poem that displays this logic more clearly.

Oenone and Paris

Thomas Heywood's *Oenone and Paris* is one of a number of epyllia that follow the pattern of *Venus and Adonis*, centred around the wooing of an uninterested mortal by a love-stricken nymph. The poem is remarkable in that there is even less narrative in this narrative poem than in Shakespeare's, which is itself unusually static. Oenone is the nymph whom Paris leaves for Helen. The entire poem consists of a single encounter between them, where Oenone argues for the unjustness of Paris's broken promise, and Paris attempts to exonerate himself: 'Persist, fayre Nimph, attentiuely to heare me / And thou shalt see how well as I can cleare me' (33.5–6). Not surprisingly, rhetoric becomes a central subject of the poem, especially with regard to Paris's former 'deceite and flatterie' (64.2), witnessed even by the trees, which bear 'in their barkes thy solemne protestations / Which, now I finde, were meere dissimulations' (56.5–6). And as with Shakespeare's poem, the language is remarkably legalistic. Early in the poem, for example, the nymph rounds on Paris:

And art thou come to prosequute the cause
Of well or woe? my loosing or my winning?
Say gentle Trojan, wordes that may delight me,
And for thy former lust I will acquite thee.

(10.3–6)

There is talk of pleading (27.2), parleys (27.6), suits (31.4, 105.6), promises past (49.1), breeches (12.3), just complaints (31.1), miscarriages (32.6), 'credite, faith, and vowes' (98.4). None of these, of course, are exclusively legal terms, but the accumulation of them does have a certain force.

The legal lexicon is appropriate given that the poem is about a marriage and a rape. Oenone was Paris's 'quondam wife' (26.5), left behind for 'that forreine hecfar of the Greekes, / Who, yet a youngling, was braue Theseus rape' (12.1–2). This description of Helen is notable for two reasons. First, it identifies her as foreign. Foreignness is often associated with, or is the product of, rape. Second, the phrase 'Theseus rape' seems to make of 'rape' a category or role, on the order of 'wife' or 'mistress.' This usage follows an earlier reference to Helen as Paris's 'beauteous rape' (4.1) and is echoed later when Oenone refers to her as 'thy rape': 'Thou and thy rape haue done me double wrong; / But were she here, howe sore would I assault her?' (95.1–2). Rape, at least insofar as it concerns Helen, is not so much a violation of the woman as it is an identity category. Helen is, in the early modern period and in this poem, not a victim but a notorious whore: 'Nought else saue lust, and breach of loue shee seekes' (12.3), says Oenone; Lucrece, gazing on a picture of the fall of Troy, says in a similar vein, 'Show me the strumpet that began this stir, / That with my nails her beauty I may tear' (1471–2). Rape, as Oenone intimates, creates divisions; breach of love in the first instance, but also war: 'The lust of Laeda summons thee to fight / I, and be sure the Greekes will be reuenged' (72.1–2). Whereas the exchange of women works to consolidate bonds between men, the theft of women – ravishment or rape – creates divisions. Rape in the epyllion often functions as a dividing line, either geographic, temporal, or political, between different groups of men. This is especially clear in *Oenone and Paris*, where Helen, the embodiment of rape, marks the divide between two different spaces, which correspond to two versions of Paris.

As in *Hero and Leander*, the poem traces out two distinct geographic realms. The geographical difference is marked at the beginning of the poem, when 'Phrigian Paris ... [rises] from th'imbracements of his new-stolne bryde' (2.1–2) and travels 'as farre as Ida mountaine' (2.5). The landscape that Oenone inhabits, and which Paris formerly inhabited, is resolutely pastoral in contrast to the corrupt urban spaces of Troy:

> Grace to these hilles, and dales, & louely brookes,
> Disgrace to walled cities, traffique townes,
> Fame to the swift foote huntresses in these nookes,
> Shame to the girles yclad in gorgeous gownes.
>
> (29.1–4)

The vales of Ida are stocked with the usual pastoral personnel, including nymphs, satyrs, and 'Fayries' (52.4). Before the arrival of Mercury, the three goddesses, and the golden ball, Paris was a simple unknown swain, 'Drowsilie leaning on my shepheardes crooke' (36.1), tending his goats (52.2), and carving his love's name into the bark of trees. He is bribed by the three goddesses with offers of wisdom, wealth, or love, and as befits an Ovidian hero, he chooses love. (As it is, he gets wealth anyway as a result of his new-found patrimony, and if his rhetorical command is any evidence, he acquires some wisdom as well.)

It is Paris's choice of Venus, love, and the 'beautous rape' Helen that effects the metamorphosis in this poem. Paris gains a new identity, discovering that he is 'Sonne to King Priamus, and Queene Hecuba' (51.2). He tells Oenone, 'I knewe not this when first of all I knewe thee / Which had I knowne, I had disdain'd to view thee' (52.5–6). Oenone protests, 'Is not my byrth equiualent with thine? / I am a Nimph, thou but a mortall creature' (90.1–2), but she misses the point that elsewhere

she seems to understand. The pastoral world and Troy are two fundamentally different places, and as a result of his new identity, Paris now
belongs irretrievably to the latter: in the pastoral world 'Cinthia liues,
that loues the painefull farmour, / Not braue Bellona, glistring in her
armour' (70.5–6). The difference is between the realm of pastoral poetry and epic poetry, and the schemes of law, masculinity, and desire
associated with each.

Chief among these differences is the way the law functions. Oenone
cannot understand why the gods did not intervene and sink the boat
carrying Helen:

Band bee that barke that brought from Lacedemon
That snowt-fayre Princesse with her tempting face!
Could neither chaungeling Proteus, nor Palemon,
Seas soueraigne Neptune, with thy three-forkt mace, –
Why would not some fayre sea-god make a motion
To drench that painted Idoll in the Ocean?

(13.1–6)

The answer to Oenone's question comes later. Paris tells her that love is a
stronger force than justice:

What made the gods to trewant it from heauen
And shift them subtillie into sundrie shapes
But he that roues his shaftes at sixe and seuen,
Laughing at riot, revelling, and rapes?
His force made Ioue with Danaes to iest,
Beguiling faire Alcmena and the rest.

(109.1–6)

Here as elsewhere, rape is seen as a characteristic part of the activities of
the gods, accompanied as usual by metamorphosis. Just as Venus smiles
at Mirrha's incest, Cupid laughs 'at riot, revelling, and rapes' (109.4).
The upshot, says Paris, is that 'loue is in no lawe contained' (111.2), and
therefore Oenone's complaints, at least from the perspective of an epic
or Ovidian universe, are meaningless. It is Cupid, whose force is irresistible, that should be blamed, not Paris: 'If on the ragged rockes a shippe
be splitted, / The sternesman, not the Carake, should be twitted' (117.5–
6). By pleading an Ovidian approach to desire, Paris acquits himself of
any responsibility in the matter.

Paris, in effect, demonstrates the particular mode of chaste thinking characteristic of the Ovidian narrator. In the pastoral world, as a pastoral swaine, Paris lives according to the Petrarchan rules. In the Ovidian world he is able to separate himself from himself, or from previous versions of the self. He is able to distance himself from his own desire, to the point where he can assert that it is not even his own. He is merely the boat, not the 'sternesman' (117.6), and he has nothing to do with the cruelties of desire. It is this separation that allows him to both recognize Oenone's claim and refuse its logic. It is this separation and refusal that allows both the marriage to Helen and his activity in the public sphere of Troy. In spite of what we know to be the outcome of this particular narrative, the poem suggests that such a refusal is a necessary accompaniment of maturity and the marker of the division between youth and adult. In the epic mode, as we have observed, rape frequently features as the mark of a political change. Rape is associated with tyranny, and male friendship with its opposite. Rape may thus be productive of male friendship, and of the political subjectivity that accompanies it; it acts as the negative matrix out of which the friends emerge, or against which they define themselves. In the epyllion, although rape may still mark or create divisions between groups of men, the more important divide is between two competing literary ideologies and schemes of desire, which also marks a division in or distance from the self.

The Rape of Lucrece

Shakespeare's version of the Lucretia story, critics have observed, differs from most other sources both in its attention to psychology and its relative lack of interest in the political dimensions of the narrative. Other critics have drawn attention to its highly rhetorical language, particularly its use of chiasmus, and linked this to its relatively flat characterizations of the central figures. Certainly the poem, like other epyllia, is greatly interested in rhetoric; as Richard Lanham observes, in this version it is not the sight of Lucrece that inflames Tarquin's lust, but rather Collatine's description of her; other key moments in the poem, particularly the rape, are also figured as rhetorical events. It is to some degree, as Lanham argues, a poem 'about the rhetoric of display, about the motives of eloquence.'[13] In his deconstructionist approach to *The Rape of Lucrece*, Joel Fineman pays close attention to the poem's theorizing of its own rhetoric, 'so as to guard against a variety of naturalistic or naturalizing accounts that might be advanced to explain both the causes and the consequences of Shakespeare's version of the rape of Lucrece.'[14]

Fineman's caution is useful, although at the same time other critics have pointed out the problems of seeing the poem *only* as rhetoric, or focusing strictly upon the action of the rhetoric at the expense of ethical considerations.[15] Considering the poem in the context of the genre of the epyllion prompts us to steer a middle course through these two approaches, and to see the poem as interested not so much in rape itself as in the representation or the cultural meanings of rape, and the uses to which those representations can be put.

The Rape of Lucrece is most often considered as a complaint, but it shares enough with the epyllion (particularly with *Venus and Adonis*) that it is useful and revealing to read it according to the expectations of that genre.[16] The poem contains, for example, an aetiological myth, observations about gender ('men have marble, women waxen minds, / And therefore are they form'd as marble will' [1240–1]), and many of the genre's favourite rhetorical devices. Most importantly, as with many epyllia, *The Rape of Lucrece* has as one of its narratives rhetorical education.[17] Whereas this usually is the education of a youth, in this poem it is a married woman; as Enterline argues, Lucrece's 'entry into the poem's discourse follows the perverse logic of a violent pedagogical curriculum.'[18] As a consequence of the rape, Lucrece gains over the course of the poem a deeper sense of the power of rhetoric and a greater rhetorical ability. For example, the climax of the long address in front of the painting of Troy is her sudden awareness of both the limitations of representation and its potential duplicity.

All of the major events of the narrative are figured as determined by or in some way implicated in the processes of rhetoric.[19] The villain of the piece, Tarquin, is to some degree figured as a poor rhetorician. As critics frequently note, it is the 'name of 'chaste'' (8) that enflames Tarquin, rather than Lucrece's beauty. Prior to the rape, Tarquin's lengthy struggle is dramatized specifically as a debate with himself: 'in his inward mind he doth debate / What following sorrow may on this arise' (185–6). The rape is effected through threats of what rhetoric will accomplish ('thou, the author of their obloquy, / Shalt have thy trespass cited up in rhymes' [523–4]) and resisted by reminders of rhetoric's memorializing power:

And wilt thou be the school where Lust shall learn?
Must he in thee read lectures of such shame?
Wilt thou be glass wherein it shall discern
Authority for sin, warrant for blame,
To privilege dishonor in thy name?

(617–21)

What little description there is of the action of the rape is entirely given over to two accounts, one metaphoric and one literal, of the silencing of Lucrece's speech:

> The wolf hath seiz'd his prey, the poor lamb cries,
> Till with her own white fleece her voice controll'd
> Entombs her outcry in her lips' sweet fold.

> For with the nightly linen that she wears
> He pens her piteous clamors in her head,
> Cooling his hot face in the chastest tears
> That ever modest eyes with sorrow shed.

>   (677–83)

The aftermath of the rape is an explosion of this pent-up rhetoric, which some critics, notably Lanham, have read as evidence of Lucrece's insincerity: 'we are meant to see a woman carried away as much by the language of feeling as by feeling itself.'[20] At some considerable length, Lucrece denounces what she sees as the abettors of her rape, Night, Opportunity, and Time, and launches into an ecphrastic excursus on a painting of the Fall of Troy. Finally, her suicide is understood as a way of controlling future rhetorical exploitations of her story ('no dame hereafter living / By my excuse shall claim excuse's giving' (1714–15); she understands that the rape has inevitably made her the subject of rhetoric, so it is imperative that she determine precisely what she will mean.

Tarquin is only too obviously a bad humanist subject, a negative exemplum for the reader. Not just a tyrant, he is also a betrayer of the bonds of male friendship, which for the humanists were often figured as the foundation of civil society. In the literature of male friendship, tyranny is incompatible with this particular kind of homosocial bond, and thus Tarquin's betrayal of his friend Collatine is the first of many divisions that the rape effects. But this poem is less interested in political structures than in the subjectivities that correspond to them, and so Tarquin's tyranny manifests itself in other ways as well. As in *Mirrha* and *Oenone*, one of these ways is through an association with Petrarchan poetry. The author of the anonymous *Love's Complaint* (1597), a long address to the lover's cruel Petrarchan mistress Julia, makes a similar (if gender-reversed) association. The poet clearly has Shakespeare's poem in mind when he refers to himself as '*Lucrece* chast' and his mistress as 'proud *Tarquin*,'

Who by disdainfull frownes and tyrannie
My loue and life to wofull end doth bring;
  Slaying my harmless loue with cold disdain ...

(sig. C2v)

A.D. Cousins observes of Shakespeare's Tarquin, 'Expressing his will to tyranny, his proto-tyrannic role, Tarquin's desire makes him a brutal parody of the Petrarchan lover as a species and his pursuit of Lucrece a sexual heightening/violation of the Petrarchan discourse of love.'[21] These associations are a little complicated: not only does Tarquin's rape represent an extension of the tyrannies of desire in Petrarchan discourse, but Tarquin himself represents the Petrarchan lover who is tyrannized, either by desire or by his cruelly chaste mistress. In the debate with himself that precedes the rape, Tarquin in effect allows himself to be tyrannized by his own desire. As was the case in our earlier discussion of *Cephalus and Procris*, it is a question of the management of the self, and especially of desire. In this poem, however, this failure is figured as an inability to manage a divided self.

In *The Rape of Lucrece*, a form of this self-division is first evident in Lucrece, in the 'silent war of lilies and of roses' (71) in her face, the description of which becomes the motivating cause of Tarquin's desire.[22] This self-division is connected quite quickly to the rhetorical figure of chiasmus and transferred to Tarquin: – 'for himself himself he must forsake' (157), 'he himself himself confounds' (160) – and the drama of the opening section of the poem becomes Tarquin's war with himself. Critics such as Joel Fineman, Heather Dubrow, and Catherine Belsey have drawn attention to the way 'the poem ostentatiously foregrounds its chiastic matter and manner';[23] chiasmus is appropriate, in the context of the present argument, for the way it neatly figures self-division, but also for how it can be used to figure transference or exchange or even a contract; this is appropriate enough given Shakespeare's perennial fascination with economics, but also pertinent given the economic significance of rape in the laws.

Through chiasmus, the poem suggests that the burden of Tarquin's failed masculinity, which culminates in the rape, is in effect transferred to Lucrece. Directly following the rape, Tarquin and Lucrece are consistently contrasted and paralleled through a series of one-line descriptions: 'She bears the load of lust he left behind, / And he the burthen of a guilty mind' (734–5). Chiasmus, the figure so characteristic of the poem, is here used to suggest an exchange or transference between Lucrece and Tarquin. Tarquin's failure to manage himself and the damage this causes to his soul is paradoxically described in terms of a rape, and the parallel is further emphasized by referring to his soul in the feminine:

> For now against himself he sounds this doom,
> That through the length of times he stands disgraced;
> Besides, his soul's faire temple is defaced,
> To whose weak ruins muster troops of cares,
> To ask the spotted princess how she fares.
>
> She says her subjects with foul insurrection
> Have batter'd down her consecrated wall,
> And by their mortal fault brought in subjection
> Her immortality, and made her thrall.
>
> (717–25)

The self-division seen earlier in Tarquin is now characteristic of Lucrece, and it is up to her to effectively manage the division that Tarquin could not: 'Myself thy friend will kill myself thy foe' (1196). Just as 'She bears the load of lust he left behind' (734), Lucrece will also be forced to bear the burden of Tarquin's failed masculinity and to manage it better than he has.

The legend of Lucretia, rehearsed in the argument that precedes the poem, demonstrates that the proper sphere of women's activity is the home. As various critics have observed, and as we see in such poems as Thomas Edwards's *Cephalus and Procris*, there is a connection between women in the public sphere and women's rhetoric. Women's errancy is connected to women's errant discourse. Tarquin's violation of Lucrece is also a violation of the private sphere from which, in effect, she is forcibly ejected. Tarquin's threat to Lucrece was to make her the subject of rhetoric, but as she realizes afterwards, this is the inevitable effect of the rape anyway. According to the early modern cultural logic of rape, to ravish a woman is to remove her from the private sphere and carry her into the public: it is a making-public of the woman, or a publishing of her. This, we remember, is what spurs on the rape in the first place, when Collatinus unwisely praises his wife in public and why, presumably, Lucrece's rape is figured in rhetorical terms. Once the woman has been forced into the public sphere, there is no return, which accounts for the fear that a woman ravished is likely to decline into some version of whoredom, and why the early modern law needed to carefully guard against a rape victim's post-facto consent.

Lucrece, as a woman removed from the private sphere, becomes in effect rhetoric. In the context of the genre, her narrative is not dissimilar to that of youths such as Narcissus, or Adonis, or other characters in the genre whose fate it is to become iconic. Lucrece certainly shows an awareness of this process of becoming-iconic, and her suicide is her way of becoming a positive rather than a negative exemplum. Much as the rape of Helen moves Paris from the genre of pastoral to the genre of epic, Lucrece's rape has forced her out of the genre she both occupied and embodied (Xenophon-inspired household management tract, perhaps) and into the world of epic. Lanham argues that in her excessive rhetoric after the rape 'she exposes her former selfhood. It was entirely rhetorical. She was only a role; that gone, she is as good as dead.'[24] In the rhetorically self-conscious world of the epyllion, however, many characters are aware of themselves as characters or as rhetorically constituted. Lucrece's problem, after the rape which forces her into the public sphere of rhetoric, or the world of the Lacanian Symbolic, is to find a role that is both available and acceptable to her.

Lucrece's violation results in something like a birth then, hinted at in the way the poem explains her incessant talking: 'True grief is fond and testy as a child ... Old woes, not infant sorrows, bear them mild' (1094, 1096). Her situation is like that of the youth, in that she now occupies a middle term or transitional state and her gender, through the rhetorical transaction with Tarquin, has become complicated. Unlike the youth, however, there is for Lucrece no possible metamorphosis into adult male. Lucrece realizes that she has undergone a transformation, as she compares her present situation with the past:

> But when I fear'd, I was a loyal wife:
> So am I now – O no, that cannot be,
> Of that true type hath Tarquin rifled me.

> (1048–50)

Tarquin's ravishment takes her away from her husband, and leaves her on her own: 'I am the mistress of my fate' (1069). Robbed of the 'type' of 'loyal wife,' Lucrece must find a new iconic destiny, which is for the genre one definition of subjectivity. This is the function of the long scene in front of the painting, which, as Lanham observes, Lucrece uses as a mirror. Lucrece's ventriloquism of the various selves represented there can be seen to some degree as serial acts of identification, as she attempts to find a suitable role or subjectivity for herself in the public, masculine world of the epic. She seizes first upon Hecuba: 'On this sad shadow Lucrece spends her eyes, / And shapes her sorrow to the beldame's woes' (1457–8). Obviously thinking of her own situation, she questions, 'Why should the private pleasure of some one / Become the public plague of many moe?' (1478–9). As a wife, Hecuba occupies a familiar role, but one which is no longer available to Lucrece. Rejecting 'the strumpet' Helen (1471) as site of identification, or rather using her as a site of negative identification, she moves on to the many other faces in the painting, using her initial identification with Hecuba as a template for further identifications:

> So Lucrece, set a-work, sad tales doth tell
> To pencill'd pensiveness and color'd sorrow;
> She lends them words, and she their looks doth borrow.
>
> (1496–8)

These identifications take place at the level of the body – 'she their looks doth borrow' – but they are at the same time achieved through narrative, as Lucrece tells 'sad tales' of the self. The development of Lucrece's new ego, then, is at the same time a rhetorical education and a rhetorical process, a successive layering of versions of the self.

Ultimately, however, there is no acceptable role for Lucrece within the public sphere except as martyr to chastity and she resolves upon revenge by proxy, and death. The figure of chiasmus is iconically appropriate for the story of a martyr, but its crossed structure is also suggestive, as we have seen, of an ironic transference or exchange. Although Lucrece states, 'Mine enemy was strong, my poor self weak' (1646), her suicide is a mastery of both her body and her destiny, a mastery that Tarquin could not manage, and her death is figured in the same phallic terms as that of Adonis. As she stabs herself she says, ''tis he, / That guides this hand to give this wound to me' (1721–2). In a chiastic fashion, the suicide both replays and undoes the rape, giving Lucrece back the control of her self-representation, which she temporarily had lost.

Lucrece's death scene replays to some degree both her and Tarquin's struggles for self-control, and this is replayed yet again as her father and husband fight both over her and over their own emotions:

> The one doth call her his, the other his,
> Yet neither may possess the claim they lay.
> The father says, 'She's mine.' 'Oh, mine she is,'
> Replies her husband, 'do not take away

My sorrow's interest, let no mourner say
He weeps for her, for she was only mine,
And only must be wail'd by Collatine.'

(1793–9)

Although both have in the past owned Lucrece, neither now 'may possess' Lucrece. Lucrece has been stolen or ravished, has fully entered the public sphere, and in death has become rhetoric. As Collatinus and Lucretius repeat Tarquin's failure to manage himself, replaying their loss of Lucrece through a loss of control over their emotions, Brutus mimics or seizes Lucrece's self-control. He does this in part by managing the self-division that Lucrece, as a woman in the public sphere, could only solve through the knife. In particular, Brutus uses the occasion of her death to abandon his duplicity, which took the form of a public performance of witlessness. Brutus 'pluck'd the knife from Lucrece' side ... Burying in Lucrece' wound his folly's show' (1807, 1810). Just as Lucrece bears the burden of Tarquin's failed masculinity but resolves it through self-mastery, Brutus seizes, when her husband and father do not, the legacy of Lucrece's discipline and converts it into epic action. Brutus is an ostentatiously divided subject who can nonetheless tolerate and master this division; moreover, unlike Lucrece's father and husband, he can sufficiently distance himself from himself to convert personal calamity to public, epic activity. The predominance of the figure of chiasmus in the poem, and the concern with the future rhetorical deployment of the self, both foreground the centrality of the notion of exchange in the development of these particular subjectivities, subjectivities that are born out of the contract that Lucrece makes with her kinsmen to avenge her death.

Significantly, Shakespeare's version does not mention the founding of the republic and so in this version, neither Brutus nor Collatinus are in any way beneficiaries of her death. And, in contrast to Ovid's version, revenge is first mentioned by Lucrece, not Brutus.[25] Lucrece's body is carried through the streets and the result of this, the final lines of the poem report, is that 'The Romans plausibly did give consent / To Tarquin's everlasting banishment' (1854–5). The conclusion of the poem then is simply that the vow made to Lucrece has been fulfilled, and that she has made good on her declaration that she will be 'the mistress of my fate' (1069). While her chosen fate has struck many readers and critics as an unlikely and undesirable exchange of life for reputation, an exchange which, moreover, seems designed to shore up patriarchal ideologies,[26] we must at the same time be attentive to the rhetorical nature of the world of the poem. According to the symbolic economy of the poem, Lucrece has achieved rhetorical mastery through becoming iconic and thus has achieved something like a full subjectivity. In the epyllion as in Tarot, death does not always mean death.

Hiren: or the Faire Greeke

The author of the *Lawes Resolution of Womens Rights* distinguishes between the two species of rape in English law, using two of the most famous classical examples of rape as illustrations, Lucrece and Helen. The first category of rape is 'when a woman is enforced violently to sustaine the furie of bruitish concupiscence; but she is left where she is found, as in her owne house or bed, as Lucrece was, and not hurried away, as Helen by Paris,'[27] which represents the latter form of rape. The history of rape laws in the Middle Ages and the early modern period is complicated because of the law's early failure to distinguish rape from abduction. In the various laws passed concerning rape since the Statutes of Westminster,[28] we can isolate two key trends. One is the concern with property, especially inherited property, and the other is the problem of consent. These two concerns are obviously related. 6 Richard II, c. 6 ruled that 'whensoever such Ladies, Daughters, and other Women aforesaid be ravished, and after such Rape do consent to such Ravishers ... they that be ravished ... be from thenceforth disabled, and by the same Deed be unable to have or challenge all Inheritance, Dower, or Joint Feoffment after the Death of their Husbands and Ancestors.' The author of the *Lawes Resolution* argues that the new elements of the statute are necessary for the protection of women, who might otherwise, out of pity, protect their rapist from the harshness of the law by saying that they consented to the rape.[29] (They might also, he hints, do it for gain.) Other interests are clearly being protected, however, in the increasingly detailed laws concerning, as the statute of Philip and Mary puts it, 'suche as shall take awaye Maydens that bee Inheritoures' (4 & 5 Philip and Mary, c. 8). Coke in his *Institutes* specifies that this law does not apply to all women, but only those who have property, are taken against their will, are married to the offender, and are not the ward of the offender. The law seems most clearly directed at women under the age of sixteen, for whom the issue of consent is crucial. If she marry without her guardian's consent, her property and inheritance revert to her next of kin. If she is under the age of twelve, her consent has no effect whatsoever. The seriousness of this offence is indicated by 39 Elizabeth, c. 9, which denied the abductor and any accomplices benefit of clergy. The separation of rape from abduction in fact seems more concerned with the protection of property than with the protection of women, and 'the law's desire to have it both ways – as a crime against property and as a crime against the person – reveals a crisis in the Early Modern construction of woman's subjectivity: she is both property or passive object and a person invested with agency, with the will and discernment that define consent.'[30]

The issue of consent is clearly a thorny one, especially so given the common perception that conception demonstrated consent. Scholars such as Norman Bryson and Barbara J. Baines have highlighted the extent to which consent complicates the Lucretia story, in light of the belief that the body may consent (through pity or pleasure) even when the mind does not. Clearly, the existence of what we might call involuntary consent testifies to the existence of a different construction of the body and selfhood. At the same time, it complicates the notion of will, and should caution us away from equating our notion of consent, which implies free choice, with earlier notions of consent, which do not necessarily preclude coercion. The seeming uncontrollability of consent thus makes the already fraught connection between women and property in the period even more anxiety ridden. The literature of the period gives ample evidence of a culture fascinated by the economics of marriage, especially as regards dowries and dowagers, and as Amy Louise Erickson shows, lawmakers continually struggled to define the property rights of women.[31]

Involuntary consent is a problem for the woman's male relatives, and the laws are written to protect against the possibility of the woman's consent leading to the loss of inherited property, mostly by ruling consent immaterial. Whereas the rape laws attempt to manage the problem of consent through severely circumscribing it, the poems handle it through refashioning subjectivity. If rape in epic literature frequently figures as a foundational moment for a new community, one which has overthrown tyranny, in the epyllion, with its more restricted focus, rape figures as a foundational moment for a new subjectivity, one which has conquered the tyranny of desire. In the poems, the problem of involuntary consent is associated with the victims (most obviously Lucrece), but also, in a curious act of transference, with the rapists, as rape becomes a problem of male subjectivity. Rape in the poems is often figured as a failure on the part of the rapist to manage the problem of self-division that sits at the heart of the notion of involuntary consent, and this failure of management in the poems is read as a failure of masculinity; managing self-division appropriately signals an ability to act in the social.

Some of the anxieties around women and property that are evident in the rape laws, especially around the notion of consent, help to make sense of what is at stake in William Barksted's *Hiren: or the Faire Greeke* (1611). The poem parallels the rape of Hiren with the rape of Constantinople, devoting much of its attention to Mahomet's ravishment and seduction of the maid, and of her subsequent consent. Seeing these anxieties around rape at work in the poem demonstrates how the thinking around the changes in the rape laws is connected to broader social concerns. The narrative, which is divided into two parts, is set against the fall of Constantinople in 1453, and so is clearly not Ovidian in origin. Like Beaumont's *The Metamorphosis of Tobacco*, it is an Ovidian treatment of a non-Ovidian subject, and thus it shows us how amenable or transferable Ovidian attitudes are to non-Ovidian concerns. As with the author's *Mirrha*, this poem is obviously indebted to Shakespeare, and to the genre of the epyllion in general. It is full of references to Ovidian gods and goddesses, it employs many of the favourite rhetorical devices, and it demonstrates many of the usual concerns around women, rhetoric, and desire.

As Samuel C. Chew points out in one of the few mentions of the poem, the legend of Hiren, also known as Irene or Hyerenee, became early on an accepted part of the history of the fall of Constantinople.[32] Hiren, goes the legend, was a beautiful Greek virgin presented to the conqueror Mahomet by one of his soldiers. He falls hopelessly in love with her, to the neglect of his affairs and the consternation of his people and his soldiers. One faithful retainer, Mustapha, finally gets up the courage to remind the fearsome tyrant of his ancestors and his responsibilities. Mahomet commands Hiren to dress in her finest, and presenting her to the assembled nobles, asks who would not fall in love with such a beauty. 'And having so said, presently with one of his hands catching the fair Greek by the hair of the head, & drawing his falchion with the other, at one blow strook off her head, to the great terror of them all: and having so done, said unto them, *Now by this iudge whether your Emperour is able to bridle his affections or not.*'[33]

There were at least two well-known versions of the story in English, in William Painter's *Palace of Pleasure* and Richard Knolles's *Generall Historie of the Turke* (1603). It is generally assumed that a version of the story was the basis of a lost play by George Peele, entitled *The Turkish Mahomet and*

Hyrin the fair Greeke, which was probably the source of references to Hiren in plays by Shakespeare, Jonson, and Middleton.[34] Since Barksted was an actor, if such a play existed, this would likely be one of his principal sources. Painter's and Knolles's versions of the story agree on all the major details. In both, the bulk of the narrative is concerned with Mustapha's oration to Mahomet, and the point of the story, aside from the conflict between public duty and private passion, is to show, in Painter's words, 'the beastlie crueltie of an infidell lover towards his ladie.'[35] Barksted's version of the story differs quite dramatically from these two – Mustapha's charge to Mahomet, for example, which takes up more than half of Painter's tale, takes less than three stanzas in Barksted's poem – but because of the lost Peele play, it is impossible to know which of the innovations he is responsible for, and which he is simply copying from Peele.[36]

The fall of Constantinople was formerly seen by historians as the end of the Middle Ages and the beginning of the Renaissance. Lisa Jardine's material history of the Renaissance restores it to that position, showing the importance of the event for the development of a European commodity culture.[37] Within the period, the Ottoman Empire was, quite naturally, viewed with some concern, as it conquered more and more territory while the Christian European states squabbled amongst themselves. At the same time, as Jardine notes, 'The fact that Christendom failed to come to Constantinople's rescue probably caused no surprise to any of the politicians involved,'[38] since few powers aside from the Catholic Church had a stake in keeping the city Christian, and many states had commercial interests or aspirations in this important trade link. Nonetheless, Christian monarchs occasionally found it in their interest to hypocritically and half-heartedly make threatening gestures towards the Ottomans. Popular representations of the Turk, Chew writes, emphasized their cruelty, their territorial rapaciousness, their single-mindedness as displayed in the discipline of their armies, and their licentiousness as demonstrated by their harems. The Ottoman Empire was frequently seen as the scourge of God, a punishment either for the Byzantine Empire's worship of images, or for Christian Europe's disunity. When a combination of Venetian and Spanish forces successfully fought the Turkish navy at Lepanto in 1571, England along with the rest of Christian Europe rejoiced. The victory was memorialized by James VI of Scotland in a narrative poem of over nine hundred lines, as well as in a number of Spanish epics.[39]

Nabil Matar has shown how highly schizophrenic the English relation to Islam and the Turkish Empire was, alternately deploring and admiring this vastly powerful non-Christian empire.[40] If on the public stage, the Turk was a figure of tyranny, within Elizabeth's government attitudes towards the Ottomans were considerably different: 'Commercial rivalry with Venice, political and economic rivalry with Spain, religious differences with all the Catholic countries of Europe, and the general calculations of trade-interests alike dictated a policy of neutrality if not of actual friendship with the Turks';[41] Matar argues that 'the late 1580s and 1590s witnessed the golden age of Anglo-Muslim relations.'[42] Elizabeth maintained highly cordial and lucrative relations with a number of Islamic states, while overlooking both religious difference and the actions of English privateers making raids off the Barbary coasts, and Muslim pirates off of hers.[43] In 1575 the London merchants Edward Osborne and Richard Staper sent their agents Joseph Clements and John Wight to Constantinople to obtain permission to trade. In 1578 William Harborne returned to establish the basis for ongoing trade, an enterprise to which 'the English government unquestionably gave its unofficial backing.'[44] In 1581 Elizabeth granted a patent for the Turkey Company, which in 1592 would become the highly lucrative Levant Company. Friedenreich argues that the travel books and geographies of the Levant, unlike other genres which deal with the region, accept the fall of the city and look past it: 'taking a disaster for Christian peoples and turning it around to promote trade and tourism is the genius which made the British empire successful for so long.'[45]

Others in England were less comfortable, as Matar notes: 'English writers and strategists recognized, from the first establishment of the Turkey Company until the Great Migration and well into the rest of the seventeenth century, that their colonial ideology was winning against the Indians but losing against the Muslims; they were enslaving Indians while Muslims were enslaving them.'[46] Clearly, if the English were to succeed in their imperial ambitions, some change of thinking was required. There is, then, an ambivalence, not to say hypocrisy, in English attitudes towards the Turk at the time, because of the clash between religious and mercantile interests. While Barksted's poem does not explicitly reflect this dilemma, it does perhaps surface in its conflicted portrayal of Mahomet, who is at once luxurious Oriental tyrant and exemplary male subject.

The poem begins by rehearsing many of the usual themes around the Turks, mentioning famous battles, identifying Mahomet as 'the fatall scourge' (3.1), noting the current threat to Europe and especially Italy because the European nations 'for trifles iarre' (4.6), and glancing at the atrocities committed during the sack of Constantinople. The narrative proper then begins, as Mahomet, the son of Amurath, falls in love with the beautiful Greek virgin Hiren. In this version, it is Mahomet himself who finds Hiren, saves her from the fate of other young ladies – 'rape with murder, stalk't about the land' (8.4) – and woos her. In his tent at night he is overcome with desire, Petrarchan-style: 'sinking downe, he set a soule-taught grone, / And sigh'd, and beat his heart' (31.2–3). He orders Hiren brought to him, and woos her in terms both Petrarchan ('But say I languish faint, and grow forlorne ... Wouldst then for euer hold me yet in scorne?' [35.1, 3]) and Ovidian (echoing Gaveston's plans in *Edward II*):

> At home shall comick Masques, & night-disports
> Conduct thee to thy pillow, and thy sheetes,
> And all those reuels which soft loue consorts,
> Shall entertaine thee with their sweetest sweets.
> And as the warlike God with *Venus* meetes,
> And dallies with her in the Paphian groue,
> Shall *Mahomet* in bed shew thee such sports,
> As none shall haue, but she which is his loue.
>
> (42.1–8)

Mahomet spends a considerable amount of time persuading her, which Hiren resists by citing the case of 'Prince-forc'd chaste *Lucretia*': 'Ere I like her be rap'd, ô reaue my breath' (49.2, 3). Mahomet continues the comparisons to famous rape victims when he offers her the compliment – 'Not halfe so faire was *Hellen*, thy pre'cessor' (53.1) – and then offers a blazon to her beauty, ending with her lips, which he proceeds to kiss. (The Helen reference is especially pointed, as one of the commonplaces of narratives of the fall of Constantinople was a reference to the fact that the city had been founded by Constantine, son to Helen, and lost by Constantine, son to another Helen.)[47]

Mahomet's kiss lasts for three stanzas, and by the end of it, Hiren has consented to her ravisher:

> twas the hidden vertue of that kisse,
> That her chast lips were nere vs'd to beforne
> That did vnframe her, and confime her his.
>
> (57.6–8)

This results in an aside to youths regarding the power of lips – 'After fifteene, who kisses a faire maide, / Had need to haue friends trusty of the fates' (58.2–3) – and a pronouncement on the fickleness of women:

> Seldome prove women friends vnto their foes,
> But when with our kindnesse they are tane,
> So weake professors swalow their owne bane:
> Shew them the axe they'l suffer martyrdome,
> But if promotion to them you propose,
> And flattery, then to the lure they come.
>
> (60.3–8)

Hiren's consent is no doubt what leads Chew to conclude that 'in style and psychology this poem is beneath contempt.'[48] It is worth noting the terms in which the kiss itself is described:

> breathles now, he breath'd into her loue,
> Who scorn'd to take possession by degrees,
> No law with her strange passion, will he prove,
> But having interest, scorn'd one inch to leese,
> *Cupid*, sheele set thee free withouten fees.
>
> (56.1–5)

The language is strikingly legalistic, and has to do principally with property. This is appropriate given that the rape of Hiren allegorizes the rape of Constantinople, but it also conveys one of the central anxieties of sixteenth-century rape law: that the woman's consent will yield to her ravisher her family's property.

In neither Painter's nor Knolles's version of the story is the wooing given much attention, and there is never any suggestion that she has consented, although in Painter they are lovers for three years. Here, Mahomet's passion is not even consummated until stanza 79, more than two-thirds of the way into the poem, and Mustapha finally enters to voice his objection to the affair in stanza 90. The prolonged debate and seduction narrative between Hiren and Mahomet changes the focus of the story considerably, moving it away from being simply a fable of the extraordinary cruelty of the Turk and more towards the usual concerns of the epyllion.

Part II of the poem opens with Hiren, though won, still resisting. The consummation of their passion takes place against the backdrop of an attack by the Christians, to which Mahoment is oblivious; the stichomythia between him and his frantic advisors further emphasizes the political significance of the whole ravishment narrative:

> One tels him that the Christians are in field.
> You do not marke her beauty, he replies.
> Two mightie Cities to their power doth yeeld:
> Note but the lustre sparkling from her eyes
>
> (71.1–4)

The juxtaposition of private pleasure and public service is common enough, and Mahomet, much like the Roman Antony, becomes effeminized by his passions:

> If she but speake to him, he low doth bend,
> And such a seruitude he doth discouer.
> Neglecting of himselfe in that grosse measure,
> That *Hiren* clips her slaue, no Emperour
>
> (85.5–8)

The comparison with Antony becomes more pointed a few stanzas later: '*Mahomet* to have his pleasure fed, / Doth loose the worlds sway for a fickle woman' (90.7–8). Unlike Antony, however, Mahomet listens to his trusty advisor Mustapha. He assembles his 'Bashaes, and the noble bloud' (98.1) and, after anatomizing Hiren's beauty for them – 'View but her hand, her lip, her brow, her eyes, / The smalnesse of her waste, and comely stature' [104.1–2] – he cuts off her head. (This would seem a fairly literal demonstration of the connection made by literary critics between the blazon and the dismembering of the beloved.) For Mahomet, this is a demonstration that shows while 'mortall men are subiect to loues rod,' he is 'natures conquereour, and a perfect God' (106.6, 8). He then runs through his trusty advisor with a sword, but is prevented from killing himself. Regaining his senses ('Awake dull mate, [awake] and leave this trance' [112.1]), he vows never to love again, and to shun pity in his conquest of the world. Mahomet's transformation is similar to that of Glaucus and other male figures in the genre, who escape enslavement by Petrarchan mistresses and gain or regain an ability to act in the public sphere.

There are many familiar elements of the epyllion here (ecphrasis, highly rhetorical speeches, blazon) and many familiar themes: love versus public service, the effeminizing power of desire, the fickle nature of women. The narrative makes the familiar point that desire must be mastered if one is not to end up as a womanish slave, excluded from the world of masculine activity; the horrifying destiny, as Shakespeare's Tarquin puts it, of 'A martial man to be soft fancy's slave!' (200). In this poem, Mahomet manages to play the roles of both Tarquin and Brutus, a confusion related to his simultaneous roles in the poem as proper masculine subject and feared political enemy. As Tarquin, he ravishes Hiren and then successfully seduces her. The political tyranny that Tarquin stands for is, for the early modern period, well represented by the Turk, but it also corresponds to the tyranny of desire, which renders Mahomet a slave. Mahomet becomes his own Brutus then, castigating his own tears and controlling his emotions, but it is Hiren who is slain in order to overthrow the tyranny. Much as Helen seems to embody the essence of rape in *Oenone and Paris*, Hiren here through an act of transference seems to absorb the tyranny that is typically associated with rape in the classical tradition. At the same time, Hiren in effect becomes Mahomet's body, the site of the unruly desires that threaten to overwhelm the self, and which Mahomet must therefore overcome. It is for this reason that the killing of Hiren is necessary, and why it is posed as a proof that Mahomet is a god rather than a human. One key difference between human and god is of course the body itself, or what the body represents: that 'mortall men are subject to loues rod' (106.6). Mahomet, much like Coriolanus, desires to be beyond desire.[49] Hiren's enslavement of Mahomet represents then a familiar if extreme example of the threat that desire poses to the masculine self, and of the necessity of triumphing over that desire.

While Hiren is another example of the dangers of women, she is clearly at the same time a synechdoche for Constantinople: 'Who reads or heares the losse of that great town / *Constantinople*, but doth wet his eyes ... O mourne her ruine' (6.1–2, 6). Hiren and Constantinople are yet two more examples of the parade of ruined maids that tramps disconsolately through the genre. The Christian states failed to protect Constantine, and the city was ravished by the Turk. The Turk is for the early modern period a figure of rapaciousness, and the fall of Constantinople is the archetypal example of this rapacity. As a result of this rape, writes Barksted, the rest of Europe, and especially Rome, is now in danger of being overrun as well. Here we see a parallel to the rape laws. The initial ravishment may, through the consent of the ravished, lead to further ravishments, specifically the property of the victim's family, which the victim may legally possess. Consent, as the poem shows, is for all intents and purposes beyond the woman's control and thus the only recourse, if one is not to lose one's property to strangers, is strict control by laws or other means. The solution, paradoxically enough, is to emulate Mahomet and at least psychologically to turn Turk. Only by mastering pity and pleasure and even conscience, like Brutus or Mahomet, can the male subject avoid the losses attendant upon involuntary consent. The subjectivity represented by Mahomet, both tyrant and ideal subject, echoes England's contradictory attitude towards the Turk, simultaneously fearful and envious, but it also provides a model for the kind of male subject useful and necessary in England's dream of empire, a dream that at the time of writing was only being realized by the Turk.

Unlike the Lucretia narrative, the story of Hiren does not end in the overthrow of a political tyranny, although Mahomet's reference to Helen as Hiren's 'pre'cessor' (53.1) does imply that Hiren will participate in the founding of a dynasty. Mahomet uses the death of Hiren as a means to further his own political tyranny and to quell dissent in his ranks. The rape does, however, mark the divide between two political systems, those of Europe and the Ottoman Empire, and between two versions of masculine subjectivity. Just as in *Oenone and Paris*, in this poem rape marks the line between the pastoral and the epic, between the Petrachan swain and the epic warrior. And as with other poems, it is not just the central character that is rendered into a potent, speaking subject through the ruin of a maid. Ultimately it is not only Mahomet who is the Brutus of this narrative but also Barksted, who uses the occasion of rape to warn Europe of the dangers of this tyrannical foe and, not incidentally, to publish at the same time a semi-pornographic poem.

Embracing Contradiction

In the poems looked at in this chapter we can observe a few common phenomena. The first we might characterize as contradiction. This exists in *Mirrha* at a basic level, in the disjuncture revealed in Bagnall's comment that Barksted gilds Mirrha's crime with delight, a contradiction registered in the poem by Mirrha's transformation; as Hopkins notes, 'Although the myrrh tree into which Myrrha is transformed is twisted and weeping it is also beautiful and fragrantly-perfumed, part of the fabled sumptuous opulence of Arabia.'[50] In *Oenone and Paris*, contradiction can be seen in Paris's recognition of the justice of Oenone's claim, a justice that he can at the same time disregard because of his new identity and new sphere of activity. Existing in the epic world of masculine activity, Paris has a different sense of justice and law, one that allows for an easy coexistence with contradiction. This sense of contradiction exists on a number of levels in the Hiren story and in contemporary attitudes towards the Ottoman Empire. In failing to rescue Constantinople and then in subsequently pursuing trade relations with the Turk while at the same time deploring the empire's rapaciousness and false religion, Christian Europe demonstrates a similar capacity for contradiction. In the poem, this is echoed to some degree by the ambivalent presentation of Mahomet, whose cruelty, while represented, is significantly downplayed in favour of other narratives. We might also see contradiction in the presentation of Hiren, who in this version becomes a willing captive, betrayed by her own body in the moment of seduction. Hiren, representative to some degree of Christian Europe, is willing to be seduced by the Turkish menace, especially, we might note, when this seduction is accompanied by the promise of riches. The problem of contradiction is to some degree solved by transferring the tyranny associated with rape to Hiren herself, who is then conveniently killed.

Related to contradiction is the problem of involuntary consent. Consent has been an issue in the poems, although in the case of Helen, who is characterized as the embodiment of rape, consent never seems to be in question. Mirrha and Hiren consent (as does Lucrece, in Barbara J. Baines's argument) but the circumstances of their consenting show how problematic an issue it is. Aside from Helen, all the victims of ravishment may be said to have consented against their will. A brief survey of early modern rape law suggests that the issue of consent gains an increasing attention in the statutes, and commentators have observed that the laws increasingly recognize women's will, as they gradually come to see the woman as the principal victim of rape, rather than her family. This change, argues these writers, is seen in the legal separation of rape and abduction. But it can also be argued that the separation allows for a useful distinction between those ravishments that involve property and those that do not. The statutes on abduction allow the law to manage or guard against the problem of consent in those cases where property is at stake.

In *Hiren* there is something of an analogy in the relations between Hiren and her body, with regard to her consent, and Mahomet and Hiren, with regard to his enslavement. Mahomet becomes enslaved by his desire, just as Hiren consents against her will. The tyranny of desire is a frequent subject of these poems, associated in both *Mirrha* and *Oenone* (and to some degree in *Hiren*) with Petrarchanisms. Desire is persistently figured as a threat to the will. What *Hiren* allows us to see is the continuum between managing desire or managing the body, and what we have called managing contradiction. The Ovidian world view is premised on the acceptance of the contradictory nature of desire and the acceptance of the inevitability of riots, incests, and rapes. Being an Ovidian means being able to manage one's desire, which is to say, being able to tolerate self-division or to establish a distance from the self that allows for the possibility of contradiction or indeed, hypocrisy. Such distance allows Brutus to castigate the Romans, Paris to abandon Oenone, Mahomet to kill Hiren, and Barksted to gild Mirrha's crime with such delight. The psychological transference or exchange that is accomplished by the figure of chiasmus in *The Rape of Lucrece* becomes a notable feature of the contractual subject, who in contracting for himself to some degree commodifies the self by making the self an object of exchange. The benefits of this psychological mechanism are, in any case, quite clear, both in the epyllion and in international trade, something which we will observe again in *The Metamorphosis of Tobacco*.

Conclusion:
Nymphs and Tobacconalias

Most serviceable *Hempseed,* but for thee,
These helpes for man could not thus scattered be.
Tobaccoes fire would soone be quenched out,
Nor would it leade men by the *Nose* about:
Nor could the *Merchants* of such heathen *Docks*
From small beginnings, purchase mighty Stockes:
By follies daily dancing to their *Pipe*
Their States from rotten stinking *Weedes* grow ripe:
By which meanes they have into Lordships run
The Clients being beggered, and vndone:
Who having smoak'd their land to Fire and Aire
They whiffe and puffe themselves into dispaire.
Ovid 'mongst all his *Metamorphosis**
Ne're knew a transformation like to this,
Nor yet could *Oedipus* e're vnderstand,
How to turne Land to Smoake, or Smoake to Land.
For by the meanes of this bewiching smother,
One Element is turn'd into another,
As Land to Fire, Fire into Aiery matter,
From Aire, (too late repenting) turnes to water.

John Taylor, *The Praise of Hempseed,* 9

*A strange change, and yet not stranger then for the women of these times to be
turned to the shapes of men

According to John Taylor, tobacco is the source of powerful metamorphoses, as tobacco merchants become lords while prodigals smoke their

family fortunes away. For many writers, this new and expensive import was a cause for concern, and tobacco comes to embody many of the problems of the new economy. In the Taylor poem as in the epyllion, these economic changes are connected with more fundamental shifts: the violations of the social hierarchy, the transformations of the rich man to the beggar and the merchant to the lord, are compared to violations of the gender hierarchy, in the form of cross-dressing women. In early modern England, one didn't have to go all the way back to the classical myth to see shapes transformed to bodies strange.

As a way of concluding, in this chapter we will look at a poem that takes the concerns of the genre and extends them outward into the contemporary world of the poem. John Beaumont's *The Metamorphosis of Tobacco* (1602) is not a typical epyllion, as it does not retell an episode of Ovid, nor does it feature any of the genre's favourite stories, the maturation of a youth or the ruination of a maid. Nonetheless, as we shall see, it is very closely allied to the genre.[1] Beaumont's poem is a mock encomium to the plant that was still something of a novelty in England. The literature of the 1590s is replete with references to tobacco-smoking gallants;[2] Henry Buttes, for example, writes:

> It chaunc'd me gazing at the Theater
> To spie a Lock-Tabacco-Chevalier,
> Clowding the loathing ayr with foggie fume
> Of Dock-Tabacco, friendly foe to rume,
> I wisht the Roman lawes seuerity
> *Who smoke selleth, with smoke be don to dy.*[3]

Smoking appears on Francis Lenton's list of the favourite activities of the fashion-obsessed Inns of Court gentlemen: 'Plaies, Dancing, Fencing, Tauerns, Tobacco.'[4] In the Middle Temple Revels of 1597–8, John Hoskyns's Tuftaffeta speech makes a certain amount of nonsensical reference to tobacco, reflecting, no doubt, the participation of Sir Walter Ralegh in the festivities.[5] Often attributed (incorrectly) with introducing tobacco into England, Ralegh was its most visible proponent.

Tobacco was almost from the moment of its introduction into England a controversial commodity, and its controversial nature was almost inevitably linked to its foreign origins. Although foreign goods had been a source of anxiety for English rulers for some time, tobacco more than most import commodities was caught up in nationalist discourses. For those who hated it, it was usually because of its non- or even anti-English nature: 't'is a toy to mocke an Ape in deed, / That English men should love a stranger weed.'[6] Or, as the title page of *Work for Chimny-sweepers* proclaims, 'Better be chokt with English hemp, / then poisoned with Indian Tabacco.' Because of its origins in the New World and its connection to pagan cultures, tobacco was associated by some with the devil: 'this hearbe seemed to bee first found out and inuented by the diuell, and first used and practised by the diuels priests, and therefore not to be used of us Christians.'[7] It was also caught up in emerging racial discourses. In *Bartholomew Fair*, Justice Overdo objects to tobacco because its 'complexion is like the Indian's that vents it!' (and secondarily, because alligators might have pissed on it).[8] In a similar vein, the satirist Joseph Hall writes in his discussion of the fictional land of Moronia: 'some think that the Indians of the torrid zone were the originators of this famous smoke, to make themselves black inside. For their color pleased them, and it did not seem right that the inside of the same body should be different in color from the outside.'[9] Tobacco, as the John Taylor epigraph demonstrates, was a commodity with a dangerously transformative power; in that sense, tobacco epitomized many of the dangers of the emerging commodity culture, dependent as it was on international trade, and the resultant changes in subjectivity connected with this new economy.

Just as it emblematized the problems of international trade, tobacco summoned up many of the current problems of international diplomacy. England had been in open conflict with Spain since 1585, and much of that conflict was carried out at sea. Barbara Fuchs argues that 'under Elizabeth, England pursued a highly aggressive para-naval policy towards Spain; in the 1570s and 80s, piracy became England's belated answer to Spain's imperial expansion.'[10] Tobacco was inevitably caught up in these activities since, as Beaumont observes, the '*Spaniards* have the royaltie, / Where glorious gold, and rich *Tabacco* be' (971–2). In the 1590s, the main supply of tobacco came from the Spanish colonies of Cumaná and Caracas, and from Trinidad, where privateers and traders bartered first with native suppliers, and after 1592, with Spanish colonists.[11] Lorimer argues that 'the trade developed, as did all other English activities in the region, out of Elizabethan privateering.'[12] Relatively small amounts of tobacco were officially imported into England from Spain, but due to the expense of the commodity, the bulk arrived via the Caribbean contraband trade.[13] Consumption of tobacco thus either enriched the enemy Spain or was dependent upon the ethically dubious activities of privateers. Given that the setting of Beaumont's poem is Virginia, it is curious to note that tobacco would not be produced in any appreciable quantities there until at least ten years after the poem's publication. In the 1590s, tobacco and Trinidad were so closely associated in the English mindset as to be synonyms.[14] Tobacco and Virginia were connected, however, in the enthusiastic propaganda for settlement in North America, where England would challenge the Spanish overseas empire.[15] By planting tobacco in Virginia, Beaumont proleptically bypasses the Spanish.

We see a similar attempt to circumvent the nationalist dilemmas caused by tobacco in Henry Buttes's *Dyets Dry Dinner*: 'By their meanes [i.e., the Spaniards] it spred farre and neare: but yet wee are not beholden to their tradition. Our English Ulisses, renomed Syr Walter Rawleigh, a man admirably excellent in Navigation, of Natures privy counsell, and infinitely reade in the wide booke of the worlde, hath both farre fetcht it, and deare bought it.'[16] In his reference to Ralegh as Ulysses, Buttes thus echoes the epyllion's desire to circumvent the Italians and claim for England an epic foundation and national destiny, only now with the Spanish as rivals rather than the Italians. His text thus participates in the 'bitter rivalry between emerging empires, especially Spain and England, to portray themselves as the true inheritors of Rome, assuming the epic mantle of empire.'[17] The same distinction surfaces in Beaumont's *Tabacco*. Because of the poem's focus westward, the rivals for empire are not the sodomitical Italians but the '*Gotthish Spaniards*' (971), 'A Nation worse then the *Laestrygones*, / And farre more sauage then the *Sauages*' (973–4). This fairly common characterization of the Spanish in the New World – more savage than the savages – does much of the same work as accusations of sodomy, placing the Spanish on the level of the subhuman and disallowing any claims to imperial glory. At the same time as it denigrates the Spanish, the poem seeks to take on the literary heritage of classical Rome by employing Ovid for the colonial enterprise.

Beaumont's panegyric to tobacco is very much in the spirit of the epyllion. Like the other poems, it is to a great degree about invention and rhetoric. This perhaps is the point of the competing aetiological narratives the poem contains: why invent only one story, when you can have three instead? Whereas other epyllia are content to spin out thirty lines of Ovid into nine hundred lines of witty self-display, Beaumont goes one better and writes an Ovidian poem that is not based on a story from Ovid at all (although portions of the poem are in fact almost direct translations from the first book of the *Metamorphoses*). As is signalled in the fleeting references to 'our wittie *Mores*' (907) and 'the learned *Rott'rodame*,' Erasmus (908), the poem is to some degree in the tradition of *The Praise of Folly*: here the subject is one frequently allied with folly, or with trifling. Beaumont reminds us, however, that if it is a trifle, it is a fashionable one, consumed by gallants rather than 'that corrupted artificiall drug, / Which euery Gull as his owne soule doth hug' (19–20), dock-tobacco. In his *Counter-Blaste to Tobacco* (1604), published a couple of years later, James I attributes tobacco's popularity to people's 'foolish affectation of any noueltie': 'Doe we not dayly see, that a man can no sooner bring ouer from beyond the Seas any new forme of apparell, but that hee can not bee thought a man of spirit, that would not presently imitate the same? And so from hand to hand it spreades, till it be practised by all, not for any commoditie that is in it, but only because it is come to be the fashion.'[18] As we saw in the first chapter, the young gentlemen of the Inns of Court were known to be obsessed with the latest trend. This poem, itself part of a fashionable genre, is able to combine the fashionable commodity with yet another current source of fascination, literature from or about the New World.

The poem begins with some opening lines of praise to the plant, and then goes on to offer three differing histories of tobacco. The first has to do with Prometheus and Earth who, along with her sisters, creates an herb that inspires life into Prometheus's creation. The second is a tale of a Virginian nymph whose beauty causes Apollo to hide his head in the ocean, and Jove to come a-wooing. Juno changes the nymph to a plant, which Jove imbues with mystical powers that cause the golden age to begin. (Included in this narrative is a long courtroom scene, in which Suadia, Jove's solicitor, indicts Apollo for dereliction of duty.) The third tale denies that the gods ever had knowledge of the plant or the history of the world would certainly have been different; this is then demonstrated at length. The poem as a whole ends with the suggestion that a new golden age has appeared in England, as a result of Elizabeth's colonial endeavours, and this golden age is crowned with tobacco.

In the poem, tobacco is both literally and figuratively an inspirational commodity: it is life-giving and life-restoring and it rivals rhetoric and song in its civilizing effects. Beaumont persistently links rhetoric and tobacco in the poem. Sometimes rhetoric's effects are transferred to tobacco, other times tobacco renders rhetoric dumb. Had the ancients known of tobacco, the narrator asserts, Homer and Anacreon would have had no need of writing. Invoking one of the cherished topoi of humanist writing and one of its exemplars of rhetoric, the poem argues that tobacco would have replaced rhetoric as the origin of civil society:

Nor needed *Hermes* with his fluent tongue
Haue ioin'd in one a rude vnciuill throng,
And by perswasions made that companie
An order'd Politike societie,
When this dumbe Oratour would more perswade
Then all the speeches *Mercurie* had made.

(703–8)

Similarly, at the sight of tobacco, '*Orpheus* himselfe would haue forsooke his Lute, / And altogether stood amaz'd, and mute' (811–12). Closer to home, tobacco would have rendered unnecessary the humanist revolution, which saw itself as founded on rhetoric:

Had great *Tabacco* pleas'd to shew her powers,
As now she doth in this blest age of ours,
Blest age, wherein the *Indian* Sunne had shin'd,
Whereby all Arts, all tongues have been refin'd:
Learning long buried in the darke abysme
Of dunsticall, and monkish barbarisme,
When once this herbe by carefull paines was found,
Sprung vp like *Cadmus* followers from the ground,
Which Muses visitation bindeth vs,
More to great *Cortez*, and *Vespucius*,
Then to our wittie *Mores* immortall name,
To *Valla*, or the learned *Rott'rodame.*

(907–18)

Learning, like tobacco itself, lingered in darkness until this age discovered it. Humanism and exploration are here set up as complementary or equivalent activities, and more particularly, rhetoric and tobacco are closely aligned. Exploration (along with its unnamed associate, overseas trade) becomes the logical corollary to humanist learning, and in some ways surpasses it. We are more indebted to Cortez and Vespucci than to More, Valla, and Erasmus for the recovery of the Muses, avers the narrator. This, argues Barbara Shapiro, was not an unusual sentiment, especially at the Inns of Court, which counted among their number the elder Richard Hakluyt, a lawyer and a member of the Middle Temple. The gentlemen of the Inns of Court were known for their interests 'in the study of anatomy, astronomy, geography, history, mathematics, theology, and foreign languages,'[19] and thus were fully aware of all the new discoveries challenging classical authority: 'the expansion of factual knowledge of the Old and New Worlds made a great impression on humanists and nonhumanists alike. Not only were the new facts interesting in and of themselves, but they seemed to suggest that the ancient world was not the repository of all knowledge. And orientation towards the future became possible.'[20] We have encountered this new orientation towards futurity in other contexts (most notably in connection to the contract); here, we might observe, it is linked with a larger historical trajectory similar to that found in the poems of Edwards and Weever, where the classical world was colonized for England's further national glory. The recourse to the Old World provides the necessary epic beginnings for England's dynastic ambitions.

The poem, as we have noted, starts with a hymn of praise to tobacco, 'The blessed offspring of an vncouth land' (16). The narrator invokes the spirit of tobacco to inspire his song, the 'great God of Indian melodie, / Which at the *Caribes* banquet gouern'st all, / And gently rul'st the sturdiest *Caniball*' (32–4), one of the first of many instances in which tobacco performs the traditional role of rhetoric or song. Tobacco has inspired the '*Indian* Priests' (41) and their 'barbrous Poetrie' (42); now it will enable the poet to 'pitch [his muse's] tents on the *Parnassian* hill' (50). The drug which can inspire Indians at their 'bloodie feasts' (35) will now assist in the colonization of the home of classical poetry.

The first story that the muse inspires begins with Ovid's account of the creation of the universe. Prometheus then creates the form of humans and steals fire from the sun, but he is condemned by Jove to be chained to the Caucasus. Earth, pitying him and his creation, calls together her sisters to create a miraculous plant: 'eu'ry Ladie shall that herbe endow / With the best gemmes that deck her glorious brow' (179–80). It is thus tobacco, and not just the divine fire, that is responsible for human life: 'thus adorn'd, by holy fire inflam'd / Sweete life and breath within that carkasse fram'd' (225–6). Jove hides the plant 'from the worlds better part' (238) but one day the Muses stumble across it in the 'palace of great *MuteZume*' (245). Entranced, they abandon Europe for 'this truest *Indian* treasure' (248). As a result, 'braules and quarrels rise' in Europe, 'All friendship banisht' (254–5). This failure of civilization is cured when tobacco is found. Tobacco, much like rhetoric in the humanist accounts, restores order to the Old World and the humanist dream of a united Christian Europe is fictionally realized.

The second, alternative tale is much longer, although it has a similar trajectory. It concerns a nymph who dwells in the valleys of Wingandekoe, 'Which now a farre more glorious name doth beare, / Since a more beautious Nymph was worshipt there' (265–6), which is to say Elizabeth, the virgin queen. The native nymph is so beautiful that she outshines the sun and the moon, and they hide themselves in shame. This dereliction of duty by the sun leads to a courtroom scene, where Apollo defends himself with a brilliant display of legal rhetoric. Jove, thus hearing of the maid, heads off to seduce her in typical Ovidian style, 'Telling her stories how the force of loue / Had bow'd the hearts of Gods that dwelt aboue' (447–8). The ever-jealous Juno transforms the nymph into an herb, to which Jove adds both earthly and celestial powers, 'And fram'd it as a *Micro-cosme* of good' (472). Tobacco then causes the golden age to begin.

The description of the golden age is largely a translation from Book I of the *Metamorphoses*. Ovid says that there was no need of law, and 'no suppliant throng gazed fearfully upon its judge's face; but without defenders lived secure' (I; 9).[21] Beaumont elaborates on this for his Inns of Court audience, satirizing the corruptions of the legal profession:

> Nor did the busie Client feare his cause,
> Nor in strong brasse did they engraue their lawes,
> Nor did the doubtfull parties faintly tremble,
> While the brib'd Iudge did dreadful looks dissemble.
>
> (481–4)

The next major feature of the golden age in Ovid is an absence of sea travel: 'Nor yet had the pine-tree, felled on its native mountains, descended thence into the watery plain to visit other lands; men knew no shores except their own. Nor yet were cities begirt with steep moats' (I; 9). Sea travel is, of course, an engrossing topic for the Elizabethans and particularly appropriate to the subject of this poem. Beaumont makes an interesting shift in emphasis here, specifying sea travel for commercial purposes:

> Then safe from harme the vaunting Pine did stand,
> And had no triall of the Shipwrights hand,
> But stood vpon the hill where first it grew,
> Nor yet was forc'd another world to view:
> Nor vnto greedie Merchants yet were knowne

The shores of any land beyond their owne:
Eu'ry defencelesse Citie then was sure,
Nor could deep ditches make it more secure.

(485–92)

In Ovid, there is something of a break between the mention of exploration and the mention of cities with moats, although they are obviously to
some degree related. In Beaumont, as in Elizabethan culture generally,
the links are a little clearer. In particular, the connection between 'greedie
Merchants' and the many 'defencelesse Citie[s]' attacked by English
pirates and government-sanctioned privateers in the pages of Hakluyt
would have been rather pointed to a late Elizabethan audience (and in
fact English pirates sometimes disguised themselves as merchants).[22]
Many of Elizabeth's foreign policy interventions were made at least
partially to secure or protect English commercial interests.[23] This connection between trade and warfare is strengthened by another addition
the poem makes to Ovid. Immediately after the mention of the lack of
war, Beaumont returns to the issue of sea travel: 'Nor did ambitious
Captaines know the way / To passe the cliffie shores of their owne sea'
(497–8). Whether these are captains of the navy or the merchant marine
is not specified. One of the most ambitious captains in Elizabeth's day
was also the one most associated with tobacco, privateering, and the
settlement of Virginia: Sir Walter Ralegh.

The golden age in this section ends when a jealous Proserpine commands the furies to set fire to the earth with torches made of tobacco:
'And euer since they by these flames did cause / Famine, dissention,
plagues, and breach of lawes' (531–2). To cover her tracks, Proserpine
hires poets to blame all of the destruction on Phaeton. This tobacco
scourge starts the iron age, and overseas exploration. Ovid says, 'Men
now spread sails to the winds, though the sailor as yet scarce knew them;
and keels of pine which long had stood upon high mountain-sides, now
leaped insolently over unknown waves' (I; 11). Beaumont once again
modifies this to mean overseas trade:

The Merchant then the boistrous sea did plow,
Spite of the frowne of *Neptunes* angrie brow,
Nor could the horrour of one iourneyes paine
Feare greedie thoughts from ventring so againe:
Neptune then grieued with the wounds and dints,

...

Made the Sea stormie, which before was mild:
Since which the ribs of broken ships doe show,
What hurts and dangers by this engine grow,
Which makes each fertile countrie want the more,
By seeming Steward of each countries store.

(547–51, 556–60)

Once again, Hakluyt lurks in the background here, with his many tales of shipwrecks and his many tales of lucrative piracy and privateering. The passage also summons up the new interest in colonization, especially England's schemes for New World plantations. As in the golden age section, overseas trade and war are implicitly connected. As in Ovid, in the iron age all civilized bonds are forgotten, greed and disease are rampant, and the goddess Ate rules the earth. Aesculapius takes it upon himself to cure man. The god:

(Enuying the glorie shepheard *Pan* had wonne,
When of his loue transform'd he did inuent
The pleasure of a Musicke instrument)
Descri'd this herbe to our new golden age,
And did deuise a pipe, which should asswage
The wounds, which sorrow in our hearts did fixe,
More than the sound of flutes, and fiddle-sticks.

(656–62)

Pan's pipe is thus surpassed by Aesculapius's, as tobacco once again rivals music and its close ally rhetoric, soothing our heartache and returning civilization to the earth. As with the first myth, the rediscovery institutes something of a golden age, which the third account of tobacco will make even more explicit.

The third account of tobacco does not give an origin for the plant, but suggests instead that the gods of the classical world could not have known about it, or the world would have evolved much differently.[24] This section of the poem is the showiest, widely ranging over classical literature and world history, offering witty accounts of what might have been. The Romans, for example, had they known of the divine herb, would have staged '*Tobacconalia*[s]' (716) instead of their usual celebrations. Beaumont takes us through the world of the *Metamorphoses*, through classical history, discoursing on medieval history and the displacement of scholastic philosophy (in a passage quoted above) until he reaches the present. Here we learn that 'our more glorious Nymph, our modern Muse' Elizabeth (921),

> Hath vncontrol'd stretcht out her mightie hand
> Ouer *Virginia,* and the *New-found-land,*
> And spread the Colours of our *English* Rose
> In the farre countries, where *Tabacco* growes,
> And tam'd the sauage nations of the West,
> Which of this iewell were in vaine possest.

$$(931-6)$$

Breezing lightly over the Spanish, Beaumont suggests that a new golden age is upon us, at least those of us in England. Or more accurately, given tobacco's oft-cited superiority to gold, a tobacco age is upon us.[25]

The three narratives do share something of a common trajectory, all tending towards the suggestion that England is the rightful heir of classical history and that England's colonial ventures are a necessary component of that. The geographic progress of the earlier poems, from the home of the gods of classical literature to Elizabeth's kingdom, is now extended even further westward. Knapp argues of the third narrative that 'the gods' ignorance of tobacco damns the classical world, by reminding Beaumont's readers of one of the first and most powerful intellectual reactions to America's discovery, the realization that the ancients had, for all their intimidating genius, proven profoundly benighted.'[26] Bearing in mind how writers of epyllia, such as Edwards and Weever, claim the classical tradition for England, we might see this less as a damning than an appropriation: Beaumont still wants to pitch tobacco's tent 'on the *Parnassian* hill' (50), after all. The importation of tobacco, much like the importation of classical literature, allows English literature to become the rightful heir of Rome. In other poems this appropriation has sometimes taken the form of a dismissal of Petrarchanism, a dismissal which rejects contemporary Rome for its classical incarnation, and reinforces this claim by Englishing Ovid. Here a similar process of national differentiation takes place, but given the subject of praise, it is the Spanish who are rejected rather than the Italians.

Another internal differentiation takes place in the poem, which we can see most prominently in the alterations to Ovid's golden age. These alterations cause some logical problems within the poem: if tobacco is so wonderful, why are the sea-faring merchants who provide it such a menace? Part of this presumably has to do with the aristocracy's desire to distance itself from the mercantile enterprises in which it was nonetheless heavily involved, which was sometimes accomplished by stressing the heroic aspects of exploration and downplaying the trade.[27] Many of the pirates plying international waters were officially sanctioned privateers, and their voyages, like Drake's circumnavigation, made many of their investors, including Elizabeth, very rich.[28] Kim F. Hall notes that the aristocracy was involved in England's economic transformation 'to a degree unprecedented in Europe. Thus the class that was in great part responsible for the great flowering of vernacular literature was simultaneously involved in laying the groundwork for Britain's future economic advancement' and much of that advancement came through the joint-stock companies and overseas trade, in which members of Beaumont's family almost certainly invested.[29] This does not mean, however, that the aristocracy enthusiastically embraced a mercantile ethos. Quite the contrary, as Fuchs argues: there is a clear anxiety in plays dealing with trade and exploration that if 'the aristocracy stoops to trade for the sake of riches, while the lower classes trade to improve their station, the hierarchies of the social echelon risk becoming meaningless in the pursuit of commerce.'[30] Another anxiety that lurks in the background is the awareness that by attacking the Spanish, English privateers are aiding the Turk, and are becoming virtually indistinguishable from the Barbary corsairs. As both Fuchs and Matar argue in different contexts, England's activities in the New World were intertwined in complex ways with the politics of the Mediterranean.[31]

In thinking about these anxieties around trade, we might remember here the two constituencies of the Inns of Court: the upper classes, like Beaumont and his brothers, for whom the Inns were something of a finishing school and fashionable residence, and another group who were actually there to learn the law, which would have included the children of wealthy merchants. As Wilfred R. Prest notes, the former community distanced itself from the latter and was given to anxious assertions of its social superiority. For this community of aristocrats and gallants, tobacco is imported in the poem not through pirates or worse yet merchants, but rather through classical learning. We can see a related project in Camões's mercantile epic, *The Lusiads*, where classical literary form is appropriated to dignify Portugal's adventures in India.[32] Here, however, the comic classical allusions are used to distance rather than to dignify the mercantile aspects of exploration.

In dignifying the commodity, the poem necessarily justifies colonialism. One of the more familiar of these justifications is that the natives 'of this iewell were in vaine possest' (936), which is linked to the idea that natives do not know the value of anything.[33] We see this as well in James's *Counter-Blaste*, combined with, among other things, the anti-Spanish objection: 'shall we, I say, without blushing, abase ourselues so farre, as to imitate these beastly *Indians*, slaues to the *Spaniards*, refuse to the world, and as yet aliens from the holy Couenant of God? Why doe we not as well imitate them in walking naked as they doe? in preferring glasses, feathers, and such toyes, to golde and precious stones, as they do?'[34] The assertion of the native's ignorance of the worth of tobacco is contradicted more than once in the poem, where we see Indian poets inspired by smoking, cannibals calmed at banquets, and others using it to overcome physiological difficulties: 'those, to whom *Plinie* no mouths did giue, / Doe only on diuine *Tabacco* liue' (1033–4). More to the point is the idea that the natives figure as a prehistory for the English. Just as tobacco was hidden among the savages, so our learning was obscured in 'monkish barbarisme' until the 'blest age' of humanism arrived. Just as the golden age of England supercedes that of the classical era, so does the nymph Elizabeth supercede the nymph of Wingandekoe. We were not given tobacco earlier, says Beaumont, 'Least mortals should no worke, nor trade professe, / But spend their daies in lust, and idlenesse' (945–6), rather like the inhabitants of the New World, according to many accounts. This belongs to another strain of early modern discourse on the New World regarding the golden age and pre-contact natives, a discourse exemplified by Thomas Harriot's *Briefe and True Report of the New Found Land of Virginia*, Montaigne's essay 'Of Cannibals,' and Shakespeare's *The Tempest*. As Stephen Orgel notes in his introduction to *The Tempest*, these texts suggest in diverse ways that 'in the New World, Europe could see its own past, itself in embryo.'[35] Here, although that is clearly signaled in some places, especially in the portrayals of the golden age, it is just as clearly contradicted elsewhere, where the natives are portrayed as 'voide of sense, / With sauage rites, and manners' (919–20).

What are we to make of these contradictions? Presumably, given the general tone of the poem, the logical inconsistencies contribute to the humour of the undertaking. The point is not to make a serious pitch for tobacco, overseas trade, or the moral superiority of the natives of North America, but rather to wittily praise a fashionable and controversial habit. At the same time, however, we might note that the humour does in fact work to acknowledge and displace the unresolveable contradictions involved in the tobacco trade and the larger changes in the economy that the tobacco industry epitomized. Which is to say: sure there are problems, but so what? The Ovidian voice is one which is peculiarly suited to such moral, or more properly amoral, stances. Just as the Ovidian narrator can acknowledge the cruelties of desire as an inevitable part of the comedy of life, so here can the world-weary nineteen-year-old recognize the ethical compromises of tobacco and continue to smoke. Here we must recognize that acknowledgment of contradiction is in fact an essential part of the genre. This allows us to see what is at work in a genre which frequently offers competing narratives without adjudicating between them ('Others affirme' [671], 'Others doe tell' [261]), and at the same time is devoted to sententiae, gnomes, and truisms ('Floods from the earths strange motions often rise' [146]; 'Who laies on colours doth the substance hide' [328]). This has less to do with some kind of commitment to the radical contingency of knowledge, and more to do with a pragmatic stance that there are some things that the narrator knows to be true, and others about which he does not care. Not deciding is precisely what enables a stance that has less to do with moral relativism than with the irrelevance of morals. Taking this stance allows the narrator to outrageously align rhetoric, which had a high moral purpose for the humanists, with tobacco, which the poem gleefully admits to be a morally questionable trifle. This is, in fact, a necessary equivalence, when the poem can see that the purposes of England's overseas voyages have less to do with the overt justification of bringing glory to the nation and civilization to the natives, tasks for which rhetoric is eminently suited, and more to do with the base desire for gold and foreign commodities.

At the same time, the poem's play with matters of truth and knowledge reflects the developing notion of fact within the period.[36] Barbara Shapiro hypothesizes connections between refinements in legal method and larger intellectual developments, which were spurred on to some degree by the expansion of factual knowledge that was the result of exploration. 'There can be no doubt,' she writes, 'that many leading lawyers in England were familiar with, and participated in, major intellectual movements of the sixteenth and seventeenth centuries. In the area of evidence and proof, these intellectual movements clearly influenced the development of the law itself. Judges and lawyers, no less than philosophers, scientists, historians, and theologians, had a major commitment to finding methods and procedures which best elucidated and established truth.'[37] The fact, with its claim to objectivity, is akin to both

perspectivism in painting, which offers a purely mathematical representation of space, and the plain style in rhetoric. We can argue then, that
the genre's interest in vision and painting is linked to its interest in
sententiae and aetiological digression. More importantly, however, we
can link it to a certain attitude towards knowledge and desire that is
characteristic of the Ovidian narrator, which is most clearly on display in
those poems that deal with sexual violence. The management of contradiction characteristic of the narrators in those poems is clearly related to
the narrator's relation to tobacco in this poem. The narrator's distance
from his own desire is exactly analogous to the distance between the
disinterested, observing eye and its discrete object of knowledge. In
neither case is the self morally implicated in its own activities.

   The Metamorphosis of Tobacco demonstrates that the attitude that the
Ovidian poet takes towards desire is transferable to other aspects of its
existence. The version of subjectivity constructed across this poem, especially in the narrative voice, is certainly congruent with the sexual and
political subjects we have seen in other poems. While it is simplistic to
suggest that Ovidian poetry is inherently colonialist, we can see that the
particular moral pose that Elizabethan Ovidian poetry affects is one that
is amenable to overcoming the dilemma that colonialist activities posed
for thinking Christians. The same rhetorical ploys and psychological
mechanisms involved in Ovidian love poetry are at work here in the
service of colonial exploitation. More broadly, we can see that the literary nationalism of the other poems exists on a continuum with a range
of nationalisms, ones that oppose the English not just to Petrarchans but
to the '*Gotthish Spaniards*' (961). Just as Thomas Edwards writes in *Narcissus* that it is the job of English poets to send to 'Nations farre, / The
greatnes of faire *Albions* praise' (L'Envoy 12.5–6), this poem applauds
Elizabeth's attempt to 'spread the Colours of our *English* Rose' (933)   .
over the globe. The two are clearly related ventures.

The rapid rise and fall of the epyllion is an interesting question for
literary history, although, as I suggested in the introductory chapter, it is
by no means an isolated case. A number of reasons might be submitted
for why the epyllion ceased to be written in any significant numbers after
1603. The first is simply the vicissitudes of literary fashion, compounded
by the interests of the genre itself. Because the appeal of the genre was to
a large degree its self-consciously fashionable nature, it consequently
had a built-in obsolescence. In a related vein, it may also have been
affected by the fortunes of Petrarchan poetry in England. The death of

Elizabeth has often been seen to have coincided with changes in literary taste, either because she was no longer around to favour particular poetic modes, or because there were wider changes in mood accompanying a new regime at court. The epyllion's fashionably cynical approach to desire, which was to some degree based on a satiric distance from the poetic mainstream, now passes *into* the poetic mainstream, in the works of Donne, Jonson, and the metaphysical poets.

Why does any genre disappear? If we see literature as having serious (if perhaps unconscious) social aims, we might hypothesize that genres disappear when the cultural work they were performing has been accomplished or is no longer seen as necessary, or when the grounds on which they staged their cultural interventions have shifted. The latter would appear to be the case with the epyllion, if the previous paragraph is correct in its surmises. But what, ultimately, was the cultural work the epyllion was performing?

Lynn Enterline points to a fascinating quirk of cultural history in the period: although Virgil and the *Aeneid* were regarded as the pinnacle of an Elizabethan schoolboy's education, the 1590s witnessed a boom not in epic but in its minor cousin.[38] Why did this generation retreat from the serious, public concerns of the epic to the trivial dalliances of the epyllion? And what is it that distinguishes the aims of these two genres, other than length? In his study *Epic and Empire*, David Quint identifies 'two rival traditions of epic ... associated with Virgil and Lucan. These define an opposition between epics of the imperial victors and epics of the defeated, a defeated whose resistance contains the germ of a broader republican or antimonarchical politics.'[39] Like the epics of the victors, the epyllion is attached to England's imperial project, but we have at the same time identified in the genre a form of republican politics, especially in those poems that deal with the matter of empire. The epyllion paradoxically embodies opposing principles; it is a genre, as we have seen, that is founded on the embrace of contradiction. In the introduction, I suggested that one difference between the epic and the epyllion was the kind of political subject at the centre: while both see self-mastery as essential for the masculine subject and both see women, especially those from the east, as a threat to that subject, the epic typically features the ideal subject of nationhood, a hero who embodies key elements of the national ideology. The cynical tone of the epyllion, on the other hand, rules out any idealism; its principal target is the idealistic Petrarchan poet, but this cynicism radiates outwards into the world.

This leads to a crucial distinction between the two genres. While the subject of the epyllion is an imperialist subject, it is at the same time a cynical subject, in Slavoj Žižek's terms. According to Žižek, the cynical subject is marked by a paradoxical stance towards ideology: 'one knows the falsehood very well, one is well aware of a particular interest hidden behind an ideological universality, but still one does not renounce it.'[40] Thus, for example, the narrator of *Tobacco* knows that the idealistic claims for imperialism are false, but nonetheless remains committed to the project. Such a cynicism depends upon the self-division we have observed in the Elizabethan Ovidian subject, a self-division based on an abstraction, Žižek would argue, that is ultimately preceded and structured by the commodity form.

Quint observes that the epic as a form ends in the Renaissance. Given the epyllion's connection to the epic, this would provide another reason for the former's disappearance. But given the distinction we have just elucidated, the epyllion's appearance may at the same time announce the end or the impossibility of epic, at least in the Virgilian mode. Following our earlier logic, we could surmise that the epic disappeared because it could no longer perform the cultural work for which it was most suited, since the grounds for its intervention had shifted. In particular, the kind of subject it was designed to produce, one with an idealistic attachment to nationhood, was no longer necessary, useful, or even possible in this new form of empire. Although Spenser wanted his epic to fashion an ideal English gentleman, the project had to be abandoned after Book VI. The epyllion does a far better job of producing the subject necessary for England's overseas commercial ventures, which is perhaps why it flourishes in the dying moments of the epic. Although the epyllion is positioned at the end of several traditions – of the epic, of Petrarchan poetry, of a certain version of humanism – it nonetheless announces the beginning of others, heralding an approach to desire, to the self, and to the world whose time, evidently, had come.

Notes

Introduction: Heterosexuality and Citizenship in the Elizabethan Epyllion

1 Brown, '"Tradition and the Individual Talent": Teaching Ovid and the Epyllion in the Context of the 1590s,' 93.
2 Traub, 'Afterword,' 266.
3 Bredbeck, *Sodomy and Interpretation*, 118.
4 Maslen, 'Myths Exploited: The Metamorphoses of Ovid in Early Elizabethan England,' 28.
5 The first example of the genre, Thomas Lodge's, was published in 1589; the last major example, Francis Beaumont's, in 1602. As might be expected, lesser productions sporadically appeared until 1646, when James Shirley's *Narcissus, or the Self-Lover* appeared, which seems to be the end of the road. Some critics have identified Tennyson's 'Oenone' as an epyllion, but in structure and tone it more closely resembles a complaint.
6 Walter Allen, Jr., 'The Non-Existent Classical Epyllion.' The use of the term in classical literary studies continues to be a matter of some minor controversy. The most prominent candidate for the term is Catullus 64, 'The Marriage of Peleus and Thetis': see, for example, Pavlock, *Eros, Imitation, and the Epic Tradition*, 69–146; and Kenneth Quinn, *Texts and Contexts*, 74. Critics of the English examples, by contrast, generally agree that there is a genre but disagree on its name and its characteristics.
7 Hulse, *Metamorphic Verse*; Keach, *Elizabethan Erotic Narratives*, 119.
8 Enterline, '"Embodied Voices": Petrarch Reading (Himself Reading) Ovid.'
9 Bate offers a lucid survey of the history of Ovid in Renaissance England in chapter 1 of his *Shakespeare and Ovid*, 1–47. Other early Elizabethan translations of single tales include the following: *The fable of Ovid treting of Narcissus* (1560); Thomas Underdowne, *Excellent historye of Theseus and Ariadne*

(1566); and William Hubbard, *Tragicall and lamentable historie of Ceyx, kynge of Thrachine, and Alcione his wife* (1569).

10 For a recent discussion of Golding's translation and the extent to which it moralizes, see Lyne, *Ovid's Changing Worlds: English* Metamorphoses, *1567– 1632*, 27–79. In quoting the *Metamorphoses*, I have depended upon two editions, depending on whether an early modern or a modern translation seemed most appropriate. References to Ovid in the text will be either to Golding's edition, and will include book and line number, or to Mary M. Inne's prose translation, in which case the citation will refer to page number.

11 This example comes from Barkan, *Transuming Passion*, 39.

12 For a discussion of Petrarchism in England, see Dubrow, *Echoes of Desire*.

13 Full bibliographic information for the editions of epyllia used can be found in the first section of the Works Cited. Many of the epyllia referred to in this study are available in Elizabeth Story Donno's (now out of print) anthology, *Elizabethan Minor Epics*. Because Donno's anthology excludes surrounding matter such as title pages and dedicatory poems (and in the case of Weever's *Faunus and Melliflora*, the concluding poems), I have cited editions that reproduce the original texts more fully. In general, I will provide line numbers as they appear in the editions used, either lines or stanza and line numbers, or page numbers. Some later examples of the epyllia can be found in Paul W. Miller, ed., *Seven Minor Epics of the English Renaissance*.

14 In contrast to the present study, Georgia E. Brown argues that the epyllion consciously defines itself in opposition to the epic, flaunting its status as trivial and marginal, and thus effeminizes its author ('Gender and Voice in "Hero and Leander"'). On the emergence of the English nation in Eliza- bethan England, see Helgerson, *Forms of Nationhood*.

15 Nor, the reader will have noticed, does this one: the press thought it inadvis- able to have such an obscure word in the title.

16 In a recent discussion of Chapman, John Huntington discusses Chapman's hostility to what could be seen as the dominant tendencies of the genre, although he does argue that the poem is at heart Ovidian (*Ambition, Rank and Poetry in 1590s England*, 128–46). As I argue above, however, there are a number of different Ovids corresponding to different cultural milieux.

17 Osborne, *The Life, Letters and Writings of John Hoskyns, 1566–1638*, 152.

18 As we shall see in chapter 5, in another tradition of interpretation the Orpheus myth was also read as a story about the civilizing power of rhetoric, generally seen in Orpheus charming the wild beasts. This does not tend to be the Orpheus that appears in the epyllion.

19 Marotti, '"Love Is not Love": Elizabethan Sonnet Sequences and the Social Order.'

20 Warner, 'New English Sodom,' 347.

21 Traub, 'The (In)Significance of "Lesbian" Desire in Early Modern England,' 72–3.

22 Rocke, *Forbidden Friendships: Homosexuality and Male Culture in Renaissance Florence*.

23 On Hobbes, see Macpherson, *Political Theory of Possessive Individualism*. By contrast, in Sir Thomas Smith's *De Republica Anglorum*, perhaps the most important work of political philosophy in the Elizabethan period, the family (really the married couple) is quite clearly the smallest unit and the foundation of society. See Book I, chapters 11–15, where he offers a natural history of government.

24 Pye, *The Vanishing: Shakespeare, the Subject and Early Modern Culture*, 8.

25 Dubrow, *Echoes of Desire*, 37.

26 Lewis, *The Allegory of Love*.

27 The most obvious evidence of this emergence is the increasing power of parliament over the course of Elizabeth's reign, and especially the House of Commons's changing conception of its role in the governance of the nation. See, for example, MacCaffrey, *Queen Elizabeth and the Making of Policy, 1572–1588*, 463–99.

1. The Metamorphosis of the Subject

1 Ovid, *Sorrows of an Exile*, 4.x. Patrick Cheney notes, 'As a young man, Ovid served Rome by holding minor offices: he was a *triumvir capitalis* or member of a board presiding over prisons; a member of a centrumviral court presiding over questions of inheritances; and a judge in private lawsuits' (*Marlowe's Counterfeit Profession*, 59).

2 This is the case even with Marlowe and Shakespeare. Lucy Gent, for example, draws attention to the influence of the Inns of Court culture on *Venus and Adonis* in 'Venus and Adonis: The Triumph of Rhetoric,' 721–2.

3 Richardson, *A History of the Inns of Court*, 69; Finkelpearl, *John Marston of the Middle Temple*, 18–31; Marotti, *Manuscript, Print, and the English Renaissance Lyric*, 35–7.

4 Tubbs, *The Common Law Mind*, 129–67; Helgerson, *Forms of Nationhood*, 63–104.

5 For a discussion of the role and development of these various courts, see Plucknett, *Concise History*, 83–190.

6 Smith, *De Republica Anglorum* (1583), 142.

7   Baker, *Reports*, 51.
8   Ibid., 85.
9   Ibid., 142.
10 Plucknett, *Early English Legal Literature*, 103.
11 Tubbs, *The Common Law Mind*, 45.
12 Baker, *Reports*, 124.
13 Ibid., 135.
14 Tubbs, *The Common Law Mind*, 193.
15 Ibid., 166.
16 Bate, *Shakespeare and Ovid*, 19–25; Enterline, *Rhetoric of the Body from Ovid to Shakespeare*, 164–7. For a much fuller account of grammar school education, see Baldwin's *William Shakespeare's Small Latine and Less Greek*.
17 Quoted in Tubbs, *The Common Law Mind*, 234n3.
18 Quoted in Tubbs, *The Common Law Mind*, 151.
19 See Bland, 'Henry VIII's Royal Commission on the Inns of Courts'; and Fisher, 'Thomas Cromwell, Humanism and Educational Reform, 1530–40.'
20 Knafla, 'The Influence of Continental Humanists and Jurists on the English Common Law in the Renaissance,' 66.
21 DeNeef, 'The Poetics of Orpheus: The Text and a Study of *Orpheus His Journey to Hell* (1595),' 27.
22 Donno, Introduction, *Elizabethan Minor Epics*, 9.
23 Stone, *The Crisis of the Aristocracy, 1558–1641*, 240; Stretton, *Women Waging Law in Elizabethan England*, 6.
24 Barkan, *Transuming Passion*, 18–19.
25 Barkan, 'Diana and Acteon: The Myth as Synthesis,' 318.
26 Lacan, *The Seminar of Jacques Lacan. Book VII*, 143.
27 Barkan, *Transuming Passion*, 27.
28 Ibid., 18.
29 de Grazia, 'Weeping for Hecuba,' 359.
30 Greenblatt, 'Psychoanalysis and Renaissance Culture,' 144, 135.
31 Skura, 'Understanding the Living and Talking to the Dead: The Historicity of Psychoanalysis'; Sedinger, 'Historicism and Renaissance Culture'; Davis, 'On the Lame'; and Bellamy, *Translations of Power*. Two recent essay collections address in various ways psychoanalysis in early modern studies: Valeria Finucci and Regina Schwartz, eds, *Desire in the Renaissance* (Princeton, NJ: Princeton University Press, 1994); and Carla Mazzio and Douglas Trevor, eds, *Historicism, Psychoanalysis, and Early Modern Culture* (New York: Routledge, 2000).
32 Greenblatt, 'Psychoanalysis and Renaissance Culture,' 136–7.
33 Davis, 'On the Lame,' 602.

34 Roper, *Oedipus and the Devil*, 13.
35 Skura, 'Understanding the Living and Talking to the Dead,' 83–4.
36 Silverman, *Male Subjectivity at the Margins*, 41.
37 Ibid., 27.
38 Ibid., 23.
39 Guth, 'The Age of Debt, the Reformation and the English Law,' 69.
40 Plucknett, *Concise History*, 141–2.
41 Radin, *Reinterpreting Property*, 55.
42 Enterline, *Rhetoric of the Body*, 158.
43 Bashar, 'Rape in England between 1550 and 1700,' 33.
44 *Statutes of the Realm*, 5 & 6 Phil & Mary c. 8; 18 Eliz. c. 7.
45 Porter, 'Rape – Does It Have a Historical Meaning?' 217.
46 Walker, 'Rereading Rape,' 2, 4. A recent example of such an ahistorical
   reading of rape is Barbara J. Baines's claim, extraordinary in an essay on the
   representation of rape, that 'the very meaning of rape eludes' the author of
   the *Lawes Resolutions of Womens Rights*, as if such a meaning were singular
   and self-evident ('Effacing Rape in Early Modern Representation,' 77).
47 Manning, *Village Revolts*, 33.
48 Gowing, *Domestic Dangers: Women, Words, and Sex in Early Modern London*.
49 Žižek, *The Sublime Object of Ideology*, 25.
50 Greenblatt, 'Psychoanalysis and Renaissance Culture,' 136–7.
51 Radin, *Reinterpreting Property*, 41.
52 Lacan, *The Language of the Self*, 134.
53 Žižek, *The Sublime Object of Ideology*, 16–17.
54 Lacan, *The Seminar of Jacques Lacan. Book I*, 74, 79. The fullest account of this
   process is Lacan's essay on the mirror stage, *Ecrits: A Selection*, 1–7.
55 Freud, 'The Ego and the Id,' 364.
56 Lacan, *The Seminar of Jacques Lacan. Book I*, 151.
57 Lacan, 'Some Reflections on the Ego,' 13.
58 Lacan, *The Seminar of Jacques Lacan. Book I*, 151.
59 Fisher, 'The Renaissance Beard: Masculinity in Early Modern England.'
60 Lacan, *The Seminar of Jacques Lacan. Book I*, 96.
61 Thomas Lacquer's account of the Galenic one-sex model of the body is
   perhaps the most influential example of this historicizing of the body
   (*Making Sex: Body and Gender from the Greeks to Freud*); some recent studies
   have questioned the extent to which this understanding informed popular
   beliefs about the body. Bruce R. Smith notes, for example that 'the fact that
   Helkiah Crooke in his encyclopedic *Microcosmographia: A Description of the
   Body of Man* (1616) can test the one-sex model against the evidence of
   recent anatomical studies and summarily reject it (249–50) suggests that

Galen's idea may have had less currency than some critics have assumed'
('Premodern Sexualities,' 322). Winfried Schliener suggests that during this
period the one-sex model was being seriously challenged but was still widely
accepted ('Early Modern Controversies About the One-Sex Model'). Janet
Adelman surveys English medical and gynecological tracts and finds little
evidence for the Galenic understanding of the body in 'Making Defect
Perfection.' See also Gowing, *Domestic Dangers,* 5–9; and Schoenfeldt, *Bodies
and Selves in Early Modern England,* 1–39.

62 Smith, 'Premodern Sexualities,' 325.
63 Shapiro, 'The Concept "Fact": Legal Origins and Cultural Diffusion.'
64 Adelman, 'Making Defect Perfection,' 25.
65 On the sumptuary laws, see Harte, 'State Control of Dress and Social
   Change in Pre-Industrial England.'
66 See, for example, *Virgidemiarum,* satire IV.ii.
67 Walker, 'Rereading Rape,' 13. Miranda Chaytor observes that 'in story after
   story ... The rape victim's work was disrupted, their clothing stolen, tum-
   bled, trampled on, soiled, "slitted from top to bottom"' ('Husband[ry]:
   Narratives of Rape in the Seventeenth Century,' 383). There is the possibility that torn clothing was a legal fiction: *The Lawes Resolution* says that the
   victim must 'with Hue and Cry complaine to the good men of the next
   towne, shewing her wrong, her garments torne' (392). Addressing this
   point, Chaytor argues that even if there is a necessity to demonstrate torn
   garments, this still cannot account for all of the references to clothing in
   the rape narratives (404n16).
68 Kiernan, 'State and Nation in Western Europe,' 27.
69 Holdsworth, *A History of English Law,* 3: 457. Holdsworth's 'free and lawful
   man' was certainly gendered male: the status category of 'woman' was an
   exceptionally durable one, arguably lasting well into this century.
70 Pye, *The Vanishing,* 116.
71 On the outlines of absolutism in England, see Perry Anderson, *Lineages of
   the Absolutist State,* 85–112.
72 Baker, *Reports,* 48.
73 Atiyah, *An Introduction to the Law of Contract,* 3.
74 Teeven, *A History of the Anglo-American Common Law of Contract,* 1.
75 Ibid., 9.
76 Atiyah, *An Introduction to the Law of Contract,* 1–2.
77 Atiyah, *The Rise and Fall of Freedom of Contract,* 37.
78 Sacks, 'The Promise and the Contract in Early Modern England,' 31.
79 Wilson, 'Ben Jonson and the Law of Contract,' 144.
80 Sacks, 'The Promise and the Contract in Early Modern England,' 38.

81 Wilson, 'Ben Jonson and the Law of Contract,' 145.
82 Polito, 'Wit, Will and Governance in Early Modern Legal Literature.'
83 Rose, *States of Fantasy*, 9.

2. 'Bold sharpe Sophister[s]': Rhetoric and Education

1 Guilpin, *Skialetheia*, 6.
2 Overbury, 'An Innes of Court man,' *The 'Conceited Newes' of Sir Thomas Overbury and his Friends*, ed. James E. Savage, 146.
3 Finkelpearl, *John Marston of the Middle Temple*, 16, 61. A comprehensive account of the Inns of Court educational system can be found in Richardson, *A History of the Inns of Court*, esp. 91–166.
4 Prest, *The Inns of Court under Elizabeth I and the Early Stuarts*, 21–2.
5 Hall, *Virgidemiarum* IV.ii.1–2, in *The Collected Poems of Joseph Hall.*
6 Baker, *Readings*, xxx.
7 Dugdale, *Origines juridiciales*, 141.
8 Knafla, 'The Matriculation Revolution.'
9 'I am not of the opinion of most of the Nobilitie and Gentrie of this Kindome, who whenas their Sonnes leave the Universities, omitt the Innes of Court and send them beyond the Seas. Travaile is a necessary accomodation for a gentleman and an especial part of his education; but what is it to be conversant abroad and a straynger at home. These Innes of Court are vertuous and fruitefull semynaries for the breeding of youth where they study the knowne Lawes of the land and other noble exercises ... There are more noble Families raised by the profession of the Lawe in this Kindgome than by all other professions whatsoever' (Higford, *Institutions*, f. 54r–v).
10 Gilbert, *Queene Elizabethes Achademy*, 7, 10.
11 Shapiro, *Probability and Certainty in Seventeenth-Century England*, 170. See also Prest, *The Inns of Court*, 137–73.
12 Shoeck, 'The Elizabethan Society of Antiquaries and Men of the Law.' Shoeck lists early members who were associated with the Inns. See also Fussner, who differs on the founding date of the society (*The Historical Revolution*, 93).
13 For an account of 'the normal career of a successful lawyer' at Gray's Inn, and further details on the legal exercises, see Fletcher, *The Pension Books of Gray's Inn 1569–1669*, xxxii–xxxv.
14 Baker, *Spelman*, 129.
15 Buck, *The Third Universitie of England*, 977.
16 Ibid., 968–9.
17 See Sorlien, ed., *The Diary of John Manningham of the Middle Temple, 1602–1603.*

248 Notes to pages 45–8

18 On the various kinds of learning exercises, see Richardson, *A History of the Inns of Court*, 128–66.
19 Baker, *Readings*, xlix.
20 Ibid., lvii. The Pension Books of Gray's Inn state that 'none shalbe callyd to the barre but soch as be of convenient contynuance & have performyd exercises three years before they be called, that is to saie have gon abroad to Grand Mootes sixe tymes, have mooted at the utter barre in the library sixe times, & have put cases at bolts in terme sixe times & thereof bring due certifycatte: of the first from the Reader, the Auncient [that] goeth wyth hym, & the principalls in the Inns of Chancerie: of the second from those two that sitt at the bench: & of the thirde from those three that sytt at the Bolt' (102).
21 Ibid., lxxii.
22 Bland, 'Rhetoric and the Law Student in Sixteenth-Century England,' 508.
23 For an analysis of the evidence, see Richardson, *A History of the Inns of Court*, 54–60, 211–44.
24 Ibid., 220, where Richardson refers to the report.
25 Heywood, *An Apology for Actors*, sig. C3v.
26 MacCaffrey, *Elizabeth I*, 170. For a lengthier account of the masque itself, see Brooks, *Sir Christopher Hatton*, 31–49. The opportunities for display that such spectacles offered were clearly attractive; see Hammer's discussion of Essex's use of the 1595 Accession Day celebrations to promote his own career at court, 'Upstaging the Queen.'
27 Whitted, 'Transforming the (Common)place,' 153. On the conditions of performance of these revels, see Knapp and Kobialka, 'Shakespeare and the Prince of Purpoole;' and Burkhart, 'The Surviving Shakespearean Playhouses.'
28 Osborn, *The Life, Letters, and Writings of John Hoskyns, 1566–1638*, 98.
29 Quoted in ibid., 98.
30 Rae, *Thomas Lodge*, 46. A.B. Taylor argues that Marlowe was influenced by the poem as well in 'A Note on Christopher Marlowe's "Hero and Leander."'
31 A.B. Taylor argues that Peend's claim to have written this before Golding is spurious, and that in fact Peend's translation is influenced by Golding's ('Thomas Peend and Arthur Golding').
32 Runsdorf, 'Transforming Ovid in the 1560s,' 125.
33 A.B. Taylor notes that at one point in the tale Peend changes Ovid's octopus into a more familiar crab. He suggests, however, that Peend is merely copying from Golding ('Thomas Peend and Arthur Golding,' 19). However,

we also get hares and hounds, hawks and partridges, and pikes and roaches, which we don't find in Golding. Michael Pincombe argues that these animal images work to emphasize Salmacis's bestial desire ('The Ovidian Hermaphrodite,' 162). On Golding's Englishing of Ovid, see Lyne, *Ovid's Changing Worlds*, 53–79.

34 Keach, *Elizabethan Erotic Narratives*, 56.
35 Silberman, 'Mythographic Transformations in Ovid's Hermaphrodite,' 646.
36 Maslen, 'Myths Exploited,' 19.
37 Keach, *Elizabethan Erotic Narratives*, 32.
38 F.L., *The Young Gallants Whirligigg* (London, 1627), 3.
39 L[enton], *Characterismi*, sig. F5v.
40 Hawarde, *Les Reportes del Cases in Camera Stellata*, 47, 48. In his introduction to the play, Richard Levin argues that this case was the basis for Thomas Middleton's *Michaelmas Term* (Lincoln: University of Nebraska Press, 1966), xi–xiii. Joseph Hall retells a similar scamming of 'needy Gallants' in his 1599 *Vergidemiarum* IV.v.115–30.
41 Helgerson, *The Elizabethan Prodigals*, 108–9.
42 Lodge, 'An Alarum against usurers,' *The Complete Works of Thomas Lodge*, 1:20.
43 Keach, *Elizabethan Erotic Narratives*, 36.
44 Moulton, *Before Pornography*, 37.
45 Golding for some reason changes Tethys to Thetis (a different aquatic deity), and this is followed by Lodge. Sandys has Tethys.
46 Barkan, 'Diana and Acteon: The Myth as Synthesis,' 328.
47 Sandys, *Ovid's Metamorphosis Englished*, 645.
48 Parker, *Literary Fat Ladies*, 110, 107.
49 Vickers, 'Diana Described.'
50 Cain, 'Spenser and the Renaissance Orpheus,' 25.
51 Finkelpearl, *John Marston of the Middle Temple*, 101.
52 Keach, *Elizabethan Erotic Narratives*, 20.
53 Dubrow, *Echoes of Desire*, 37.
54 Enterline, '"Embodied Voices,"' 122, 122.
55 See, for example, Jones and Stallybrass, 'The Politics of *Astrophel and Stella*'; and Marotti, '"Love is not Love": Elizabethan Sonnet Sequences and the Social Order.'
56 Irigaray, *This Sex Which Is Not One*, 172.
57 Sedgwick, *Between Men: English Literature and Male Homosocial Desire*.
58 Wittig, *The Straight Mind and Other Essays*, 28–9, 29.
59 Butler, *Gender Trouble*, 113.

60 Irigarary, *This Sex Which is Not One*, 192.
61 Creet, 'Sexual Subordination.'
62 DiGangi, *The Homoerotics of Early Modern Drama*, 1–23.

3. 'More lovely than a man': The Metamorphosis of the Youth

1 Bate, 'Sexual Perversity in *Venus and Adonis*,' 80. Catherine Belsey similarly notes of criticism of Shakespeare's poem that, 'a substantial proportion of twentieth-century criticism, by endorsing the opposition Adonis formulates [between love and lust] and finding in it the thematic truth of the poem, reproduces the taxonomy he helps to cement; such criticism thereby enlists Shakespeare in support of family values, the naturalization of the nuclear family as the only legitimate location of desire' ('Love as Trompe-l'oeil: Taxonomies of Desire in *Venus and Adonis*,' 274).
2 Lacan, *Ecrits*, 151–2.
3 Ibid., 143.
4 Žižek, *Enjoy Your Symptom!* 159.
5 Ibid., 152.
6 Ibid., 156.
7 Ibid., 160.
8 Williams, 'The Coming of Age of Shakespeare's Adonis,' 770.
9 Dubrow, *Captive Victors*, 34.
10 Williams, 'The Coming of Age of Shakespeare's Adonis,' 776.
11 Lacan and the *école freudienne*, *Feminine Sexuality*, 144.
12 Ibid., 137.
13 Keach on Finkelpearl, *Elizabethan Erotic Narratives*, 138.
14 Sandys, *Ovid's Metamorphosis Englished*, 484.
15 Lacan, *The Seminar of Jacques Lacan. Book VII*, 151.
16 Grosz, *Jacques Lacan*, 43.
17 Bush, *Mythology and the Renaissance Tradition in English Poetry*, 180.
18 Bal, *Lethal Love*, 61.
19 Plato, *The Symposium*, 90.
20 Boose, 'The 1599 Bishops' Ban, Elizabethan Pornography, and the Sexualization of the Jacobean Stage,' 192.
21 Lacan, *Ecrits*, 148.
22 Wilson, *The Arte of Rhetoricke*, 17.
23 Hoskins, *Directions for Speech and Style*, 2.
24 Ibid., 7.
25 Lacan, *The Language of the Self*, 134.
26 Lacan, *Ecrits*, 15.

27 Ibid., 142.
28 Irigaray, *This Sex Which Is Not One*, 192.
29 Rose in Lacan and the *école freudienne, Feminine Sexuality*, 47.
30 Ibid., 151.
31 Keach, *Elizabethan Erotic Narratives*, 5.
32 Stern, *Gabriel Harvey*, 127.
33 Duncan-Jones, 'Much Ado with Red and White,' 490–7.
34 Taylor, 'Shakespeare's Cousin, Thomas Greene, and his Kin,' 81.
35 'Often of an afternoon groups of young Inns of Court men would head for the public playhouses in the London suburbs, where a personal acquaintance with the players helped to distinguish the real bloods among them. Probably it was on some such excursion that William Shakespeare and the young Earl of Southampton first saw each other' (Akrigg, *Shakespeare and the Earl of Southampton*, 31).
36 Akrigg, *Shakespeare and the Earl of Southampton*, 195–7; Martindale and Burrow, 'Clapham's *Narcissus.*'
37 Martindale and Burrow, 'Clapham's *Narcissus*,' 150. A.L. Rowse's argument that Leander is modelled on Southampton suggests a further connection between Clapham's and Marlowe's poems (*Shakespeare's Southampton*, 78–80).
38 Akrigg, *Shakespeare and the Earl of Southampton*, 195.
39 Martindale and Burrow, 'Clapham's *Narcissus*,' 152.
40 On *Venus and Adonis* as an admonitory fiction, see Akrigg, *Shakespeare and the Earl of Southampton*, 33–4, 194–5 and, more recently, Murphy, 'Wriothesley's Resistance.'
41 Fisher, 'The Renaissance Beard,' 175.
42 Gent, 'Venus and Adonis,' 726.
43 See, for example, the Nurse's speech in *Romeo and Juliet*, 1.3.16–48, 50–7.
44 Enterline, *The Rhetoric of the Body from Ovid to Shakespeare*, 129.
45 Lewis, *English Literature in the Sixteenth Century, Excluding Drama*, 236–7.
46 Grosz, *A Feminist Introduction to Jacques Lacan*, 50–1.
47 Lewis, *English Literature in the Sixteenth Century*, 238.
48 Don Cameron Allen argues that the horse narrative is the replacement for the Atalanta/Hippomenes tale. As Venus does not narrate that particular part of the poem, and as it has as its likely source Clapham's *Narcissus*, it makes more sense that this episode be seen as the substitution ('On Venus and Adonis,' 100).
49 Smith in Evans, *Riverside Shakespeare*, 1704.
50 Mortimer, *Variable Passions*, 15.
51 Fienberg, 'Thematics of Value in *Venus and Adonis*,' 26.

52 Quoted in Hamilton, 'Venus and Adonis,' 7.

53 Hamilton, 'Venus and Adonis,' 7.

54 Ibid., 13.

55 Sheidley, '"Unless It Be a Boar,"' 11.

56 Williams, 'The Coming of Age of Shakespeare's Adonis,' 770.

57 Sheidley, '"Unless It Be a Boar,"' 13.

58 Ibid., 14.

59 Asals, 'Venus and Adonis,' 46.

60 Hulse, Metamorphic Verse, 166.

61 The Legend of Orpheus and Euridice in [...] Loues Complai[nts] London: 1597. For a discussion of the poem in relation to R.B.'s Orpheus His Journey to Hell, see Kenneth Borris, 'R[ichard] B[arnfield]'s Homosocial Engineering,' 346–8. Borris speculates that the anonymous author wrote this homophobic poem in direct response to R.B.'s homoerotic verses.

62 Lanham, The Motives of Eloquence, 88.

63 In a parallel argument, Catherine Belsey writes that the poem participates in the emergence of family values in the period. 'The family promises gratification in exchange for submission to the rules: true love is desire that is properly regulated; it is for an appropriate (heterosexual) object; and its story is told in Shakespearean comedy' ('Taxonomies of Desire,' 275).

64 Campbell, '"Desunt nonnulla": The Construction of Marlowe's Hero and Leander as an Unfinished Poem.' See also Bredbeck, Sodomy and Interpretation, 128.

65 Cheney, Marlowe's Counterfeit Profession, 241.

66 In David Lee Miller's influential reading of the poem, the Hellespont figures as one of the many 'empty spaces' of the poem, which organize 'all the structures of antithesis, whether rhetorical, topographic, or sexual' ('The Death of the Modern,' 764).

67 Wilson, Arte of Rhetoric, 416.

68 Haber, '"True-loves blood": Narrative and Desire in Hero and Leander.'

69 Brown, 'Gender and Voice in "Hero and Leander,"' 154–5.

70 Gregory Bredbeck and Claude J. Summers see the poem functioning in a similar way with regard to heterosexuality, but make rather different arguments about how this works. Bredbeck argues that the poem denaturalizes heterosexuality and demonstrates its relativity, whereas Summers argues that the poem works to destabilize the dominant constructions of sexuality of the day. See Bredbeck, Sodomy and Interpretation; and Summers, '"Hero and Leander": The Arbitrariness of Desire.'

71 Quoted in Yates, Art of Memory, 10.

72 Vickers, 'Diana Described: Scattered Woman and Scattered Rhyme,' 266.

73 Godshalk, 'Hero and Leander: The Sense of an Ending,' 305.

74 On the other hand, both rude peasants (at least in pastoral) and soldiers
    from Thrace (where Orpheus instituted pederasty) are chief among the
    literary types generally attracted to youths.
75 Wilson, *The Arte of Rhetoric*, 315.
76 Freud, *On Sexuality: Three Essays on the Theory of Sexuality and Other Works*, 61.
77 Haber, '"True-loves blood": Narrative and Desire in *Hero and Leander*,' 381.
78 Steane, *Marlowe: A Critical Study*, 326.
79 Tuve, *Elizabethan and Metaphysical Imagery*, 157. On this now notorious
    reading, see Haber, '"True-loves blood,"' 381; and Bredbeck, *Sodomy and
    Interpretation*, 131–2.
80 Hulse, *Metamorphic Verse*, 99.
81 Ibid., 107.
82 Steane, *Marlowe*, 326.
83 Hulse, *Metamorphic Verse*, 108.
84 Leech, *Marlowe*, 256.
85 Barkan, *Transuming Passion: Ganymede and the Erotics of Humanism*, 48–9.
86 Spenser, *Poetical Works*, 422.
87 Ibid., 455.
88 Irigaray, *This Sex Which Is Not One*, 193.
89 Ariès, 'Thoughts on the History of Homosexuality.'
90 Hulse, *Metamorphic Verse*, 31.
91 Bredbeck draws attention to the repeated attention given to the
    commodification of women in the poem (*Sodomy and Interpretation*, 122–8).
92 Leishman, ed. *The Three Paranassus Plays*.
93 Hulse, *Metamorphic Verse*, 99; Cheney, *Marlowe's Counterfeit Profession*, 261–2.
    Four years after Marlowe's death, Thomas Beard identifies Marlowe as 'one
    of our own nation, of fresh and late memory, called Marlin, by profession a
    scholler, brought up from his youth in the Universitie of Cambridge, but by
    practise a playmaker, and a Poet of scurrilitie' (quoted in Cheney, *Marlowe's
    Counterfeit Profession*, 261).
94 He goes on to suggest that 'the Oratour may lead his hearers which way he
    list, and draw them to what affection he will: he may make them to be
    angry, to be pleased, to laugh, to weep, and lament ... and briefely to be
    moved with any affection that shall serve best for his purpose' (Peacham,
    The Garden of Eloquence 1577, sig. Aiii).
95 Leonard, 'Marlowe's Doric Music: Lust and Aggression in *Hero and Leander*,'
    64–5.
96 Klause, 'Venus and Adonis: Can We Forgive Them?' 359–60.
97 Enterline, *The Rhetoric of the Body from Ovid to Shakespeare*, 190.
98 Sheidley, '"Unless It Be a Boar,"' 14.
99 Hulse, *Metamorphic Verse*, 120.

100 Ibid., 123.
101 Miller, 'The Death of the Modern,' 763.
102 Godshalk, '*Hero and Leander*: The Sense of an Ending,' 294.
103 Lewis, *English Literature in the Sixteenth Century, Excluding Drama*, 240.
104 Ibid., 250.
105 Ibid., 246.
106 Barkan, *Transuming Passion*, 113.
107 Ibid., 114.

4. 'Yon's one Italionate': Sodomy and Literary History

1 Buckley, ed., '*Cephalus and Procris*' and '*Narcissus*' by Thomas Edwards, xxvi.
2 Ibid., xxv.
3 Stopes, in arguing for a candidate born in 1540, makes the dubious argument that the reference to himself as a 'young beginner' is 'a bit of fun, a specimen of his peculiar humour' ('Thomas Edwards, Author of "Cephalus and Procris, Narcissus,"' 215).
4 Eccles, 'Brief Lives,' 46.
5 Hughey, *John Harington of Stepney*, 172.
6 Vinge, *The Narcissus Theme*, 174.
7 Bush, 'The Influence of Marlowe's *Hero and Leander* on Early Mythological Poems,' 212.
8 Vinge notes that the 'transvestism motif' has appeared elsewhere in 'secondary renderings of the mythological theme' (*The Narcissus Theme*, 175).
9 Orgel, 'Nobody's Perfect.' On the antitheatricalists generally, see Barish, *The Anti-theatrical Prejudice*.
10 Vinge, *The Narcissus Theme*, 176.
11 Helgerson, *Forms of Nationhood*, 2.
12 See Bray, *Homosexuality in Renaissance England*; Barkan, *Transuming Passion*; Stewart, *Close Readers*.
13 Orgel, 'Nobody's Perfect.'
14 Stewart, *Close Readers*, xxviii.
15 Ibid., 3–37.
16 Pettie, *A Petite Pallace of Pettie His Pleasure*, 73–4.
17 Ibid., 82, 83.
18 See Fish, *Surprised by Sin*.
19 Pettie, *A Petite Pallace of Pettie His Pleasure*, 82.
20 Hutson, *The Usurer's Daughter*, 21–2.
21 Parker, *Literary Fat Ladies*, 98.
22 Ibid., 105.
23 Quoted in Hutson, *The Usurer's Daughter*, 46.

24 Weever, *Faunus and Melliflora ('1600)*, ed. Davenport, vii.
25 Keach, *Elizabethan Erotic Narratives*, 162.
26 Honigmann, *John Weever*, 21.
27 Weever, *Faunus and Melliflora* (1600), ed. Davenport, vi. On the Bishops' Ban, see Boose, 'The 1599 Bishops' Ban.'
28 Keach, *Elizabethan Erotic Narratives*, 174.
29 Ibid., 163.
30 Ibid., 167.
31 Ibid., 168.
32 Ibid., 171.
33 Ascham, *The Scholemaster*, 66.
34 Boose, 'The 1599 Bishops' Ban,' 195. On the reputation of Aretino in England, see McPherson, 'Aretino and the Harvey-Nashe Quarrel,' 1551–8, and Moulton, *Before Pornography*, 144–57.
35 Moulton, *Before Pornography*, 116–17; McPherson, 'Aretino and the Harvey-Nashe Quarrel,' 1553–4. Another more famous example occurs in E.K.'s gloss on the January eclogue of Spenser's 'The Shepheardes Calender,' which refers to Lucian's 'develish disciple Unico Aretino' in a discussion of the 'disorderly love, which the learned call paederastice' (422–3). Although Unico Aretino and Pietro Aretino were in fact two different people (the former, whose real name was Bernardo Accolti, appears in the first book of *The Courtier*; the latter wrote the pornographic sonnets), McPherson argues that they were often confused in England, and almost certainly were in the case of E.K.
36 On this, see Stewart, *Close Readers*, especially 84–121. See also Barkan, *Transuming Passion*.
37 Marston, *Scourge of Villanie*, III.75–8 ('In Lectores ...,' 7, 77–8).
38 Goran V. Stanivukovic offers a sensitive discussion of the relation between the two poems, although he overstates the case a bit when he argues Venus and Adonis are the models for Gale's lovers; 'Shakespeare, Dunstan Gale, and Golding,' *Notes and Queries* n.s. 41 (1994): 35–7.

5: 'The *Thracian* fields and company of men': The Erotics of Political Fraternity

1 Anderson, *Imagined Communities*, 7.
2 The author of the poem is not on the title page but was identified as early as 1640 as Beaumont; see Finkelpearl, 'The Authorship of *Salmacis and Hermaphroditus*'; and Thompson, 'Death by Water,' 100.
3 Thompson, 'Death by Water,' 102.
4 Ann Rosalind Jones and Peter Stallybrass argue that in this version Salmacis 'is present not as the female half of a hermaphrodite but as the drainer

away of Hermaphroditus' masculinity; she defines him through negation. Thus Hermaphroditus' change is presented as a problem of male identity' ('Fetishizing Gender,' 97). While Jones and Stallybrass are no doubt correct to read this as a problem of identity, it is important to note more accurately the terms of the problem and its location at the level of the body or the bodily ego ('Fetishizing Gender,' 97).

5 See, for example, Jones and Stallybrass, 'Fetishizing Gender'; Daston and Park, 'The Hermaphrodite and the Orders of Nature'; Parker, 'Gender Ideology, Gender Change'; and Greenblatt, *Shakespearean Negotiations*, 66–93.

6 Greenblatt, *Shakespearean Negotiations*, 73–86.

7 Keach, *Elizabethan Erotic Narratives*, 196.

8 See Thompson, 'Death by Water.'

9 Daston and Park, 'The Hermaphrodite and the Orders of Nature,' 120. These connections appear in nonmedical literature as well, as seen in a more prurient and judgmental way in George Sandys's gloss on the legend, where hermaphrodites and sodomites seem to be the same thing. 'There are many at this day in *Aegypt*, but most frequent in *Florida*; who are so hated by the rest of the *Indians*, that they use them as beasts to carry their burthens; to suck their wounds, and attend on the diseased. But at *Rome* they threw them as soone as borne into the river; the Virgins singing in procession, and offering sacrifice unto *Juno*' (*Ovid's Metamorphosis Englished*, 208–9).

10 Middleton's satirical portrait of Pyander contains many of the same characteristics of the youth as seen in epyllia: attractive, androgynous, and fatally seductive to men. Satan, writes Middleton, has left Pyander in London ('Troynovant') as a memorial to Sodom:

> The still memorial, if I aim aright,
> Is a pale chequer'd black hermaphrodite.
> Sometimes he jets it like a gentleman,
> Other whiles much like a wanton courtesan;
> But, truth to tell, a man or woman whether,
> I cannot say, she's excellent at either;
> But if report may certify a truth,
> She's neither of them, but a cheating youth.
> Yet Troynovant, that all-admired town,
> Where thousands still do travel up and down,
> Of beauty's counterfeits affords not one,
> So like a lovely smiling paragon,
> As is Pyander in a nymph's attire,
> Whose rolling eye sets gazers' hearts on fire. (V. 21–34)

11 Sandys, *Ovid's Metamorphosis Englished*, 209.

12 Ibid., 206.

13 Thompson, 'Death by Water,' 113.

14 Krier, 'Sappho's Apples,' 9

15 Hammill, *Sexuality and Form*, 36–7.

16 Alberti, *On Painting*, 61.

17 The literature on perspective in painting is immense. For a brief overview of some of the more important theoretical questions, see Jay, 'Scopic Regimes of Modernity.' For a more philosophical approach to Panofsky's study, see Damisch, *The Origin of Perspective*.

18 Panofsky, *Perspective as Symbolic Form*, 67–8.

19 Ibid., 30–1.

20 Jay, 'Scopic Regimes of Modernity,' 9.

21 Panofsky, *Perspective as Symbolic Form*, 68.

22 Pye, *The Vanishing*, 68.

23 Silverman, *The Threshold of the Visible World*, 14.

24 Ibid., 13, 16.

25 Brennan, *History after Lacan*, 49.

26 'The sixteenth century's enthusiastic belief in proportion is the justification for new requirements concerning physical bearing. The body's microcosm must evoke, by the subtleties and wealth of measures and relationships among its parts, those of the world at large' (Vigarello, 'The Upward Training of the Body from the Age of Chivalry to Courtly Civility,' 154).

27 Hammill, *Sexuality and Form*, 41.

28 'The idea of a sociological organism moving calendrically through homogeneous, empty time is a precise analogue of the idea of the nation, which also is conceived as a solid community moving steadily down (or up) history' (Anderson, *Imagined Communities*, 26).

29 Hulse, *Metamorphic Verse*, 74.

30 Keach, *Elizabethan Erotic Narratives*, 205.

31 See Stretton, *Women Waging Law in Elizabethan England*.

32 Cioni, *Women and Law in Elizabethan England*, i. On the other hand, Spring (*Law, Land, and Inheritance*) shows that courts like Chancery were also used to circumvent the common law in order to deny heiresses potential inheritances. Similarly, Stretton argues that 'it is misleading to represent equity as women's legal saviour, just as it is misleading to represent the common law as their legal downfall' (*Women Waging Law in Elizabethan England*, 28).

33 Cioni, *Women Waging Law in Elizabethan England*, 18.

34 Gowing, *Domestic Dangers*.

35 Keach, *Elizabethan Erotic Narratives*, 205–6.

36 Jay, 'Scopic Regimes of Modernity,' 8.

37 The attribution of the poem to Barnfield is an ongoing debate. The most
   recent editor of the poem, A. Leigh DeNeef, in 'The Poetics of Orpheus,' does
   not offer a candidate for its authorship. For a fuller discussion of these issues,
   see the essays by Kenneth Borris and Wes Folkerth in Borris and Klawitter, eds,
   The Affectionate Shepherd. Although my argument does not depend on identifying R.B. as Richard Barnfield, the homoerotic content of the poem, its interest
   in pastoral male conversation, and the connection of the genre with the Inns
   of Court all tend to support the attribution to Barnfield.
38 DeNeef, 'The Poetics of Orpheus,' 49.
39 Worrall, 'Biographical Introduction: Barnfield's Feast of "all Varietie,"' 30–1.
40 Prest, *The Inns of Court*, 41.
41 N.B. is generally identified as Nicholas Breton, who had lodgings in
   Holborne. Although there is no record of him attending the Inns of Court,
   his name does appear in William Covell's *Polimanteia* (1595) in a list of
   writers associated with the Inns.
42 In his introduction to the poem, Hyder Edward Rollins argues that 'this
   long time of vacation' refers to the plague in 1594, and that Jones is addressing himself to the courtiers forced to leave town (Breton, *The Arbor of
   Amorous Devices*, xiv). This is an equally plausible reading of the introduction, and one which would not preclude the address to the gentlemen of
   the Inns, many of whom attended court or aspired to courtly service.
   However, one year earlier Jones entered two other works in the Stationer's
   Register that reflect in contrasting moods the economic effects of the
   vacations: 'A Sorrowful songe of London's Lamentation for the Loss of the
   term, &c,' entered on 8 October 1593; and 'A newe songe of London's
   joyfull wellcome to the Nobilitie, gentelemen and Communalitie to Hillarye
   Term,' entered 22 January 1593 [1594].
43 Dekker, *The Dead Tearme*, 4: 27. These complaints also seem to have a long
   history. J.H. Baker notes that when the courts were moved by Edward I to
   York Castle, 'we learn from the complaints of shopkeepers in Westminster
   and Fleet Street that the exodus of lawyers and officials was so great as to be
   seriously damaging to business' (*The Third University of England*, 10).
44 DeNeef, 'The Poetics of Orpheus,' 22.
45 Cain, 'Spenser and the Renaissance Orpheus,' 25.
46 Puttenham, *The Arte of English Poesie*. 1589, 22.
47 Elyot, *The Boke Named the Gouernour*. 1531, 65.
48 Gros Louis, 'The Triumph and Death of Orpheus,' 65.
49 DeNeef writes that 'Orpheus becomes a poet for the first time in line 115
   [after Eurydice's death]; previously, he has only been a musician. The

implication is that Orpheus' experience of woe is both the stimulus and matter for his art' ('The Poetics of Orpheus,' 25). It is not clear why DeNeef should argue this, since Orpheus's singing has in fact been mentioned a number of times prior to this point. In the opening golden age section the ocean is still 'whil'st he sang' (46); we are told that '*Orpheus* often in his ditties praised' Eurydice (68); at the wedding, the guests 'sit to heare how Orpheus sings' (90). While Eurydice's death may well have given Orpheus new material for his songs, it is not in this version the origin of his singing career.

50 The relevant section from the end of the third book of Boethius reads: 'Orpheus, seeing on the verge of night / Eurydice, doth lose and kill / Her and himself with foolish love. / But you this feigned tale fulfil, / Who think unto the day above / To bring with speed your darksome mind. / For if, your eye conquered, you move / Backward to Pluto left behind, / All the rich prey which thence you took, / You lose while back to hell you look' (*The Consolation of Philosophy*, 297).

51 See Warden, 'Orpheus and Ficino.'

52 Quoted in Mills, *One Soul in Bodies Twain*, 203.

53 Gros Louis, 'The Triumph and Death of Orpheus,' 65.

54 For this reading of Lucrece, see Jed, *Chaste Thinking.* Jed notes that on Lucrece's death, her body is borne through the streets by her male relatives as an occasion for speaking against tyranny and for the foundation of republican Rome. The same political valences are generally at work in friendship texts, which stress the incompatibility of friendship and tyranny.

55 DeNeef, 'The Poetics of Orpheus,' 27.

56 Stephen Guy-Bray in *Homoerotic Space* argues that pastoral elegy in particular was a key genre in the period for the negotiation of male relations.

57 Harding, *A Social History of English Law*, 249.

58 Goodrich, 'Eating Law: Commons, Common Land, Common Law,' 246, 251.

59 Louise Schleiner, 'Pastoral Male Friendship and Miltonic Marriage.'

60 Borris, 'R[ichard] B[arnfield]'s Homosocial Engineering in *Orpheus His Journey to Hell.*'

61 Montrose, 'Of Gentlemen and Shepherds,' 417–18.

62 MacCaffrey, *Queen Elizabeth and the Making of Policy, 1572–1588*, 463–99.

63 Thomas Wilson, *The Arte of Rhetoricke*, 17.

64 Keach, *Elizabethan Erotic Narratives*, 131–2.

65 Bacon, *Essays or Counsels Civil and Moral* and *The Wisdom of the Ancients*, 6: 722.

66 Quoted in Bray, 'Homosexuality and the Signs of Male Friendship,' 55.

67 Stewart, *Close Readers*; Barkan, *Transuming Passion.*

68 Bacon, *Essays*, 437, 443.
69 Ibid., 443.
70 Ibid., 442.
71 Masten, *Textual Intercourse*, 37. More recently, Laurie Shannon looks at the political dimensions of early modern male friendship in *Sovereign Amity*.
72 Derrida, 'The Politics of Friendship.'
73 I am depending here on David M. Halperin's revisionist account of Platonic pederasty in *One Hundred Years of Homosexuality*. Halperin argues that, in spite of the various classical and critical objections, the relation between philosopher and pupil was a sexual one.
74 Holdsworth, *A History of English Law*, 3: 457, 456.
75 Laurie Shannon notes the connections between friendship and the contract in the period, drawing attention to the phrase 'meeting of the minds' in both discourses (*Sovereign Amity*, 39–40).
76 Warner, 'New English Sodom,' 346.
77 Ibid., 347.

6. 'Riot, revelling and rapes': Sexual Violence and the Nation

1   Walker, 'Rereading Rape,' 2.
2   In order to maintain a distinction between the legend and Barksted's version of it, I will use the more usual spelling of Myrrha's name except when referring to the character in the poem.
3   Flinker, 'Cyniras, Myrrha and Adonis,' 62–3. As Flinker notes, there were two other substantial early modern versions of the Myrrha story that followed Barksted's: H[enry] A[ustin]'s *The Scourge of Venus* (1613), and James Gresham's *The Picture of Incest* (1626). On the divergent opinions of Ovid's treatment of the story, see Hopkins, 'Nature's Laws and Man's,' 787.
4   Freud, 'Some Psychical Consequences of the Anatomical Distinction Between the Sexes,' *On Sexuality*, 341.
5   Baines, 'Effacing Rape in Early Modern Representation.'
6   On this point see Lefkowitz, 'Seduction and Rape in Greek Myth.'
7   Enterline, *The Rhetoric of the Body from Ovid to Shakespeare*, 158.
8   Bryson, 'Two Narratives of Rape in the Visual Arts.'
9   Karen Bamford offers a similar analysis of rape in Jacobean drama in *Sexual Violence on the Jacobean Stage*, esp. 6–10.
10 Jed, *Chaste Thinking*, 3.
11 Ibid., 11.
12 See Bamford, *Sexual Violence on the Jacobean Stage*, for examples of this phenomenon on the Jacobean stage, 81–122.

13 Lanham, *The Motives of Eloquence*, 82.

14 Fineman 'Shakespeare's Will,' 34.

15 In particular, Marion Trousdale offers a concise critique of Fineman's approach in 'Reading the Early Modern Text.' For an example of the opposite approach, one that reads the poem almost purely as a psychological case study, see Kietzman, 'What is Hecuba to Him or [S]he to Hecuba.'

16 For example, Kietzman, in 'What is Hecuba to Him or [She] to Hecuba,' makes the case for *Lucrece* as complaint; Lanham, on the other hand, in *The Motives of Eloquence*, calls it an epyllion. Thomas Middleton, cashing in on the success of Shakespeare's poem, published *The Ghost of Lucrece* in 1600. Middleton's poem is more obviously in the complaint genre, with the ghost of Lucrece returning from hell to bemoan her shame. Kietzman usefully discusses Shakespeare's poem in the tradition of Ovidian complaint (25). Lynn Enterline, who labels it an epyllion, discusses it in the broader tradition of Ovidian poetry in *The Rhetoric of the Body*, 152–97.

17 At one point, Lucrece's dismissal of the uselessness of rhetoric seems to conjure up the Inns of Court educational system:

> Out, idle word, servants to shallow fools,
> Unprofitable sounds, weak arbitrators!
> Busy yourselves in skill-contending schools;
> Debate where leisure serves with dull debaters;
> To trembling clients be you mediators:
> For me, I force not argument a straw,
> Since that my case is past the help of law. (1016–22)

18 Enterline, *Rhetoric of the Body*, 158.

19 Middleton in *The Ghost of Lucrece* echoes this emphasis on rhetoric, but unlike Shakespeare, never seems to afford Lucrece any agency:

> Lo, under that base type of Tarquin's name
> I cipher figures of iniquity.
> He writes himself the shamer, I the shame;
> The actor he, and I the tragedy;
> The stage am I, and he the history;
> > The subject I, and he the ravisher.
> He, murd'ring me, made me my murderer. (337–43)

20 Lanham, *The Motives of Eloquence*, 104. Katherine Eiseman Maus discusses this typically modern judgment on the poem in 'Taking Tropes Seriously.'

21 Cousins, 'Subjectivity, Exemplarity, and the Establishing of Character in Lucrece,' 48.

22 On this, see Vickers, '"The blazon of sweet beauty's best."

23 Fineman, 'Shakespeare's Will,' 39; see also Dubrow, *Captive Victors*, 80–168; and Belsey, 'Tarquin Dispossessed,' 323.
24 Lanham, *The Motives of Eloquence*, 104.
25 *Ovid's Fasti*, 2: 711–852.
26 For example, in a recent reading of the poem that focuses on Lucrece primarily as victim, Coppélia Kahn argues that the story of Lucrece is 'one of the founding myths of patriarchy' (*Roman Shakespeare*, 27).
27 *Lawes Resolution*, 376–7.
28 Post, 'Ravishment of Women and the Statutes of Westminster.'
29 *Lawes Resolution*, 381–2.
30 Baines, 'Effacing Rape in Early Modern Representation,' 72–3.
31 Erickson, *Women and Property.*
32 Chew, *The Crescent and the Rose*, 478–90.
33 Knolles, *The Generall Historie of the Turkes*, 353.
34 Chew, *The Crescent and the Rose*, 483.
35 Painter, *Palace of Pleasure.*
36 Based on a 1618 reference to the play by Thomas Gainsford, John J. O'Connor argues that one difference between the play and the poem is that Mustapha escapes with his life in the play: Mahomet, 'with a sterne repining at *Mustaphas* audaciousnesse, with much a doe pardoned him from cruell execution' ('A Jacobean Allusion to *The Turkish Mahoment and Hiren the Fair Greek*,' 428).
37 Jardine, *Worldly Goods*, esp. 37–90.
38 Ibid., 41.
39 James I, *His Maiesties Lepanto, or Heroicall Song.* For a recent discussion of the politics of this poem, see Bell, 'Writing the Monarch.' On Lepanto in Spanish epics, see Quint, *Epic and Empire*, 49.
40 See, in particular, Matar, *Islam in Britain, 1558–1685.*
41 Chew, *The Crescent and the Rose*, 104.
42 Matar, 'English Accounts of Captivity in North Africa and the Middle East: 1577–1625,' 557.
43 Matar, *Turks*, 19–20.
44 Brenner, *Merchants and Revolution*, 60. Alfred C. Wood notes that Elizabeth paid for Harborne's journey (*A History of the Levant Company*, 10).
45 Friedenreich, 'English Renaissance Accounts of the Fall of Constantinople,' 115.
46 Matar, *Turks*, 103.
47 Friedenreich, 'English Renaissance Accounts of the Fall of Constantinople,' 111.
48 Chew, *The Crescent and the Rose*, 486.

49 For this reading of *Coriolanus*, see Cavell, 'Who Does the Wolf Love?'

50 Hopkins, 'Cyniras and Myrrha,' 789.

Conclusion: Nymphs and Tobacconalias

1 Roger Sell attempts to cast some doubt on the attribution of tobacco to
   Beaumont, suggesting instead that it might be by George Sandys ('The
   Authorship of "The Metamorphosis of Tobacco" and "Salmacis and Herm-
   aphroditus'"). Mark Eccles, who concludes that the poem is probably by
   Beaumont, notes that 'a copy owned by George Chalmers was marked, in a
   contemporary hand, "By John Beaumont"' ('A Biographical Dictionary of
   Elizabethan Authors,' 295). For brief biographies of Beaumont, see Eccles,
   294–300, or Sell, ed., *The Shorter Poems of Sir John Beaumont*, 3–26.

2 Dickson, *Panacea*.

3 Buttes, 'A satyricall Epigram upon the wanton, and excessive use of
   Tabacco,' *Dyets Dry Dinner*, sig. P3b.

4 L[enton], *Characterismi, or, Lentons leasures*, sig. F5.

5 Osborn, *The Life, Letters and Writings of John Hoskyns*, 101.

6 J.H., *Work for Chimny-sweepers*, sig. B1r.

7 Ibid., sig. F4r. See also Dickson, *Panacea*, 139–62 for further examples.

8 Jonson, *Bartholomew Fair*, 2.6.22, 25.

9 Quoted in Dickson, *Panacea*, 171.

10 Fuchs, *Mimesis and Empire*, 118.

11 Andrews, *Trade, Plunder and Settlement*, 295; and Lorimer, 'The English Contraband Tobacco Trade, 124.

12 Lorimer, 'The English Contraband Tobacco Trade,' 124.

13 Andrews, *The Spanish Caribbean*, 229.

14 Lorimer, 'The English Contraband Tobacco Trade,' 125.

15 Davis, *The Rise of the Atlantic Economies*, 85.

16 Buttes, *Dyets Dry Dinner*, sig. P5a–b

17 Fuchs, *Mimesis and Empire*, 7.

18 James I, *A Counter-Blaste to Tobacco*, sig. C1r.

19 Shapiro, *Probability and Certainty*, 170.

20 Ibid., 17.

21 Because a fairly literal translation will be useful here, in this chapter I will be
   referring to Frank Justus Miller's edition of Ovid in the Loeb Classical
   Library. References are to book and page number.

22 Fuchs, *Mimesis and Empire*, 120–1.

23 Quinn and Ryan, *England's Sea Empire*, esp. 92–153.

24 'The Triumph of Tobacco over Sack and Ale,' attributed (probably wrongly)

to Francis Beaumont in a posthumous collection, contains much the same thought: 'The poets of old / Many fables have told / of the Gods and their symposia: / But Tobacco alone, / Had they known it had gone / For their nectar and ambrosia' (Beaumont, *Poems*, poem 135). On the attributions of the poems in this volume, see Hammersmith, 'The Printer's Copy for Francis Beaumont's *Poems*, 1653.'

25 In his 'De Guiana, Carmen Epicum,' an epic fragment prefixed to Lawrence Keymis's *Relation of the second Voyage to Guiana* (1596), George Chapman employs the rhetoric of the golden age in an attempt to convince Elizabeth to accept Guiana:

> Then most admired Soueraigne, let your breath
> Goe foorth upon the waters, and create
> A golden worlde in this our yron age.
>
> *The Poems of George Chapman* (30–2)

26 Knapp, 'Elizabethan Tobacco,' 46.

27 Richard Helgerson notes the distinction in the period between merchants and gentlemen, the two groups involved in the trade: 'Where merchants were motivated by relatively uncomplicated desire for profit, gentlemen needed the impulse of glory. Gentlemen chose to support riskier and more glamorous ventures, exploration and colonization rather than settled trade. And they were more strongly influenced by ideas of national enterprise' (*Forms of Nationhood*, 172).

28 Quinn and Ryan, *England's Sea Empire*, 139.

29 Hall, *Things of Darkness*, 18. Theodore K. Rabb similarly notes that by investing in overseas trade, 'the gentry broke with the most persistent traditions of their class throughout western Europe' (*Enterprise & Empire*, 13). In Rabb's list of overseas investors a number of Beaumonts from Leicester County appear, including possibly John's older brother Sir Henry. Two of the Beaumonts listed invested in the Virginia Company (see 243–4).

30 Fuchs, *Mimesis and Empire*, 137.

31 Nabil Matar argues that the representation of Islam in England changes significantly in the early modern period, at least partly as a result of England's encounter with the natives of North America. Viewing the Turk as equivalent to the North American native, Matar suggests, acted as psychological compensation for English fears in the face of the vastly more powerful Ottoman empire (*Turks*).

32 *The Lusiads*'s attitude to commerce has been debated, although one of its early translators called it in 1776 'the epic poem of the birth of commerce' (Rajan, '*The Lusiads* and the Asian Reader,' 5). For the opposing view, see Helgerson, who argues that the *Lusiads*'s attempts to downplay the obvious

commercial interests of the voyage in favour of an aristocratic ethos (*Forms of Nationhood*, 155–63). In either case, the epic's strategy for dealing with the troubling connection between commerce and heroism differs from that of the epyllion.

33 Knapp, 'Elizabethan Tobacco,' 35.
34 James I, *A Counter-Blaste to Tobacco*, sig. B2r.
35 Orgel, ed., *The Tempest*, 35.
36 On this epistemological development, see Poovey, *A History of the Modern Fact.*
37 Shapiro, *Probability and Certainty*, 17.
38 Enterline, 'Epic, Epyllia, and the Erotics of Early Modern Pedagogy.' My thanks to Prof. Enterline for allowing me to see a copy of this paper, which is part of larger project on rhetorical education in the grammar schools.
39 Quint, *Epic and Empire*, 8.
40 Žižek, *The Sublime Object of Ideology*, 29.

Works Cited

1. Editions of Epyllia

Barksted, William. *The Poems of William Barksted.* Edited by Alexander B. Grosart. Occasional Issues of Unique or Very Rare Books. London, 1876.

[Beaumont, Francis]. *Salmacis and Hermaphroditus.* London, 1602.

Beaumont, John. *The Metamorphosis of Tobacco.* Amsterdam: Theatrum Orbis Terrarum, 1971.

Edwards, Thomas. *'Cephalus and Procris' and 'Narcissus.'* Edited by W.E. Buckley. London: Roxburghe Club, 1882.

Gale, Dunstan. *Pyramus and Thisbe.* In *Seven Minor Epics of the English Renaissance,* edited by Paul W. Miller, 37–60.

Heywood, Thomas. *Oenone and Paris* (1594). Edited by Joseph Quincy Adams. Washington: The Folger Shakespeare Library, 1943.

Lodge, Thomas. *The Complete Works of Thomas Lodge.* 4 vols. New York: Russell and Russell, 1963.

Marlowe, Christopher. *The Complete Works of Christopher Marlowe.* Edited by Roma Gill. 3 vols. Oxford: Clarendon Press, 1987.

Marston, John. *The Poems of John Marston.* Edited by Arnold Davenport. Liverpool: Liverpool University Press, 1961.

Petowe, Henry. *The Second Part of Hero and Leander.* London, 1598.

Philos and Licia. In *Seven Minor Epics of the English Renaissance,* edited by Paul W. Miller, 1–36.

R.B., Gent. *Orpheus His Journey to Hell.* 1595. In A. Leigh Deneef, 'The Poetics of Orpheus: The Text and a Study of *Orpheus His Journey to Hell* (1595).' *Studies in Philology* 89 (1992): 20–70.

Shakespeare, William. *The Riverside Shakespeare.* Edited by G. Blakemore Evans. Boston: Houghton Mifflin, 1974.

Weever, John. *Faunus and Melliflora (1600)*. Edited by A. Davenport. London: University Press of Liverpool, 1948.

2. Secondary Sources

Adelman, Janet. 'Making Defect Perfection: Shakespeare and the One-Sex Model.' In *Enacting Gender on the English Renaissance Stage*, edited by Viviana Comensoli and Anne Russell, 23–52. Urbana: University of Illinois Press, 1999.

Akrigg, G.P.V. *Shakespeare and the Earl of Southampton*. Cambridge, MA: Harvard University Press, 1968.

Alberti, Leon Battista. *On Painting*. Translated by Cecil Grayson. Harmondsworth: Penguin, 1991.

Allen, Don Cameron. 'On Venus and Adonis.' In *Elizabethan and Jacobean Studies Presented to Frank Percy Wilson*, 100–11. Oxford: Clarendon Press, 1959.

Allen, Walter, Jr. 'The Non-Existent Classical Epyllion.' *Studies in Philology* 55 (1958): 515–18.

Althusser, Louis. *Lenin and Philosophy and Other Essays*. Translated by Ben Brewster. London: NLB, 1971.

Anderson, Benedict. *Imagined Communities: Reflections on the Origin and Spread of Nationalism*. Rev. ed. London: Verso, 1991.

Anderson, Perry. *Lineages of the Absolutist State*. London: Verso, 1974.

Andrews, Kenneth R. *The Spanish Caribbean: Trade and Plunder 1530–1630*. New Haven, CT: Yale University Press, 1978.

– *Trade, Plunder and Settlement: Maritime Enterprise and the Genesis of the British Empire, 1480–1630*. Cambridge: Cambridge University Press, 1984.

Ariès, Phillippe. 'Thoughts on the History of Homosexuality.' In *Western Sexuality: Practice and Precept in Past and Present Times*, edited by Philippe Ariès and André Béjin, translated by Anthony Forester, 62–75. Oxford: Basil Blackwell, 1985.

Asals, Heather. '*Venus and Adonis*: The Education of a Goddess.' *Studies in English Literature* 13 (1973): 31–51.

Ascham, Roger. *The Scholemaster*. Edited by R.J. Shoeck. Toronto: Dent, 1966.

Atiyah, P.S. *An Introduction to the Law of Contract*. 4th ed. Oxford: Clarendon Press, 1989.

– *The Rise and Fall of Freedom of Contract*. Oxford: Clarendon Press, 1979.

Bacon, Francis. *Essays or Counsels Civil and Moral* and *The Wisdom of the Ancients*. Vol. 6, *The Works of Francis Bacon*. Edited by James Spedding, Robert Leslie Ellis, and Douglas Denon Heath. London: Longman, 1859.

Baines, Barbara J. 'Effacing Rape in Early Modern Representation.' *English Literary History* 65.1 (1999): 69–98.

Baker, J.H. 'English Law and the Renaissance.' *Cambridge Law Journal* 44 (1985): 46–61.
– 'Introduction' to *Readings and Moot at the Inns of Court in the Fifteenth Century*, edited by Samuel E. Thorne and J.H. Baker. Vol. 2, xv–lxxvi. London: Seldon Society, 1990.
– *The Third University of England: The Inns of Court and the Common-law Tradition*. London: Selden Society, 1990.
Baker, J.H., ed. *The Reports of Sir John Spelman*. Vol. 2. London: Selden Society, 1978.
Bal, Mieke. *Lethal Love: Feminst Literary Readings of Biblical Love Stories*. Bloomington: Indiana University Press, 1987.
Baldwin, T.W. *William Shakespeare's Small Latine and Less Greeke*. 2 vols. Urbana: University of Illinois Press, 1944.
Bamford, Karen. *Sexual Violence on the Jacobean Stage*. New York: St Martin's Press, 2000.
Barish, Jonas A. *The Antitheatrical Prejudice*. Berkeley: University of California Press, 1981.
Barkan, Leonard. 'Diana and Acteon: The Myth as Synthesis.' *English Literary Renaissance* 10 (1980): 317–59.
– *The Gods Made Flesh: Metamorphosis and the Pursuit of Paganism*. New Haven, CT: Yale University Press, 1986.
– *Transuming Passion: Ganymede and the Erotics of Humanism*. Stanford, CA: Stanford University Press, 1991.
Bartlett, Phyllis Brooks, ed. *The Poems of George Chapman*. New York: Russell and Russell, 1962.
Bashar, Nazife. 'Rape in England between 1550 and 1700.' In *The Sexual Dynamics of History*, edited by the London Feminist History Group, 28–46. London: Pluto Press, 1983.
Bate, Jonathan. 'Sexual Perversity in *Venus and Adonis*.' *Yearbook of English Studies* 23 (1993): 80–92.
– *Shakespeare and Ovid*. Oxford: Clarendon Press, 1993.
Beaumont, Francis. *Poems*. London, 1653.
Bell, Sandra. 'Writing the Monarch: King James VI and *Lepanto*.' In *Other Voices, Other Views: Expanding the Canon in English Renaissance Studies*, edited by Helen Ostovich, Mary V. Silcox, and Graham Roebuck, 193–208. Newark: University of Delaware Press, 1999.
Bellamy, Elizabeth J. *Translations of Power: Narcissism and the Unconscious in Epic History*. Ithaca, NY: Cornell University Press, 1992.
Belsey, Catherine. 'Love as Trompe-l'oeil: Taxonomies of Desire in *Venus and Adonis*.' *Shakespeare Quarterly* 40 (1995): 257–76.

- 'Tarquin Dispossessed: Expropriation and Consent in *The Rape of Lucrece.*' *Shakespeare Quarterly* 46 (2001): 315–35.
Bevington, David, and Peter Holbrook, eds. *The Politics of the Stuart Court Masque.* Cambridge: Cambridge University Press, 1998.
Bland, D.S. 'Henry VIII's Royal Commission on the Inns of Courts.' *Journal of the Society of Public Teachers of Law* 10 (1969): 179–94.
- 'Rhetoric and the Law Student in Sixteenth-Century England.' *Studies in Philology* 54 (1957): 498–509.
Boethius. *The Theological Tractates and The Consolation of Philosophy.* Translated by H.F. Stewart and E.K. Rand. Loeb Classical Library. London: William Heinemann, 1953.
Boose, Lynda E. 'The 1599 Bishops' Ban, Elizabethan Pornography, and the Sexualization of the Jacobean Stage.' In *Enclosure Acts: Sexuality, Property, and Culture in Early Modern England,* edited by Richard Burt and John Michael Archer, 185–200. Ithaca, NY: Cornell University Press, 1994.
Borris, Kenneth. 'R[ichard] B[arnfield]'s Homosocial Engineering in *Orpheus His Journey to Hell,*' in Borris and Klawitter, eds, 332–60.
Borris, Kenneth, and George Klawitter, eds. *The Affectionate Shepherd: Essays in Celebration of Richard Barnfield.* Selinsgrove: Susquehanna University Press, 2001.
Bray, Alan. 'Homosexuality and the Signs of Male Friendship in Elizabethan England.' In *Queering the Renaissance,* edited by Jonathan Goldberg, 40–61. Durham, NC: Duke University Press, 1994.
Bredbeck, Gregory. *Sodomy and Interpretation.* Ithaca, NY: Cornell University Press, 1991.
Brennan, Teresa, *History After Lacan.* London: Routledge, 1993.
Brenner, Robert. *Merchants and Revolution: Commercial Change, Political Conflict, and London's Overseas Traders, 1550–1653.* Princeton, NJ: Princeton University Press, 1993.
Breton, Nicholas. *The Arbor of Amorous Devices, 1597, by Nicholas Breton and Others.* Edited by Hyder Edward Rollins. New York: Russell and Russell, 1968.
- *Brittons Bower of Delights, 1591.* Edited by Hyder Edward Rollins. New York: Russell and Russell, 1968.
Brooks, Eric St John. *Sir Christopher Hatton.* London: Jonathan Cape, 1946.
Brown, Georgia E. 'Gender and Voice in "Hero and Leander."' In *Constructing Christopher Marlowe,* edited by J.A. Downie and J.T. Parnell, 148–63. Cambridge: Cambridge University Press, 2000.
- '"Tradition and the Individual Talent": Teaching Ovid and the Epyllion in the Context of the 1590s.' In *Approaches to Teaching Shorter Elizabethan Poetry,* edited by Patrick Cheney and Anne Lake Prescott, 93–7. New York: MLA, 2000.

Bryson, Norman. 'Two Narratives of Rape in the Visual Arts: Lucretia and the Sabine Women.' In *Rape*, edited by Sylvana Tomaselli and Roy Porter, 152–73. Oxford: Basil Blackwell, 1986.

Buck, George. *The Third Universitie of England.* London, 1615.

Burkhart, Robert E. 'The Surviving Shakespearean Playhouses: The Halls of the Inns of Court and the Excavation of the Rose.' *Theatre History Studies* 12 (1992): 173–96.

Bush, Douglas. 'The Influence of Marlowe's *Hero and Leander* on Early Mythological Poems.' *Modern Language Notes* 42 (1927): 211–17.

– *Mythology and the Renaissance Tradition in English Poetry*. Minneapolis: University of Minnesota Press, 1932.

Butler, Judith. *Gender Trouble: Feminism and the Subversion of Identity*. London and New York: Routledge, 1990.

Buttes, Henry. *Dyets Dry Dinner*. London, n.d.

Cain, Thomas H. 'Spenser and the Renaissance Orpheus.' *University of Toronto Quarterly* 41 (1971): 24–47.

Campbell, Marion. '"*Desunt nonnulla*": The Construction of Marlowe's *Hero and Leander* as an Unfinished Poem.' *ELH* 51 (1984): 241–68.

Cavell, Stanley. 'Who Does the Wolf Love? Reading *Coriolanus*.' *Representations* 3 (1983): 1–20.

Chapman, George. *The Poems of George Chapman*. Edited by Phyllis Brooks Bartlett. New York: Russell and Russell, 1962.

Chaytor, Miranda. 'Husband(ry): Narratives of Rape in the Seventeenth Century.' *Gender and History* 7 (1995): 378–407.

Cheney, Patrick. *Marlowe's Counterfeit Profession: Ovid, Spenser, Counter-Nationhood*. Toronto: University of Toronto Press, 1997.

Chew, Samuel C. *The Crescent and the Rose: Islam and England during the Renaissance*. 1937. Reprint, New York: Octagon Books, 1965.

Chute, Anthony. *Tabacco*. Edited by F.P. Wilson. Oxford: Basil Blackwood, 1961.

Cioni, Maria L. *Women and Law in Elizabethan England with Particular Reference to the Court of Chancery*. New York and London: Garland, 1985.

Cousins, A.D. 'Subjectivity, Exemplarity and the Establishing of Character in Lucrece.' *Studies in English Literature* 38 (1998): 45–60.

Creet, Gerald W. 'Sexual Subordination: Institutionalized Homosexuality and Social Control in Melanesia.' In *Reclaiming Sodom*, edited by Jonathan Goldberg, 66–94. New York and London: Routledge, 1994.

D'Amico, Jack. *The Moor in English Renaissance Drama*. Tampa: University of South Florida Press, 1991.

Damisch, Hubert. *The Origin of Perspective*. Translated by John Goodman. Cambridge, MA: MIT Press, 1994.

Daston, Lorraine, and Katharine Park. 'The Hermaphrodite and the Orders of Nature: Sexual Ambiguity in Early Modern France.' In *Premodern Sexualities*, edited by Louise Fradenburg and Carla Freccero, 117–36. London: Routledge, 1996.

Davis, Natalie Zemon. 'On the Lame.' *American Historical Review* 93.3 (1988): 572–603.

Davis, Ralph. *The Rise of the Atlantic Economies*. London: Weidenfeld and Nicolson, 1973.

de Grazia, Margreta. 'Weeping for Hecuba.' In *Historicism, Psychoanalysis, and Early Modern Culture*, edited by Carla Mazzio and Douglas Trevor, 350–75. New York: Routledge, 2000.

Dekker, Thomas. *The Dead Tearme*. In *The Non-Dramatic Works of Thomas Dekker*, edited by Alexander B. Grosart. Vol. 4, 1–84. New York: Russell and Russell, 1963.

DeNeef, A. Leigh. 'The Poetics of Orpheus: The Text and a Study of *Orpheus His Journey to Hell* (1595).' *Studies in Philology* 89 (1992): 20–70.

Derrida, Jacques. 'The Politics of Friendship.' *American Imago* 50 (1993): 641–2.

Dickson, Sarah Augusta. *Panacea or Precious Bane: Tobacco in Sixteenth Century Literature*. New York: New York Public Library, 1954.

DiGangi, Mario. *The Homoerotics of Early Modern Drama*. Cambridge: Cambridge University Press, 1997.

Donno, Elizabeth Story. *Elizabethan Minor Epics*. New York: Columbia University Press, 1963.

– 'The Epyllion.' In *The History of Literature in the English Language*. Vol. 2. Edited by Christopher Ricks, 82–100. London: Barrie and Jenkins, 1970.

Dubrow, Heather. *Captive Victors: Shakespeare's Narrative Poems and Sonnets*. Ithaca, NY: Cornell University Press, 1987.

– *Echoes of Desire: English Petrarchism and Its Counterdiscourses*. Ithaca, NY: Cornell University Press, 1995.

Dugdale, William. *Origines juridiciales, or, Historical memorials of the English laws*. London, 1666.

Duncan-Jones, Katherine. 'Much Ado with Red and White: The Earliest Readers of Shakespeare's *Venus and Adonis* (1593).' *Review of English Studies* 44 (1993): 479–501.

Eccles, Mark. 'A Biographical Dictionary of Elizabethan Authors.' *Huntington Library Quarterly* 5 (1942): 281–302.

– 'Brief Lives.' *Studies in Philology* 79.4 (1982): 1–135.

Elyot, Sir Thomas. *The Boke Named the Gouernour*. 1531. Reprint, London: J.M. Dent, 1907.

Enterline, Lynn. '"Embodied Voices": Petrarch Reading (Himself Reading)

Ovid.' In *Desire in the Renaissance,* edited by Valeria Finucci and Regina Schwartz, 120–45. Princeton: Princeton University Press, 1994.

– 'Epic, Epyllia, and the Erotics of Early Modern Pedagogy.' Paper presented at the 117th Modern Languages Association Convention, New Orleans, 27 December 2001.

– *The Rhetoric of the Body from Ovid to Shakespeare.* Cambridge: Cambridge University Press, 2000.

Erickson, Amy Louise. *Women and Property in Early Modern England.* London: Routledge, 1993.

Fienberg, Nona. 'Thematics of Value in *Venus and Adonis.' Criticism* 31 (1989): 21–32.

Fineman, Joel. 'Shakespeare's Will: The Temporality of Rape.' *Representations* 20 (1987): 25–76.

Finkelpearl, Philip J. 'The Authorship of *Salmacis and Hermaphroditus.' Notes and Queries* 214 (1969): 367–8.

– *John Marston of the Middle Temple.* Cambridge, MA: Harvard University Press, 1969.

Fish, Stanley. *Surprised by Sin: The Reader in 'Paradise Lost.'* Berkeley: University of California Press, 1967.

Fisher, R.M. 'Thomas Cromwell, Humanism and Educational Reform, 1530–40.' *Bulletin of the Institute of Historical Research* 50 (1997): 151–63.

Fisher, Will. 'The Renaissance Beard: Masculinity in Early Modern England.' *Renaissance Quarterly* 54 (2001): 155–87.

Fletcher, Reginald J., ed. *The Pension Book of Gray's Inn 1569–1669.* London: Chiswich Press, 1901.

Flinker, Noam. 'Cyniras, Myrrha and Adonis: Father-Daughter Incest from Ovid to Milton.' *Milton Studies* 14 (1980): 59–74.

Folkerth, Wes. 'The Metamorphosis of Daphnis: The Case for Richard Barnfield's *Orpheus,*' in Borris and Klawitter, eds, 305–21.

Freud, Sigmund. 'The Ego and the Id.' In *On Metapsychology: The Theory of Psychoanalysis.* Pelican Freud Library, vol. 11, 341–407. Translated by James Strachey. Harmondsworth: Penguin, 1984.

– *On Sexuality: Three Essays on the Theory of Sexuality and Other Works.* Pelican Freud Library, vol. 7. Translated by James Strachey. Harmondsworth: Penguin, 1977.

Friedenreich, Kenneth. 'English Renaissance Accounts of the Fall of Constantinople.' *English Miscellany* 26–7 (1979): 105–27.

Fuchs, Barbara. *Mimesis and Empire: The New World, Islam, and European Identities.* Cambridge: Cambridge University Press, 2001.

Fussner, F. Smith. *The Historical Revolution: English Historical Writing and Thought 1580–1640.* New York: Columbia University Press, 1962.

Gent, Lucy. 'Venus and Adonis: The Triumph of Rhetoric.' *Modern Language Review* 69 (1974): 721–9.

Gilbert, Sir Humphrey. *Queene Elizabethes Achademy, A Booke of Precedence, &c.* Edited by Frederick J. Furnivall. Early English Text Society, Extra Series 8. London, 1869.

Godshalk, W.L. '*Hero and Leander*: The Sense of an Ending.' In '*A poet and a filthy play-maker': New Essays on Christopher Marlowe,* edited by Kenneth Friedenreich, Roma Gill, and Constance B. Kuriyama, 293–314. New York: AMS, 1988.

Golding, Arthur, trans. *The .xv. Bookes of P. Ovidius Naso, Entitled, Metamorphosis.* 1584. Reprinted as *Shakespeare's Ovid.* Edited by W.H.D. Rouse. Carbondale, IL: Southern Illinois University Press, 1961.

Goodrich, Peter. 'Eating Law: Commons, Common Land, Common Law.' *Journal of Legal History* 12 (1991): 246–67.

Gowing, Laura. *Domestic Dangers: Women, Words and Sex in Early Modern London.* Oxford: Clarendon Press, 1996.

Greenblatt, Stephen. 'Psychoanalysis and Renaissance Culture.' In *Learning to Curse: Essays in Early Modern Culture,* 131–45. London: Routledge, 1990.

– *Shakespearean Negotiations: The Circulation of Social Energy in Renaissance England.* Berkeley: University of California Press, 1988.

Gros Louis, Kenneth R.R. 'The Triumph and Death of Orpheus.' *Studies in English Literature* 9 (1969): 63–80.

Grosz, Elizabeth. *Jacques Lacan: A Feminist Introduction.* London: Routledge, 1990.

Guilpin, Everard. *Skialetheia.* Edited by D. Allen Carroll. Chapel Hill: University of North Carolina Press, 1974.

Guth, Delloyd J. 'The Age of Debt, the Reformation and the English Law.' In *Tudor Rule and Revolution,* edited by Delloyd J. Guth and John McKenna, 69–86. Cambridge: Cambridge University Press, 1982.

Guy-Bray, Stephen. *Homoerotic Space: The Poetics of Loss in Renaissance Literature.* Toronto: University of Toronto Press, 2002.

H., J. *Work for Chimny-sweepers, or A warning for Tabacconists.* 1601. London: Shakespeare Association, 1936.

Haber, Judith. '"True-loves blood": Narrative and Desire in *Hero and Leander*.' *English Literary Renaissance* 28 (1998): 372–86.

Hall, Joseph. *The Collected Poems of Joseph Hall.* Edited by A. Davenport. Liverpool: Liverpool University Press, 1949.

Hall, Kim F. *Things of Darkness.* Ithaca, NY: Cornell University Press, 1995.

Halperin, David M. *One Hundred Years of Homosexuality and Other Essays on Greek Love.* London: Routledge, 1991.

Hamilton, A.C. 'Venus and Adonis.' *Studies in English Literature* 1 (1961): 1–15.

Hammersmith, James P. 'The Printer's Copy for Francis Beaumont's *Poems*, 1653.' *Papers of the Bibliographic Society of America* 72 (1978): 74–88.

Hammer, Paul E.J. 'Upstaging the Queen: The Earl of Essex, Francis Bacon and the Accession Day Celebrations of 1595.' In Bevington and Holbrook, 41–66.

Hammill, Graham L. *Sexuality and Form: Caravaggio, Marlowe, and Bacon.* Chicago: University of Chicago Press, 2000.

Harding, Alan. *A Social History of English Law.* Gloucester, MA: Peter Smith, 1973.

Harrison, William. *The Description of England.* Edited by Georges Edelen. Ithaca, NY: Cornell University Press, 1968.

Harte, N.B. 'State Control of Dress and Social Change in Pre-Industrial England.' In *Trade, Government and Economy in Pre-Industrial England*, edited by D.C. Coleman and A.H. John, 132–65. London: Weidenfeld and Nicolson, 1976.

Hawarde, John. *Les Reportes del Cases in Camera Stellata.* Edited by William Pailey Baildon. London: 1894.

Helgerson, Richard. *The Elizabethan Prodigals.* Berkeley: University of California Press, 1976.

– *Forms of Nationhood: The Elizabethan Writing of England.* Chicago: University of Chicago Press, 1992.

Heywood, Thomas. *An Apology for Actors.* London, 1612.

Higford, William. *Institutions, or, Advice to his grandson.* London, 1658.

Holdsworth, William. *A History of English Law.* 5 vols. London: Methuen, 1937.

Honigmann, E.A.J. *John Weever.* Manchester: Manchester University Press, 1987.

Hopkins, David. 'Nature's Laws and Man's: The Story of Cinyras and Myrrha in Ovid and Dryden.' *Modern Language Review* 80.4 (1985): 786–801.

Hoskins, John. *Directions for Speech and Style.* Edited by Hoyt H. Hudson. Princeton, NJ: Princeton University Press, 1934.

Hughey, Ruth Willard. *John Harington of Stepney: Tudor Gentleman: His Life and Works.* Columbus: Ohio State University Press, 1971.

Hulse, Clark. *Metamorphic Verse: The Elizabethan Minor Epic.* Princeton, NJ: Princeton University Press, 1981.

Huntington, John. *Ambition, Rank and Poetry in 1590s England.* Chicago: University of Chicago Press, 2001.

Hutson, Lorna. *The Usurer's Daughter: Male Friendship and Fictions of Women in Sixteenth-Century England.* New York: Routledge, 1994.

Irigaray, Luce. *Speculum of the Other Woman.* Translated by Gillian C. Gill. Ithaca, NY: Cornell University Press, 1985.

– *This Sex Which Is Not One.* Translated by Catherine Porter. Ithaca, NY: Cornell University Press, 1985.

James I. *A Counter-Blaste to Tobacco*. London, 1604.

– *His Maiesties Lepanto, or heroicall song*. London, 1603.

Jardine, Lisa. *Worldly Goods: A New History of the Renaissance*. New York: Norton, 1996.

Jay, Martin. 'Scopic Regimes of Modernity.' In *Vision and Visuality*, edited by Hal Foster, 3–23. Seattle: Bay Press, 1988.

Jed, Stephanie H. *Chaste Thinking: The Rape of Lucretia and the Birth of Humanism*. Bloomington: Indiana University Press, 1989.

Jones, Ann Rosalind, and Peter Stallybrass. 'Fetishizing Gender: Constructing the Hermaphrodite in Renaissance England.' In *Body Guards*, edited by Julia Epstein and Kristina Straub, 80–111. London: Routledge, 1991.

– 'The Politics of *Astrophel and Stella*.' *Studies in English Literature* 24 (1984): 53–68.

Jonson, Ben. *The Alchemist*. Edited by Elizabeth Cook. New Mermaids. New York: W.W. Norton, 1991.

– *Bartholomew Fair*. Edited by G.R. Hibbard. New Mermaids. New York: W.W. Norton, 1977.

Kahn, Coppélia. *Roman Shakespeare: Warriors, Wounds and Women*. London: Routledge, 1997.

Keach, William. *Elizabethan Erotic Narratives*. New Brunswick, NJ: Rutgers University Press, 1977.

Kiernan, V.G. 'State and Nation in Western Europe.' *Past and Present* 31 (1965): 20–38.

Kietzman, Mary Jo. '"What Is Hecuba to Him or [S]he to Hecuba": Lucrece's Complaint and Shakesperean Poetic Agency.' *Modern Philology* 97 (1999): 21–45.

Klause, John. 'Venus and Adonis: Can We Forgive Them?' *Studies in Philology* 85 (1988): 353–77.

Knafla, Louis A. 'The Influence of Continental Humanists and Jurists on the English Common Law in the Renaissance.' In *Actus Conventus Neo-Latini Bononiensis*, edited by R.J. Shoeck, 60–71. Binghamton, NY: Medieval and Renaissance Texts and Studies, 1985.

– 'The Matriculation Revolution and Education at the Inns of Court in Renaissance England.' In *Tudor Men and Institutions*, edited by Arthur J. Slavin, 232–64. Baton Rouge: Louisiana State University Press, 1972.

Knapp, Jeffrey. 'Elizabethan Tobacco.' *Representations* 21 (1988): 27–66.

Knapp, Margaret, and Michal Kobialka, 'Shakespeare and the Prince of Purpoole: The 1594 Production of *The Comedy of Errors* at Gray's Inn Hall.' *Theatre History Studies* 4 (1984): 71–81.

Knolles, Richard. *The Generall Historie of the Turkes*. 5th ed. London, 1635.

Krier, Theresa M. 'Sappho's Apples: The Allusiveness of Blushes in Ovid and Beaumont.' *Comparative Literature Studies* 25 (1988): 1–22.

Lacan, Jacques. *Ecrits: A Selection.* Translated by Alan Sheridan. New York: Norton, 1977.

– *The Language of the Self: The Function of Language in Psychoanalysis.* Edited and translated by Anthony Wilden. New York: Dell, 1968.

– *The Seminar of Jacques Lacan. Book I: Freud's Papers on Technique.* Edited by Jacques-Alain Miller, translated by John Forrester. New York: Norton, 1991.

– *The Seminar of Jacques Lacan. Book II: The Ego in Freud's Theory and in the Technique of Psychoanalysis.* Edited by Jacques-Alain Miller, translated by Sylvana Tomaselli. Cambridge: Cambridge University Press, 1988.

– *The Seminar of Jacques Lacan. Book III: The Psychoses.* Edited by Jacques-Alain Miller, translated by Russell Grigg. New York: Norton, 1988.

– *The Seminar of Jacques Lacan. Book VII: The Ethics of Psychoanalysis, 1959–1960.* Edited by Jacques-Alain Miller, translated by Dennis Porter. New York: Norton, 1992.

– 'Some Reflections on the Ego.' *International Journal of Psychoanalysis* 34 (1953): 11–17.

Lacan, Jacques, and the *école freudienne. Feminine Sexuality.* Edited by Juliet Mitchell and Jacqueline Rose, translated by Jacqueline Rose. New York: Norton, 1982.

Lacquer, Thomas. *Making Sex: Body and Gender from the Greeks to Freud.* Cambridge, MA: Harvard University Press, 1992.

Lanham, Richard. *The Motives of Eloquence: Literary Rhetoric in the Renaissance.* New Haven, CT: Yale University Press, 1976.

Lefkowitz, Mary R. 'Seduction and Rape in Greek Myth.' In *Consent and Coercion to Sex and Marriage in Ancient and Medieval Societies,* edited by Angeliki E. Laiou, 17–38. Washington: Dumbarton Oaks, 1993.

Leishman, J.B., ed. *The Three Paranassus Plays.* London: Ivor Nicholson and Watson, 1949.

L[enton], F[rancis]. *Characterismi, or, Lentons leasvres: expressed in essayes and characters, neuer before written on.* London, 1631.

– *The Young Gallant's Whirligig.* London, 1627.

Leonard, John. 'Marlowe's Doric Music: Lust and Aggression in *Hero and Leander.*' *English Literary Renaissance* 30 (2000): 55–76.

Lewis, C.S. *The Allegory of Love: A Study in Medieval Tradition.* Oxford: Oxford University Press, 1958.

– *English Literature in the Sixteenth Century, Excluding Drama.* Oxford: Clarendon Press, 1954.

Lorimer, Joyce. 'The English Contraband Tobacco Trade in Trinidad and

Guiana, 1590–1617.' In *The Westward Enterprise: English Activities in Ireland, the Atlantic, and America 1480–1650*, edited by K.R. Andrews, N.P. Canny, and P.E.H. Hair, 124–50. Liverpool: Liverpool University Press, 1978.

[...] *Loues Complai[nts,] With The Legend of Orpheus and Euridice*. London: 1597.

Lyne, Raphael. *Ovid's Changing Worlds: English* Metamorphoses, *1567–1632*. Oxford: Oxford University Press, 2001.

MacCaffrey, Wallace. *Queen Elizabeth and the Making of Policy, 1572–1588*. Princeton, NJ: Princeton University Press, 1981.

– *Elizabeth I*. London: Edward Arnold, 1993.

Macpherson, C.B. *Political Theory of Possessive Individualism: Hobbes to Locke*. Oxford: Clarendon Press, 1962.

McPherson, David. 'Aretino and the Harvey-Nashe Quarrel.' *PMLA* 84 (1969): 1551–8.

Manning, Roger B. *Village Revolts: Social Protest and Popular Disturbances in England, 1509–1640*. Oxford: Clarendon Press, 1988.

Marotti, Arthur F. '"Love Is not Love": Elizabethan Sonnet Sequences and the Social Order.' *English Literary History* (1982): 396–428.

– *Manuscript, Print, and the English Renaissance Lyric*. Ithaca, NY: Cornell University Press, 1995.

Martindale, Charles, and Colin Burrow. 'Clapham's *Narcissus*: A Pre-Text for Shakespeare's *Venus and Adonis*? (text, translation, and commentary).' *English Literary Renaissance* 22.2 (1992): 147–76.

Maslen, R.W. 'Myths Exploited: The Metamorphoses of Ovid in Early Elizabethan England.' In *Shakespeare's Ovid: The* Metamorphoses *in the Plays and Poems*, edited by A.B. Taylor, 15–30. Cambridge: Cambridge University Press, 2000.

Masten, Jeffrey. *Textual Intercourse: Collaboration, Authorship and Sexuality in Renaissance Drama*. Cambridge: Cambridge University Press, 1997.

Matar, Nabil. 'English Accounts of Captivity in North Africa and the Middle East: 1577–1625.' *Renaissance Quarterly* 54 (2001): 553–72.

– *Islam in Britain, 1558–1685*. Cambridge: Cambridge University Press, 1998.

– *Turks, Moors and Englishmen in the Age of Discovery*. New York: Columbia University Press, 1999.

Maus, Katherine Eisaman. 'Taking Tropes Seriously: Language and Violence in Shakespeare's *Rape of Lucrece*.' *Shakespeare Quarterly* 37 (1986): 66–82.

Middleton, Thomas. *The Ghost of Lucrece*. Edited by Joseph Quincy Adams. New York: Charles Scribner's Sons, 1937.

– *Michaelmas Term*. Edited by Richard Levin. Lincoln: University of Nebraska Press, 1966.

– *Micro-Cynicon. Sixe Snarling Satyres.* In *The Works of Thomas Middleton,* edited by A.H. Bullen, vol. 8, 111–36. New York: AMS Press, 1964.

Miller, David Lee. 'The Death of the Modern: Gender and Desire in Marlowe's "Hero and Leander."' *South Atlantic Quarterly* 88 (1989): 757–87.

Miller, Paul W., ed. *Seven Minor Epics of the English Renaissance.* Gainesville, FL: Scholars' Facsimiles and Reprints, 1967.

Mills, Laurens J. *One Soul in Bodies Twain: Friendship in Tudor Literature and Stuart Drama.* Bloomington, IN: Principia Press, 1937.

Montrose, Louis Adrian. 'Of Gentlemen and Shepherds: The Politics of Elizabethan Pastoral Form.' *English Literary History* 50 (1983): 415–59.

Mortimer, Anthony. *Variable Passions: A Reading of Shakespeare's* Venus and Adonis. New York: AMS Press, 2000.

Moulton, Ian Frederick. *Before Pornography: Erotic Writing in Early Modern England.* Oxford: Oxford University Press, 2000.

Murphy, Patrick M. 'Wriothesley's Resistance: Wardship Practices and Ovidian Narratives in Shakespeare's *Venus and Adonis.*' In Venus and Adonis*: Critical Essays,* edited by Philip C. Kolin, 323–40. New York: Garland, 1997.

O'Connor, John J. 'A Jacobean Allusion to *The Turkish Mahoment and Hiren the Fair Greek.*' *Philological Quarterly* 35 (1956): 427–9.

Orgel, Stephen. 'Nobody's Perfect: Or, Why Did the English Stage Take Boys for Men?' *South Atlantic Quarterly* 88.1 (1989): 7–29.

Orgel, Stephen, ed. *The Tempest.* By William Shakespeare. Oxford: Oxford University Press, 1987.

Osborn, Louise Brown. *The Life, Letters and Writings of John Hoskyns 1566–1638.* New Haven, CT: Yale University Press, 1937.

Ovid. *Metamorphoses.* Translated by Frank Justus Miller and G.P. Goold. Loeb Classical Library. 2 vols. Cambridge, MA: Harvard University Press, 1984.

Ovid. *Sorrows of an Exile.* Translated by A.D. Melville. Oxford: Oxford University Press, 1995.

Ovid's Fasti. Translated by James George Frazer. Loeb Classical Library. London: William Heinemann, 1959.

Painter, William. *Palace of Pleasure.* Edited by Joseph Jacobs. 3 vols. London: 1890.

Panofsky, Erwin. *Perspective as Symbolic Form.* Translated by Christopher S. Wood. New York: Zone, 1991.

Parker, Patricia. 'Gender Ideology, Gender Change: The Case of Marie Germain.' *Critical Inquiry* 19 (1993): 337–64.

– *Literary Fat Ladies: Rhetoric, Gender, Property.* London: Methuen, 1987.

Pavlock, Barbara. *Eros, Imitation, and the Epic Tradition.* Ithaca, NY: Cornell University Press, 1990.

Peacham, Henry. *The Garden of Eloquence.* 1577. Menston, England: The Scholar Press, 1971.

Peend, T[homas]. *The Pleasant fable of Hermaphroditus and Salmacis.* London, 1565.

Pettie, George. *A Petite Pallace of Pettie His Pleasure ...* Edited by I. Gollancz. 2 vols. London: Chatto and Windus, 1908.

Pincombe, Michael. 'The Ovidian Hermaphrodite: Moralizations by Peend and Spenser.' In *Ovid and the Renaissance Body,* edited by Goran V. Stanivukovic, 155–70. Toronto: University of Toronto Press, 2001.

Plato. *The Symposium.* Translated by Walter Hamilton. Harmondsworth: Penguin, 1951.

Plucknett, T.F.T. *A Concise History of the Common Law.* 5th ed. Boston: Little, Brown and Company, 1956.

– *Early English Legal Literature.* Cambridge: Cambridge University Press, 1958.

Polito, Mary. 'Wit, Will and Governance in Early Modern Legal Literature.' *Mosaic* 27.4 (1994): 15–34.

Poovey, Mary. *A History of the Modern Fact.* Chicago: University of Chicago Press, 1998.

Porter, Roy. 'Rape – Does It Have a Historical Meaning?' In *Rape,* edited by Sylvana Tomaselli and Roy Porter, 216–36. Oxford: Basil Blackwell, 1986.

Post, J.B. 'Ravishment of Women and the Statutes of Westminster.' In *Legal Records and the Historian,* edited by J.H. Baker, 150–64. London: Royal Historical Society, 1978.

Prest, Wilfred R. *The Inns of Court under Elizabeth I and the Early Stuarts 1590–1640.* London: Longman, 1972.

Puttenham, George. *The Arte of English Poesie.* 1589. Kent, OH: Kent State University Press, 1988.

Pye, Christopher. *The Vanishing: Shakespeare, the Subject and Early Modern Culture.* Durham, NC: Duke University Press, 2000.

Quinn, David B., and A.N. Ryan. *England's Sea Empire, 1550–1642.* London: George Allen and Unwin, 1983.

Quinn, Kenneth. *Texts and Contexts: The Roman Writers and their Audience.* London: Routledge and Kegan Paul, 1979.

Quint, David. *Epic and Empire: Politics and Generic Form from Virgil to Milton.* Princeton, NJ: Princeton University Press, 1993.

Rabb, Theodore K. *Enterprise and Empire: Merchant and Gentry Investment in the Expansion of England, 1575–1630.* Cambridge, MA: Harvard University Press, 1967.

Radin, Margaret Jane. *Contested Commodities.* Cambridge, MA: Harvard University Press, 1996.

– *Reinterpreting Property.* Chicago: University of Chicago Press, 1993.

Rae, Wesley D. *Thomas Lodge.* New York: Twayne, 1967.

Ragland-Sullivan, Ellie. *Jacques Lacan and the Philosophy of Psychoanalysis.* Urbana and Chicago: University of Illinois Press, 1987.

Rajan, Balachandra. '*The Lusiads* and the Asian Reader.' *English Studies in Canada* 23.1 (1997): 1–19.

Richardson, W.C. *A History of the Inns of Court: With Special Reference to the Period of the Renaissance.* Baton Rouge, LA: Claitor's Publishing Division, 1975.

Rocke, Michael. *Forbidden Friendships: Homosexuality and Male Culture in Renaissance Florence.* Oxford: Oxford University Press, 1996.

Roper, Lyndal. *Oedipus and the Devil: Witchcraft, Sexuality and Religion in Early Modern Europe.* London: Routledge, 1994.

Rose, Jacqueline. *States of Fantasy.* Oxford: Clarendon Press, 1996.

Rowse, A.L. *Shakespeare's Southampton.* London: Macmillan, 1965.

Runsdorf, James H. 'Transforming Ovid in the 1560s: Thomas Peend's *Pleasant Fable.*' *American Notes and Queries* 5 (1992): 124–6.

Rye, William Benchley, ed. *England as Seen by Foreigners in the Days of Elizabeth and James the First.* 1865. Reprint, New York: Benjamin Blom, 1967.

Sacks, David Harris. 'The Promise and the Contract in Early Modern England: Slade's Case in Perspective.' In *Rhetoric and Law in Early Modern Europe*, edited by Victoria Kahn and Lorna Hutson, 28–53. New Haven, CT: Yale University Press, 2001.

Sandys, George. *Ovid's Metamorphosis Englished, Mythologized and Represented in Figures.* 1632. Edited by Karl K. Hulley and Stanley T. Vandersall. Lincoln, NE: University of Nebraska Press, 1970.

Savage, James E., ed. *The 'Conceited Newes' of Sir Thomas Overbury and his Friends.* Gainesville, FL: Scholars' Facsimiles and Reprints, 1968.

Schleiner, Louise. 'Pastoral Male Friendship and Miltonic Marriage: Textual Systems Transposed.' *Literature, Interpretation, Theory* 2 (1990): 41–58.

Schleiner, Winfried. 'Early Modern Controversies about the One-Sex Model.' *Renaissance Quarterly* 53 (2000): 180–91.

Schoenfeldt, Michael C. *Bodies and Selves in Early Modern England.* Cambridge: Cambridge University Press, 1999.

Sedgwick, Eve Kosofsky. *Between Men: English Literature and Male Homosocial Desire.* New York: Columbia University Press, 1985.

Sedinger, Tracey. 'Historicism and Renaissance Culture.' In *Discontinuities: New Essays on Renaissance Literature and Criticism*, edited by Viviana Comensoli and Paul Stevens, 117–38. Toronto: University of Toronto Press, 1998.

Sell, Roger. 'The Authorship of "The Metamorphosis of Tobacco" and "Salmacis and Hermaphroditus."' *Notes and Queries* 19 (1972): 10–14.

– ed. *The Shorter Poems of Sir John Beaumont.* Åbo: Åbo Akademi, 1974.

Shannon, Laurie. *Sovereign Amity: Figures of Friendship in Shakespearean Contexts.* Chicago: University of Chicago Press, 2002.

Shapiro, Barbara. 'The Concept "Fact": Legal Origins and Cultural Diffusion.' *Albion* 26.2 (1994): 227–52.

– *Probability and Certainty in Seventeenth-Century England.* Princeton, NJ: Princeton University Press, 1983.

Sheidley, William E. '"Unless It Be a Boar": Love and Wisdom in Shakespeare's *Venus and Adonis*.' *Modern Language Quarterly* 35 (1974): 3–15.

Shoeck, R.J. 'The Elizabethan Society of Antiquaries and Men of the Law.' *Notes and Queries* 119 (1954): 417–21.

Silberman, Lauren. 'Mythographic Transformations in Ovid's Hermaphrodite.' *Sixteenth Century Journal* 19 (1988): 643–52.

Silverman, Kaja. *Male Subjectivity at the Margins.* London: Routledge, 1992.

– *The Threshold of the Visible World.* London: Routledge, 1996.

Skura, Meredith Anne. 'Understanding the Living and Talking to the Dead: The Historicity of Psychoanalysis.' *Modern Language Quarterly* 54.1 (1993): 77–89.

Smith, Bruce R. 'Premodern Sexualities.' *PMLA* 115.3 (2000): 318–29.

Smith, Thomas. *De Republica Anglorum.* 1583. Edited by Mary Dewar. Cambridge: Cambridge University Press, 1982.

Sorlien, Robert Parker, ed. *The Diary of John Manningham of the Middle Temple 1602–1603.* Hanover, NH: University of Rhode Island Press, 1976.

Spenser, Edmund. *Poetical Works.* Edited by J.C. Smith and E. De Selincourt. Oxford: Oxford University Press, 1970.

Spring, Eileen. *Law, Land, and Inheritance: Aristocratic Inheritance in England, 1300 to 1800.* Chapel Hill, NC: University of North Carolina Press, 1993.

Steane, J.B. *Marlowe: A Critical Study.* Cambridge: Cambridge University Press, 1964.

Stern, Virginia F. *Gabriel Harvey: His Life, Marginalia and Library* Oxford: Clarendon Press, 1979.

Stewart, Alan. *Close Readers: Humanism and Sodomy in Early Modern England.* Princeton: Princeton University Press, 1997.

Stone, Lawrence. *The Crisis of the Aristocracy, 1558–1641.* Oxford: Clarendon Press, 1965.

Stopes, Charlotte Carmichael. 'Thomas Edwards, Author of "Cephalus and Procris, Narcissus."' *Modern Language Notes* 16 (1921): 209–23.

Stretton, Tim. *Women Waging Law in Elizabethan England.* Cambridge: Cambridge University Press, 1998.

Summers, Claude J. '"Hero and Leander": The Arbitrariness of Desire.' In *Constructing Christopher Marlowe,* edited by J.A. Downie and J.T. Parnell, 133–47. Cambridge: Cambridge University Press, 2000.

Taylor, A.B. 'A Note on Christopher Marlowe's "Hero and Leander."' *Notes and Queries* 16 (1969): 20–1.
– 'Thomas Peend and Arthur Golding.' *Notes and Queries* 16 (1969): 19–20.
Taylor, John. *The Praise of Hempseed.* London, 1623.
Taylor, Rupert. 'Shakespeare's Cousin, Thomas Greene, and his Kin: Possible Light on the Shakespeare Family Background.' *PMLA* 60 (1945): 81–94.
Teeven, Kevin M. *A History of the Anglo-American Common Law of Contract.* New York: Greenwood Press, 1990.
Thompson, Ann. 'Death by Water: The Originality of *Salmacis and Hermaphroditus.*' *Modern Language Quarterly* 40 (1979): 99–114.
Traub, Valerie. Afterword. In *Ovid and the Renaissance Body*, edited by Goran V. Stanivukovic, 260–8. Toronto: University of Toronto Press, 2001.
– 'The (In)Significance of "Lesbian" Desire in Early Modern England.' In *Queering the Renaissance*, edited by Jonathan Goldberg, 62–83. Durham, NC: Duke University Press, 1994.
Trousdale, Marion. 'Reading the Early Modern Text.' *Shakespeare Survey* 50 (1997): 135–45.
Tubbs, J.W. *The Common Law Mind: Medieval and Early Modern Conceptions.* Baltimore, MD: Johns Hopkins University Press, 2000.
Tuve, Rosamund. *Elizabethan and Metaphysical Imagery: Renaissance Poetics and Twentieth-Century Critics.* Chicago: University of Chicago Press, 1947.
Vickers, Nancy J. '"The blazon of sweet beauty's best": Shakespeare's *Lucrece.*' In *Shakespeare and the Question of Theory*, edited by Patricia Parker and Geoffrey Hartman, 95–115. New York: Methuen, 1985.
– 'Diana Described: Scattered Woman and Scattered Rhyme.' *Critical Inquiry* 8 (1981): 265–79.
Vigarello, George. 'The Upward Training of the Body from the Age of Chivalry to Courtly Civility.' In *Fragments for a History of the Human Body, Part Two*, edited by Michel Feher, 148–99. New York: Zone Books, 1989.
Vinge, Louise. *The Narcissus Theme in Western European Literature up to the Early 19th Century.* Translated by Robert Dewsnap. Lund: Gleerups, 1967.
Walker, Garthine. 'Rereading Rape and Sexual Violence in Early Modern England.' *Gender and History* 10 (1998): 1–25.
Warden, John. 'Orpheus and Ficino.' In *Orpheus: The Metamorphoses of a Myth*, edited by John Warden, 85–110. Toronto: University of Toronto Press, 1982.
Warner, Michael. 'New English Sodom.' In *Queering the Renaissance*, edited by Jonathan Goldberg, 330–58. Durham, NC: Duke University Press, 1994.
Whitted, Brent E. 'Transforming the (Common)place: The Performance of William Browne's *Ulysses and Circe* in Inner Temple Hall.' *Theatre History Studies* 19 (1999): 151–66.

Williams, Gordon. 'The Coming of Age of Shakespeare's Adonis.' *Modern Language Review* 78 (1983): 769–76.

Wilson, Luke. 'Ben Jonson and the Law of Contract.' In *Rhetoric and Law in Early Modern Europe*, edited by Victoria Kahn and Lorna Hutson, 143–65. New Haven, NJ: Yale University Press, 2001.

Wilson, Thomas. *The Arte of Rhetoricke (1553)*. Edited by Thomas J. Derrick. New York: Garland, 1982.

Wittig, Monique. *The Straight Mind and Other Essays*. Translated by Louise Turcotte. Boston: Beacon Books, 1992.

Wood, Alfred C. *A History of the Levant Company*. Oxford: Oxford University Press, 1935.

Worrall, Andrew. 'Biographical Introduction: Barnfield's Feast of "all Varietie."' In Borris and Klawitter, 25–40.

Yates, Frances A. *The Art of Memory*. Chicago: University of Chicago Press, 1966.

Žižek, Slavoj. *Enjoy Your Symptom! Jacques Lacan in Hollywood and Out*. New York: Routledge, 1992.

– *The Sublime Object of Ideology*. London: Verso, 1989.

Index